Irish Home Rule
1867–1921

Alan O'Day

Manchester University Press

Manchester and New York

Distributed exclusively in the USA by St. Martin's Press

Published by Manchester University Press
Oxford Road, Manchester M13 9NR, UK
and Room 400, 175 Fifth Avenue, New York, NY 10010, USA

Distributed exclusively in the USA by
St. Martin's Press, Inc., 175 Fifth Avenue, New York,
NY 10010, USA

Distributed exclusively in Canada by
UBC Press, University of British Columbia, 6344 Memorial Road,
Vancouver, BC, Canada V6T 1Z2

British Library Cataloguing-in-Publication Data
A catalogue record for this book is available from the British Library

Library of Congress Cataloging-in-Publication Data
O'Day
    Irish home rule. 1867–1921 / Alan O'Day.
      p.   cm. — (New frontiers in history)
    Includes bibliographical references and index.
    ISBN 0–7190–3775–1 (hardback).—ISBN 0–7190–3776–X (pbk.)
    1. Ireland—Politics and government—1837–1901. 2. Ireland—Politics and government—1901–1910. 3. Ireland—Politics and government—1910–1921. 4. Home rule—Ireland.
    I. Title. II. Series.
    DA957.O24   1998
    941.508—dc21   97–47404

ISBN 0 7190 3775 1 hardback
    0 7190 3776 X paperback

First published 1998

05 04 03 02 01 00   10 9 8 7 6 5 4 3 2 1

Typeset in Great Britain
by Northern Phototypesetting Co. Ltd, Bolton
Printed in Great Britain
by Bell & Bain Ltd, Glasgow

For my aunt, Helen E. O'Day

Acknowledgements

the Catholic University of America, the School of Advanced Study, University of London and the University of Dublin (Trinity College). I continue to owe much to the European Science Foundation, especially my colleagues in the project on 'Comparative Studies on Governments and Non-Dominant Ethnic Groups in Europe, 1850–1940', to Christoph Mühlberg now in Bonn, and Geneviève Schauinger in Strasburg. Some of the work was done during a year as a Visiting Professor at Concordia University, Montreal. As a reminder of both the passage of time and of our mortality, my mother, who was still relatively young and healthy when this work began, is now elderly and in nursing care, and my son, Andrew, then a young child, is now a university graduate student. I owe a huge debt to my relatives Mary and Reg Green and Georgiania Wiegley. My aunt has been a source of encouragement and support over many years and I take pleasure in making this long overdue tribute to her.

Alan O'Day

Note on terminology

A number of conventions are followed. Catholic(s) and Protestant(s) are in upper case. Catholic rather than Roman Catholic is employed while Derry not the legal designation Londonderry is used. Unionist is in upper case, but nationalist, a term used sparingly is in lower case. Home Rule always appears in upper case. This label is used for a party, movement, ideology and specific formula for governing Ireland and at various points is interchangeable with Irish party and the Irish parliamentary party. After December 1890 Parnellite refers to those who supported Parnell, anti-Parnellite for his Irish national opponents. Occasionally, Redmonite is substituted for Parnellite. The context makes clear what is meant.

Glossary

People

Abraham, William, b. 1840, d. 1915. A Methodist from County Limerick, he was active in the Land League. He sat in the House of Commons from 1885 to 1892, 1895 to January 1910, and between June 1910 and his death. In December 1890 Abraham supported Justin McCarthy against Parnell.

Acland, Arthur Herbert, b. 1847, d. 1926. A Liberal MP from 1885 to 1899, he sat in the Cabinet of 1892–95.

Adams, W. G. S., b. 1874, d. 1966. A Professor of Economics, he served on the Committee of the Cabinet on Irish Finance in 1911. Subsequently he was a founder and editor of the *Political Quarterly* between 1914 and 1916 and Secretary to the Prime Minister from 1916 to 1919.

Addison, Christopher, b. 1869, d. 1951. Liberal MP 1910–22, he subsequently joined the Labour party, being an MP under its banner from 1922 to 1931. He was created first Viscount Addison in 1945.

Agar-Robartes, Thomas, b. 1880, d. 28 September 1915 (from wounds suffered in military action). He was a Liberal MP for Austall, Cornwall from 1908 until his death. Agar-Robartes was sympathetic to the exclusion of north-east Ulster from a Home Rule regime.

Ambrose, Dr Daniel, b. 1843, d. 1895. He was an Anti-Parnellite MP from 1892 until his death.

Andrews, Thomas, b. 1834, d. 1914. He was a member of the Recess Committee.

Ardilaun, first Baron (Arthur Edward Guinness), b. 1840, d. 1915. Prior to being created a Baron in 1880, he was a Conservative MP for Dublin 1868–69 and from 1874 to 1880.

Arnott, Sir John, b. 1853, d. 1940. As well as being chairman of the *Irish Times*, he had extensive commercial interests.

Glossary

Asquith, Herbert H., b. 1852, d. 1928. A Liberal MP from 1886 to 1918, he re-entered the House of Commons in February 1920. Asquith was Home Secretary, 1892–95, Chancellor of the Exchequer 1905–08 and Prime Minister, 1908–December 1916.

Bagehot, Walter, b. 1826, d. 1877. An influential commentator on political economy, Bagehot authored *The English Constitution*.

Balfour, Arthur J., b. 1848, d. 1930. Balfour entered the Cabinet in his uncle Lord Salisbury's government of 1885. In March 1887 he became Chief Secretary of the Irish Office, remaining there until November 1891 when he was appointed leader of the House of Commons. He succeeded Salisbury as Prime Minister in 1902, resigned the leadership of the Conservative party in November 1911 but rejoined the Cabinet in May 1915, remaining in it until 1922. He was created the first Earl of Balfour in 1922.

Balfour, Gerald, b. 1853, d. 1945. A nephew of Lord Salisbury and younger brother of Arthur Balfour, Gerald became Chief Secretary of the Irish Office in 1895, holding this post until 1900. He was in the Cabinet between 1900 and 1905. Gerald succeeded his brother as the second Earl of Balfour in 1930.

Barnes, George, b. 1882, d. 1940, A Labour MP, he was in the War Cabinet from August 1917 to January 1920.

Barrie, Hugh, b. 1860, d. 1922. MP for North Londonderry from 1906, Barrie was Vice-President of the Department of Agricultural and Technical Instruction. He headed the Ulster delegation in the Irish Convention, 1917–18.

Barry, Kevin, b. 1902, d. 1 November 1920 (by hanging). Barry was a medical student at University College, Dublin, who participated in a raid in which several people were killed. His execution occasioned widespread protests.

Barton, Robert, b. 1861, d. 1975. An Irish Protestant and cousin of Erskine Childers, he was elected for Sinn Féin in 1918 but declined to take his seat, instead sitting in the first Dáil Éireann in January 1919. Barton was a member of the delegation sent to London in October 1921 to negotiate the Treaty.

Beaverbrook, first Baron (William Maxwell Aiken), b. 1879, d. 1964. Canadian-born, influential British newspaper proprietor. An intimate of Lloyd George, he received his title in 1917.

Bernard, Archbishop John Henry, b. 1860, d. 1927. He was Church of Ireland Archbishop of Dublin, 1915–19 and President of the Royal Irish Academy between 1916 and 1921. Bernard was a member of the Irish Convention, 1917–18.

Glossary

Bessborough, seventh Earl, b. 1821, d. 1906. An Irish Liberal Peer, he chaired the Commission created in August 1881 to examine the Irish land question.

Biggar, Joseph G., b. 1828, d. 1890. Biggar was a prominent Ulster Protestant Home Ruler who subsequently converted to Catholicism. He took a major part in the National Conference in November 1873, being an MP from 1874 until his death. He was a key participant in the obstruction struggles of the 1870s and a prominent figure in the Irish party during the 1880s.

Birrell, Augustine, b. 1850, d. 1933. He was an MP from 1889 to 1900 and from 1906 to 1918. After serving as President of the Board of Education from December 1905 in Campbell-Bannerman's government, he became Chief Secretary of the Irish Office in February 1907, resigning at the beginning of May 1916.

Blake, Edward, b. 1833, d. 1912, was a major Canadian politician who was induced to accept an Irish seat in 1892, remaining an MP until 1907. Blake was an authority on the Constitution and an intimate political adviser to John Dillon. He was a Protestant.

Blennerhassett, Rowland P., b. 1850, d. 1913. He was a Protestant who captured the Kerry constituency in the Home Rule interest at a by-election in February 1872, holding the seat until 1885. An early supporter of the Home Rule League, he was never closely associated with Parnell, joining Shaw and the other nominal Home Rulers in withdrawing from the Irish party in January 1881.

Blunt, Sir Wilfrid Scawen, b. 1840, d. 1922. A noted adventurer with access to a sector of the political Establishment, Blunt had good contacts with some members of the Irish party. He was arrested in Ireland in 1887 and imprisoned for two months in Kilmainham gaol.

Bradlaugh, Charles, b. 1833, d. 1891. He was elected to the House of Commons for Northampton in 1880 but as a declared atheist he declined to take the oath of allegiance, insisting instead of being allowed to affirm. This was denied. His quest to take up his seat was not successful until 1886. He retained his seat for Northampton until his death. Catholics and the Irish party generally were hostile to Bradlaugh's admission to Parliament.

Breen, Dan, b. 1894, d. 1969. Part of the gang that murdered two policemen in Tipperary in January 1919, marking the first engagement since the Easter Rising of 1916.

Bright, John, b. 1838, d. 1889. Bright, a Quaker, was a well-known Liberal politician who sat in Gladstone's Cabinet between 1880 and July 1882 when he resigned in protest at the bombardment of Alexandria. He had supported disestablishment of the Irish Church and the Land Act of 1870. Until the mid-1880s Bright was regarded as favourable to Irish claims. In 1886 he became a Liberal Unionist.

Glossary

Brodrick, W. St John (Lord Middleton), b. 1856, d. 1942. He was a prominent southern Irish Unionist who became the 9th Viscount Middleton in 1907. His was a key spokesman for southern Unionism after 1914. In 1920 he was created the Earl of Middleton.

Bryce Killen, James, b. 1841, d. 1923. Bryce was a noted intellectual who was an MP between 1906 and 1918. An Ulster Presbyterian, Bryce served as Chief Secretary of the Irish Office from December 1905 to February 1906.

Buller, Sir Henry Redvers, b. 1839, d. 1908. He was Under-Secretary of the Irish Office in 1887.

Burke, Thomas Henry, b. 1829, d. 6 May 1882 (assassinated in Phoenix Park). Burke, a Catholic, joined the Irish Administration in 1857 and rose to being Under-Secretary of the Irish Office, an appointment he held at the time of his assassination.

Butt, Isaac, b. 1813, d. 1879. Protestant leader of Home Rule party from March 1874 to May 1879. First returned as an MP briefly in 1850, then sat in the House of Commons from 1852 to 1865 and finally for Limerick City from September 1871 until his death. He was counsel for several Young Ireland prisoners in the late 1840s and defended a number of Fenians in the 1860s. He also served as the head of the Amnesty Association and Tenant League in the later 1860s.

Callan, Philip, b. 1837. Callan was returned to the House of Commons in 1868, sitting until 1880. He was an early recruit to the Home Rule movement and member of the Irish party formed in March 1874. During the obstruction crisis he aided Biggar and Parnell. Callan was never on good terms with influential figures in the Irish party and was ousted from his seat in 1885.

Campbell-Bannerman, Sir Henry, b. 1836, d. 1908. He was returned to the House of Commons in 1868, sitting until his death. Campbell-Bannerman was Chief Secretary of the Irish Office (without a seat in the Cabinet) from October 1884 to June 1885. He became leader of the Liberal party in 1899 and Prime Minister in December 1905, an office he surrendered only a few days before dying. Campbell-Bannerman was committed to Home Rule and enjoyed good relations with senior figures in the Irish party, particularly with T. P. O'Connor.

Carnarvon, fourth Earl of, b. 1831, d. 1890. Carnarvon, who was known to be sympathetic to Home Rule ideas, was Lord Lieutenant in the Salisbury government of 1885–6.

Casement, Sir Roger, b. 1864, d. 1 August 1916 (by hanging at Pentonville Prison, London). Born into an Ulster Protestant family, Casement was a distinguished civil servant and humanitarian who gradually became converted to radical nationalism. During the First World War he recruited Irish prisoners of war to serve under the German flag. He was convicted and executed for this activity. Casement was captured in

Glossary

Kerry where he was attempting to land with a shipment of German arms.

Castledown, Baron (Bernard Edward Barnaby Fitz-Patrick), b. 1849, d. 1937. He sat for Portarlington borough from 1881 until succeeding to the title in 1883. Castledown was a southern Unionist.

Cave, Sir George, b. 1856, d. 1928. He was Solicitor-General from November 1915 to December 1916 and Home Secretary from December 1916 to January 1919 when he became Lord Justice of Appeal, receiving the title of Viscount Cave.

Cavendish, Lord Frederick, b. 1836. Second son of the Duke of Devonshire, d. 6 May 1882. He was the younger brother of Lord Hartington and a Liberal MP from 1865 until his assassination. Cavendish was married to Gladstone's niece and enjoyed close personal relations with the Prime Minister. He had just succeeded W. E. Forster as Chief Secretary of the Irish Office when he was killed.

Cecil, Lord Hugh, b. 1869, d. 1956. A son of the Marquess of Salisbury, he was an MP between 1895 and 1906 and again from 1910 to 1937. In 1944 he was created Baron Quickswood.

Cecil, Lord Robert, b. 1864, d. 1954. A son of the Marquess of Salisbury, he was an MP between 1906 and 1910 and from 1911 to 1923, becoming a member of the government in May 1915. In 1923 he was created Viscount Cecil of Charlwood; he was awarded the Nobel Peace Prize in 1937.

Chamberlain, Austen, b. 1863, d. 1937. Oldest son of Joseph Chamberlain, he was a highly influential Unionist political figure. At various points he was a member of the War Cabinet and on Andrew Bonar Law's retirement in 1921 leader of the Conservative party.

Chamberlain, Joseph, b. 1836, d. 1914. He was elected to the House of Commons in 1876, retaining his seat until dying. Chamberlain was a member of the Cabinet between 1880 and 1885 and again in the early months of 1886 but resigned in March 1886. He opposed Home Rule in 1886 and thereafter. He subsequently was a Cabinet Minister from 1895 until he resigned in 1906, suffering a severe stroke in 1906 which effectively closed his active political life. His older son, Austen, played a significant role in Irish affairs.

Childers, Erskine, b. 1870, d. 1922 (by firing squad). He was born into a southern Irish Protestant family but made his early reputation in Britain. He became converted to nationalism and was a confidant of Eamon de Valera. Childers acted as Secretary to the delegation sent to London to negotiate the Treaty in October 1921. Declining to support the Treaty, he was captured in 1922 and executed by the Irish Free State.

Childers, H. C. E., b. 1827, d. 19 January 1896. He was in the Gladstone Cabinet, 1880–05, serving as Chancellor of the Exchequer from 1882 and Home Secretary in the government of 1886. He chaired the Royal Commission on the Financial Relations between Great Britain and Ireland appointed in 1894, but died before it reported.

Churchill, Lord Randolph, b. 1849, d. 1895. Son of the Duke of Marlborough, Lord Lieutenant of Ireland, 1876–80, he spend considerable time in Dublin and became well acquainted with Irish politicians. He was one of the Tory ginger-group, the Fourth party, during the Parliament of 1880–85. Churchill was a member of the Cabinet in 1885–6 and again in the Salisbury government formed in 1886, though he resigned as Chancellor of the Exchequer late in the year never regaining ministerial office. He married Jenny Martin in 1874 and had one son, Winston. He was an MP from 1874 until his death in 1895.

Churchill, Winston, S., b. 1874, d. 1965. Son of Lord Randolph Churchill, he became a Liberal MP. Between 1905 and 1921 he held several ministerial posts.

Clancy, J. J., b. 1847, d. 1928. He was on the editorial staff of the *Nation* between 1870 and 1885. Subsequently be became a lawyer, being called to the Irish Bar in 1887 and becoming a KC in 1906. Clancy authored numerous pamphlets for the party and was an MP between 1885 and 1918, supporting Parnell in December 1890.

Clark, Sir Ernest, b. 1864, d. 1951. A civil servant who was Assistant Secretary at the Inland Revenue in 1919 when he transferred to being Assistant Under-Secretary in the Irish Office in 1920, becoming Secretary of the Treasury of Northern Ireland on its creation in 1921.

Clarke, Sir Edward, b. 1841, d. 1933. He was a Conservative MP from 1880 to 1900 and from January to June 1906. He was Solicitor-General between 1886 and 1892. He acted for *The Times* before the Commission on Parnellism and Crime.

Clarke, Thomas J., b. 1852, d. 1916 (3 May by firing squad). Clarke, a Fenian, was arrested in 1883 for his role in the dynamite campaign and released in 1898. He settled in Dublin in 1907 and was a leader of the Easter Rising in 1916.

Collins, Michael, b. 1880, d. 1922 (assassination). Collins's reputation as the organiser of intelligence and murder squad activities in Dublin after 1919 gave him immense prestige in republican circles. A member of de Valera's provisional government, he was part of the team dispatched to London to negotiate with the British government in October 1921, signing the Treaty on 6 December 1921.

Connolly, James, b. 1868, d. 12 May 1916 (by firing squad). A Marxist, trade-union organiser and head of the Irish Citizen Army, Connolly was one of the thirteen men executed in Dublin for his role in the Easter Rising. He was and remains revered by the political left.

Cosgrave, William, b. 1880, d. 1965. Elected to the Dublin Corporation in 1909, he was involved in radical national politics, being sentenced to death for participation in the Easter Rising in 1916. This was commuted to penal servitude for life, but he was released under the general amnesty in January 1917. Cosgrave was elected to the House of Commons in August 1917 but declined to take his seat. He sat in the Dáil on its creation in January 1919.

Craig, Sir James, b. 1871, d. 1940. Craig was returned to the House of Commons as a Unionist for East Down in 1906, holding this seat until 1918 when he moved to the mid-Down constituency. He resigned in June 1921 on becoming Prime Minister of Northern Ireland, a post he retained until his death on 24 November 1940. Craig was made a baronet in 1918 and created Viscount Craignavon in 1927.

Cranbrook, Viscount (Gathorne Hardy), b. 1814, d. 1906. Member of the Conservative Cabinets 1885–86 and 1886–92. Raised to an Earldom in 1892.

Crawford, William Sharman, b. 1781, d. 1861. Sharman Crawford was a Protestant Ulsterman who was involved in Radical causes. He was an MP from 1834 to 1837 and again between 1841 and 1852. Known as the father of tenant-right, he was popular with Ireland's farmers. In the early 1830s and again in the 1840s he advocated a form of federal Home Rule.

Crewe, first Marquess, b. 1858, d. 1945. An influential Liberal peer.

Croke, Thomas William, b. 1824, d. 1902. He served as Archbishop of Cashel from 1875 until his death. Croke worked tirelessly for national causes, sometimes antagonising the papacy. He was patron to the Gaelic Athletic Association when it was founded.

Cullen, Cardinal Paul, b. 1803, d. 1878. Created Archbishop of Armagh in 1850 he was translated to Dublin in 1852 where he remained until he died. Cullen placed Catholic issues above the national question and was unsympathetic to movements that rivalled his influence. He kept his distance from the Home Rulers and they in turn mistrusted him.

Curran, T. B., b. 1840, d. 1913. He resided in Australia for many years where he accumulated a fortune. Curran was a substantial contributor to anti-Parnellite funds and was returned as an anti-Parnellite MP in 1892, remaining in the House of Commons until 1900.

Curzon, first Marquess, b. 1859, d. 1925. Influential Conservative politician and member of the War Cabinet.

Daly, James (of Castlebar), b. 1835, d. 1910. A Poor Law Guardian, grazier, merchant and proprietor of the *Connaught Telegraph*, Daly was a leading exponent of the tenant cause in Mayo and a founder with Michael Davitt of the land movement in 1879.

D'Arcy, Most Revd Charles Frederick, b. 1859, d. 1938. He was Church of Ireland Archbishop of Dublin 1919–20 and then Archbishop of Armagh from 1920.

Glossary

Daunt, William O'Neill, b. 1801, d. 1885. Born into a prominent Protestant family, O'Neill Daunt was a convert to Catholicism. He was a writer and active supporter of national causes.

Davis, Thomas, b. 1814, d. 1845. A leader of Young Ireland and critic of Daniel O'Connell, Davis, an intellectual and ardent advocate of national rights was an inspiration to later generations of nationalists.

Davitt, Michael, b. 1846, d. 1906. He joined the Fenians in 1865 and was sentenced to fifteen years imprisonment in 1870, being released on a ticket of leave in December 1877. Davitt was a founder of the Land League in October 1879, remaining a prominent figure in the struggle against the Irish landlords. He was elected an MP in February 1882 but declared ineligible as an undischarged felon. He was elected as an anti-Parnellite in December 1892, but was unseated on petition. He became an MP in February 1893 but resigned in May 1893 on being declared bankrupt. He was elected in 1895 and sat until resigning in 1899.

Derby, fourteenth Earl of, b. 1799, d. 1869. Conservative Prime Minister, 1866–68.

Desart, fifth Earl, b. 1848, d. 1934. He held various public offices.

de Valera, Eamon, b. in New York 1882, d. 1975. Condemned to death for his role in the Easter Rising of 1916, he was reprieved. He was a leading figure in the Sinn Féin movement between 1919 and 1921.

Devlin, Joseph, b. 1872, d. 1934. A Belfast Catholic, Devlin used the power of the Ancient Order of Hibernians to great effect. He was a close ally of John Dillon and succeeded him as Irish party chairman when Dillon lost his seat in December 1918.

Devoy, John, b. 1842, d. 1928. Devoy, a Fenian, was imprisoned in the 1860s and resided in the United States after his release. He remained active in national politics throughout the remainder of his life.

Dicey, Albert Venn, b. 1835, d. 1922. Dicey was a noted constitutional authority and fervent opponent of Home Rule. His writings were influential.

Dickson, Thomas Alexander, b. 1833, d. 1909. Sat as a Liberal MP, 1874–80, and was defeated at the general election of 1880 but returned to Parliament at the Tyrone by-election in September 1881, remaining an MP until the general election of 1885. He was a Protestant advocate of tenant-right and showed sympathy with the Home Rule ideal. In May 1888 he was returned to the House of Commons in the by-election for St Stephen's Green, Dublin, and sat until 1892. He was an anti-Parnellite during the O'Shea divorce crisis.

Dilke, Sir Charles, b. 1843, d. 1911. During the Gladstone administration of 1880–05 he was Under-Secretary for Foreign Affairs until December 1882 when he entered the Cabinet as President of the Local Government Board. A close political associate of Joseph Chamberlain, Dilke's career was ruined when he was named co-respondent in the Crawford divorce suit in 1885.

Dillon, John, b. 1851, d. 1927, son of the Young Ireland leader and MP, John Blake Dillon. He took an active part in the Home Rule movement in the 1870s and was first elected an MP in 1880 resigning his seat in 1883, but was returned to Parliament at the general election of 1885, sitting continually until being defeated in December 1918. Though never personally close to Parnell he was among the most prominent members of the Irish party, a major figure in the Land League and along with William O'Brien the chief organiser of the Plan of Campaign. Dillon became chairman of the anti-Parnell majority in succession to Justin McCarthy in February 1896, resigning in 1899 to make way for the unification of the national party. He succeed John Redmond as party chairman in March 1918.

Dillon, John Blake, b. 1816, d. 1866. A Young Ireland leader, he was an MP at the time of his death and the father of John Dillon.

Disraeli, Benjamin, b. 1805, d. 19 April 1881. He was the Conservative Prime Minister in 1868 and again between 1874 and 1880. Disraeli was created the Earl of Beaconsfield in 1876.

Dolan, Charles J., b. 1881. A former school teacher he became an MP in 1906 but resigned his seat in January 1907 in protest against the policy of the Irish party. He stood as a Sinn Féin candidate for the Leitrim North seat he vacated in the by-election on 21 February 1908, losing to the Irish party nominee.

Donelan, Captain Anthony J. C., b. 1846, d. 1924. He was a Protestant who sat for Cork East between 1892 and 1911 when he was unseated on petition. He was then elected for Wicklow East in July 1911 which he held until 1918. He was an Irish party Whip for a period.

Doran, C. G. A prominent Home Ruler and alderman of Queenstown, he took part in the National Conference in November 1873.

Dudley, second Earl, b. 1867, d. 1932. Between 1906 and 1908 he was Parliamentary Secretary to the Board of Trade then chaired the commission on congestion in Ireland.

Duffy, Sir Charles Gavan, b. 1816, d. 1903. A founder of the *Nation* newspaper in 1843, Duffy was a leading member of Young Ireland. During his long residence in Australia he became a prominent political figure, being knighted for his labours. Duffy returned to Ireland in the 1880s and promoted moderate self-government ideas. He had good connections with leading British politicians.

Duffy, George Gavan, b. 1882, d. 1951. Son of Sir Charles Gavan Duffy, he joined Sinn Féin and was returned at the general election of 1918 but declined to take his seat. Duffy sat in the Dáil created in January 1919 and was a member of the negotiating team which signed the Treaty on 6 December 1921.

Duggan, Eamonn, b. 1874, d. 1936. A solicitor he was elected to the House of Commons in 1918 but as a Sinn Féin MP he declined to take his seat, instead sitting in the first Dáil Éireann in January 1919. Duggan was a member of the delegation sent to London in October 1921 to negotiate the Treaty.

Duke, Henry E., b. 1855, d. 1939. A Barrister who became a QC in 1889, Duke was a Conservative MP, serving as Chief Secretary of the Irish Office from 31 July 1916 to April 1918 when he was appointed a Lord Justice of Appeal.

Dunraven, fourth Earl of, b. 1841, d. 1926. A prominent southern landlord and Unionist, he played a large role in Irish affairs. Dunraven represented landowners' interests at the conference in December 1902 and founded the Irish Reform Association in the following year.

Dyke, Sir William Hart, b. 1837, d. 1931. He was a Conservative Whip from 1868 to 1874 and then Chief Whip between 1874 and 1880. Dyke was appointed Chief Secretary of the Irish Office in June 1885, resigning in January 1886 shortly before the fall of the Conservative government.

Edward VII, b. 1841, d. 1910. Monarch, 22 January 1901 to 6 May 1910.

Egan, Patrick, b. 1841, d. 1919. Proprietor of a Dublin bakery, he had been a member of the Supreme Council and was Treasurer of the Irish Republican Brotherhood until 1877. Egan became Treasurer of the Land League, subsequently emigrating in 1883 to America where he eventually became the Minister to Chile.

Esmonde, Thomas H. Grattan, b. 1862, d. 1935. MP 1885–1918, he was an Irish party Whip, a post he resigned in disgust in June 1907.

Farrell, James Patrick, b. 1865, d. 1921. A journalist, he was an Irish party MP from 1895 to 1918.

Finigan, James L., He was a journalist who captured Ennis as a supporter of Parnell in July 1879, retiring from Parliament in 1882.

Finlay, the Revd John, b. 1842, d. 1921. A Church of Ireland Rector of Carlow, he served on the Recess Committee.

Fisher, Herbert, b. 1865, d. 1940. Elected a Fellow of the British Academy in 1907, Fisher was a Liberal MP from December 1916 to 1926. He was President of the Board of Education between December 1916 and October 1922.

Flynn, James C., b. 1852, d. 1922. Elected an Irish party MP for the North Division of Cork in 1885, he joined the anti-Parnellites in December 1890, remaining a member of Parliament until 1910.

Foster, William E., b. 1818, d. 1886. A Quaker, Foster had been active in the relief effort during the Great Irish Famine. He had been a member of the Cabinet during Gladstone's first government and was appointed Chief Secretary of the Irish Office in 1880, resigning on 2 May 1882 in protest at the release of Parnell from prison. Thereafter he was a bitter critic of the Irish party.

Fry, Sir Edward, b. 1827, d. 1918. A judge, he chaired the commission charged with investigating Trinity College, Dublin in 1906–07.

Garvin, J. L., b. 1868, d. 1947. Garvin was a prominent Unionist and editor of the *Observer*. Subsequently he authored the first volumes of the life of Joseph Chamberlain.

George V, b. 1865, d. 1936. Monarch, 6 May 1910 to 1936.

George, David Lloyd, b. 1863, d. 1945. He became an MP in 1890 and remained in the House of Commons until his death. Lloyd George was Chancellor of the Exchequer from 1908 to December 1916 and then Prime Minister until 1922.

Gibson, Edward (Baron Ashbourne from July 1885), b. 1837, d. 1913. Gibson was a Conservative and distinguished member of the Irish Bar. He was MP for the University of Dublin between 1875 and 1885. Gibson was Attorney-General for Ireland, 1877–80, and Lord Chancellor of Ireland, 1885–86, 1886–92, 1895–1905. His views on Irish matters carried great weight among senior Conservatives, especially before 1886.

Gilhooly, James P., b. 1845, d. 1916. He was an MP for Cork West from 1885 until his death. Gilhooly supported Justin McCarthy against Parnell in December 1890.

Gill, T. P., b. 1868, d. 1931. He was a journalist who sat in Parliament between 1885 and 1892, supporting the anti-Parnellites in December 1890. Gill became involved with the Irish co-operative movement and other groups promoted by Sir Horace Plunkett. He was secretary to the Recess Committee in 1896.

Ginnell, Laurence, b. 1854, d. 1923. A founder of the Irish Literary Society and a barrister, Ginnell was arrested several times. He was a leading advocate of 'cattle driving' during the ranch war, 1907–09. First elected to the House of Commons in 1906 Ginnell was expelled from the Irish party in 1909 and suffered defeat at the polls in 1910. He was elected under the Sinn Féin banner in 1918, but declined to take his seat.

Gladstone, Herbert, b. 1854, d. 1930. Son of William Gladstone, he was an MP from 1885 to 1910 when he became Viscount Gladstone. Herbert Gladstone took a keen interest in Irish affairs in the 1880s and enjoyed his father's confidences. At the turn of the century he was Chief Whip of the Liberal party.

Gladstone, William E., b.1809, d. 1898. Prime Minister, 1868–74, 1880–5, 1886, and 1892–94.

Gordon, General Charles George, b. 1833, d. 1885. Known as Chinese Gordon, he was a popular military leader who lost his life at Khartoum in 1885.

Glossary

Goschen, George J., b. 1831, d. 1907. A former Cabinet Minister in Gladstone's first government, he became a Liberal Unionist in 1886, serving as Chancellor of the Exchequer from January 1887 until 1892. He was created the first Baron Goschen in 1900.

Granville, second Earl (George Levenson Gower), b. 1815, d. 1891. Earl Granville was an intimate colleague of Gladstone's, serving as Foreign Secretary in the government of 1880–05, and was a member of the Cabinet in 1886.

Grattan, Henry, b. 1746, d. 1820. Grattan was the leader of the Irish Parliament created in 1782 and also served in the Westminster House of Commons. The eighteenth-century Irish Parliament is often referred to as Grattan's Parliament.

Grey, Sir Edward, b. 1862, d. 1933. He became an MP in 1885. From 1905 to 1916 Grey was Foreign Secretary. He was created Viscount Grey of Fallodon in 1916.

Griffith, Arthur, b. 1872, d. 1922. A leader and Vice-President of the Sinn Féin movement, Griffith was editor of *Sinn Féin* from 1906 to 1915 and of *Nationality* in 1916. He was the head of the Irish delegates to the Treaty conference in London between October and December 1921.

Grosvenor, Lord Richard, b. 1837, d. 1912. The youngest son of the Marquess of Westminster, he was a Liberal MP and Chief Whip between 1880 and 1885. He retired as an MP in February 1886.

Haldane, R. B., b. 1856, d. 1928. As a young Liberal he had a formidable reputation for his intellect and legal talents. He first entered Parliament in 1885, retaining his seat until 1911. He was Lord Chancellor from 1912 to 1915.

Hamilton, Sir Edward Walter, b. 1847, d. 1908. Private Secretary and then Principal Private Secretary to Gladstone between 1880 and 1885, he was knighted in 1885 and moved to the Treasury. He was personally close to both Gladstone and Lord Rosebery. His journals are an important source of information about Gladstone and Rosebery.

Harcourt, Lewis V., b. 1863, d. 1922 Son of Sir William Harcourt and an influential Liberal in his own right, he acted as his private secretary and confidant, entering the House of Commons in 1904 and leaving in 1917 when he was created the First Viscount Harcourt.

Harcourt, Sir William, b. 1827, d. 1904. He entered the House of Commons in 1868 and with brief interruptions remained a member until his death. Harcourt sat in several Liberal Cabinets, was Home Secretary, 1880–05, Chancellor of the Exchequer, 1886 and again 1892–95; he wanted to succeed Gladstone as Prime Minister. His relations with Gladstone's successor, Lord Rosebery, were very sour. Harcourt was Liberal leader of the House of Commons from March 1894 until resigning in December 1898, and informal leader of the Liberal party after Rosebery's resignation in 1896. Never an enthusiast for Home Rule, he none the less declined to repudiate it in public.

Harrington, Timothy C., b. 1851, d. 1910. A key figure in the Land League and subsequently in the National League, he began as a journalist in Tralee and was returned to Parliament in 1883, remaining an MP until his death. He was Lord Mayor of Dublin in 1901, 1902 and 1903. Harrington supported Parnell in December 1890.

Hartington, Marquess of, b. 1833, d. 1908. He served as Chief Secretary of the Irish Office from January 1871 to 1874, succeed Gladstone as Liberal leader in the House of Commons in 1875, was second only to Gladstone in importance between 1880 and 1885, but declined office in the Liberal administration of 1886. His younger brother Lord Frederick Cavendish was assassinated in Phoenix Park on 6 May 1882. Hartington became a Liberal Unionist in 1886, being chairman of the Liberal Unionist Council between 1886 and 1904. He became the Duke of Devonshire in 1891.

Healy, Maurice, b. 1859, d. 1923. He was the younger brother and confidant of T. M. Healy. He was elected to Parliament in 1885, sitting until 1900 and once again from 1909 to 1918. Healy was a solicitor and married a daughter of A. M. Sullivan.

Healy, T. M., b. 1855, d. 1931. Healy was an ambitious young journalist who was initially mesmerised by Parnell and briefly served as his private secretary. He was returned to Parliament in 1881, lost the seat in 1886 but was elected in 1887, sitting from then until 1910 when he was defeated, but was returned once more in 1911, retaining his seat until 1918. Healy became a barrister, being called to the Irish Bar in 1884, becoming a QC in 1899 and a KC at the English Bar in 1910. He took the lead against Parnell in December 1890 and played the largest role in the vitriolic attack on him. Healy was closely connected with the Sullivan clan to whom he was linked by family and then marriage to T. D. Sullivan's daughter, but was widely mistrusted. His clashes with John Dillon were legendary. Healy defended the employers in the Dublin lock-out of 1913. He was governor-general of the Irish Free State from 1922 to 1928.

Hennessy, Sir John Pope, b. 1834, d. 1891. An MP between 1859 and 1865, he was already the nominee of the Irish party for the Kilkenny by-election in December 1890 when the divorce crisis split the movement. He opted to identify with the anti-Parnellite faction, winning the by-election on 28 December.

Henry, Sir Charles, b. 1860, d. 1919. Returned as a Liberal MP in 1906, he remained in Parliament until his death. Henry was created a baronet in 1911.

Henry, Mitchell, b. 1826, d. 1910. Henry, a Protestant, was born into a Lancashire merchant family with recent Ulster connections. He purchased Kylemore Castle in Galway and was elected as a Home Ruler in

1871, retaining his seat until 1885. Henry won Glasgow Blackfriars as a Liberal in 1885 but lost his seat the following year, never returning to Parliament. During the 1870s he often acted as Isaac Butt's unofficial second in command.

Hewart, Sir Gordon, b. 1870, d. 1943. A Liberal MP between 1913 and 1922, Hewart was Solicitor-General from December 1916 to January 1919 when he became Attorney-General. He was knighted in 1916, becoming Viscount Hewart in 1940.

Hicks Beach, Sir Michael, b. 1837, d. 1916. He was Chief Secretary of the Irish Office without a seat in the Cabinet between 1874 and February 1878 and again though a member of the Cabinet from August 1886 to early March 1887. During 1885–86, 1892–95 and 1895 to 1902 he was Chancellor of the Exchequer. Hicks Beach had a reputation for favouring Irish reform. He was created Viscount St Aldwyn in 1906.

Hyde, Douglas, b. 1860, d. 1949. The son of a Church of Ireland clergyman, Hyde in 1893 was the leading force in the foundation of the Gaelic League and its first President. He became the first President of Ireland in 1937, retaining this office until 1945.

Jackson, William L., b. 1840, d. 1917. He succeeded Arthur Balfour as Chief Secretary in the Irish Office in November 1891, remaining in this post until the resignation of the Salisbury government in August 1892.

Johnson, William, b. 1829, d. 1902. He was called to the Irish Bar in 1872. A Protestant Conservative MP for Belfast between 1868 and 1878 he then sat for Belfast South from 1885 until his death.

Kennedy, Patrick J., b. 1864, d. 1947. A landowner and gentleman, he chaired the Meath County Council from 1900 to 1902. Kennedy was an MP between 1892 and 1895 and again from 1900 to 1906.

Kettle, Thomas M., b. 1880 the son of Andrew Kettle, a leading associate of Parnell, d. 9 September 1916 on the Western Front. Called to the Bar in 1906, Kettle was Professor of Economics in the National University from 1910. He was an MP between July 1906 and December 1910, being regarded as a leading intellectual and something of a young turk.

Killen, James Bryce, b. 1845, d. 1916. A journalist and Fenian, Bryce, a Presbyterian, helped Michael Davitt found the Land League.

Kitchener, first Earl, b. 1850, d. 5 June 1916. From 1914 Secretary of State for War, he was lost at sea in 1916.

Kruger, Paul, b. 1825, d. 1904. A Boer leader and sometime head of the Transvaal.

Labouchere, Henry, b. 1831, d. 1912. He was a newspaper proprietor and Liberal MP for Northampton from 1880 until 1906. He was on friendly terms with several Irish MPs, notably T. M. Healy, and a self-designated conduit between the Irish party and Gladstone.

Lalor, James Fintan, b. 1807, d. 1849. Fintan, a Protestant, was an advocate of national principles in the 1840s but is chiefly known for his radical views on the land question. He became a source of inspiration to subsequent agrarian radicals.

Lamb, Edmund, b. 1863, d. 1925. Liberal MP between 1906 and 1910.

Lansdowne, fifth Marquess of, b. 1845, d. 1927. A southern Irish Unionist who exerted immense influence in the post-1912 years.

Larkin, James, b. 1876, d. 1947. The organiser of the trade-union movement in Dublin, he took the lead in employees' resistance to the Dublin lock-out in 1913. Larkin sought to built a political movement devoted to the interests of labour and was mistrusted by conventional nationalists.

Lavelle, Father Patrick, b. 1825, d. 1886. A well-known Mayo priest who supported the Fenian movement. He was frequently in conflict with his superiors.

Law, Andrew Bonar, b. 1858 in Canada, d. 1923. He was an MP from 1900 to 1910 and from 1911 until he died. Law, from Ulster Presbyterian origins, was leader of the Conservative party from November 1911 to March 1921 and subsequently from October 1922. He served in the Cabinet from May 1915 to January 1919. In 1922 he became Conservative Prime Minister.

Lecky, W. E. H., b. 1838, d. 1903. Known primarily as an intellectual and historian, he was a Unionist MP from December 1895 until his death. A fine statue of Lecky graces the front quadrangle of Trinity College, Dublin.

Logue, Cardinal Michael, b. 1840, d. 1924. Bishop of Raphoe from 1879, he was created a Cardinal in 1893.

Londonderry, Lady, b. 1879, d. 1959. The influential wife of Lord Londonderry she did most of the social arrangements for Andrew Bonar Law during his tenure as leader of the Conservative party.

Long, Walter, b. 1854, d. 1924. A Conservative with close ties with southern Irish landowners, Long was Chief Secretary of the Irish Office from March to December 1905, Chairman of the Irish Unionist Party, 1906–10, and its Vice-Chairman from then until May 1921. He chaired the committee in 1919 charged with drawing up a plan for Irish self-government. In May 1921 he was created Viscount Long of Wraxall.

Loreburn, first Earl, b. 1846, d. 1923. A Liberal MP (as Robert Reid) from 1880, he served as Lord Chancellor from 1905 to 1912.

Lough, Thomas, b. 1850, d. 1922. He was born in Ireland where he attend a Wesleyan School. Lough was Liberal MP for Islington South from 1892 to 1918.

Lucy, Sir Henry, b. 1848, d. 1924. Lucy, a Liberal, was the most renowned parliamentary journalist of his age.

McCabe, Cardinal Edward, b. 1816, d. February 1885. McCabe succeeded Cardinal Cullen as Catholic Archbishop of Dublin. He mistrusted Parnell and worked to limit Land League and Irish party influence.

MacCarthy, John George, b. 1829., d. 1892. A solicitor in Cork, he was an early member of the Home Rule movement and MP from 1874 until 1880.

McCarthy, Justin, b. 1830, d. 1912. A journalist and novelist, McCarthy entered politics relatively late, being returned at a by-election in 1879 and retiring from Parliament in 1900. He became Vice-Chairman of the Irish party in December 1890 when the office was created for him and Chairman of the anti-Parnellites in December 1890, a position he resigned in February 1896. McCarthy was on close personal terms with numerous British Liberals.

McCarthy, Justin Huntly, b. 1859, d. 1936. Only son of Justin McCarthy, he was, like his father, a novelist and popular historian of his own age. He was elected at a by-election in 1884 and remained an MP until retiring in 1892. He supported the anti-Parnellites in December 1890.

MacDonnell, Sir Antony, b. 1848, d. 1925. An Indian civil servant who was appointed Under-Secretary of the Irish Office in 1902, holding this post until resigning in summer 1908. A Catholic and brother of an Irish party MP, MacDonnell was vested with unusual authority for an Under-Secretary. He was created first Baron MacDonnell in 1908.

McGhee, Richard, b. 1851 An anti-Parnellite MP for Louth between 1896 and 1900 when he was defeated, he was elected again to the House of Commons in December 1910, retaining his seat until 1918.

McKillop, William, b. 1860, d. 1909. An Irish party MP between 1900 and 1909.

MacSwiney, Terence J., b. 1880, d. 1920 (on hunger strike). He was elected as a Sinn Féin MP for mid-Cork in 1918, but declined to take his seat instead serving in the first Dáil Éirrean in January 1919. He was Lord Mayor of Cork when he died on hunger strike.

Mahaffy, Sir John Penland, b. 1839, d. 1919. He was the Provost of Trinity College and President of the Royal Irish Academy from 1911 to 1918. Mahaffy had a formidable intellectual reputation and was a member of the Irish Convention of 1917–18. He was knighted in 1918.

Mahon, Charles James Patrick, known as the O'Gorman Mahon, b. 1800, d. 1891. First returned to Parliament in 1830, he was soon unseated, but was then an MP between 1847 and 1852, returning to the House of Commons in 1879. The O'Gorman Mahon retired in 1885 but was returned at a by-election in 1887, retaining his seat until he died. He had a colourful career and was on good personal terms with Gladstone and Parnell.

Manners, Lord John, b. 1818, d. 1906, second son of the Duke of Rutland, He was a member of the Conservative Cabinets of 1874–80, 1885–86 and 1886–92.

Glossary

Manning, Henry Edward Cardinal, b. 1808, d. 1892. Manning a convert to Catholicism, became Archbishop of Westminster in 1865, retaining this appointment until his death. He was made a Cardinal in 1875.

Markievicz, Countess (Constance Gore-Booth), b. 1868, d. 1927. Sentenced to death for her participation in the Easter Rising of 1916, this was commuted and she was released in the general amnesty of January 1917. Countess Markievicz was elected a Sinn Féin MP in 1918 but declined to sit in the House of Commons, instead being a member of the first Dáil Éireann.

Marlborough, Duchess of, b. 1843, d. 1899. She was the wife of the Lord Lieutenant of Ireland and began a fund for the relief of the distressed peasants in December 1879.

Marlborough, seventh Duke of, b. 1822, d. 1883. Father of Lord Randolph Churchill and Lord Lieutenant of Ireland 1876–80.

Martin, John, b. 1812, d. 29 March 1875. An Ulster Presbyterian, Martin had been a Young Irelander in the 1840s. He founded the National League of Ireland in 1864 to advance self-government ideas and was an early supporter of Home Rule. He won the Meath by-election as an Independent Nationalist in January 1874 and subsequently acted as Secretary of the Home Rule League after its formation in late 1873. John Mitchel was his brother-in-law.

Maxwell, General Sir John, b. 1859, d. 1929. Sent to Ireland in the wake of the Easter Rebellion of 1916, he was in command when the executions of the leaders took place and the policy of internment implemented.

Mayo, seventh Earl of, b. 1851, d. 1927. He succeeded to the title in 1872. A prominent southern landlord and Unionist, he represented the owners at the land conference in December 1902.

Meath, twelfth Earl of, b. 1841, d. 1929. A prominent southern landlord and Unionist, he represented the owners at the land conference in December 1902.

Merry, Tom. Conservative Political cartoonist. During the 1880s his work frequently appeared in the *St Stephen's Review*.

Milner, first Viscount (Alfred), b. 1854, d. 1925. Milner was created a Baron in 1901 and served in the War Cabinet between 1916 and 1918.

Mitchel, John B., b. 1815, d. March 1875. An Ulster Presbyterian, he joined the Repeal Association in 1843 but seceded along with other members of the Young Ireland group. He was convicted in 1848 and sentenced to fourteen years' transportation to Australia from which he escaped in 1853, thereafter living in the United States. Mitchel was revered in radical national circles. He stood and was twice elected MP for Tipperary in early 1875 but his election was declared invalid because he was an undischarged convict. Martin returned to Ireland in March 1875, but died. His brother-in-law John Martin caught cold at Mitchel's funeral and died shortly afterwards.

Molloy, Bernard C., b. 1842, d. 1916. He was an MP from 1880 to 1900, supporting Parnell in December 1890 despite his being identified with issues sponsored by the Catholic Church. He was a private Chamberlain at the Court of the Pope.

Monteagle, second Baron, b. 1849, d. 1926. An Irish landlord, he represented the landowners interest at the land conference in December 1902.

Montgomery, Hugh de Fellenberg, b. 1844, d. 1924. Influential Ulster landlord who succeeded to family estates of 12,448 acres in 1868. Montgomery as a prominent Unionist.

Moore, George Henry, b. 1811, d. 19 April 1870. Moore was an MP for Mayo between 1847 and 1857, returning to Parliament for the same constituency in 1868 until his death. He was a popular figure who commanded immense influence among nationally minded Catholics.

Moore, Stephen, b. 1836. A Conservative, he became MP for Tipperary in Mayo 1875 when John Mitchel was unseated on petition, retaining the seat until 1880.

Moriarty, Bishop David, b. 1814, d. 1877. He was made Bishop of Kerry in 1856, a post he held until his death. Moriarty was a renown critic of Fenianism and supported the Liberals.

Morley, John, b. 1838, d. 1923. A well-known journalist, intellectual and Radical politician, Morley entered Parliament in 1883, serving as Chief Secretary of the Irish Office in 1886 and between 1892 and 1895. A close associate of Gladstone's, he published the classic three-volume biography of his life in 1903. Morley sat in Liberal Cabinets from 1905 to 1914 when he resigned in protest at the decision to declare war.

Nolan, John P., b. 1838, d. 1923. Following his first election to the House of Commons for Galway he was unseated following the notorious trial of the election petition by Judge Keogh. He captured the seat in 1874 and remained an MP until 1895 when he was defeated. Nolan supported Parnell in December 1890. He returned to the House of Commons in October 1900 but was defeated in 1906. Nolan was a military officer, retiring in 1881 with the rank of Lieutenant Colonel.

Northcliffe, first Viscount (Alfred Hamsworth), b. 1865, d. 1922. An influential newspaper proprietor who received his title in 1904.

Northcote, Sir Stafford, b. 1818, d. 1887. He was a member of the Conservative Cabinet, 1874–80 and 1885–86, serving as Tory leader of the House of Commons from August 1876 until June 1885. Northcote was created the Earl of Iddesleigh in 1886.

O'Brien, J. F. X., b. 1831, d. 1905. A Fenian, he was sentenced to death in 1867, but reprieved. He was elected to Parliament in 1885, retaining his seat until 1891. An anti-Parnellite during the divorce split, he was Treasurer of the United Irish League.

Glossary

O'Brien, the Revd Richard, b. 1809, d. 1885. As the Catholic Dean of Limerick he was known for his religious and philanthropic work. O'Brien was an advocate of Home Rule ideas in the late 1860s and 1870s.

O'Brien, William, b. 1852, d. 1928. He was a journalist and author who took a vigorous role in the Land League and along with John Dillon was the principal leader of the Plan of Campaign. O'Brien was in and out of Parliament several times: he won the Mallow by-election in 1883, lost his seat in 1886, was returned in May 1887 and sat until 1895 when he resigned, was elected again in 1900 but resigned in 1909, finally sitting again from January 1910 until 1918. O'Brien was the first editor of *United Ireland* and much of its vigour was due to his energy. He founded the United Irish League in 1898. O'Brien and Dillon were close associates and friends, but fell out in the aftermath of the Wyndham land purchase legislation of 1903, becoming bitter enemies subsequently. O'Brien became the leading nationalist advocate of conciliation of Unionists.

O'Connor, Arthur, b. 1844, d. 1923. A former civil servant, O'Connor was returned to the House of Commons in 1880 as a supporter of Parnell. He was a close associate of T. M. Healy, joining the anti-Parnellite ranks in December 1890. O'Connor was Chairman of the Public Accounts Committee of the House of Commons between 1895 and 1900 when he lost his seat. He became a QC in 1899 and was later an English county court judge.

O'Connor, John, b. 1850, d. 1928. He was returned at the by-election for Tipperary in January 1885 after Parnell overturned the selection of a local man as the party candidate. O'Connor supported Parnell in December 1890 and lost his seat in 1892 but was returned to Parliament in 1905 where he remained until 1918. He became a KC in 1918.

O'Connor, T. P., b. 1849, d. 1929. O'Connor was a noted London journalist who entered the House of Commons as a supporter of Parnell in 1880, remaining an MP until his death. O'Connor was President of the Irish National League of Great Britain and successor organisations from October 1883. He joined the anti-Parnellite majority in December 1890. A close friend and support of John Dillon, O'Connor was also on good terms with Sir Henry Campbell-Bannerman and David Lloyd George.

O'Donnell, Frank Hugh, b. 1848. He sat in Parliament from June 1877 to 1885, being in the 1870s one of the most persistent of the obstructionists. He fell out with Parnell. T. M. Healy labelled him Crank Hugh O'Donnell.

O'Donnell, John, b. 1840, d. 1895. He was a journalist, organiser for the United Irish League and later its General Secretary for five years. He was elected to the House of Commons in 1900, retiring in December 1910.

O'Donnell, Cardinal Patrick, b. 1856, d. 1927. Created Catholic Bishop of Raphoe in 1888, he presided over the Irish Race Convention in 1896 and the National Convention in 1900. He was the chief clerical representative

Glossary

at the Irish Convention of 1917–18, breaking with John Redmond on the question of Ireland's financial autonomy under Home Rule. He effectively forced Redmond to retreat on this question. Subsequently, he was translated to the Archbishopric of Dublin.

O'Kelly, James J., b. 1845, d. 1916. O'Kelly was a journalist with a colourful past. He was in close contact with John Devoy in the late 1870s. O'Kelly was returned to Parliament in 1880, supported Parnell with whom he was on good personal terms in December 1890 and lost his seat in 1892. However, O'Kelly returned to the House of Commons in 1895 and remained there until his death.

Oliver, F. S., b. 1864, d. 1934. An influential writer who advocated federalist ideas.

O'Neill, Charles, b. 1849, d. 1918. A Unionist MP for South Armagh from 1909 to his death.

O'Shaughnessy, Richard, b. 1843. He was called to the Irish Bar in 1866, becoming MP for Limerick in 1874 until resigning in 1883. He was a supporter of Isaac Butt during the obstruction controversy and also upheld the Land Act of 1881.

O'Shea, Katharine, b. 1845, d. 1921. An Englishwoman of prominent family, she was married to Captain O'Shea from whom she was often estranged. Her liaison with Parnell started at the beginning of the 1880s. After the divorce, she and Parnell married on 25 June 1891.

O'Shea, Captain William Henry, b. 1840, d. 1905. Husband of Katharine O'Shea, he was elected MP for Clare in 1880, holding the seat until 1885. O'Shea was odious to the Irish party. In 1885 he narrowly lost his bid to be elected as a Liberal for a Liverpool constituency where Parnell campaigned vigorously on his behalf. Parnell then insisted that O'Shea be returned for the Galway City by-election on 10 February 1886. Captain O'Shea declined to vote on the second reading of the Government of Ireland Bill, walking out of the House of Commons. In December 1889 he filed for divorce naming Parnell as co-respondent, and was granted a *decree nisi* on 17 November 1890, precipitating the crisis ending in the split of the Irish party.

Parnell, Charles Stewart, b. 1846, d. 1891. First elected MP in April 1875 he remained in Parliament until his death. Parnell became party chairman in May 1880. As a consequence of the divorce, on 6 December 1890 a majority of nationalist MPs joined Justin McCarthy in rejecting Parnell's leadership.

Parnell, John Howard, b. 1843, d. 1923. The older brother of Charles Steward Parnell, he lived mostly in America. John Howard contested Wicklow in 1874. He returned to Ireland after his brother's death, sitting as a Parnellite MP from 1895 to 1900.

Pearse, Patrick, b. 1879, d. 1916 (3 May by firing squad). Founder of a

Glossary

Gaelic-speaking school and active advocate of Irish cultural ideas, he was the Provisional President of the Irish Republic in 1916 and chief author of the Proclamation of the Irish Republic.

Peel, Sir Robert, b. 1788, d. 1850. Peel served as Chief Secretary of the Irish Office and then was the Conservative Prime Minister, 1842–6, being in office when the Great Irish Famine began. Gladstone left the Conservative party with him in the aftermath of the repeal of the Corn Laws and his later Irish ideas were influenced by Peel's policies.

Pigott, Richard, b. c.1828, d. 1889 (suicide). Pigott was a journalist who ran Fenian newspapers. These he sold to Parnell and associates in 1881 who converted them into *United Ireland*, a newspaper devoted to supporting the policies of Parnell and the Land League. Pigott was a shadowy figure on the fringes of national politics. In February 1889 he was exposed as the forger of the Parnell facsimile letters reproduced in *The Times* in 1887 under the title 'Parnellism and Crime'.

Plunkett, David, b. 1838, d. 1919. Third son of Baron Plunkett. He was called to the Irish Bar in 1862 and became a QC in 1868. In 1868 he was a Law Adviser to the Crown, Solicitor-General for Ireland 1875–77, First Commission of Works 1885–86 and 1886–92, and MP for the University of Dublin from 1870 to 1895.

Plunkett, George Noble (Count), b. 1851, d. 1948. Plunkett was made a Count of Rome in 1884. He stood unsuccessfully as a Parnellite candidate for Parliament in 1892, 1895 and 1898, being returned in 1917 supported by Sinn Féin but declined to take his seat. He was the father of one of the executed leaders of the Easter Rising.

Plunkett, Sir Horace Curzon, b. 1854, d. 1932. Third son of sixteenth Baron Dunsany. Attended Eton, where he was a contemporary of Gerald Balfour, and Oxford. After a period ranching in Wyoming, he returned to Ireland. He was elected Unionist MP for Dublin South in 1892 but was defeated in 1900. Plunkett was chairman of the Recess Committee in 1896, Vice-President of the Department of Agricultural and Technical Instruction between 1899 and 1907 and Chairman of the Irish Convention of 1917–18. John Dillon was very antagonistic towards him.

Power, John O'Connor, b. 1856, d. 1919. He was elected an MP in 1875, retaining his seat until 1885. O'Connor Power visited America with Parnell in 1876 and toured the cities of England and Scotland with him in autumn 1877. During the late 1870s he was active in the obstruction struggle. However, he fell out with the Irish party and became an active supporter of Gladstone after 1881, standing unsuccessfully as a Liberal candidate at the general election of 1885.

Powerscourt, seventh Viscount, b. 1836, d. 1904. A prominent Wicklow landlord, he was a representative Irish peer in the House of Lords from 1869. At the land conference in December 1902 he represented the interests of landowners.

Glossary

Primrose, Sir Henry, b. 1846, d. 1923. A civil servant and sometime private secretary to Gladstone, Primrose is credited with preparing the financial clauses of the Government of Ireland Bill in 1886. In 1911 he chaired the committee commissioned to examine the financial proposals for a new Home Rule measure.

Redmond, John E., b. 1852, d. 6 March 1918. Redmond was the eldest son of William Archer Redmond, MP, and brother of W. H. K. Redmond, MP. He was a clerk in the House of Commons in the late 1870s but gave up his post and became involved in Home Rule politics. He was an MP from 1881 to 1918. Redmond supported Parnell in December 1890 and became leader of the Parnellites after Parnell's death. In February 1900 he assumed the chairmanship of the United Irish party, a position he retained until a few days prior to his death.

Redmond, William Archer, b. 1825, d. 1880. Father of John and W. H. K. Redmond, he was from a distinguished Wexford Catholic family, sitting as a Home Ruler for Wexford borough from 1874 until his death.

Redmond, Captain William Archer, b. 1886, d. 1932. Son of John Redmond, he was returned to the House of Commons for East Tyrone in 1910 but resigned this seat in March 1918 in order successfully to contest his father's former constituency of Waterford City, holding it until 1921.

Redmond, W. H. K., b. 1861, d. 1917. The younger brother and close confidant of John Redmond, he was the son of William Archer Redmond, MP. Willie Redmond was an MP from 1883 until his death on the Western Front in Belgium on 9 June 1917.

Reid, Sir Thomas Wemyss, b. 1842, d. 1905. A Liberal journalist and editor of the *Speaker*, he was knighted in 1893.

Rendel, Stuart, b. 1844, d. 1913. Rendel was a Welsh Liberal MP from 1880 until his creation as Lord Rendel in 1894.

Richmond, sixth Duke of, and first Duke of Gordon, b. 1818, d. 1903. He held various ministerial posts and was chairman of the commission appointed in 1879 charged with investigating the condition of agriculture in the United Kingdom.

Roberts, (John) Bryn, b. 1843, d. 1931. A Liberal MP from 1885 to 1906 when he was appointed a judge.

Robinson, Sir Henry, b. 1857, d. 1927. He was Vice-President of the Local Government Board for Ireland from 1898 to 1920. Robinson was regarded as an authority on Irish affairs.

Robinson, Seámus. Part of the gang that murdered two policeman in Tipperary in January 1919, marking the first engagement since the Eater Rising of 1916.

Ronayne, Joseph P., b. 1822, d. 1876. Ronayne exerted considerable influence in Home Rule circles and upon Parnell. He was an MP from December 1872 until his death.

Rosebery, fifth Earl, b. 1849, d. 1929. Brought into the Cabinet in 1885, he was Foreign Secretary in the Liberal government of 1886 and again between 1892 and 1894 when he succeeded Gladstone as Prime Minister. Rosebery resigned the leadership of the Liberal party in November 1896 but remained an influential figure.

Russell, Thomas Wallace, b. 1841, d. 1920. He was a Unionist MP for Tyrone from 1886 to January 1910 and an Irish party MP for North Tyrone from October 1911 to 1918. Russell was Secretary to the Local Government Board, 1895 to 1900, and Vice-President of the Department of Agricultural and Technical Instruction in succession to Sir Horace Plunkett from 1907 to 1918. Russell, an Ulster Protestant, was a strong advocate of compulsory land purchase.

St Albans, Duchess of, d. 1926. Widow of the Duke of St Albans.

Salisbury, third Marquess of, b. 1830, d. 1902. Lord Salisbury was the Conservative Prime Minister in 1885–86, 1886–92, 1895–1902, when he retired because of declining health.

Samuel, Herbert, b. 1870, d. 1963. First elected an MP in 1902 he remained in Parliament until defeated at the general election of 1918. From 1906 to December 1916 Samuel held several ministerial posts. He was created the first Viscount Samuel in 1937.

Saunderson, Col. Edward, b. 1837, d. 1906. Serving first as a Liberal MP from 1865 to 1875, Saunderson was returned to Parliament as a Conservative for North Armagh in 1885, holding the seat until he died. He was Chairman of the Ulster Unionist party.

Scott, C. P., b. 1846, d. 1925. He was the editor of the *Manchester Guardian* from 1872 until 1929.

Selborne, second Earl, b. 1859, d. 1942. He was an influential Liberal Unionist.

Sexton, Thomas, b. 1848, d. 1932. Sexton was a journalist and was first returned to Parliament in 1880, remaining an MP until 1896 when he retired. He was High Sheriff of Dublin in 1887, Lord Mayor in 1888 and 1889 and chairman of the *Freeman's Journal* between 1892 and 1912. Sexton had immense influence within the Irish party and supported the anti-Parnellites in December 1890. In the Edwardian era party leaders were ever conscious to placate Sexton because he often determined the stance of the *Freeman's Journal*, sometimes in opposition to official party policy.

Shaw, William, b. 1823, d. 1895. Shaw, a Cork Protestant, was returned to Parliament in 1868, retaining his seat until 1885. He was elected Chairman of the Irish party following Butt's death but lost the leadership to Parnell on 17 May 1880. He withdrew from the party in January 1881 thereafter sitting and generally supporting the Liberals. Shaw was chairman of the failed Muster Bank; he was declared bankrupt in January 1886.

Shaw-Lefevre, George J., b. 1831, d. 1928. A Radical who sat in several Liberal Cabinets, he was an MP from 1866 to 1885 when he lost his seat, returning to the House of Commons between 1886 and 1895. He was created Baron Eversley in 1906. As Eversley he wrote a major account of the Irish land question.

Shawe-Taylor, John, b. 1866, d. 1911. Son of a County Galway squire, Shawe-Taylor's letter in 1902 initiated the land conference in December where he represented the landowners' interests.

Sheehan, Daniel Desmond, b. 1874, An ally of William O'Brien, Sheehan was the Honorary Secretary of the All-for-Ireland League and President of the Irish Land and Labour Association. He was an MP from 1901 to 1918.

Sheehy, David, b. 1844, d. 1932. He was an MP between 1885 and 1900 and again from 1903 until 1918. Brother of the nationalist priest Father Sheehy, he sided with the anti-Parnellites in December 1890.

Sinclair, Thomas, b. 1839, d. 1914. An Ulster Liberal until 1886, Sinclair was thereafter an active Liberal Unionist.

Smith, Abel Henry, b. 1862, d. 1930. Smith had been an unpaid private secretary to Walter Long between 1895 and 1900 and sat as a Conservative MP from 1900 to January 1910.

Smith, F. E., b. 1872, d. 1930, he became a member of the government as Solicitor-General in May 1915, Attorney-General in October 1915 and Lord Chancellor as Baron Birkenhead (created Viscount in 1921, Earl in 1922) in October 1919.

Smith, Goldwin, b. 1823, d. 1910. A notable historian and intellectual, he emigrated to Canada in 1871 but maintained a close interest in Home Rule which he opposed.

Smith, W. H., b. 1825, d. 1892. Smith was head of W. H. Smith newsagents and a Conservative MP. He was in the Cabinet in 1885–86, being Chief Secretary of the Irish Office for a few days in January 1886 after William Hart Dyke's resignation. Between 1887 and 1891 Smith was leader of the House of Commons.

Smuts, General, b. 1850, d. 1950. Smuts was a South African leader and member of the War Cabinet.

Smyth, Patrick J., b. 1823, d. 1885. Though principally a Repeal advocate since the 1840s, Smyth was elected to the House of Commons as a Home Ruler in 1871, sitting until 1884 when he resigned. Smyth became disillusioned over the land war and with Parnell.

Southborough, first Baron, b. 1860, d. 1947. He was a civil servant.

Spencer, fifth Earl, b. 1835, d. 1910. Spencer was twice Lord Lieutenant of Ireland, 1868–74 and 1882–85. He was an influential Gladstonian, sitting in the Cabinet in 1886 and between 1892 and 1895.

Glossary

Stack, Austin, b. 1880, d. 1929. Elected a Sinn Féin MP in 1918 he declined to take his seat, sitting instead in the first Dáil. Stack was Secretary of Home Affairs in the Dáil between 1919 and 1921 and a member of the delegation sent to London in October 1921 to negotiate the Treaty.

Sullivan, Alexander Martin, b. 1830, d. 1884. Sullivan was the brother of T. D. Sullivan and Donal Sullivan. He succeeded Charles Gavan Duffy in 1874 as editor of the *Nation* newspaper, handing over control to T. D. Sullivan in 1876. A. M. Sullivan was a pious Catholic who turned the newspaper into a voice of the Catholic hierarchy as well as being an advocate of self-government principles. He was detested by Fenians. Sullivan attended the private meeting at the Bilton Hotel on 19 May 1870 which founded the Home Government Association. He was an MP from 1874 to February 1882 when he resigned.

Sullivan, Donal, b. 1838, d. 1907. He was the brother of A. M. and T. D. Sullivan and closely linked to T. M. Healy. Sullivan was returned to Parliament in 1885, retaining his seat until he died. He supported the anti-Parnellites in December 1890.

Sullivan, T. D., b. 1827, d. 1914. He was the oldest of the three Sullivan brothers who sat in the House of Commons. He succeeded A. M. Sullivan as proprietor of the *Nation*. Sullivan was returned to Parliament in 1880, sitting until 1900 when he retired. Despite being a moderate, he was imprisoned for a short period during the Plan of Campaign. Like his son-in-law T. M. Healy, Sullivan, a pious Catholic who devoted considerable energy to cleric interests, disliked Parnell and sided with his opponents in December 1890.

Tone, Theobald Wolfe, b. 1773, d. 1798 (suicide). An Protestant Irishmen, Wolfe Tone was an advocate of Catholic rights in the 1790s and a republican. He was created a general in the French Army and captured during the French invasion of 1798. Pleading the right as a soldier to be executed by firing squad, he was condemned to be hanged, drawn and quartered. Prior to his execution he committed suicide. Subsequently he became an icon to nationalists and especially to republicans.

Tracey, Séan. Part of the gang that murdered two policemen in Tipperary in January 1919, marking the first engagement since the Easter Rising of 1916.

Trevelyan, George Otto, b. 1838, d. 1928. Son of Sir Charles Trevelyan, who has a chequered reputation in Irish history because of his part in famine measures and their absence, G. O. Trevelyan entered parliament in 1865 and was noted as an advocate of franchise reform. He became Chief Secretary of the Irish Office in May 1882 after the assassination of Lord Frederick Cavendish, leaving this post in October 1884. In the Gladstone administration of 1886 he was Secretary for Scotland, but resigned with Joseph Chamberlain in March. Trevelyan was initially a Liberal Unionist, losing his seat in 1886. In 1887 he rejoined the Liberal party and sat again in the House of Commons from 1887 until 1897. He is chiefly remembered for his historical writings.

Glossary

Victoria, b. 1819, d. 1901. Monarch, 1837 to 22 January 1901.

Walsh, William J., b. 1841, d. 1921. Walsh succeeded Cardinal McCabe as Archbishop of Dublin. He had been the President of St Patrick's College, Maynooth (the national seminary) since 1881. Walsh's reputation as a nationalist made him a controversial choice for the see of Dublin. After his accession he was a supporter of the Irish party and deeply involved in political calculations.

Webb, Alfred, b. 1837, d. 1908. A Quaker, Webb was one of the founders of the Home Government Association in 1870 and remained part of all subsequent Home Rule organisations. He served most as Treasurer. Webb was a founder of the Protestant Home Rule Association in 1886. He wrote numerous pamphlets and articles on Irish questions, serving as an MP between 1890 and 1895 when he resigned. Webb supported the anti-Parnellites in December 1890.

Welby, Baron, b. 1837, d. 1905. A civil servant, he was Permanent Secretary to the Treasury, 1885–94, being created a Baron in 1894.

Willoughby de Brooke, nineteenth Baron (Richard Grenville Verney), b. 1869, d. 1923. He succeeded to the title on his father's death in 1902. During the Constitutional crisis of 1909–11, and subsequently over Home Rule he was a vocal critic of concessions.

Wyndham, George, b. 1871, d. 1913. First elected to the House of Commons in 1889, Wyndham was Chief Secretary (with a seat in the Cabinet, 1902) from 1900 to 6 March 1905 when he resigned. Wyndham had close connections with the Balfour brothers; his progressive ideas made him suspect to Ulster Unionists.

Principal acts and bills referred to in the text

Coercion legislation
Criminal Law and Procedure Act, 1887
Criminal Law and Procedure Act, 1887 invoked, 1902 denominational
Peace Preservation Act (Westmeath Act), 1872
Peace Preservation Act (Arms Act), 1881
Prevention of Crime Act, 1882
Protection of Person and Property Act, 1881

Education
Education Act, 1892: made attendance compulsory
Education Act, 1902: provided rate-supported funds for denominational schools in England and Wales.
Education Endowments Act, 1885
Intermediate Education Act, 1878: created a commission to act as an examining body for all intermediate schools
Irish Universities Act, 1908: created the National University of Ireland consisting of the former Queen's Colleges at Cork and Galway along

with the former Catholic University in Dublin. The Queen's College, Belfast became free-standing as The Queen's University of Belfast
Royal University of Ireland Act, 1879: created the Royal University comprising the Queen's Colleges

Land

Arrears Act, 1882
Compensation for Disturbance Bill, 1880 (defeated in House of Lords)
Evicted Tenants Bill, 1894 (defeated in House of Lords)
Evicted Tenants Act, 1907
Irish Land Act, 1909
Land Act, 1903
Land Law Act, 1881
Land Law Act, 1887
Land Law Act, 1896
Landlord and Tenant Act, 1870
Land Purchase Bill, 1886 (withdrawn)
Purchase of Land Act, 1885
Purchase of Land Act, 1891
Purchase of Land Amendment Act, 1888
Tenants' Relief Bill, 1886 (defeated)

Other measures and bills

Agricultural and Technical Instruction Act, 1898
Ballot Act, 1872: established secret ballot.
Corrupt and Illegal Practices Act, 1883
Housing of the Working Classes Act, 1908
Irish Church Act, 1869: disestablished Church of Ireland
Irish Reform Act, 1868: lowered franchise requirement
Labourers' Act, 1883: authorised acquisition of land to construct cottages for agricultural labourers
Labourers' Act, 1906: extended previous labourers' acts, including that of 1883
Light Railways and Technical Instruction Act, 1891
Local Government Act, 1898
National Insurance Act, 1911
Old Age Pensions Act, 1908
Parliament Act, 1911
Poor Law Guardians Act, 1896: women qualifed for election
Redistribution Act, 1885: redrew parliamentary constituencies
Reform Act, 1884: tripled size of Irish electorate
Registration Act, 1898: women and peers received local government franchise
Representation of the People Act, 1918
Town Tenants Act, 1906

Chronology

1864
21 January   National League founded.
29 December   National Association founded.

1866
28 June   Fourteenth Earl of Derby appointed (Conservative) Prime Minister.

1867
1 February   Abortive Fenian raid on Chester Castle.
17 February   Bishop David Moriarty denounces Fenians.
5–6 March   Fenian Rising.
20 June   Clan na Gael founded in New York.
18 September   Manchester Rescue attempt; Sergeant Brett killed; 23 November, 3 Irishmen hanged for the incident.
13 December   Clerkenwell House of Detention explosion (12 killed, more than 50 injured).

1868
27 February   Benjamin Disraeli succeeds Earl of Derby as (Conservative) Prime Minister.
19 March   Irish Reform Bill introduced in House of Commons (enacted 13 July).
23 March   William Gladstone calls for disestablishment of Church of Ireland.
26 May   Michael Barrett executed for Clerkenwell explosion (last public execution).
3 August   Amnesty movement begins in Cork.
17 November–   General election (Gladstone appointed (Liberal) Prime
2 December   Minster on 3 December; C. S. Fortescue appointed Chief Secretary on 16 December; Earl Spencer sworn as Lord Lieutenant on 18 December).

1869

22 February	Announcement of release of 49 non-military imprisoned Fenians.
1 March	Irish Church Bill introduced in the House of Commons (enacted 26 July to take effect on 1 January 1871).
29 June	Amnesty Association founded (Isaac Butt elected President).
28 September	Irish Tenant League founded with Butt at its head.
8 December	Vatican Council opens in Rome.

1870

12 January	Papal condemnation of Fenians.
15 February	Land Bill introduced in House of Commons (enacted 1 August).
19 April	George Henry Moore dies.
19 May	Private meeting at Bilton Hotel, Dublin marks founding of Home Rule movement.
29 July	Michael Davitt sentenced to 15 years imprisonment.
1 September	First public meeting of Home Government Association.
20 September	Fall of Rome; end of temporal rule of the Pope.

1871

12 January	Marquess of Hartington appointed Chief Secretary in succession to Fortescue.
17 January	John Martin wins County Meath by-election as an Independent Nationalist (first Home Rule victory).
20 September	Isaac Butt wins Limerick City by-election.

1872

8 February	J. P. Nolan wins County Galway by-election.
12 February	Rowland P. Blennerhassett wins co. Kerry by-election.
1 April–27 May	Galway election petition trial; Nolan unseated on 27 May.
18 July	Ballot Act introduces secret voting.
19 August	Local Government Board Act.
26 November	Catholic Union of Ireland founded.

1873

12 March	Irish University Bill defeated in House of Commons.
26 May	University of Dublin Tests Act.
18–21 November	National Conference establishes Home Rule League.

1874

31 January–12 February	General election in Great Britain (Disraeli appointed (Conservative) Prime Minster 20 February; created Earl of Beaconsfield, 21 August 1876; Sir Michael Hicks Beach appointed Chief Secretary on 27 February).

3 March	Irish party founded.
30 June–2 July	First major debate in the House of Commons on Home Rule.
30 July	Joseph Biggar resorts to obstruction on Expiring Laws Continuance Bill and is criticised by Butt.

1875

13 January	Gladstone retires as Liberal party leader; succeeded by Marquess of Hartington on 3 February.
20–1 January	Tenant-right Conference in Dublin.
16 February	John Mitchel returned unopposed at Tipperary by-election (returned second time on 12 March; declared ineligible on both occasions).
19 April	Charles Stewart Parnell wins County Meath by-election (makes maiden speech in House of Commons on 26 April).
22 April	Joseph Biggar engages in obstruction of Peace Preservation Bill (enacted 28 May).
5–7 August	O'Connell centenary celebrations.

1876

30 June–1 July	Home Rule debate in House of Commons.
20 August	Supreme Council of Irish Republican Brotherhood (IRB) put in force early decision that republicans should cease being MPs by 5 March 1878.
11 December	Duke of Marlborough sworn in as Lord Lieutenant.

1877

31 July–1 August	Parnell and Biggar spearhead obstruction.
27–8 August	Annual Convention of the Home Rule League of Great Britain held at Liverpool; Parnell elected President for the coming year.
17 October–12 November	Gladstone makes only visit to Ireland; presented with Freedom of Dublin.
19 December	Davitt released from prison on ticket of leave.

1878

14–15 January	National Conference meets to consider parliamentary policy.
15 February	James Lowther succeeds Hicks Beach as Chief Secretary.
21 June	Intermediate Education Bill introduced by the government (enacted 16 August).
24 October	Paul Cardinal Cullen dies (appointed Archbishop of Dublin, 3 May 1852; succeeded by Edward McCabe.

1879

4 February	Butt attends his last Home Rule League meeting.
20 April	Tenant Right Association meeting at Irishtown, County Mayo.

Chronology

5 May	Butt dies (succeed by William Shaw as party chairman on 22 May).
1 June	Parnell meets John Devoy, resulting in the New Departure.
8 June	Parnell speaks at Westport land meeting.
26 July	James Lysaght Finigan wins Ennis by-election.
14 August	Richmond Commission appointed (reports 14 January 1881; 11 July 1882).
15 August	Irish Universities Bill enacted.
16 August	National Land League of Mayo founded.
21 October	Irish National Land League founded; Parnell elected President.
19 November	Davitt, James Daly and James Bryce Killen charged with sedition (case ends without convictions).
18 December	Duchess of Marlborough's Appeal for relief of distress founded.

1880

2 January	Parnell arrives in New York to begin his North American tour.
2 January	Mansion House Committee for relief of distress founded.
2 February	Parnell addresses American House of Representatives.
20 February	Parnell when speaking at Cincinnati, Ohio is alleged to have called for breaking 'the last link' between Ireland and Britain (he would deny using this phrase).
1 March	Seed Supply (Ireland) Act.
8 March	Government announces dissolution of Parliament.
15 March	Relief of Distress Act.
21 March	Parnell returns to Ireland.
31 March–13 April	General election (Gladstone appointed (Liberal) Prime Minister on 23 April; W. E. Forster appointed Chief Secretary on 30 April. Earl Cowper sworn in as Lord Lieutenat on 4 May).
17 May	Parnell elected sessional chairman of Irish party by 23 votes to 18.
28 May	John O'Connor Power introduces Land Bill in House of Commons.
1 June	Peace Preservation Act expires.
19 June	Government introduces Compensation for Disturbances Bill.
29 July	Bessborough Commission appointed (reports 4 January 1881).
3 August	Compensation for Disturbances Bill defeated in the House of Lords.
19 September	Parnell's speech at Ennis advocates what becomes

xli

	known as 'boycotting'.
24 September	Beginning of ostracism of Captain Boycott.
14 October	Parnell's 'coats off' speech at Galway.
2 November	Fourteen leaders of the Land League (including Parnell) indicted for conspiracy to prevent payment of rent (trial begins 29 December, collapses when jury fails to reach verdict on 25 January).

1881

4 January	Bessborough Commission reports.
14 January	Richmond Commission preliminary report.
16–17 January	William Shaw and other 'nominal' Home Rulers leave Irish party.
24 January	Protection of Person and Property Bill introduced in House of Commons (enacted 2 March).
31 January	Ladies' Land League launched in Dublin.
3 February	Michael Davitt's ticket of leave (parole) suspended; he is returned to prison.
21 March	Peace Preservation Act.
7 April	Land Bill introduced in House of Commons (enacted 22 August).
2 May	John Dillon arrested (released 8 August).
13 August	First issue of *United Ireland*.
7 September	T. A. Dickson, the Liberal candidate, wins the County Tyrone by-election; Parnell's candidate polls weekly.
15–17 September	Land League Convention in Dublin adopts Parnell's formula to 'test' the Land Act.
13–14 October	Parnell and leading Land League figures imprisoned without trial under the provisions of the Protection of Person and Property Act.
18 October	'No Rent Manifesto'.
20 October	Land Court opens; government suppresses Land League.

1882

10–24 April	Parnell free on parole.
28 April	Lord Cowper resigns as Lord Lieutenant (replaced by Lord Spencer on 4 May).
2 May	Parnell released from Kilmainham gaol; W. E. Forster resigns as Chief Secretary (replaced by Lord Frederick Cavendish on 6 May).
6 May	Cavendish and Thomas Burke, Under-Secretary, murdered in Phoenix Park.
9 May	George Otto Trevelyan appointed Chief Secretary.
11 May	Prevention of Crime Bill introduced in House of Commons (enacted 12 July).
15 May	Arrears Bill introduced in House of Commons (enacted 18 August).
6 June	Davitt makes initial speech advocating land national-

isation.

11 July	Richmond Commission final report.
8 August	Joyce family murdered (Maamtrasna Murders).
18 August	Labourers' Cottages and Allotments Act.
17 October	Irish National League founded.

1883

13 January	Arrest of 17 members of 'Irish Invincibles' (executions, 14 May–9 June).
30 June	T. M. Healy wins Monaghan by-election.
25 August	Labourers' Act; Corrupt and Illegal Practices Act.
11 December	Parnell presented with testimonial of more than £37,000.

1884

1 October	Episcopal Hierarchy formally requests Irish party to represent its education interests in the House of Commons.
17 October	A. M. Sullivan dies.
23 October	Sir Henry Campbell-Bannerman appointed Chief Secretary in succession to Trevelyan.
1 November	Gaelic Athletic Association founded.
1 December	Redistribution Bill introduced in House of Commons (enacted 25 June 1885; eliminates 22 small boroughs in Ireland).
6 December	Representation of the People Bill enacted (Irish electorate increased from 126,000 to 738,000 as a consequence).

1885

21 January	Parnell's speech at Cork.
11 February	Cardinal McCabe dies (succeeded by William Walsh on 23 June).
1 May	Irish Loyal and Patriotic Union founded.
9 June	Liberal government resigns (Salisbury appointed (Conservative) Prime Minster on 23 June; 25 June, Sir William Hart Dyke appointed Chief Secretary; Earl of Carnarvon sworn in as Lord Lieutenant on 30 June;.Edward Gibson created Lord Ashbourne on becoming Lord Chancellor of Ireland on 27 June).
17 July	Ashbourne introduces the Irish Land Purchase Bill in the House of Lords (enacted 14 August).
25 June	Redistribution of Seats Act.
1 August	Parnell has secret meeting with Carnarvon.
14 August	Labourers' Housing and Education Endowments Acts.
5 October	First National League convention to select parliamentary candidates; Parnell emphasises the 'single plank' of Home Rule.

21 November	Irish National League of Great Britain Manifesto to the Irish in Britain to vote against the Liberals.
24 November–9 December	General election; Liberals returned with largest number which is exactly equalled by the total of Conservatives and Home Rulers.
17 December	Herbert Gladstone announces that his father is converted to Home Rule (Hawarden Kite).

1886

23 January	W. H. Smith succeeds Hart-Dyke as Chief Secretary.
25 January	Ulster Unionist party founded; Colonel Edward J. Saunderson is elected leader.
28 January	Salisbury's Ministry resigns.
1 February	Gladstone appointed (Liberal) Prime Minister; John Morley appointed Chief Secretary on 6 February.
1–10 February	Galway borough by-election, Captain O'Shea returned.
22 February	Lord Randolph Churchill speaks in Belfast.
27 March	Joseph Chamberlain and Trevelyan put resignations from Ministry into effect.
8 April	Home Rule Bill introduced in House of Commons.
17 April	Land Purchase Bill introduced in House of Commons (withdrawn 11 June). Irish Protestant Home Rule Association founded.
8 June	Home Rule Bill defeated on its Second Reading in the House of Commons.
26 June	Parliament dissolved.
1–17 July	General election (Salisbury appointed Prime Minister on 25 July; Hicks Beach appointed Chief Secretary on 5 August).
20 September	Parnell's Tenants' Relief Bill defeated in the House of Commons.
29 September	Royal Commission (Cowper Commission) appointed to consider land question.
23 October	Plan of Campaign published in *United Ireland*.
18 December	Plan of Campaign proclaimed 'an unlawful and criminal conspiracy'.

1887

21 February	Cowper Commission reports.
7 March	Arthur Balfour becomes Chief Secretary in succession to Hicks Beach; *The Times* begins series 'Parnellism and Crime'.
28 March	Criminal Law and Procedure Bill introduced in House of Commons (enacted 19 July).
31 March	Irish Land Bill introduced in House of Lords (enacted 23 August).
18 April	Facsimile letter purported to be in Parnell's hand published in *The Times*.
19 August	National League proclaimed as 'dangerous associa-

xliv

	tion'.
9 September	Mitchelstown incident (3 fatalities).

1888

20 April	Papal Rescript condemns Plan of Campaign.
8 May	Parnell addresses the Liberal 80 Club.
13 August	Special Commission on 'Parnellism and Crime' established.
24 December	Land Purchase Act.

1889

20–2 February	Pigott unmasked as forger of letters published in *The Times*.
30 April–8 May	Parnell's testifies before Special Commission.
30 August	Light Railways and Technical Instruction Acts.
25 October	Tenants' Defence Association launched in Dublin.
22 November	Final session of Special Commission.
24 December	Captain William H. O'Shea files a petition for divorce, naming Parnell as co-respondent.

1890

13 February	Special Commission reports.
19 February	Biggar dies.
12 April	'New Tipperary' opens.
17 November	O'Shea granted a *decree nisi* in his divorce petition.
24 November	Gladstone informs Justin McCarthy via Morley that if Parnell remains his own leadership will be a 'almost a nullity'.
25 November	Parnell re-elected Chairman of Irish party.
28 November	Parnell's 'Manifesto to the Irish People'.
1–6 December	Irish party meets in Committee Room 15, Palace of Westminster and splits on the 6th when 44 MPs withdraw to form a separate party, leaving 28 behind with Parnell.
3 December	Catholic episcopal standing committee denounces Parnell.
22 December	Anti-Parnellite candidate, Sir John Pope Hennessy, wins Kilkenny by-election.
30 December	Negotiations between William O'Brien and Parnell begin in Boulogne (ends without agreement 11 February 1891).

1891

7 March	*National Press* (anti-Parnellite) launched.
10 March	Irish National Federation (anti-Parnellite) founded.
2 April	Anti-Parnellite candidate wins Sligo North by-election.
6 April	Irish Loyal and Patriotic Union becomes Irish Unionist Alliance.
25 June	Parnell and Katharine O'Shea marry.

8 July	Anti-Parnellite wins Carlow by-election.
5 August	Purchase of Land Act; creates Congested Districts Board.
27 September	Parnell's last public speech at Creggs.
1–2 October	National Liberal Federation's Newcastle Programme.
6 October	Parnell dies (funeral, 11 October).
9 November	W. L. Jackson succeeds Balfour as Chief Secretary.

1892

22 February	Irish Education Bill introduced in House of Commons (enacted 27 June).
17 June	Belfast Convention opposes Home Rule.
12–26 July	General election (Gladstone appointed (Liberal) Prime Minister on 15 August; Morley returns as Chief Secretary on 22 August).
25 November	Douglas Hyde addresses National Literary Society.

1893

13 February	Home Rule Bill introduced in the House of Commons.
31 July	First meeting of Gaelic League.
2 September	Home Rule Bill passes in House of Commons.
8 September	Home Rule Bill defeated in House of Lords.

1894

3 March	Gladstone resigns.
5 March	Lord Rosebery becomes (Liberal) Prime Minister.
12 March	Rosebery's 'predominant partner' speech in the House of Lords.
18 April	Irish Agricultural Organisation Society founded by Sir Horace Plunkett.
19 April	Evicted Tenants Bill introduced in House of Commons (defeated in House of Lords 14 August).
26 May	Royal Commission on the Financial Relations between Great Britain and Ireland appointed (H. C. E. Childers chairman).

1895

21 June	Government loses vote on Army estimates.
23 June	Liberal Ministry resigns.
25 June	Salisbury appointed (Conservative) Prime Minister.
12–26 July	General election (Salisbury remains Prime Minister; Gerald Balfour appointed Chief Secretary 4 July).
27 August	Plunkett proposes formation of 'Recess Committee'.
7 November	Healy expelled from executive of Irish National League of Great Britain and on 13 November from Irish National Federation.

1896

2 February	McCarthy resigns as chairman of anti-Parnellite party.
18 February	John Dillon elected (31 to 21) Chairman of anti-Parnellites.
31 March	Poor Law Guardians Bill enacted (women qualified for election as Poor Law Guardians).
1 August	Recess Committee reports.
14 August	Land Law Act.
1–3 September	Convention of the Irish Race held in Dublin.
5 September	Publication of Royal Commission on Financial Relations report.
6 October	Rosebery resigns as Liberal leader.

1897

12 January	People's Rights Association founded.

1898

23 January	William O'Brien launches United Irish League at Westport.
21 February	Local Government (Ireland) Bill introduced in House of Commons (12 August).
29 March	Registration Act (women and peers receive local government franchise).

1899

7 February	Dillon resigns as chairman of anti-Parnellites.
March	Commemoration of 1798.
9 August	Agricultural and Technical Instruction Act.
11 October	Boer War begins.

1900

30 January	Irish party reunited; 6 February, John Redmond elected chairman.
3–26 April	Queen Victoria visits Ireland.
19–20 June	United Irish League convention; Redmond elected President and it is confirmed as organisational arm of Irish party.
6 August	Intermediate Education Act.
29 September–11 October	General election (Salisbury remains Prime Minster; George Wyndham appointed Chief Secretary 9 November).
11 December	Healy expelled from Irish party.

1901

22 January	Queen Victoria dies; succeeded by King Edward VII.
1 July	Royal Commission (Lord Robertson chairman) on University Education in Ireland appointed.
4 December	United Irish League of America founded in New York.

xlvii

1902

14 February	Rosebery at Liverpool repudiates Home Rule policy.
31 May	Boer War ends.
11 July	Salisbury resigns; Arthur Balfour on 12 July appointed (Conservative) Prime Minister.
3 September	Captain John Shawe-Taylor publishes letter suggesting land settlement.
8 November	Sir Antony McDonnell appointed Under-Secretary.
20 December	Land Conference convened in Dublin (reports 3 January 1903).

1903

28 February	Robertson Commission final report.
25 March	Land Bill (the Wyndham Act) introduced in House of Commons (enacted 14 August).
11 July–1 August	Edward VII visits Ireland.
4 November	William O'Brien announces withdrawal from public life.

1904

26 April–5 May	Edward VII visits Ireland.
21 August	Dunraven letter on devolution.
26 August	Irish Reform Association founded.
27 September	Wyndham rejects idea of devolution.

1905

3 March	Ulster Unionist Council formed.
6 March	Wyndham resigns as Chief Secretary (Walter Long appointed 12 March).
4 December	Balfour resigns.
5 December	Sir Henry Campbell-Bannerman appointed (Liberal) Prime Minister; James Bryce appointed Chief Secretary 14 December.

1906

13–27 January	General election (Campbell-Bannerman remains Prime Minister).
9 April	Education Bill introduced (defeated in House of Lords 19 December).
5 May	First number of *Sinn Féin* published.
18 May	Town Tenants Bill introduced in House of Commons (enacted December).
28 May	Labourers' Housing Bill introduced in House of Commons (enacted 4 August).
31 May	Davitt dies.
2 June	Royal Commission (Sir Edward Fry chairman) on Trinity College appointed.
14 October	Laurence Ginnell, MP denounces grazing system.
21 October	Col Saunderson dies; 1 November, Walter Long elected leader of Irish Unionists.
31 December	Peace Preservation Act, 1881, expires.

1907

12 January	Fry Commission reports.
29 January	Augustine Birrell appointed to succeed James Bryce as Chief Secretary.
7 May	Irish Council Bill introduced in House of Commons.
21 May	National Convention follows Redmond's advice and rejects the Council Bill.
3 June	Government announces withdrawal of Council Bill.
27 June	Evicted Tenants Bill introduced in House of Commons (enacted 28 August).
2 August	Pius X issues *Ne Temere*.
13 December	O'Brien and John Redmond hold discussions on O'Brien's return to the Irish party.
19 December	Joint Committee of Unionist Associations of Ireland founded.

1908

17 January	O'Brien and Healy rejoin Irish party.
21 February	C. J. Dolan Sinn Féin candidate for North Leitrim by-election is defeated.
31 March	Irish University Bill introduced in House of Commons (enacted 1 August).
3 April	Campbell-Bannerman resigns; H. H. Asquith appointed (Liberal) Prime Minister on 8 April.
1 August	Old Age Pensions Act.
21 December	Housing of the Working Classes (Ireland) and Children's Acts.

1909

9–10 February	United Irish League Convention; O'Brien shouted down.
29 March	People's Budget introduced in House of Commons (rejected by House of Lords, 30 November).
20 September	Labour Exchanges Act.
3 December	Irish Land Act.
10 December	Asquith speaks at the Albert Hall endorsing Home Rule.

1910

15–28 January	General election (Asquith remains Prime Minister).
21 February	Edward Carson elected leader of Ulster Unionists.
31 March	All-For-Ireland League founded by O'Brien.
6 May	King Edward VII dies; succeeded by George V.
17 June–4 November	Constitutional Conference (Irish party is not invited to send representatives).
10 November	Failure of Constitutional Conference publicly announced.
3 December–13 January 1911	General election (Asquith remains Prime Minister).

1911

22 February	Parliament Bill introduced (royal assent 18 August).
7–12 June	George V visits Dublin.
23 September	Unionist rally at Craigavon.
1 October	Official dedication of Parnell Monument in Dublin.
27 October	Sir Henry Primose's Committee reports.
8 November	Balfour resigns as leader of Conservative party; succeeded on 13 November by Andrew Bonar Law.
16 December	Local Authorities Qualification and National Insurance Acts.

1912

8 February	Winston Churchill speaks in Belfast.
11 April	Government of Ireland Bill introduced.
11, 13, 18 June	Parliamentary debate on Thomas Agar-Robartes motion to exclude parts of north-east from Home Rule Bill.
27 July	Unionist rally at Blenheim Palace.
28 September	Ulster Day.

1913

1 January	Edward Carson's motion in the House of Commons to exclude Ulster from the Home Rule Bill.
16 January	Home Rule Bill passes third reading in House of Commons.
30 January	House of Lords rejects Home Rule Bill.
31 January	Ulster Volunteer Force formed.
7 July	Home Rule Bill passes in House of Commons.
15 July	Home Rule Bill defeated in House of Lords.
17 September	Carson's speech at Newry on provisional Ulster government.
14 October, 6 November, 10 December	Asquith and Bonar Law hold secret talks.
19 November	Irish Citizen Army launched.
25 November	Irish Volunteers formed.
4 December	Royal Proclamation prohibits importation of military arms to Ireland.

1914

15 January	Bonar Law announces end of meetings with Asquith.
9 March	Asquith announces that Home Rule Bill will be amended.
20–5 March	Curragh incident.
24–5 April	Larne gunrunning.
12 May	Asquith announces that an amending bill is to be brought forward (introduced in House of Lords on 23 June; postponed indefinitely on 30 July).
25 May	Home Rule Bill passes third reading in House of

1

	Commons.
21–4 June	Buckingham Palace Conference.
28 June	Archduke Franz Ferdinand assassinated.
26 July	Four people killed and 37 wounded by military at Bachelors Walk after Howth gunrunning.
3 August	Germany declares war on France.
4 August	Belgium invaded; the United Kingdom declares war.
10 August	Education (Provision of Meals) Act.
18 September	Suspending and Home Rule Acts.

1915

25 May	Formation of first coalition government.

1916

24–9 April	Rising in Ireland.
3 May	Birrell resigns.
3–12 May	Executions of 13 leaders of revolt.
10 May	Asquith announces Royal Commission on the Rebellion (opens 18 May, reports 3 July).
12–18 May	Asquith visits Ireland.
23 May	David Lloyd George given task of seeking an agreement between Irish parties.
12 June	Ulster Unionist Council accepts Lloyd George proposals.
26–9 June	Trial in London of Sir Roger Casement (executed 3 August).
1 July	Somme offensive begins (concludes 13 November).
3 August	H. E. Duke appointed Chief Secretary.
7 December	Lloyd George appointed to succeed Asquith as Prime Minster (2nd coalition formed).
22–3 December	About 600 untried internees released.

1917

1 February	Unrestricted Germany submarine campaign begins.
3 February	Sinn Féin candidate, Count Plunkett, wins Roscommon North by-election.
6 April	United States enters war.
9 May	Sinn Féin candidate wins Longford South by-election.
21 May	Lloyd George announces establishment of Irish Convention.
7 June	William Redmond killed on the Western Front.
16 June	Government announces release of Sinn Féin prisoners.
10 July	Eamon de Valera wins Clare East by-election.
25 July	Opening of Irish Convention at Trinity College.
10 August	William Cosgrave wins Kilkenny by-election.
25 September	Thomas Ashe dies on hunger strike in Mountjoy prison.
25–6 October	De Valera elected President of Sinn Féin.

27 October	De Valera elected President of Irish Volunteers.

1918

8 January	President Wilson announces the 14 points.
13 January	Several Nationalist members of Irish Convention break with Redmond on question of fiscal autonomy.
2 February	Irish party candidate wins Armagh South by-election.
6 February	Representation of the People Act.
20 February	Southern Unionist committee formed.
6 March	Redmond dies (12 March Dillon elected Chairman of Irish party).
5 April	Final meeting of Irish Convention (12 April reports).
9 April	Military Services Bill introduced in House of Commons (enacted 18 April).
23 April	One-day strike against conscription.
17–18 May	Arrests of Sinn Féin leaders, including de Valera.
20 June	Arthur Griffith wins Cavan East by-election; conscription and Home Rule plans dropped.
4 October	Germany seeks armistice (effected 11 November).
21 November	Parliamentary (Qualification of Women) Act.
4 December	Nominations for parliamentary representation close (25 Sinn Féin candidates are unopposed).
14 December	General election (results announced on 28 December).

1919

18 January	First full meeting of Paris Peace Conference.
21 January	Two Tipperary policemen killed; Dáil Éireann meets at Mansion House Dublin.
1 April	De Valera escapes from Lincoln jail.
1 April	Second session of Dáil Éireann; de Valera elected President.
3 June	Local Government Act.
18 June	Dáil Éireann establishes 'arbitration courts'.
21 June	Treaty of Versailles signed.
10 September	Proclamation of Sinn Féin, Irish Volunteers, Gaelic League and other bodies.
12 September	Government declares Dáil Éireann illegal.
20 September	Republican newspapers suppressed.
7 October	Cabinet sub-committee on Ireland appointed.

1920

2 January	Formation of Black and Tans.
15 January	Borough and Urban Council Elections.
25 February	Better Government of Ireland Bill introduced in House of Commons (enacted 23 December).
10 March	Ulster Unionist Council accepts six county exclusion area.

| 12 June | Elections for county councils, rural district councils and Boards of Poor Law Guardians. |

9 June Dáil Éireann meets for first time since October 1919.

9 August	Restoration of Order Act.
25 October	Terence MacSwiney dies on hunger strike.
1 November	Kevin Barry executed.
21 November	'Bloody Sunday'.

1921

1 January	British government policy of reprisals implemented.
4 February	Carson resigns Ulster Unionist leadership (replaced by James Craig).
9 April	Archbishop William Walsh dies.
5 May	Craig and de Valera hold private talk in Dublin.
24 May	General election for Northern Ireland Parliament.
7 June	First meeting of Northern Ireland House of Commons; James Craig appointed Prime Minister.
22 June	King George V ceremonial opening of Northern Ireland Parliament.
28 June	Southern Ireland Parliament meets and adjourns indefinitely.
9 July	British government and republicans agree to truce (effected 11 July).
14–21 July	De Valera meets Lloyd George in London.
16 August	Second Dáil Éireann meets.
11 October	Anglo-Irish Conference opens, lasts until 6 December.
17–18 November	Unionist Association conference in Liverpool.
6 December	Treaty signed.
16 December	Treaty approved by British Parliament.

1922

| 7 January | Dáil Éireann approved Treaty by 64 votes to 57. |

1

Definitions, interpretations, terminology and theoretical concepts

We can not, under the British Constitution, ask for more than the restitution of Grattan's Parliament. But no man has the right to fix the boundary to the march of a nation; no man has a right to say to his country: 'Thus far shalt thou go and no further', and we have never attempted to fix the *ne plus ultra* to the progress of Ireland's nationhood, and we never shall. (Charles Stewart Parnell, 21 January 1885)[1]

The demand for national self-government is ... founded by us, first of all, upon right, and we declare that no ameliorative reforms, no number of land acts, or labourers' acts, or education acts, no redress of financial grievances, no material improvements or industrial development, can ever satisfy Ireland until Irish laws are made and administered upon Irish soil by Irishmen. (John Redmond, 4 September 1907)[2]

Introduction

Home Rule has been explored from many angles, but most authorities concur with John Redmond that it was a demand standing independent and above other Irish grievances. Parnell's timeless anthem at Cork City in January 1885, a phrase from which adorns his monument in Dublin, exemplifies another feature of the standard interpretation: what Ireland demanded was delimited by the British Constitution. Home Rule was expedient, the minimum that Irishmen were prepared to accept because this was the maximum that England might concede. From another vantage point, Parnell's position was reiterated in a newspaper editorial on the eve of the 1918 general election:

1

Viewed from another point of view, the present election cannot be said to be concerned about any real vital issue. It is a question, not so much of the end in view, as the means for the attainment of that end. It resolves itself, for the most part, into a domestic dispute as to which of the two courses is better in the long run for the attainment of the most extensive measure of freedom which may be attainable for their beloved country. Parliamentarians would be satisfied, for the present at all events, with Irish autonomy within the Empire. Sinn Féiners wish to sever with one stroke the chain that binds Ireland to England, and will not be content with anything less.[3]

F. S. L. Lyons gives the imprimatur of modern scholarship to the orthodox interpretation, writing 'if the Irish question did not change in its essentials, it is clear that the context within which it was debated and fought was very different in, say, 1914, from what it had been in 1800, or even in 1850'.[4] His verdict would now require qualification. James O'Shea suggests that the idea of Home Rule suited tenant farmers admirably as an expression of anti-English feelings, while R. V. Comerford maintains: 'in the early 1870s, as for long before and long after, popular Irish nationalism was a matter of the self-assertiveness of the Catholic community and of a search for material benefits, rather than a question of yearning for constitutional forms'.[5] Home Rule was an ideal or aspiration to which Parnell and Redmond gave voice, a constitutional formula that would grant Ireland autonomy in most local matters, while maintaining the overarching supremacy of the Westminster Parliament. It was a movement and party that gave expression to the objective, an umbrella affording refuge to a range of particularised interests, a net that allowed Irish society to be dominated by the Catholic bourgeoisie and clergy, and a parliamentary device that was driven by the imperatives of Westminster alignments.

This work analyses the content and context of the various Home Rule schemes, examines the opposition to self-government, assesses other institutional and ameliorative reforms – which either offered some form of self-rule or were intended as substitutes for it – and explores the functions and understanding of what a Dublin Parliament was expected to accomplish. There is no other single study that analyses these questions.[6]

Five themes run through the narrative: first, chronology and context are crucial to the way Home Rule unfurled; second, Home Rule was the means by which disparate national interests were formulated, mobilised and directed; third, the intersection of institutional structures with the world of ideas was important; fourth, the dispute shaped the discourse and rhetoric about self-government, civil and majoritarian rights and the concept of citizenship; and fifth, British politicians responded imaginatively to the challenge. Margaret O'Callaghan draws attention to the importance of how ideas are represented, a conclusion that is echoed in the present work.[7] Home Rule was integral to British political discourse in the late nineteenth and early twentieth centuries. John Morley in 1868 pinpointed Ireland's centrality, observing:

> [T]here is the Irish question, for example. Underneath the surface of this, and wrapped up in it, are nearly all the controversies of principle which will agitate the political atmosphere of our time. It is a microcosm of the whole imperial question. It is the test of our fitness to deal with the other problems which modern circumstances, pressing hard against the old order of ideas and traditions, is forcing upon our attention. The functions of the State, the duties of property, the rights of labour, the question whether the many are born for the few, the question of a centralised imperial power, the question of the pre-eminence of morals in politics – all these things lie in Irish affairs.[8]

Debates about Home Rule took place on the political hustings, in Parliament, through the medium of opinion journals and the press. Words rather than bloodshed were the chosen weapon. The issue inspired both high-minded and ignoble sentiments, blending ideas, pragmatic plans, political scheming, electioneering and appeals to public sentiment. In an age of emergent democracy, Home Rule pre-eminently brought into the public arena the problem of the respective rights of majorities and minorities. This book focuses mainly on the politics of Home Rule, pointing to the interaction of, and need to convince and maintain the allegiance of eight identifiable groups, each of which was vital to the legitimacy of self-government. First, the national movement had to persuade and retain the conviction of its own people, the Catholics of Ireland; second, implementation could only take place when a major political group in Great Britain adopted the programme; third, the House of Commons had to pass a self-government measure, implying the need for an electoral strategy and public consent; fourth, the presumed opposition of the House of Lords had to be modified; fifth, a substantial section of public opinion in Britain had to be converted to the idea; sixth, it had to be accepted by influential elements of the press; seventh, southern Irish Unionist opposition had to be moderated; and, finally, Ulster Unionist interests needed to be satisfied. In the first two attempts to initiate Home Rule, too few of these groups were convinced, in 1912 the question became hamstrung by the problem of Ulster, though by 1914 at least the main outline of a settlement was reached. The next two attempts to introduce Home Rule, between 1916 and 1918, revealed once and for all the difficulty of addressing the concerns of

3

all eight groups simultaneously. Only after April 1918, when British leaders divided the question into its constituent parts, were the requisite conditions in place, and a settlement, no matter how imperfect and contentious, completed.

I devote less systematic attention to how Home Rule was interpreted in Ireland at the grassroots, to developments in the rhetoric of self-determination and to the role of the diaspora, all interesting questions in their own right. The theme underlined here is that the debate on Home Rule was carried out within an Anglo-Irish political context by elites who when necessary, enlisted the support of wider groups for their respective positions, but usually pursued their aims with only limited reference to these external elements.

This book does not fit into any single interpretative or methodological 'school', but is syncretic. Underpinning the study is Parnell's observation in 1874 that he 'put Home Rule first because it embodied everything else'.[9] Conventionally, Home Rule is seen as a two-sided coin – national demands and British responses – coupled to the theme espoused by Redmond and Lyons of whether self-government would be won through constitutional agitation or physical force.[10] Patriots are arranged along a continuum – radical revolutionaries at one end, constitutionalists at the other, linked together by their common goal. Here, instead, an alternative model is substituted, emphasising internal dynamics within the national movement, and a distinction is made between those who advocated self-government primarily on moral grounds, and those who did so on material grounds. Contrary to its originators' intentions, Home Rule contributed to polarisation in Ireland. The division was not purely ethnic, but in the longer term the issue of self-government became the instrument of the Catholic rural middle classes, a development that was advanced by the land question and by a redistribution of parliamentary seats which reduced urban influences. The class base of Home Rule is often recognised, but its implications receive little attention. Ulster Unionism has often been seen in this light, and here Home Rule is to be subjected to analysis using a similar conceptual framework. Home Rule was not founded upon rural grievances, but drew strength from these and came to reflect agrarian values.

According to Philip Bull, the land issue was the gateway to questions of nationality and its relationship to the landowning class.[11] A cohesive national movement was able to set the pace of events, as happened in the three agrarian agitations: the land war, Plan of Campaign and the United Irish League from 1898 to 1903. Bull suggests that the structures of these agrarian movements, especially in the last instance, effectively created the basis for an alternative system of government, but that this system proved unable to adapt to changes resulting from the Wyndham Act of 1903 and its corollary, a co-operative future between the Protestant Ascendancy and bourgeois Catholicism. William O'Brien sought to build upon the foundation laid in 1903, but this was resisted by John Dillon, who preferred the reassuring formula of conflict based upon polarisation on agrarian questions. Bull argues that reversion to a redundant political strategy eventually destroyed the Irish party, narrowing support, and shifting emphasis away from patriotic ideology to a movement that merely expressed class and sectional interests. Catholic sectarianism was reinforced, and under Dillon's influence the arguments used by the Irish party shifted 'from nationalism to class, from a priority for Irish autonomy to a multi-British alliance against privilege and old elites. They had … returned the journey of O'Connell from Repeal to the Whig alliance … linking the future of their cause inextricably to a British party. As with O'Connell, the consequences of this was to be the undermining of the political basis of their movement.'[12]

Consonant with older Irish patriotic interpretations, this argument emphasises the limitations of parliamentarianism, the shortcomings of British responses and a fossilised Irish party by the mid-Edwardian years.[13] In this book, in contrast, Home Rule is presented as a more varied and complex phenomenon: the Irish party is seen promoting sectional interests from the time of its foundation, and Catholic sectarianism is evident from the outset, with its growing virulence owing more to Irish Ireland and the Gaelic revival than to Dillon. R. F. Foster anticipates the question of how the Irish party retained its grip, suggesting that it continued to work effectively on behalf of constituents; the reforms it promoted appealed to the dominant elite.[14] Paul Bew throws light on the problem, observing, 'the party represented the accumulated political capital of an increasingly self-confident, middle-class, Catholic Ireland'.[15] Preoccupation with routine conventional politics, focusing to a considerable degree on obtaining practical reforms, provided a firm link between leaders and local elites. Moreover, David Fitzpatrick points out that, despite the absence of formal local structures in 1914, virtually all independent groups claimed loyalty to the party, a condition mirrored in Alvin Jackson's analysis of Ulster Unionists in Edwardian Ireland.[16] The Home Rule movement, Fitzpatrick observes, had a well-established place in local communal life, a vitality that it maintained through a delicate equilibrium of potentially antagonistic forces.

Definitions

Irish self-government has a distant lineage. It was given flesh in the late eighteenth century when Ireland enjoyed substantial though not complete autonomy. The British Crown remained head of state in Ireland and the Irish Parliament did not engage in independent relations with foreign potentates. Considerable authority was retained by the English government, which could decline to accept legislation passed by in Dublin, and neither the Viceroy nor the Chief Secretary was accountable to the Irish Parliament. Only Protestants comprised the Irish Parliament, though Catholics able to meet the high property qualification were granted the ballot in 1793. Ireland possessed representative but not responsible institutions. As an alternative to such limited autonomy, Protestant republicans such as Theobald Wolfe Tone sought complete separation from Great Britain. His aim was 'to break the connection with England, the never-failing source of all our political evils'.[17] He was followed by Robert Emmet, another disaffected Protestant, who tried 'to effect a total separation between Great Britain and Ireland – to make Ireland totally independent of Great Britain'.[18] Republicans might dream of an unambiguous break, but they usually failed to address the matter of Ireland's place within a British-dominated North Atlantic imperium.

After the success of Catholic emancipation in 1829, Daniel O'Connell attempted to revive a Repeal of the Union campaign, anticipating that even if this could not be achieved, the issue would at least be a lever with which to squeeze concessions out of British leaders. In 1831 he announced, 'we only want a Parliament to do our private business, leaving the national business to a national assembly'.[19] O'Connell's formula, called 'simple Repeal', entailed a reversion to the Constitution of 1782, which would make the Irish and Westminster Parliaments co-equal, leaving the Crown the sole connection between the two countries. His movement was almost entirely composed of Catholics. When he attempted to lure the prominent Ulsterman, William Sharman Crawford, into the campaign in November 1831, he was rebuffed. Sharman Crawford could support 'a national principle of local legislation', but not 'two parliaments with equal powers in all matters'.[20]

When O'Connell revived the Repeal campaign in 1843, the movement sought:

> the restoration of a separate and local Parliament for Ireland – the restoration of the independence of Ireland. The first would necessarily include the making of all laws that should be of force within the entire precincts of Ireland – by the Sovereign, the Lords, and the Commons of Ireland, and the total exclusion of any other legislature from any interposition in affairs strictly Irish. The second would necessarily include the final decision of all questions in litigation by Irish tribunals seated in Ireland, to the total exclusion of any species of appeal to British tribunals.[21]

O'Connell's more mundane goal was 'a Parliament inferior to the English Parliament but vested with powers of "independent legislation"'.[22] But, he was prepared to accept 'a subordinate Parliament'. While O'Connell conceived of an Irish Parliament in which popular influences, at least in the lower chamber, would be substantial, he did not resolve how relations between Great Britain and Ireland in areas such as foreign and military affairs would be harmonised, or the degree of independence that an Irish executive might exercise. Isaac Butt, then an opponent, took O'Connell to task, pointing out that he 'had never told them what was the national independence at which he aimed – whether he was to be contented with the settlement of 1782 ... or whether they were to sue for something beyond and inconsistent with that settlement'.[23] Like its predecessor, this Repeal campaign appealed principally to Catholics.

An alternative federalist campaign was the handiwork of a mainly Protestant counter-movement. In November 1844 Sharman Crawford drew up a plan heavily influenced by the model recently established for Canada. Under this scheme, Irish representation would be retained at Westminster. In his view:

> [T]he principle of self-government by representation should be carried out through every institution of the state; and local taxation, whether in a parish or a town, should be imposed and managed, and the by-laws affecting the locality enacted by a body representing the locality which taxation or these laws affect, and the whole kept under control and regulation, by the central power of Imperial representation.[24]

In 1844 O'Connell briefly took up Sharman Crawford's ideas on federalism, though these never achieved popularity among Repealers, perhaps because advocates lacked both cohesion and an agreed definition of what was intended.[25] By late November, O'Connell was anxious to distance himself from the federalist adventure: '"Federalists", I am told, are still talking and meeting – much good may it do them, I wish them all manner of happiness; but I don't expect any good from it. ... I wish them well. Let them work as well as they can but they are none of my children. I have nothing to do with them.'[26] O'Connell's flirtation with federalism helped open a breach with Young Ireland – the group of intellectuals associated with his movement – which then deserted him, in part, as a response to his vacillations and modest ambitions. Thomas Davis one of Young Ireland's original leaders, rejected the federalist project, arguing that 'the aspiration of Ireland is for unbounded nationality. ... The destiny of Ireland ... is for no qualified freedom.'[27] Davis declared that he would 'never contribute one shilling, or give my name, heart, or hand, for such an object as the simple Repeal by the British Parliament of the Act of Union';[28] nothing short of 'independence' would satisfy him. James Fintan Lalor was even more scathing about Repeal. Indeed, Young Ireland as a whole had as much difficulty as advocates of Repeal in giving precision to what it demanded and especially in defining the future connection between the two countries.

The foray into constructing a federal constitution has been largely forgotten. However, it merits closer attention. Sir Charles Gavan Duffy's retrospective, *Young Ireland*, affords a useful glimpse of the episode by one who was critical of O'Connell's deviation.[29] He saw federalism as a construct of Irish Protestants and English Radicals in need of a means to be associated with a 'national' issue in order to salvage their prospects at the forthcoming general election. Duffy suggested that:

> [F]ederalism as it was then commonly understood meant little more than the creation of a Legislative Council with fiscal powers somewhat in excess of the fiscal powers of the grand jury, but not authorised to deal with the greatest concerns of a nation – domestic and international trade, the land code, education, national defences, and the subsidies to religious denominations.[30]

Thus, he could see that the lasting legacy of federal self-government would be something less than what Catholics desired. Federalism, like Repeal, fell into abeyance after 1846.

Fenians – members of a secret oath-bound Irish Republican Brotherhood committed to the establishment of a republic in Ireland – also had little grasp of finely calibrated structures. Their Proclamation in 1867 decreed:

> [A]ll men are born with equal rights, and in associating to protect one another and share public burdens, justice demands that such associations should rest upon a basis which maintains equality instead of destroying it.
>
> We therefore declare that, unable longer to endure the curse of Monarchical Government, we aim at founding a Republic based on universal suffrage, which shall secure to all the intrinsic value of their labour.
>
> The soil of Ireland in the possession of an oligarchy, belongs to us, the Irish people, and to us it must be restored.
>
> We declare, also, in favour of absolute liberty of conscience, and complete separation of Church and State.[31]

A republic was the professed goal, though individual Fenians were less committed to a precise formula and open to variations on the self-government principle. It was their methods more than the programme which frightened the respectable classes.

In 1870 the Home Government Association tried to formulate its aims, which under Butt's guidance were defined as 'federal Home Rule'. In spite of Butt's legal and academic credentials, not to mention his critique of O'Connell's ambiguity more than twenty-five years earlier, he was no more than partially successful in constructing a precise definition. His rationale was that 'England, Scotland and Ireland, united as they are under one sovereign should have a common executive and a common national council for all purposes necessary to constitute them, to other nations, as one state, while each of them should have its own domestic administration and its own domestic Parliament for its own internal affairs.'[32] He sought an autonomous, responsible Parliament of two chambers. There was to be a House of Commons of 250–300 MPs and an upper chamber composed of resident peers. The authority of the Irish body would be like that of the old Irish Parliament under Grattan, but it would surrender some powers of taxation for specified imperial needs. The Westminster Parliament would have authority over imperial expenditure, the national debt, civil list, the cost of the military, nomination and maintenance of ambassadors and the colonial establishment. Ireland was to retain its present number of MPs in the Westminster House of Commons. Butt saw his plan as 'the outline ... a crude and imperfect one ... to originate discussion, and to draw out more complete suggestions'. No more than its predecessors did this new movement succeed in drafting proposals that answered key questions such as the proportion of taxation payable by Ireland or the powers of intervention a British regime might retain. Nor were the functions of the Crown carefully illuminated. Butt did not maintain absolute fidelity to the scheme and it never received more than polite acquiescence from Irish patriots.

At the National Conference in November 1873, federalism was accepted as the official platform but some delegates expressed preferences for other plans.[33] The commitment to details was sufficiently vague for Parnell to say in 1875 that he could see no difference between Home Rule and Repeal, as they were practically the same thing.[34] Parnell was unwilling to define what he meant by Home Rule, though he denied being a separatist and promised that the 'Queen would be our Queen'.[35] John Redmond articulated the broad principle of Home Rule, but was not enlightening about the exact relationship between the two countries after its implementation. Parnell's testament at Cork in January 1885 was the fullest definition he offered in public prior to 1886. Typically, it is more remarkable for sentiment than detail.

Home Rule was given reasonably finite form not by Irishmen, but in Gladstone's Government of Ireland bill in 1886. Gladstone held 'that there is such a thing as local patriotism, which in itself is not bad, but good'.[36] In order to enable that local sentiment to flourish, he proposed to 'establish a Legislative Body sitting in Dublin for the conduct of both legislation and administration in Irish as distinct from Imperial affairs'. In his proposed structure many powers permanently or for a specified time were retained by the Westminster Parliament. It was acknowledged, even by national representatives, that the Dublin assembly could be suspended or revoked, as became the fate of the Northern Ireland Parliament in 1972. Before the second reading of the bill Parnell in his final speech accepted it as a 'final' solution, but he was soon repudiated by some of his own supporters.[37] Subsequently, the meaning of Home Rule was well understood, though the details changed over time. Thomas Sexton in 1893 stated that the 1886 proposal had 'narrowed ... the area of the controversy'.[38] When Irish Home Rule was placed before Parliament again in 1912, it was as the first instalment of a devolution of powers to local assemblies in the United Kingdom.

Often, critics, rather than the advocates of Home Rule, were more precise in their understanding of what it would imply – none more so than A. V. Dicey, the then Professor of Constitutional Law at Oxford University, who in 1886 pointed out that Gladstone's plan meant:

> The creation of an Irish Parliament which shall have Legislative authority in matters of Irish concern, and of an Irish executive responsible (in general) for its acts to the Irish Parliament or the Irish people. Hence every scheme of Home Rule which merits that name is marked by three features – *first*, the creation of an Irish Parliament; *secondly*, the right of the Irish Parliament to legislate within its own sphere (however that sphere may be defined) with the habitual freedom from the control of the Imperial or British Parliament; and *thirdly*, the habitual responsibility of the Irish executive for its acts to the Irish people or to their representatives.[39]

Dicey observed that Home Rule was not 'local self-government; Home Rule does not mean national independence but it forms a halfway house to separation'. He analysed the various possibilities – federalism, colonial independence, revival of Grattan's constitution, and Gladstone's proposal – finding them all wanting. His discussion, if partisan, had the merit of clarifying the existing notions, reducing the confusion about what Home Rule implied. He also formulated the requirements of a satisfactory Home Rule scheme, stating:

> It must in the first place be consistent with the ultimate supremacy of the British Parliament.

It must in the second place be just; it must provide that each part of the United Kingdom take a fair share of Imperial burdens; that the citizens of each part have equality of rights; that the rights both of individuals and of minorities be safely guarded.

It must in the third place promise finality; it must be in the nature of a final settlement of the demands made on behalf of Ireland, and not be a mere provocation to the revival of fresh demands.[40]

By 1893 Gladstone had abandoned some aspects of his previous proposal, explaining that the new one had 'the necessary characteristics of I will not say finality, because that is a discredited word, but a real and a continuing settlement'.[41] Home Rule now no longer had to be definitive but only an advanced stage en route to a final settlement.

Both advocates and opponents of Home Rule tended to use terminology such as 'self-government', 'responsible self-government', 'local self-government', 'federalism', 'devolution' and 'independence', all without precision.[42] If greater consensus emerged after 1886, this was not invariably the case. John Redmond in 1910 could say that the concession of Home Rule was only valuable as a means to 'strengthen the arm of the Irish people to push on to the great goal of national independence', and shortly thereafter that 'by Home Rule we mean something like you have here [in the USA], where Federal affairs are governed by the Federal Government and state affairs by the state government'.[43] Alan Ward outlines the differences, noting that Irish Home Rule was an example of devolution, a system of government in which a central legislature would create subordinate regional assemblies to which it would devolve responsibility for regional affairs.[44] He distinguishes this from 'Home Rule All Round', which describes a comprehensive plan for devolution to regional legislatures in England, Scotland and Wales, something that never left the drawing board. Federalism, he suggests, is a constitutional system in which central and regional legislatures exercise co-ordinate powers, the two levels of authority being defined in a constitution that can only be revoked or amended by extraordinary means, not by ordinary legislation. Home Rule proposals after 1870s, Ward observes, were devolutionary, no matter that some were called 'federal'. Home Rulers like Butt were not purists, despite the fact that many of them were lawyers. Typically, they were blasé about institutional structures.

Defining what constituted Ireland proved no less a hurdle. Ireland the island was clearly demarcated and easily comprehensible. There is no iron law that islands, even quite small ones such as Ireland, any more than other geographical regions, are destined by nature to be single or successful nations. The world holds many contrary examples. Nor is it pre-ordained that natural geography must be a determinant in nation-building. One Sinn Féin official in 1916 conceded: 'geography has worked hard to make one nation of Ireland; history has worked against it. The island of Ireland and the national unit of Ireland simply do not coincide.'[45] Irish unity, as some have pointed out, was introduced by the English in the Middle Ages; since then, government and administration that was not purely local had been organised on a countrywide basis. Ireland had an organic unity stretching back over centuries.

Reluctantly, even national spokesmen acknowledged the existence of two Irelands, but the division was usually thought of as religious and cultural, not in territorial terms. The dominant culture of the Protestant Church of Ireland did not express the division spatially, as membership was concentrated in the southern provinces. Gladstone, whose sympathy for the minority was mainly limited to the landed order, saw Ireland's divisions not in territorial but in religious and cultural terms. When critics of the first Home Rule bill raised the idea of granting a separate status to all or the Protestant part of Ulster, Gladstone and Parnell joined forces to dismiss their demands for territorial partition. Gladstone swiftly pointed out that Ireland had always been united; there was no justification for division now. Parnell rejected the Ulster claim to territorial autonomy, citing the number of Catholics there, the historic unity of Ireland and the fact that his country could not 'spare a single Irishman'.[46] Also, he pointed out that southern Protestants relied upon their counterparts in Ulster for security, an attitude emanating from his southern Church of Ireland origins.

Increasingly, though, protagonists of a separate Ulster reinforced their claims and argued for two territorial Irelands. But Unionist separatists were never wholly persuasive, always encountering problems when defining what they meant by Ulster. Their failure to make a thoroughly convincing case, compounded by an over-hasty dismissal of the idea of the political separation of Ulster from the rest of Ireland, complicated post-1912 settlements. The Proclamation of the Irish Republic by the rebels in the Easter Rising of 1916 affirmed the national vision: 'the Irish Republic is entitled to, and hereby claims, the allegiance of every Irishman and Irishwoman', and it reiterated also the contention that present divisions were 'carefully fostered by an alien government, which have divided a minority from the majority in the past'.[47] Eamon de Valera voiced the feelings of many Catholics when he cast doubt upon the right of northern Protestants to remain in Ireland if they resisted the majority will. Home Rule intensified the need to define what was meant by 'Ireland'.

Interpretations

Writings on Home Rule are voluminous. They can be categorised by perspective, chronology, authors' origins or a combination of these approaches. Private papers, newspapers, periodicals, public records, the parliamentary debates, recollections, published diaries and letters, biographies and specialist works ensure that there is no dearth of material in which to study Home Rule. The literature can be placed in six broad schools: Unionist, liberal, Irish patriotic, 'high politics', Marxist and modern revisionist. These designations are not mutually exclusive.

Between 1886 and 1914 Unionist polemical literature was rich in volume, argument and emotion, but little of this vast body of material is consulted regularly today; the settlements of 1920–21 sapped interest in the Unionist case. Most post-1920 work, even that sympathetic to the Conservatives, is reticent about Unionist opposition to Ireland's demand for autonomy. Richard Shannon is cautious in his assessment of Tory opposition to Home Rule.[48] Lord Blake is reserved about Andrew Bonar Law's Ulster stance; his later survey of the Conservative party states: 'whatever the errors of the Liberals [1912–14], the fact remains that the Conservatives were launched on a very perilous course'.[49] John Ramsden adopts the view that Law as 'leader of the opposition in Parliament approved and supported the destruction of both the practice and authority of Parliament', a view that has also been advanced by two American writers, David Miller and L. P. Curtis, jun.[50] Traditional Unionist interpretations have been unfashionable for more than seventy-five years, though a few studies, such as those of A. T. Q. Stewart, constitute exceptions.[51] Paul Bew stresses the vitality and creative energy of Unionism, observing that its study has been hampered from being seen as a negative appendage to the national movement.[52]

Since the early 1920s liberal and Irish patriotic perspectives have dominated the field. John Morley's classic biography of Gladstone, initially published in 1903, was an impassioned defence of Home Rule. Morley, of course, was a political colleague of Gladstone, a political journalist staking out a position, not a dispassionate scholar intent on weighing up and balancing evidence before pronouncing judgement. For him, the biography had the purpose of restoring Liberals to their grand mission. In the years immediately proceeding the Second World War, George Dangerfield, R. C. K. Ensor, J. L. Hammond and Nicholas Mansergh reaffirmed and extended his perspective: Unionists were the 'guilty men' of the Irish story. For Dangerfield, they were agents in the destruction of liberal values. Hammond sees in Gladstone's Home Rule proposals the best means to avert the tragedy of the Anglo-Irish war. Mansergh replicates this attitude, writing:

[I]n the long unhappy history of Anglo-Irish relations only one event is more truly tragic than the rejection of Home Rule in 1886. The opportunity of settlement had come, perhaps the greatest of English statesmen was ready to grasp it and yet the unique chance was destroyed by a failure in perception whose consequences not even time can wholly repair.[53]

Common threads running through liberal interpretations include Gladstone's grand vision, the possibility of Home Rule ending centuries of Anglo-Irish antagonism, and a reluctance to subject the successive schemes to close scrutiny. Irish patriotic writings offer a variant. These flowered particularly in the post-1922 Irish Republic, but were visible earlier in the works of the indefatigable journalist, R. Barry O'Brien. His centre of gravity was Irish.

University-based research-driven history flowered after the Second World War. Mainstays of the academic approach can be summarised as careful sifting of evidence, fidelity to information, balance and a professed refusal to employ history as a handmaiden to politics. Lyons captured the kernel of academic professionalism, explaining: 'I have a historian's loyalty to my sources and, once having seen this material would find it impossible to behave as if it didn't exist. … A public man belongs in the last analysis to history and the ordinary rules of privacy don't apply – or at least not in the way that they do to private people.'[54] The two centres of academic interest in Home Rule in Ireland were Trinity College, Dublin, where T. W. Moody and his disciples dissected the Irish parliamentary party and The Queen's University of Belfast, where J. C. Beckett's students examined Unionist resistance to Home Rule.

'High politics' is a product of fashion in historiography at British universities. Studies by Michael Hurst and D. A. Hamer established a framework of intensive mining of private correspondence and strict adherence to chronology. Hamer concludes that Gladstone's motivation was not entirely altruistic, contending that while he believed in his plan for resolving Irish disaffection, Home Rule was primarily a means to deal with Liberal party disputes.[55] A. B. Cooke and J. R. Vincent took the approach a long step further, asserting that only personal materials are reliable guides to motives thereby challenging the usual reliance upon public as well as private pronouncements.[56] Their belief is that issues and ideas were subservient to personal quests for power. According to this thesis, Gladstone took up Home Rule as a means to outmanoeuvre inconvenient rivals. The technique is used to explain British leaders' motivations rather than

14

those of Irish politicians. Though once very influential, the 'high politics' thesis has since lost its lustre, and is only partially applied to the Irish side of Home Rule. Sophisticated restatements of the liberal interpretation, such as those of T. A. Jenkins and Colin Matthew, have drawn the sting from 'high politics'.[57]

Academic fashion has favoured emphasis upon localism and internal class divisions, an outlook inspired by Marxist and revisionist approaches. David Fitzpatrick's study of County Clare during the fraught decade 1913–23 looks on changes and their absence at grassroots level in rural Ireland; K. T. Hoppen provides a classic analysis of Irish national politics viewed from the bottom, while Tom Garvin employs an occupational and geographical analysis of participants in revolutionary activities. Paul Bew's contributions emphasises internal class conflict as the key dynamic within the national ranks. Peter Gibbon, Austen Morgan, Henry Patterson and Margaret Ward amplify issues from modern Marxist perspectives.[58] Quantitative analysis adds an ingredient to the discussion, though it has not been applied systematically to the Home Rulers over an extended period. Elsewhere, I have attempted to quantify the participation of the Parnellites between 1880 and 1885, and have interposed a concept of 'interest' pioneered by Sir Lewis Namier for explaining political behaviour at the beginning of George III's reign. William Lubenow's treatment of the Home Rule Parliament of 1886 applies chiefly to British rather than to Irish alignment.[59]

'Revisionism' as it is generally understood – reinterpretation of the patriotic past with the political intent of undermining the patriotic and revolutionary tradition – enters the debate on Home Rule indirectly.[60] The wider public has been immune to many of the changes in academic fashion, preferring familiar liberal or 'green' versions. North American academics, many from Irish ancestral origins, have mostly stood outside the fisticuffs of recent academic disputes.

Terminology and theoretical concepts

Anthony D. Smith points to five conditions necessary for entrenching national identity among a significant section of inhabitants; first, historic territory or homeland; second, common myths and historic memories; third, a common, mass public culture; fourth, common legal rights and duties for all members; and fifth, a common economy with territorial mobility for members.[61] Catholics only realised these conditions around 1867, the chronological starting point of this study. Smith's description is appropriate at the point when nationalism reaches relative maturity, but other concepts are essential to account for its progress. George Boyce points to four forms of development which are relevant to Home Rule: colonial identity, cultural identity, national identity, and nationalism.[62] These are not stages per se, but are incremental and are used in the following senses. Colonial identity, sometimes termed territorial patriotism, is felt by members of a group whose national identity takes its origins in the mother country, but whose cultural identity has been shaped by their new environment. Colonial identity is similar to and is usually transformed in the presence of ethnic forms of organisation into what Michael Hechter and Margaret Levi term regionalism.[63] Because colonial elites enjoy higher economic, social and educational status, and comprise the bulk of the early intelligentsia, they are generally found as the initiators in rediscovering the cultural origins of a national movement, but become disillusioned when goals antagonistic to their status are promoted in its later political phases. Home Rule is an illustration of those who wanted to express a colonial identity, withdrawing as it came to be seen as an attack upon their interests. Cultural identity is felt by members of a group who either have or have had a distinct or relatively autonomous existence, and who share a recognisably common way of life. However, the Irish, like other emergent nationalities, were fragmented into numerous localised subcultures. Modernising forces – literacy, education, communication, the centralising bureaucratic state and a more organised and disciplined Catholic Church – were factors facilitating the growth of a common culture; the intelligentsia were its prime agents. This is labelled 'high culture' by Ernest Gellner.[64] Miroslav Hroch observes that the purveyors of this culture lack a political programme and do not seek to mobilise the masses until a further metamorphosis has taken place.[65] Recent work necessitates some modification of these views. In Donegal, what began as a 'high' or 'Home Rule' culture was remoulded into a localised Catholic national identity. National identity is felt by members of a group who define their culture as the national one, and their group as the true legitimate inheritors of the homeland. This stage, too, is spearheaded by the intelligentsia, who now have a political agenda but have not yet converted the masses to their cause. Hroch, though he does not use the same terminology, treats the progression from cultural to national identity as the decisive shift in the progression of the movement. Nationalism is the assertion by members of a group that is seeking autonomy of its distinctive history and culture. It, of course, exists for some members at an early point, but is essential at the time when large segments of the population are converted to the patriotic programme. While the intelligentsia remains overrepresented, other middle-class groups now take up prominent leadership positions. Nationalism becomes essentially an ethnic movement, coinciding with the rise of democracy and employing democratic appeals, especially the rights of citizenship.

Several recent theorists emphasise nationalism as a rational rather than a sentimental response – individuals identify with a particular community because this serves their interest.[66] Identification may bring returns in the form of employment, physical comfort, or merely emotional satisfaction. Cultural nationalism is complementary, reinforcing political objectives and thereby elevating the return on investment in nationalism. Hechter and Levi suggest that ethnic solidarity arises in regions developed as internal colonies where there is a hierarchical cultural division of labour determining life's chances.[67] Solidarity increases when members interact within the boundaries of their own group. The movement's durability, however, depends on its ability to deliver on its promises. Hechter and Levi distinguish between regional and ethnoregional movements: the first couches claims solely in terms of material demands; the second, bases its claim on ethnic distinctiveness.

These propositions are germane to Home Rule. At early points, but most definitively during the land war between 1879 and 1881, Catholics were mobilised by a collectively held notion of the land for the people, as opposed to the 'alien' landowners, an idea imbued with the sense of 'native' dispossession. The Irish parliamentary party capitalised on the claim that it delivered the economic goods, building upon these to promote the national idea of self-government. Linkage of the land and national demands gave Home Rulers their dynamic after 1879, though, in part, at the cost of making themselves primarily a rural movement thereafter. Completion of the process of conversion to an ethnic concept of the nation was the final step in the transition from a Western European to a Central/Eastern European form of nationalism. As Hechter and Levi observe, when life chances are seen as independent of inclusion in a particular ethnic group, the subjective significance of membership recedes or disappears. Their explanation helps in understanding the very high degree of Catholic mobilisation over a long time. But Ireland was not divided into two stratified blocs. An aspiring Catholic bourgeoisie secured a niche in the British state (including Ireland) but remained receptive to patriotic appeals. John Hutchinson points to blocked mobility, arguing that the rate of Catholic advancement did not keep pace with escalating expectations.[68] He also demonstrates that blockage became acute at the beginning of the twentieth century, inflaming a younger generation of intelligentsia which vented its frustration against both the established state and those in control of patriotic organisations. Hroch shows the importance of a completed social structure for a political movement prioritising political demands. He also suggests that until a late point in its progression, autonomy not independence is the focus of national movements. His emphasis upon sequences of events and social composition accords with Ireland's experience.[69]

There is a recent disposition to see Home Rule as a bourgeois formula to strengthen its own position against the existing dominant state and also as a means to exert authority over the masses. Economic theory points to psychological events and prestige as Home Rule's 'value-added' benefits for groups receiving fewer of the direct material compensations. In practice, the benefits to individuals cannot be measured in terms of concrete material advantages, a point long articulated by Home Rulers. Treatment of the issue in the chapters that follow assesses the idea and its use in the context of these concepts within a conventional chronological narrative.

Notes

1 *The Times*, 22 January 1885.

2 R. Barry O'Brien (ed.), *Home Rule Speeches of John Redmond, MP* (London, 1910), pp. 337–8.

3 *Sligo Champion*, 14 December 1918.

4 F. S. L. Lyons, *Ireland since the Famine* (4th impression; London, 1976), p. 15.

5 James O'Shea, *Priest, Politics and Society in Post-Famine Ireland: A Study of County Tipperary 1850–1891* (Dublin, 1983), p. 211; R. V. Comerford, *The Fenians in Context: Irish Politics and Society 1848–82* (Dublin, 1985), p. 194.

6 John Kendle, *Ireland and the Federal Solution: The Debate Over the United Kingdom Constitution, 1870–1921* (Kingston and Montreal, 1989); Alan J. Ward, *The Irish Constitutional Tradition: Responsible Government and Modern Ireland, 1872–1922* (Washington, DC, 1994); also, see, Vernon Bogdanor, *Devolution* (Oxford, 1979).

7 Margaret O'Callaghan, *British High Politics and a Nationalist Ireland: Criminality, Land and the Law Under Forster and Balfour* (Cork, 1994), especially, pp. 107, 153, passim.

8 John Morley, 'Old Parties and New Policy', *Fortnightly Review*, IV, New Series (1 September 1868), p. 327.

9 *The Freeman's Journal*, 12 March 1874.

10 As an example, see, T. W. Moody, *Davitt and the Irish Revolution, 1846–82* (Oxford, 1981), pp. 26–7.

11 Philip Bull, *Land, Politics and Nationalism: A Study of the Irish Land Question* (Dublin, 1996), p. 4.

12 *Ibid.*, p. 170.

13 See, Michael Hopkinson, *Green Against Green, the Irish Civil War* (Dublin, 1988), p. 2.

14 R. F. Foster, *Paddy and Mr Punch: Connections in Irish and English History* (London, 1993), pp. 262–78.

15 Paul Bew, *Ideology and the Irish Question: Ulster Unionism and Irish*

Nationalism 1912–1916 (Oxford, 1994), p. xviii.

16 David Fitzpatrick, *Politics and Irish Life 1913–1921: Provincial Experience of War and Revolution* (Dublin, 1977), pp. 85–7, 93–4, 100; Alvin Jackson, 'Unionist Politics and Protestant Society in Edwardian Ireland', *Historical Journal*, 33 (4), p. 866.

17 Quoted in Lyons, *Ireland since the Famine*, p. 15.

18 Quoted in Alan O'Day and John Stevenson (eds), *Irish Historical Documents since 1800* (Dublin, 1992), pp. 14–16.

19 Quoted in Ward, *Irish Constitutional Tradition*, p. 42.

20 Quoted in B. A. Kennedy, 'Sharman Crawford's Federal Scheme for Ireland', in H. A. Cronne, T. W. Moody and D. B. Quinn (eds), *Essays in British and Irish History in Honour of James Eadie Todd* (London, 1949), p. 237; also, see, D. George Boyce, 'Federalism and the Irish Question', in Andrea Bosco (ed.), *The Federal Idea, Vol I: The History of Federalism from the Enlightenment to 1945* (London and New York, 1991), p. 120.

21 Quoted in Ward, *Irish Constitutional Tradition*, p. 44.

22 Quoted in O'Day and Stevenson (eds), *Irish Historical Documents*, p. 60.

23 Quoted in Kevin B. Nowlan, *The Politics of Repeal* (London, 1965), p. 8.

24 Quoted in Kennedy, 'Sharman Crawford's Federal Scheme', p. 246; for details see, pp. 250–1.

25 Oliver MacDonagh, *The Emancipist: Daniel O'Connell 1830–47* (London, 1989), pp. 254–7.

26 Quoted in Sir Charles Gavan Duffy, *Young Ireland: A Fragment of Irish History* (London, Paris and New York, 1880), p. 599.

27 Quoted in *ibid.*, p. 591.

28 Quoted in O'Day and Stevenson (eds), *Irish Historical Documents*, pp. 68–70.

29 Duffy, *Young Ireland*, pp. 575–609.

30 *Ibid.*, p. 577.

31 Quoted in O'Day and Stevenson (eds), *Irish Historical Documents*, pp. 76–7.

32 Isaac Butt, *Irish Federalism: Its Meaning, Its Objects and Its Hopes* (4th edn; Dublin, 1874).

33 *Proceedings of the Home Rule Conference held at the Rotunda, Dublin on the 18th, 19th, 20th and 21st November 1873* (Dublin, 1874), pp. 105–6.

34 *The Nation*, 23 October 1875.

35 *The Freeman's Journal*, 30 August 1883.

36 *Parliamentary Debates [PD]*, 304 (1886), cc. 1036–84.

37 *Ibid.*, 305 (1886), cc. 1168–84.

38 *Ibid.*, 4th Series, 8 (1893), cc. 1313–27.

39 A. V. Dicey, *England's Case Against Home Rule* (reprt; Richmond, Surrey, 1973), pp. 20–1.

40 *Ibid.*, p. 158.

41 *PD*, 8 (1893), cc. 241–75.

42 Kendle, *Ireland and the Federal Solution*, pp. 4–5.

43 Quoted in Ward, *Irish Constitutional Tradition*, pp. 85–6.

44 *Ibid.*, p. 51.
45 Quoted in Bew, *Ideology and the Irish Question*, p. 218.
46 *PD*, 304 (1886), cc. 1175, 1179–80.
47 Quoted in O'Day and Stevenson (eds), *Irish Historical Documents*, pp. 160–1.
48 Richard T. Shannon, *The Age of Disraeli, 1868–1881: The Rise of Tory Democracy* (London and New York, 1992); *The Age of Salisbury 1881–1902: Unionism and Empire* (London and New York, 1996).
49 Robert Blake, *The Conservative Party from Peel to Thatcher* (London, 1985), p. 195.
50 John Ramsden, *The Age of Balfour and Baldwin 1902–1940* (London, 1978), p. 85; David W. Miller, *Queen's Rebels: Ulster Loyalist in Historical Perspective* (Dublin, 1978), pp. 98–108; L. P. Curtis, jun., 'Ireland in 1914', in W. E. Vaughan (ed.), *A New History of Ireland VI: Ireland Under the Union, II, 1870–1921* (Oxford, 1996), p. 177.
51 See, A. T. Q. Stewart, *The Ulster Crisis* (London, 1967); *The Narrow Ground: Aspects of Ulster, 1609–1969* (London, 1977).
52 Bew, *Ideology and the Irish Question*, p. x.
53 Nicholas Mansergh, *Ireland in the Age of Reform and Revolution* (London, 1940), p. 150.
54 F. S. L. Lyons to Myles Dillon, 13 July 1967, F. S. L. Lyons Papers, Trinity College, Dublin.,
55 Michael Hurst, *Joseph Chamberlain and the Liberal Reunion: The Round Table Conference 1887* (London, 1967); D. A. Hamer, *Liberal Politics in the Age of Gladstone and Rosebery: A Study in Leadership and Policy* (Oxford, 1972), pp. 129–30.
56 A. B. Cooke and J. R. Vincent, *The Governing Passion: Cabinet Government and Party Politics in Britain 1885–86* (Brighton, 1974).
57 T. A. Jenkins, *Gladstone, Whiggery and the Liberal Party 1874–1886* (Oxford, 1988); H. C. G. Matthew, *Gladstone* (Oxford, 1995).
58 Fitzpatrick, *Politics and Irish Life*; K. T. Hoppen, *Elections, Politics and Society in Ireland 1832–1885* (Oxford, 1984); Tom Garvin, *The Evolution of Irish Nationalist Politics* (Dublin, 1981) and *Nationalist Revolutionaries in Ireland 1858–1928* (Oxford, 1987); Paul Bew, *Land and the National Question in Ireland 1858–1882* (Dublin, 1978); Peter Gibbon, *The Origins of Ulster Unionism: The Formation of Popular Protestant Politics and Ideology in Nineteenth-Century Ireland* (Manchester, 1975); Austen Morgan, *James Connolly: A Political Biography* (Manchester, 1988) and *Labour and Partition: The Belfast Working Class 1905–23* (London, 1991); Henry Patterson, *Class Conflict and Sectarianism: The Protestant Working Class and the Belfast Labour Movement 1868–1920* (Belfast, 1980); Margaret Ward, *Unmanageable Revolutionaries: Women and Irish Nationalism* (London, 1983).
59 Alan O'Day, *The English Face of Irish Nationalism: Parnellite Involvement in British Politics, 1880–86* (Dublin, 1977; 2nd revised edition; Aldershot, 1994); William C. Lubenow, *Parliamentary Politics and the Home Rule Crisis: The British House of Commons in 1886* (Oxford, 1988).
60 See, Desmond Fennell, 'Against Revisionism', in Ciaran Brady (ed.), *Interpreting Irish History: The Debate on Historical Revisionism*

(Dublin, 1994), pp. 184–5.

61 Anthony D. Smith, *National Identity* (London, 1991), p. 14.

62 See, D. George Boyce, *Nationalism in Ireland* (3rd edn; London, 1995), pp. 18–19.

63 See, Michael Hechter and Margaret Levi, 'Ethno-Regional Movements in the West', in John Hutchinson and Anthony D. Smith, *Nationalism* (Oxford, 1994), pp. 184–95.

64 Ernest Gallner *Nations and Nationalism* (Oxford, 1983).

65 See, Miroslav Hroch, *Social Preconditions of National Revival in Europe* (Cambridge, 1985); his main themes are restated in an amended form in 'National Self-Determination from a Historical Perspective', in Sukumar Periwal (ed.), *Notions of Nationalism* (Budapest, London and New York, 1995), pp. 65–82.

66 See the stimulating essays in Albert Breton, Gianluigi Galeotti, Pierre Salmon and Ronald Wintrobe (eds), *Nationalism and Rationality* (Cambridge, 1995).

67 Hechter and Levi, 'Ethno-Regional Movements'.

68 John Hutchinson, *The Dynamics of Cultural Nationalism: The Gaelic Revival and the Creation of the Irish National State* (London, 1987), pp. 266–76.

69 Hroch, *Social Preconditions*.

2

Rise of Home Rule, 1867–79

'Fenianism' was not a political or even a national movement, but a social one. It may be said to have been only the revelation of what has long been passing in the hearts and minds of the people. Whatever was political or national in its objects was subordinate to the social one – that of destroying landlordism. ... In all previous Irish movements the national question had been put foremost; but the mass of the people understood the 'national question' in a sense somewhat different from that put upon it by their leaders. With them landlordism and the land system was the impersonation of English domination and misrule. (Isaac Butt, 1866)[1]

The treasonable associations must be extinguished with the utmost energy and by suitable measures. Then it will be for you statesmen to adopt those remedial measures, the mottoes of which, I hope will be policy, justice, and above all a moderation which will ensure equal rights to adverse parties, without giving either a triumph. (Lord Strathnairn, General in command of the army in Ireland, 1867)[2]

Introduction

Fenianism was an unlikely catalyst for a remodelled self-government movement that was to dominate the Irish political landscape until 1916. This supposedly secret society had an indeterminate programme that contained, as Isaac Butt observes above, an implicit social message, as well as striving for an Irish republic to be won by armed rebellion.[3] Fenians gave classic expression to the moral demand for self-government even if many chose to interpret it in ways more consonant with material ambitions. Though the objective was impractical and support for Fenianism limited, the conspiracy roused no end of fear among the respectable Catholic middle class at the heart of national-minded organisations and of the British government. Fenianism appealed to, and was composed largely of, the dangerous classes – radicalised émigrés at the top and a rank-and-file of artisans and urban workers, restless young males outside the conventional social restrains of Irish life.[4] Its programme and methods were anathema to the trilogy of Church, bourgeoisie and tenant farmers who might subscribe to the ideal of self-government but not to Fenian means. On 17 February 1867 Bishop David Moriarty spoke for that concern in a much cited denunciation of Fenians for whom 'eternity is not long enough, nor hell hot enough'.[5] Yet, from this conspiracy's rebellion in early 1867 came the beginnings of a modern Home Rule movement. At the same time the Fenian revolt stirred British governments into action to relieve Catholic grievances in an attempt to placate the respectable Irish classes and build a bulwark against extremism. Though Fenianism did not mark the beginnings of a constructive or liberal unionist approach to Ireland, from this moment the concept of what became known as 'constructive Unionism' became the backstop to British anxiety about the sister island. The rebellion had several long-term effects: it brought moderates together to form organisations under the society's control; new leaders emerged to lead the movement; Fenianism provided a training ground for the future generation of constitutional leaders; national consciousness was roused by the selfless sacrifices of individual Fenians; and Britain responded boldly to the crisis with a package of reforms. These were major accomplishments for a group which eschewed conventional politics and had no hope of winning its goals though, to be sure, such achievements were not what Fenians sought.

Common currents run through the 1867–79 period – first, of finding a means to harness the whole or most of the nation to a patriotic agenda, and second, that of subverting Fenianism and substituting for it moderate middle-class control over the fortunes of the national movement. The predominant form of national identity – Catholic middle-class reformism directed towards electoralism and the Westminster Parliament – was asserted and refined during these years. Its motif was an absence of extensive mass organisation with a corresponding tendency to base political action on a strategy of activism running from the top down.

Early national revival, 1867–70

At the beginning of 1867 Catholic identity lacked cohesion and an effective programme. True, the Catholic hierarchy sought disestablishment of the Church of Ireland and increased state funding of its religious schools; tenant farmers agitated for greater security for themselves; and a small contingent remained loyal to Repeal of the Union. Groups existed for the promotion of all of these and other objectives, though they were small, exerting little general appeal. John Martin's National League, established on 21 January 1864 for the restoration of a separate and independent Irish legislature and Cardinal Cullen's National Association, founded on 29 December 1864, had been efforts to thwart the rising force of Fenianism, but neither grew into popular movements.[6] Similarly, there were farmers' clubs, mainly located in the affluent agricultural districts of Leinster and run by the large or 'strong' tenants worked for land reform; none, though, emerged as the fulcrum of national demands. Some Liberal Irish MPs advocated patriotic ideals, but they lacked any semblance of unity. There was no effective pressure group at home to make the patriotic case or to keep the parliamentarians up to the mark. National identity thrived as a sentiment, but as a coherent movement it was shambolic.

The Fenian rising on 5 March 1867 changed matters (see document 1). It had four consequences: the formation of a clemency movement on behalf of the activists who had been imprisoned as a result of the rebellion, concern by middle-class leaders to formulate a platform to contain the Fenian threat, the reanimation of clerical involvement in politics and the renewed interest of British politicians in Irish reform. Before much of this could mature two further incidents revealed the apparent extent of the menace posed by repressed Irish revolutionary forces, in these instances both in Britain itself. In the first, the rescue of Fenians from a prison van in Manchester on 18 September resulted not only in their escape but also in the accidental killing of the guard, Sergeant Brett. Three of the plotters were convicted and then executed for the murder on 23 November. Rejection of pleas for clemency and the public hangings of the three men sparked a series of indignation meetings across Ireland and in Great Britain. Father Patrick Lavelle foresaw, 'out of their ashes will spring up an army of their like'.[7] While not precisely correct about the outcome, he was certainly prescient in seeing that the tragedy would induce a new sense of common purpose among contesting national factions. The Manchester trio had not long been consigned to quicklime when on 13 December another attempted rescue of Fenians at the Clerkenwell House of Detention in London went badly awry. A misjudged explosive, which was meant to breach the walls of the gaol, killed twelve civilians, injuring fifty others. The incident set off a minor panic. Irishmen hastened to disavow the perpetrators but the shock brought home to people in Britain the seriousness of disaffection.

At the beginning of 1868 the Dean of Limerick organised a Declaration by the clergy for Repeal of the Union that was signed by 1,600 clerics.[8] At the same time the Bishop of Cloyne's pastoral proclaimed that the time was right for a truly independent political party to promote national objectives.[9] However, patriotism's fate was tied to liberalism; Bishop Moriarty observed that 'liberalism is the new religion and there is no seeking justice except through its help'.[10] That link was underlined when on 23 March Gladstone proposed an end to the established status of the Church of Ireland. The twinning of national aspirations and liberalism had profound implications for the future of Home Rule. As the year progressed, this spirit of nationality was underlined by a growing sympathy for the Fenian prisoners. On 5 November a new organisation, the Irish Liberation Society, was initiated to secure their release, being converted on 29 June 1869 into the Amnesty Association, with Isaac Butt, a Protestant barrister and former Tory MP, who had distinguished himself in the legal defence of Fenians, as President. Since the Fenian revolt British political life had been obsessed by Irish disaffection. In August 1868 Gladstone pledged to 'open a future of happiness, prosperity, and contentment which shall stand in joyful contrast with the past of that unhappy land'.[11] Nothing stirred emotions more than the Church question. The *Annual Register* for 1868 recorded:

> [I]t may, indeed, almost be said that the entire political interest of the present session was concentrated on the question of the Irish Church, and as soon as the existence of the Parliament came to an end the scene of the controversy was merely shifted, and the issue transferred from the benches of the House of Commons to the hustings of the three kingdoms.[12]

During the general election in the United Kingdom, held between 17 November and 2 December 1868, Gladstone campaigned on a platform where by 'the removal of this Establishment I see the discharge of a debt of civil justice, the disappearance of a national, almost a world-wide reproach, a condition indispensable to the success of every effort to secure the peace and contentment of that country'.[13] The outcome was a Liberal victory, making Gladstone Prime Minister. Liberals captured 382 seats overall, including 65 in Ireland, against a Conservative total of 276. Although the Conservatives suffered losses in Ireland, they were not annihilated for they secured 39 constituencies, 14 outside Ulster. Gladstone particularly had been moved by the Fenian rebellion, acknowledging:

> I am oppressed day and night with the condition of Ireland, with the sad and painful spectacle it exhibits to the world, and with the painful consciousness that this springs out of the past and present

faults in our government of the country, not out of special obliquity and vice in the people.[14]

While this election was not the only one that was dominated by the Irish question between 1868 and 1921, it was the sole occasion when Irish reform received an unequivocal mandate from a British electorate. Gladstone's sympathies were energised by a liberal unionism intent upon relieving those defects that threatened the security of the Union. For him, the prime questions involved the Church, certain conditions pertaining to land tenure and satisfying Catholic feelings on higher education. It is a considerable exaggeration to see him, as does a recent commentator, offering Home Rule to Ireland without any constitutional structures; rather, his intention was to curtail sentiment for widespread self-government.[15]

While disestablishment was the foremost election issue in Britain and amongst the Catholic clergy, in Ireland itself other questions, including land reform, amnesty and the demand for a Catholic university funded from state resources, were promoted.[16] In the rest of Britain, too, other issues were placed before the electorate. Disestablishment was accorded primacy as the symbolic demand behind which other and, for the majority of electors, more essential reforms lurked. For the bulk of electors the land was the most important matter.[17] The contest was significant because many advanced men participated in constitutional politics for the first time. In due course this led many of them towards incorporation into the Home Rule movement.

Vying with disestablishment for attention was the problem of clemency for imprisoned Fenians. Gladstone, however, did not come into office as an amnesty Prime Minister. Rather, 'our purpose & duty is to endeavour to draw a line between the Fenians & the people of Ireland, & to make the people of Ireland indisposed to cross it'.[18] The Prime Minister was inclined to allow the judicious release of some prisoners (49 were set free in March 1869 followed by a further 33 in January 1871), but this good intention ran aground on the shoals of resistance within his own administration.[19] Some Fenians, mainly Irish soldiers convicted by court martial, remained in gaol and the amnesty question continued to fester until January 1878 when the Conservative government of Lord Beaconsfield effected the final releases. The issue became increasingly hot during 1869. At least 411 public demonstrations (638,00 attended meetings between July and October alone) were held throughout Ireland to support clemency and others took place in Great Britain. One meeting in October, held in the relatively small borough of Ennis, had an estimated attendance of 40,000, and some 200,000 were present at a rally that same month in Dublin. In several instances priests were present, often chairing the meetings. A petition seeking amnesty was signed by more than 1,400 clergy.[20] The distribution of demonstrations, however, was uneven replicating the organisation and appeal of patriotic ideals. Leinster accounted for 180 separate demonstrations, another 172 took place in Munster, but only 46 were held in Connaught and a mere 8 recorded in Ulster. Amnesty proved a harbinger of the subsequent geography of patriotism. The importance of the campaign cannot be minimised. In Longford, a county which had few Fenians and little in the way of radicalised politics, the campaign dramatically increased receptiveness to these influences.[21]

The Irish Church bill was introduced in the House of Commons on 1 March 1869; when enacted, it became perhaps the single most successful major legislation for Ireland in the post-1867 period, offering something to nearly everyone. It was enacted on 26 July, taking effect from 1 January 1971. Catholics and Presbyterians shed the detested establishment, receiving compensation for the loss of their own annual grants for theological training. Generous financial compensation was awarded to the Church of Ireland. Nonconformists in Britain were gratified by the assault on Anglican privilege which they hoped might lead to disestablishment generally. The Quaker John Bright held that the Irish Church 'is anti-Protestant by reason of its unnatural position and at the same time it is as much anti-English as it is anti-Irish because it makes it impossible that the Irish people should be in perfect harmony with England'.[22] Protestants welcomed the cessation of finance for the Catholic seminary at Maynooth. Disestablishment was a remarkable event if only because it united, however briefly, the interests of Catholics and Presbyterians – no mean feat in the annals of modern Ireland. The clergy and moderate lay Catholics saw in Gladstone's administration a means of gaining their ends. Above all, Gladstone demonstrated that Ireland with its large membership in the House of Commons – 103 seats – could, in collusion with a British party, hope to win significant concessions within the framework of the Constitution. Butt recognised the possibilities when in August 1869 he noted that they should pursue the release of the prisoners 'in a temperate, moderate, yet firm manner, and leave nothing for their enemies to catch a hold on for rejecting their purposes'.[23] Despite frustrations, he would hold to this belief until his death a decade later.

Disestablishment and amnesty dominated the scene, but they were not the only issues exercising Irish minds. Land reformers looked forward to Gladstone taking up their case. Butt, who had already championed the issue, assumed the leadership of the Irish Tenant League when it was formed on 28 September 1869 in Tipperary Town.

27

According to *The Freeman's Journal* tenants' rights meetings held since the beginning of 1869 had been attended by two and a half million people.[24] Fenians resented the intrusion of the land question, seeing it as a diversion from the plight of the prisoners. They broke up several tenants' meetings during the second half of 1869. One of the difficulties confronting the formation of a national coalition, then and later, was that differing priorities of clergy, tenant farmers, Fenians and others made unity perilous; yet only through solidarity could anything effective be won. Ireland had to marshal its political strength if British leaders were to be made responsive. Butt appreciated the dilemma and in November 1869 enunciated a principle that was meant to guide Irishmen, which stated:

> [I]n my judgement it would be a great calamity to the cause of Ireland if those who are anxious to obtain the release of the political prisoners were to form the idea of promoting that object by obstructing the brave and honest efforts of the tenant farmers to obtain justice for themselves. ... I believe the two objects, so far from being antagonistic, help each other. Everything that calls out a national spirit in Ireland tends to create a power that forwards the redress of every Irish wrong.[25]

The Home Government Association, 1870–73

It was only a matter of time before self-government re-emerged as a key Irish aspiration and with it a demand for an independent Irish parliamentary party to advocate the case. Both had a lengthy, if not always honourable, lineage. Late in 1869 Butt had a further motivation for taking it up. As the head of both the amnesty and tenants' rights movements, he was acutely aware of the rivalry arising from their respective platforms. The 'national question' offered the possibility of submerging these differences under a common banner, a marquee, appealing to all patriots. Education and the land emphasised distinctions within the community. Moreover, the papal condemnation of Fenianism on 12 January 1870 made an alternative constitutional organisation more appealing. The self-government ideal might be fashioned into a tool capable of bridging divisions, filling a void resulting from the faltering and now condemned Fenianism. Butt told one audience that during 'these last three years there has been a resurrection of the Irish nation'. In another speech he affirmed: 'it is a mere question of time when we ... ought to strain every nerve to achieve for Ireland national independence. And when I say national independence I don't mean separation. I mean a self-government which gives us the entire right to manage our own affairs.'[26]

In the early months of 1870 Gladstone pushed his Irish Land Act through Parliament (it was enacted on 1 August). The new legislation disappointed Irish tenants and gave added incentive to the call for a national forum so as better to advance patriotic demands. Also, concern about the radical intentions of the democratic Parliament lead the Dean of Limerick to write to Butt on 27 February 1870 insisting there was 'one remaining chance of saving us [Ireland] from the coming confusion, and that is to permit us to make our own laws'.[27] In April, George Henry Moore, A. M. Sullivan and Lavelle conferred on the creation of a new organisation to unite all Irishmen, though Moore was to die on 19 April, before the plan could be given effect. One outcome of this ferment was that on 19 May 1870 forty-nine gentlemen, a majority of whom were Protestants, met at the Bilton Hotel in Dublin to discuss the future governing arrangements of their country.[28] From this session emerged a new Home Rule organisation: the Home Government Association. Butt, who was the foremost figure at the meeting, persuaded those present to adopt his own plan, federalism. The idea of self-government, though, exerted more appeal than did a concrete scheme of federalism. William O'Neill Daunt noted,

> [T]he Home Government Association have sent me a circular letter and prospectus. Sent them my subscription, and a letter stating that I joined their movement on the clear understanding that I looked on their Federal scheme as a provisional rather than a final arrangement of our relations with England; and that, if attained, it would help us to work out the rest. Nothing short of 1782 can or ought to satisfy Ireland.[29]

On 1 September the first public meeting of the new organisation was held in Dublin. Towards the end of the year, in order to broaden support for his panacea Butt issued a pamphlet, *Irish Federalism: Its Meaning, Its Objects and Its Hopes*, which outlined what the concept entailed, distinguishing it from Repeal. In his view, federalism would offer Ireland an opportunity for 'independence without breaking up the unity of the empire, interfering with the monarchy, or endangering the rights or liberties of any class of Irishmen'.[30] Under it, 'Ireland could enjoy all of [the] self-government and distinct national rights which would be necessary for full development of her national life'. While the idea of home government was intended to improve the condition of Ireland's institutions, Butt made it clear that 'the demand for a National Parliament rests … upon higher and more sacred grounds. Of one thing I am sure – that the desire for national independence will never be plucked or torn from the heart of the Irish nation.' He appealed to those 'who occupy the higher stations in Irish society to take their part with the people in seeking our own Parliament and in moulding and determining the forms which the Federal Constitution is to assume'. According to Butt:

> [I]t is from the joint deliberations of all classes of Irishmen that we may most confidently hope to present a plan of a national legislature, in which the just influence of property and education and rank may be harmoniously combined with popular privileges and power, so as to make the legislature the real representative of the nation.

Butt was not concerned

> whether the word Federalism, in its proper sense, be the most appropriate term to express what is proposed. I will not even stop to inquire whether the Union I suggest belongs to that class of arrangements which Lord Brougham calls Federal Unions proper or to those which he designates as improper or imperfect, or as is more probable, is one partaking of the character of both.

Though the structure he suggested was open to amendment, Butt presented a blueprint of the new arrangement. The Parliament at Westminster, where Ireland would retain its full complement of Members elected separately from those who sat in the Irish body, was to retain control over the national debt, civil list, military and foreign relations and whatever other areas the 'Federal Constitution might specially reserve to the Imperial Assembly'. Otherwise, 'the Irish Parliament consisting … of the Queen, Lords, and Commons of Ireland would have supreme control in Ireland'. The domestic House of Commons would contain 250–300 members elected on the present or an enlarged franchise. An upper chamber would be composed of the resident Irish peerage augmented, Butt suggested, by the creation of life peers. Preservation of the hereditary peerage's powers and, even more bizarre, his willingness to see the royal prerogative resuscitated, were features unlikely to find favour.

Federalism, Butt asserted, was preferable to Repeal because it devolved the same internal powers on Ireland but maintained the formal link with Great Britain and continued the current Irish role at Westminster. A justification for federalism was that since 1800 Great Britain had acquired many overseas possessions in which the Irish had a legitimate concern, an interest that could only be protected by continued representation in the Imperial Parliament. Simple Repeal, in contrast, would deprive Ireland of that representation. Furthermore, he pointed out:

> [M]any of these colonies have become the home of the exiles of the Irish race … we are bound in justice and honour, even to our own

countrymen who have settled in these colonies not to give them up.
I cannot but feel that one of the elements of the question of federalism is to be found in the vast Irish population which since the
Union has settled in the great English towns. This element is a new
one, and it is one to which every year even of those which have
passed since the days of O'Connell has added new importance.

However, he did make a genuflection in the direction of Repeal,
pointing out 'but in truth, it is an inaccuracy to say that a Federal
Constitution is not "Repeal". If we establish a Federal Constitution
we must, of course, repeal the Act of Union.' While Butt explained
how his scheme could be applied to the three kingdoms, he did not
then press the case of the others, for it 'is a matter entirely for themselves to decide'. What characterised the pamphlet and Butt's subsequent arguments was the moral purposes even more than the
material functions of home government. Butt was never as concerned
about the precise powers of an Irish government as he was about its
existence as a symbol, an object of unity and veneration. Moreover,
Butt insisted that rule from Westminster, in spite of his country's representation there, would be undesirable, for the Members would be
tempted to exercise their votes and influence for party advantage,
corrupting both themselves and Parliament. He does not elaborate
on why he believed that Irish Members who sat at Westminster after
the introduction of Home Rule would cease to act in this way.

The Bilton Hotel meeting became the basis of the Home Government Association, but this new body was not, and did not seek to
become, a popular organisation. On several occasions over the next
three years Butt pointed to the restricted purpose of this private association of gentlemen, noting also that the function was limited to
educating the mind of the country to the idea of Home Rule. John
Martin undoubtedly spoke for many when he described the Home
Government Association as 'an attempt to unite all honest and patriotic Irishmen on the only honourable and rational basis upon which
Irish could unite – the basis of their country. They might all unite
upon that basis, and they might, at the same time, hold their separate
and individual opinions upon all other points.'[31] During 1843–44
there had been a considerable debate about federalism, but a generation later widespread confusion remained. Butt's scheme roused no
more than modest enthusiasm. In October 1870 *The Nation* endorsed
Butt's proposal, but its specifics were 'no great matter at the present
stage. The one important and indispensable thing is that the popular
intellect should get hold of the project generally, and try it by the
unfailing test of examination and discussion.'[32] After the pamphlet's
publication, Butt sometimes still played down the details of his plan.
In December 1870, for instance, he said that the object of the Home

Government Association was the establishment of 'the inalienable right of self-government, and federalism was but secondary to that'.[33] Butt's appeal never lay in a specific scheme; he sought to touch patriotic emotions. He caught precisely the right mood when he told the Irish:

> [T]hey were not to crouch and whine at the feet of England, but to demand by moral force, their rights, and moral force was always strong when physical force was behind it. That physical force consisted in the existence of twelve millions of Irishmen scattered over the globe, whom England might unite in friendly federation, or whom they might make her foes.[34]

If this self-government ideal was essentially a sentiment, albeit with a moral purpose, without the apparatus of a mass organisation or political party, how could it hope to advance its objective? Also, what relationship did the concept have to other portions of the national agenda? In retrospect it is astounding that the movement survived infancy. With scarcely any finance, members, organisation and the hostility of many priests, it looked a very unpromising assemblage. Cardinal Cullen observed in autumn 1871:

> I have determined to having to do with the Home Rule movement for the present. The principle leaders in the management here are professors of Trinity College who have never heretofore manifested any good feeling towards the people of Ireland, and Orangemen who are still worse. The object appears to be to put out the present ministry and get Disraeli into power. ... The great mass of the people in Ireland are always ready to join any movement which is presented to them as something patriotic, but I think that the Home Rule movement is still looked on with suspicion by them on account of its leaders.[35]

Despite hostility and indifference, however, the Association survived and, indeed, in a limited way thrived. Although it represented itself as a single-issue organisation, almost all its members also supported other parts of the national platform, belonging simultaneously to the groups sponsoring these different issues. No one illustrated this confluence better than Butt himself, who served as head of the amnesty, land and home government movements.

The absence of funds was a liability, though one which was, in part, offset by the refusal to convert the movement into a mass organisation. Two features were apparent by the close of 1870: first, the Home Government Association was already dominated by Catholics, and the tendency of members to be identified with the whole of the denominational platform reduced their ability to reach across the sectarian divide. Second, the Association did not break away from its

Dublin roots, thus limiting its expansion and effectiveness. Alfred Webb observed in March 1871 that 'as to the cause I feel that it is making good way & forcing itself on the attention of all'. However he admitted:

[A]s to our H.G. Association I do not (privately) feel so very hopeful. We are doing our best. But somehow we have not attracted people or talent in the way I wd have hoped: the fault may be ourselves: I fear on the whole that the middle & upper classes are thoroughly demoralised here. Since the first weeks of its foundation nearly a year ago, we have not got in any new speakers of ability.[36]

By 1871 there was some interest shown in the possibility of putting forward candidates pledged to the Home Rule standard at parliamentary by-elections, though the Home Government Association declined to play a formal role in securing the nomination and election of candidates. It was the quickest route to educating the public at home and overseas because it attracted the most extensive publicity with the minimum outlay of resources and time. Home Rule advocates proved unsuccessful at the polls, losing by-elections at Mallow on 10 May, at Longford on 16 May and at Dublin City on 18 August 1870 John Martin, scoring a resounding victory as an Independent Nationalist at Meath on 17 January 1871, and Mitchell Henry in County Galway on 21 February, reversed the tide. On 17 June P. J. Smyth, really a Repealer, captured Westmeath. Butt, however, was defeated on 22 July at Monaghan, after which a vacancy occurred at Limerick City. At his adoption meeting in September 1871, Butt, typically of Home Rulers, emphasised his readiness to apply himself in Parliament to the full range of popular issues – endowment of a Catholic university, religious equality, denominational education and tenants' rights.[37] He was adopted to stand for Limerick City unopposed on 20 September.

The focus of Home Rule activity from an early point was the House of Commons. Butt again suggested that the attainment of his country's nationality would 'be won when at the next general election they would send eighty members as delegates from a united nation to demand from the justice of the English people Ireland's inalienable rights'.[38] But although the number of MPs from Ireland was considerable, it was insufficient to make more than a limited impression. Irish MPs, even it unified, could not force any British regime to adopt their ideas.

Butt, in common with Irish patriots generally, saw his movement as a free-standing 'ginger group' working outside of, though usually supporting the Liberal party. National figures at this time were predominantly concerned to achieve concrete and largely material objectives, seeking to make British leaders take account of Irish feeling and grant beneficial concessions. The fiasco over the university bill in early 1873, ending with its defeat in the House of Commons on 12 March, exemplified the difficulty in forcing Liberals to act on Irish ideas. The Catholic hierarchy professed to

> being deeply convinced of the many evils – religious, political, and social – which would flow from the establishment of the proposed university system; and being sincerely desirous to promote peace, union, and contentment amongst all classes in Ireland, do humbly pray your honourable house either to reject the University Bill [to create a state-funded Catholic University] now before you, or so to alter its character and provisions as to render it acceptable to the Catholic people of Ireland.[39]

Bruised clerical susceptibilities occasioned some readiness on the part of priests to identify with, even join, the Home Rule movement. The organisation could never penetrate rural Ireland until clerics adopted it, partly, as Bishop Moriarty pointed out, because 'the minds of the Irish people are in the hands of the Irish priests',[40] but also for the reason that the Church possessed the only institutional structure spread throughout virtually the whole country. Without the use of Church property for meetings popular movements in rural Ireland faced an uphill struggle.

Home Rule's advance in the early 1870s hinged on the fortuitous confluence of three elements: a more favourable attitude of the Church, the desire of some Fenians to play an effective political role, and a wider popular sentiment supportive of a specifically national form of political representation. The first has been treated by several writers; R. V. Comerford emphasises the second reason, while Michael Hurst's reconsideration of the impact of the secret ballot gives prominence to the third.[41] These positions are not irreconcilable but the focus of the last two diverges. Comerford pictures Fenianism and a section of Home Rulers reflecting a restlessness with authority, 'seeking political influence that was not linked with, or dependent on, their social antecedents'.[42] For him, Fenians were a 'flying column', exerting electoral pressure at by-elections in the absence of regularised political organisation. Hurst, in contrast, stresses the popular appeal of Home Rule. Both positions are tenable, though the latter is the more satisfactory. Comerford's argument overlooks the fact that the most militant men among the parliamentarians, notably Joseph Biggar and even more Parnell, were wedded to notions of status. Fenian 'flying columns' exercised only modest influence on large constituencies in which tenant farmers were the most sizeable portion of the electorate, and social restlessness, according to his own earlier study, seems linked principally to urban artisans in decaying trades and was not necessarily germane to the places where by-elections took place.[43] In any case, Home Rule successes were by such wide margins that the Fenian impact must have been negligible. In addition to the contests cited, further by-elections were fought by Home Rulers for Galway County on 8 February 1872, where J. P. Nolan won easily though he was unseated on petition on 12 June; at Kerry on 6 February 1873, when R. P. Blennerhassett triumphed by a big margin; at Wexford City on 26 April 1872, with William Redmond carrying the constituency handily; at Mallow on 7 June, when G. J. MacCarthy lost; at Londonderry on 27 November 1872, which saw Biggar beaten by a large total; and finally at Cork City on 20 December 1872, where J. Ronayne achieved a substantial win. In no instance before 1874 was Fenian influence remotely important to the outcome.

Pressure to convert the Home Government Association into a mass organisation came from two directions. First, some members were impatient with the rate of progress of the movement and wished to push it along with a revival of an organ modelled on the Repeal Association. Second, the weakness of the Association and the failure to capture by-elections in the spring and summer 1873 made activists anxious to create a stronger organisation.[44] Between 18 and 21 November 1873 a conclave, reportedly attended by more than 800 of the 900 delegates issued with admission tickets, met in Dublin to form the Home Rule League (see document 2).[45] This new group had substantial ambitions, though little money or structure. The meeting exposed many rifts and what largely held it together was a refusal to endorse any programme or strategy other than self-government. For differing reasons it was feared that a wider platform would alienate both Conservative and moral Home Rulers. At the Home Rule Conference held in Dublin in November 1873, Butt outlined the means of obtaining self-government:

> [I]f he were asked by what means he hoped to carry a federal arrangement, such as he proposed, he believed it would be carried if Ireland at the next election, sent eighty men faithfully to press the demand of the Irish nation for Home Rule. There would be a moral power in such a declaration of the national will – in the support which that demand would receive from the Irish people wherever they were scattered over the face of the globe.[46]

Another delegate, Mitchell Henry, while not dissenting from Butt's vision nevertheless held that 'it was to Mr Gladstone he looked to carry out this measure, and to nobody else'.

Butt reiterated his well-rehearsed case for self-government. For

him now, as earlier, Home Rule had moral virtues which he applied
to the situation of the aristocracy, stating:

> [I]t is impossible to estimate the effect upon the character and con-
> duct of all classes of the nation which would be produced by the
> consciousness that the nation had its destinies in its own hands, by
> the feeling that we must adjust our differences by arrangement
> between ourselves, and not by an appeal to the arbitration of an
> alien power. An aristocracy taking its place in a national parliament
> would soon become influenced by feelings and motives very differ-
> ent from those which may be indulged by men placed in the miser-
> able position in which the Irish aristocracy are now. Those who for
> the first time felt that they had a real power of action would also feel
> the real responsibility of its exercise, in the very necessity of vindi-
> cating their acts in an Irish assembly, even of their own order, the
> peers of an Irish parliament would learn to respect the public opin-
> ion to which, in every such vindication, they must really appeal.
> And brought thus into daily contact with the public opinion of their
> own country they would, of necessity, become sharers in the
> national sentiment and feeling.

His moral vision contrasts with the euphoric though pragmatic purposes outlined by another prominent participant at the Conference,
O'Neill Daunt, who observed:

> [Home Rule] means the retention of Irish money in Ireland, and the
> consequent accumulation of Irish capital. It means the residence in
> Ireland of our wealthy aristocracy, who are absentees precisely
> because they have no parliament at home to afford them legislative
> occupation, and they would speedily return when they found in
> their capital an opening for their honourable parliamentary ambi-
> tion. Home Rule means the sole control by an Irish parliament of
> Irish revenue and expenditure, subject to the condition of defraying
> our fair proportion of imperial expenses. It means the restoration of
> domestic markets for domestic manufacture.

Daunt's characterisation of what self-government would do reflects
some of the distinction emerging between the outlook of middle-
class Catholics and the never very large number of Protestant Home
Rulers.

Four major issues intruded into the conference discussions. First,
several delegates announced a preference for Repeal, arguments that
Butt attempted to counter. He and others defended not only the comparative virtues of federalism but also attempted to co-opt O'Connell's legacy for the new programme. Most, though not all of the
Repealers agreed to set aside their opinions: John Martin's compromise satisfied many for the moment. He contended that 'the present
movement must succeed by being supported by men of all opinions.

A man can join a movement and yet hold his own opinions.' Second, when some present argued for an independent and pledge-bound representation in the House of Commons, other delegates, including Martin and Butt, rejected it. Yet, a number of those present, especially Biggar, wanted something more militant than what the staid leadership seemed to offer. Third, the question of an upper chamber or House of Lords was divisive. Several delegates joined C. G. Doran of Queenstown in expressing their opposition. A dispute was forestalled by reminding those present that the details of the plan were not set in stone. Fourth, in a foretaste of the future, a controversy erupted over parliamentary policy. The Mayor of Kilkenny urged that the best course would be 'by determined action upon the part of the Irish representation – a determination that would bend to no Prime Minister's smile and would not be put down by his frown, or seduced by his blandishments'. Biggar demanded what amounted to obstruction. Butt defused the challenge, observing that 'he did not say the time may not come when Irishmen will be driven to an obstruction policy', though he cautioned, 'the power of doing it remains, and will depend on the moral support of public opinion which the world will give them'. He also expressed doubts about whether, except in extreme cases, it would be possible to justify obstruction, pointing out that even eighty Irish MPs could not carry out the tactic successfully.

For the moment the fragile unity of the movement was preserved on the wave of enthusiasm accompanying the sessions and by the realisation that any prospect of devolved government in Ireland was distant. Why argue about specifics when British acceptance of the principle seemed remote? At this stage the movement did not have a political party to represent it or any certainty of playing a substantial role in the House of Commons. Butt understood that the current euphoria would evaporate if the movement failed to maintain momentum. The problem was how to maturate national sentiment. His solution was to have patriotic MPs act in concert on an agreed set of questions. This was scarcely a novel idea; Butt had seemed to throw cold water on it at the Conference. Co-operation had pitfalls as well. Irish MPs were notoriously slack in parliamentary attendance, usually incapable of co-ordinated action, and only a minority were pledged to the Home Rule programme. In any event, the Home Rule League did not possess an agenda beyond self-government. Nevertheless, Butt pursued his idea of using the MPs to forward the national platform. In December 1873 he urged that the foremost goal should be 'to secure Ulster Tenant Right and generally to amend the Land Act'.[47] The other objects around which the MPs should rally were the restoration of Ireland's two lost parliamentary seats, assimilation of the borough and municipal franchises to those of England, endowment of the municipal corporations with the same privileges as those in England, establishment of representative county councils invested with the financial authority presently held by grand juries, creation of a fisheries board and repeal of the Convention Act in force to contain agrarian crime. He also wanted members to bring forward a motion condemning the entire system of government in Ireland. Here was an ambitious though essentially materialist programme. Patriotism was a diversified interest which could be employed to advance wide-ranging causes. Home Rule was only one element in the platform. Nevertheless, it had an exceptional place. Home Rule as a moral ideal had a particular meaning – self-government of some substantial variety in the long term – but it also acted as an ideological umbrella under which different, sometimes mutually antagonistic interests could huddle together to promote an ordered and relatively harmonious agenda. Butt's decision to opt for parliamentarianism, already implicit in his participation in elections, inevitably left the performance of the movement wedded to the effectiveness of Irish MPs.

The 1874 general election

Home Rule was put to a great test when on 24 January 1874 Gladstone dissolved Parliament. By-elections had already produced a string of Home Rule victories, even before the Ballot Act of 1872 established secret voting. These contests, along with the declarations by 26 (out of 163) Boards of Poor Law Guardians for Home Rule in 1872, demonstrated the growing popular appeal of the cry in Catholic constituencies.[48] Although the franchise was still restricted, with less than one-third of tenant farmers having the ballot, Catholic voters were able to determine the outcome of sixty-six seats.[49] Parliamentary aspirants usually sought clerical approval before publicly declaring their candidacy; priests were successful in most instances in extracting pledges from them on their two issues of greatest concern, the temporal power of the Pope and the education question.[50]

The general election held between 31 January and 12 February enlarged Home Rule numbers but did it did not transform the quality of Ireland's representatives. In total, fifty-nine professed supporters of Home Rule captured sixty constituencies (Philip Callan carried both Louth and Dundalk, choosing to sit for the latter). Nearly a third of this number – eighteen – had been elected earlier as Liberals, with a further dozen of the new MPs being of the same stripe, all ensuring their political survival by adroitly claiming adherence to Home Rule.[51] Anyone was free to claim allegiance to Home Rule ideas. One candidate who had declared himself in favour of self-government nevertheless pleaded privately that he had done this, 'for it is my only chance. I do not think any one can make much of my Home Rule'.[52] The League had no authority over local constituencies or individual candidates. Its address to the voters on the best means to advance the cause left responsibility for electoral arrangements to the localities. Supporters were informed:

> [I]t is not within our province to advise you how in each locality this can best be carried into effect. Whatever aid or advice the resources of our organisation enable us to give, will be cheerfully at the disposal of the friends of the national cause. But we cannot too strongly or too earnestly repeat that it is by the people themselves – by the people in each locality, by the electors in each constituency – that the work must be done.[53]

A curious instance of a candidate operating completely outside the League's auspices came in County Wicklow. The then High Sheriff, Charles Stewart Parnell, an unknown young grandee with no political connection, wanted to stand, but when it was discovered that he was ineligible by virtue of his office, his older brother John Howard Parnell contested the seat instead. The Home Rule League in nearby Dublin was unaware of the Parnells' political proclivities, neither brother having taken any part in national affairs, but could do nothing about the candidature. John Howard Parnell finished at the bottom of the poll.

If Home Rulers were an eclectic bunch they none the less had many traits in common. Besides adhering to self-government principles in some form, they usually supported all or most of the plethora of national issues. They only succeeded in constituencies with substantial Catholic electoral majorities. Geographically, Ulster sent two Home Rulers to Parliament, Leinster sent twenty-six, Munster sent twenty-one and Connaught a further ten. The occupational and social profile of the Home Rulers reveals an over-representation of professional men, especially journalists and lawyers, despite warnings that many of the latter sought parliamentary honours for the sake of securing government legal posts.[54] Owners of land were present in some numbers, though aristocrats, tenant farmers, shopkeepers and industrialists were largely absent. In an age when MPs were unsalaried, going into Parliament appealed mainly to men with private incomes or to those who could combine attendance at the House of Commons with employment. Some forty-six were Catholic Home Rule MPs, a further increment in the withdrawal of Protestants from the national coalition, three other Catholics were returned as Liberals. From 1874 Home Rule effectively served as an umbrella for what were essentially Catholic materialist aims.

This election also revealed the limits of potential national advances under the operative electoral system. Ireland had a large number of borough seats – thirty-seven – with mostly small, often corrupt electorates usually containing a significant proportion of Protestant voters and where, according to K. T. Hoppen, a coherent local culture flourished.[55] Hoppen contrasts this with county constituencies where politics was shaped by traditional power relationships and the national issues favoured by the farmers. In order to expand the number of patriots, some alteration of the franchise and, more importantly, redistribution of constituencies, was imperative. Butt's projections of eighty Home Rule MPs was unduly optimistic under the existing system. Nevertheless, it could scarcely be denied that Home Rulers, however designated, had achieved a magnificent success. The triumph of the movement's electoral strategy was also an endorsement of moderate materialism. Fenianism did not abjure mistrust of parliamentarians, but a section of the leadership gave Butt a trial period of three years for his policy. The reality was that the Fenians, who had been the spark for the revival of national organisation, were shoved further to the fringes of Irish affairs despite the fact that several of the new breed had received their initial political education in the movement. If parliamentarianism lasted, it could change the shape of Irish discussions in Great Britain. Past experience, however, did not augur well.

While the Home Rulers certainly gained a huge triumph in Ireland, the 1874 election exposed a flaw in Butt's strategy predicated on influencing Liberals. Conservatives captured 350 of the 652 seats in the House of Commons, and thus held a secure majority. Lord Spencer, the outgoing Liberal Lord Lieutenant of Ireland, observed that the Home Rulers' efforts 'will now be thrown away to a great extent as they will have no power in the House'.[56] Spencer could see that the presence of Home Rulers in the House of Commons would have a beneficial influence. He was 'glad on the whole that Butt is returned, as it is better that he should be in the House than out of it'. Butt attempted to put the best complexion on the situation. He insisted: 'they would be the Irish party and the Irish power in the House. They would make themselves and their country respected. They would put forward their country's wrongs. They would demand their country's rights, wholly independent of the votes of any English party.'[57]

Butt believed the new administration 'would offer them many things of material advantage to the country'.[58] Shortly after the election, at a meeting in Dublin on 3 March attended by forty-six of the

Home Rule MPs (nine others sent apologies), they formed themselves into a party. It was to be independent of all other combinations
and MPs were to take counsel together on all matters, avoiding so far
as possible isolated action.[59] An executive committee was chosen and
Butt was invited to accept the position of chairman. This event
marked the beginnings of a formal parliamentary party, although
independence from all other parties did not include sitting together
as a group in the House of Commons; two MPs actually moved with
the Conservatives to the government benches. The decision to act as
a party or interest naturally raised expectations which might prove
difficult to realise.

Butt and parliamentarianism, 1874–76

In the event the new administration did not fulfil Butt's prophesy of
bringing forward 'things of material advantage'. In the Queen's
Speech on 20 March 1874 only one comparatively minor reform for
Ireland was mentioned at all. However, the new Chief Secretary Sir
Michael Hicks Beach did sound several chords that had an impact for
some time to come. First, he repeated the widely held view that the
demand for Home Rule was ambiguous. 'It appears to me', he
declared, 'that every class in Ireland has interpreted the cry ... to
mean the fulfilment of its own particular desires.' Yet he made it clear
that this was not a regime built simply upon resistance, saying:

> I can assure them that, though an Englishman, I will endeavour in
> those duties which fall to my lot in connection with Irish affairs to
> throw off any prejudices I may have felt, and to act with a single eye
> to the welfare of Ireland. I will endeavour to act impartially between
> different creeds and different sects, whether in religion or in poli-
> tics.[60]

Hicks Beach's pledge was not fulfilled in 1874 or at any time during
the administration of 1874–80, but it opened up intriguing possibilities. It demonstrated the fact that a Conservative administration
might be as responsive to Irish wants as the Liberals. Protestants, too,
were alerted to the realisation that they could expect to be treated in
the same fashion as Catholics. The British government, in the Chief
Secretary's view, was a referee, neutral between the contending Irish
factions. The quotation from the general in command of the army in
Ireland during the Fenian revolt, cited at the beginning of the chapter, emphasises the notion of government acting as an umpire.

Despite subsequent accusations of subservience to parliamentary
forms, Butt, at least in 1874, was emphatic that representation at

Westminster was only one – and indeed a subordinate part – of the means of obtaining self-government. He warned the Irish people:

> [T]hey should not exaggerate the importance of parliamentary votes. Again and again he said that the parliamentary representation was only a part, and he believed a subordinate part, of the means by which Irish self-government would be achieved. Home rule was to be won first of all by the Irish people showing that they were in earnest in seeking it, it was also to be won by appealing to the public opinion of England and of the whole world, and to every one of those things their representatives in Parliament could very slightly contribute. What they could do was this: they could, by their presence proclaim the solemn protest of Ireland against the system under which it is governed; they could place their views fairly and distinctly before the British House of Commons, and leave to them the responsibility of rejecting the demands of the Irish people; they could destroy misrepresentation by making a statement of what Ireland really seeks; and, above all – and he was sure they would do her a most important service – they could expose the system of coercive oppression, and unconstitutional tyranny, by which England alone maintained her present system of government. By that means the Irish members could exert an important influence on public opinion. Beyond that they could do nothing – beyond that everything rested with the people.[61]

During the parliamentary session of 1874 Irish MPs introduced several bills and on 30 June staged the first substantive Home Rule debate in the House of Commons. Although morale was high, the actual result of this activity was minimal. A serious problem emerged: how could the public be persuaded to remain committed to, and vigorously to support a movement that achieved little? In March *The Nation* briefly hinted that Irish MPs might resort to 'making themselves troublesome at unexpected times' if the government ignored Irish appeals.[62] On 30 July Biggar used a stream of procedural motions during the debate on the Expiring Laws Continuance bill, which would extended existing special powers of the Irish executive to deal with disorder. The tactic, soon labelled 'obstruction', had been employed by Irish MPs in the previous decade but never gained wide currency.[63] Unhappy at Biggar's solo venture, Butt cautioned that continued use of such methods 'would not only impede the business of the House, but would bring discredit and disgrace upon the proceedings which some Irish members thought it their duty to take'.[64]

Between 1871 and 1874 electoralism and a materialist parliamentarianism had seemed a sound means of advancing the national agenda. To many like Butt, entry into the House of Commons was the logical step for a movement that had little apparatus and scant resources to build a large-scale structure in the country, even if this had been its intention; gaining seats in Parliament offered a cheap and efficient means of publicising the national cause. Butt remained cautious about what could be expected from such participation, particularly in the short term, and without clerical backing. After the 1874 general election only three of the twenty-nine Irish bishops were committed to the movement.[65] He saw that Home Rule was caught on the horns of a dilemma. If it eschewed electoralism and chose to become a mass pressure group, its power would be dissipated in public demonstrations; it was likely to prove difficult, perhaps impossible, to contain and channel such a force into purely constitutional forms. British governments and Dublin Castle could not easily suppress a peaceful parliamentary group; but they probably would try to crack down on an organisation sponsoring mass agitation. The history of the Repeal Association provided ample evidence of the state's power to curtail a popular movement. On the other hand, electoralism was detested by militants, who saw in it only corruption, vacillation and weakness. Failure to demonstrate a concrete return on participation would confirm ingrained suspicions of parliamentarianism.

Already in 1874 it was apparent that the Irish party and movement as a whole contained several defects. The parliamentary session revealed signs of disorganisation, lack of preparation and growing rifts in the party. Similar problems afflicted the Home Rule League, added to which were its meagre financial resources. David Thornley and Emmet Larkin point to divisions in the country as well.[66] The latter comments in particular on the estrangement between the urban working classes and Fenians on one side and county tenant farmers and their allies on the other. He also faults Butt's leadership capacity.

The new session opened for the Home Rulers with the embarrassment of the Tipperary by-election, which came about as a result of the resignation of Colonel White. Radical and anti-Home Rule elements determined to put forward John Mitchel, the revolutionary and undischarged felon, for the vacancy. He was returned unopposed on 16 February, only to have his election nullified. When he stood again, a Conservative joined the field. Mitchel was elected a second time on 11 March, but on being declared ineligible, the seat was awarded to Stephen Moore, the Conservative candidate, and the Home Rule party lost an MP.

During 1875 the parliamentary strategy began to sag. Part of the problem lay in Butt's absence, some in the traditional malaise of Irish members, and a good deal can be attributed to the inability to latch upon an issue capable of igniting enthusiasm in Ireland. Biggar, though, did adumbrate a promising course. In April and May, during the debates on the Westmeath Act of 1872 which implemented special or coercive measures, he reverted to obstructionist methods. Irritated by his subordinate's behaviour, Butt assured the House of Commons that Biggar was acting entirely on his own. The leader also tried to deflect mounting criticism of parliamentarianism within the Home Rule movement by pointing to a future general election and, in the meantime, he urged the need for Irish reforms on the House of Commons. But members of the Home Rule League, notably in Great Britain where the Fenian element was dominant, were increasingly critical of the Irish party and supported Biggar's actions. In June 1875, the annual conference of the Home Rule Confederation of Great Britain praised Biggar's course and called upon the party to emulate him.[67] One increasingly influential MP, John O'Connor Power, reported to his constituents that he was 'entirely in favour' of Biggar's tactics and only desisted from applying them out of 'my desire to act in accordance with the general sense of the party'.[68] Butt's personal financial difficulties caused him to be absent frequently during the session and the party's paralysis without him weakened the parliamentary strategy. Of Butt, one Home Ruler, Joseph Ronayne, observed on 8 November, 'I would trust him with my cause but not with my money. You might as well put water in a colander as money in Butt's pocket.' Butt went on to defend the virtues of the movement on the grounds of its keeping the torch of national pride alight:

> I am not sanguine of obtaining either Repeal or Home Rule by reason or argument from the English Parliament, but it is the only organisation that can keep the question before the country and prevent us from drifting bodily into whiggery, and if we get nothing in the shape of Home Rule but the payment of our own people out of our own taxes, and putting a stop to the wholesale corruption of the country going on at present, it would be the greatest step towards national independence that could be achieved.[69]

The annual party meeting on 8 February 1876 was attended by only thirty-one MPs with nine not bothering to acknowledge the invitation. The next parliamentary session was even more frustrating. Despite greater activity on the part of MPs, the outcome of these efforts remained negligible. Disquiet over Butt's patient parliamentary approach surfaced from several quarters. At the beginning of July *The Nation* stated the growing feeling that 'to us it appears that the rejection of the series of measures brought forward in the House by the Home Rule party afford a full justification for a much stronger line of action than any which they have hitherto adopted'.[70] It called for a 'policy of obstruction' to show the government that they meant business. Dissatisfaction with the state of affairs came from another direction, too. Out of loyalty to Butt, Fenians had abstained from an open attack on parliamentarianism for a trial period. However, during 1876 they began breaking up Home Rule meetings. On 20 August the supreme council of the Irish Republican Brotherhood put into action the decree passed on the meeting held on 28 May:

> that the countenance which we have hitherto shown to the Home Rule movement be from this date, and is hereby, withdrawn, as three years' experience of the working of the movement has proved to us that the revolutionary principles which we profess can be better served by our organisation existing on its own basis pure and simple; and we hereby request that all members of our organisation who may have any connection with the Home Rule movement will definitely withdraw from it their active co-operation within six months from this date.[71]

Members were given six months to dissociate themselves from the Home Rule movement. The Home Rulers had little to show for their efforts to date; patience with the experiment was drawing to a close unless some better basis of action was found. Still, in September O'Connor Power observed that 'the best platform which they could avail themselves of was the House of Commons'.[72]

Obstruction and the rise of Parnell

Prior to 1877 obstruction caused the government no more than modest concern. On 1 January 1877 Hicks Beach cited the positive side to the antics of Home Rulers, pointing out to Sir Stafford Northcote: 'their humbug has a good deal to do with keeping Ireland quiet'.[73] However, during 1877 many of the internal tensions within the national coalition surfaced. This session brought Parnell to the fore and began the next phase of parliamentarianism. Before the session opened, Butt's approach received a welcome fillip when a delegation of bishops endorsed the Home Rule movement, making it and, in particular, the leader the agent for the Church's university legislation. Already in January 1876 the Catholic hierarchy had substantially abandoned the Catholic Union (founded in 1872) as its political arm, thereby reducing the obstacles to co-operation with the Home Rule party. Acquisition of increased aid from clerics gave Butt a more than adequate replacement for declining Fenian support. The annual party meeting on 31 January 1877 was attended by thirty-two MPs. One of Butt's closest supporters, Mitchell Henry, observed:

> [I]n the next session of Parliament it would be their duty to follow a very bold course. He was not in favour of shaking hands all round,

of thankfulness for small mercies. What they wanted was their national rights, and they would be friends with those men who would assist them to gain those rights; they would not be friends with those who resisted them.[74]

Butt never rejected the principal of obstruction though he declined to endorse its implementation because in his opinion the time was not ripe. To resort to it prematurely would only discredit the weapon and, in his estimation, alienate British sympathy from the Home Rulers. He clung to a longer-term outlook centred on the role of educating opinion, on a general election to enlarge and improve Irish representation, and on the return of a Liberal government. Butt pleaded:

> [L]et us ask of the English Liberals to join us in demolishing every part of the system opposed to their principles. If we carry any measure in this way we have achieved a great triumph and can enjoy its fruits. If we fail, we have supplied another, and an unanswerable argument to Europe, to the Irish and English nations, to show that nothing but self-legislation can ever reconcile us or realise our aspirations.[75]

The chieftain suggested that the case would be advanced best in the coming session by the more frequent attendance of MPs along with the nation's display of its support for the party.

Unfortunately for Butt, in the Queen's Speech in 1877 the government had given short shrift to Ireland. The energy of the ministers began to wane following three years of intense reform and it would soon be absorbed in foreign matters.[76] This snub fanned smouldering national sentiment. Biggar found an ally in the member returned for County Meath at a by-election on 17 April 1975: Charles Stewart Parnell. The pair quickly began to exploit the parliamentary rules to draw attention to themselves. Soon *The Nation* was urging other MPs to follow their example.[77] After several Irish measures had been rejected, Parnell's intervention became more pointed and frequent. Unlike Biggar, he did not make lengthy speeches but relied upon procedural motions. By such repeated acts Biggar and Parnell brought down upon themselves the wrath of Ministers, becoming the objects of denunciation in the English press. During the spring of 1877 Butt, who took umbrage at the freelance activities of the duo, became increasingly vocal in his public criticism. The Earl of Derby noted that 'the Home Rule party as a body disclaim their tactics: but if these tactics succeed, I doubt whether they will continue to reject them', speculating that 'fifty members bent on a policy of systematic obstruction of all business would throw the whole parliamentary machine into confusion'.[78] Butt's criticism of Biggar and Parnell won the hearts of Englishmen but lost those of Irishmen when he became so incensed with their antics that he expressed his 'disapproval of the course taken by the hon. member for Meath. It was a course of obstruction – and one against which he must enter his protest.'[79] In reality, Butt and Parnell were not far apart in their approaches. Both wished to promote the national cause by the most effective means in the House of Commons, though the obstruction episode made the gap appear much wider. Whereas Butt placed emphasis upon the educative function of representation, Parnell looked to MPs to act in an expressive role, that is, he wanted them to state and re-echo Ireland's woes in unmistakable tones.[80] Parnell countered his leader's criticism by insisting that 'England respects nothing but power, and it is certain that the Irish party, comprising, as it does, so many men of talent and ability, might have the power, which attention to business, method and energy always give, if it would only exhibit these qualities.'[81] The young MP sought not to supplant parliamentarianism but to make its voice heard. This, then, was not primarily, as has been suggested, part of a rebellion against the prevailing norms of deference.[82]

On 5 June 1877 an Irish party meeting attempted to reach a compromise on obstruction, but it was quickly apparent that the differences ran too deep. Agreement did not survive long; Parnell and Biggar reverted to obstruction tactics. Following the twenty-six hour sitting, Henry Lucy noted its humorous aspect:

> [T]he difficulty of defining what Home Rule really is, and what it precisely means, has always cropped up when the matter has been debated in the House of Commons. The difficulty no longer exists. After the experience of the last twenty-six hours it is clear enough that Home Rule means not going home all night yourself, and keeping as many other people as possible out of their beds.[83]

Parnell's notoriety soared, though for different reasons, in both Britain and Ireland. On 27 July Butt threatened to resigned the leadership if the obstructionists did not desist from their course. At the beginning of August, after a renewed burst of obstruction, the young John Dillon recorded in his diary: 'this day I mark as the beginning of a new era in the history of Erin. And I wish to have in my room the portraits of the three men who pointed out to Ireland her way to freedom.'[84] Another party meeting on 6 August again tried to patch up the dispute. The obstructionists held a meeting on 21 August at the Rotunda in Dublin, where their approach was endorsed. Wounds were kept open when the Home Rule Confederation of Great Britain, a largely moribund organisation, at its annual convention on 27 and

28 August, attended by merely forty delegates, elected Parnell to take over from Butt as their President.

In previous years Parnell had impressed public opinion at home with his patriotic stance, but he had never been unusually active on the hustings. Starting in March 1877, he began to address audiences in Ireland and particularly in England with much greater frequency, and following his election as President of the Home Rule Confederation of Great Britain he barnstormed northern English and Scottish towns to promote a more vigorous parliamentary policy. Parnell's approach to this issue was setting him apart from Butt in a crucial aspect. He developed it as a means of rescuing the movement, a strategy for building popular support from the top. In the absence of an institutional structure in Ireland he substituted drama and publicity, carefully targeting his activities for the Irish press. Parnell relied upon communication, albeit at a distance via the newspapers, about events taking place in the faraway forum of Westminster. By this technique he was able to reach a nationwide audience without the uncertainties, expense and organisational apparatus required for mass demonstrations. His approach had a further virtue. Because he was utilising the House of Commons and not stumping the country he was able to circumvent the clergy, the middle classes and in some districts the Fenians who competed for control over local politics. As he was not a great orator, but grew into a solid parliamentarian, communication in this form suited Parnell's talents. The growth of literacy and the swift spread of information through newspapers distributed by the rail network afforded conditions suited to the new mode of communication.

Parnell's understanding of the possibilities enabled him to challenge Butt's policy and elevated him to the stature of a political rival. Butt's friends flooded him with advice on the way to stem Parnell's offensive. O'Neill Daunt wrote to him, urging the 'need of more vigorous and disciplined parliamentary action'.[85] Another pressed on Butt the value of an assertive parliamentary approach directed by himself:

> In my opinion the game is more in your hands than ever. The obstructionists will give you an active party & provided you keep them at work the country will be satisfied & you can guide them as your judgement dictates. Our votes and proceedings on our Irish questions will become of vital importance, and although I don't expect Home Rule to be won by throwing our swords on the scale, beyond all doubt our activity, restrained within the limits of common sense, will give us victories useful, nay necessary, for the main purpose.[86]

Butt did not revise his methods, though he displayed great resource-fulness and tenacity during the dispute.[87] Nevertheless, his perceived timidity was a source of dismay to colleagues. On 5 September O'Neill Daunt outlined the dilemma to Mitchell Henry:

> [T]he situation is just this. Firstly, Mr Butt is indispensable as a leader. No other man could take his place. Secondly, the conciliatory policy is worthless, yet our indispensable leader seems resolved to persevere in it. At any rate he has not indicated any new departure, although he certainly said at a Westminster Meeting that obstruc-tion *might* become necessary. Thirdly, Division in our army would be worse than worthless; it would be equally damaging as the milk-and-water policy, and more discreditable to ourselves.
>
> Perhaps Mr Butt knows some distinction between the precise form of obstruction practised by Mr Parnell and Mr Biggar and the obstruction which he told his Westminster visitors might become necessary. If so the public should be made aware of it, for the present condition of matters is most unsatisfactory.[88]

Increasingly, Butt relied upon out-manoeuvring the militants in the party and the Home Rule League where he enjoyed residual loy-alty. He also brought the Church to his rescue. Larkin cites Butt's open letter to Father Joseph Murphy, published on 7 September 1877, as the divisive moment in the counter-offensive. Butt contended that Parnell's version of obstruction must augur 'the abandonment of constitutional and the adoption of unconstitutional action in its stead'.[89] Larkin maintains that Parnell's more conciliatory attitude after mid-September was due to an appreciation of clerical disap-proval of the challenge to Butt's authority, though his subsequent speeches do not wholly bear out this hypothesis.[90] The struggle did not end tamely. Parnell was determined to force the issue. At a party meeting on 9 October he declared: 'I think the course the Irish party have adopted in the past has not been calculated to attract the atten-tion of the Irish people and to make them believe in our earnestness, and if we want them to support a parliamentary party we must show them that we are in earnest, and that we are determined to carry out that policy.'[91] Two days later the Home Rule League agreed to call a National Conference to adjudicate the question. A curious dispute broke out over representation at the Conference. Butt proposed six categories of delegates, consisting of clergy of all denominations, magistrates, members of corporations, town and municipal commis-sioners, Poor Law Guardians and persons who at any time had been members of the original Home Rule Association or the Home Rule League.[92] This assemblage reflects the extremely middle-class charac-ter of the movement and also made it unlikely that Parnell's views would be adopted. T. D. Sullivan proposed that the Home Rule Confederation of Great Britain be allowed to send an unlimited number of delegates, but Butt immediately objected to this attempt to pack the Conference with more radicalised, mainly working-class participants. In the end, a compromise allowed fifty delegates to attend. During the autumn Butt exploited his sources of strength among the respectable orders in Ireland.

The start of 1878 saw Butt firmly in control of the party, though the question of parliamentary policy remained very much at issue. There were thirty MPs present on 12 January at the annual party meeting, and two days later the National Conference assembled, attended by some 600 persons, including 130 Catholic clergy. Butt's leadership was sustained, even if the mood favoured a more vigorous parliamentary policy; the Conference reinforced the parliamentarianism of the Home Rule movement. If they could achieve some major legislative success when Parliament reconvened, Butt reasoned, the balance would tilt back towards himself, and Parnell's tactics would lose their potency. He began badgering Hicks Beach, who, though no longer the Chief Secretary of the Irish office, still kept a watching brief for Irish business. Butt's aim was to get the government to pass a bill to improve intermediate education in Ireland.[93] The government was alive to the potential of the situation. Naturally, English leaders, conscious of Parnell's rising stature, were not displeased at the prospect of a further fracturing of the national movement. Judicious concessions, they believed, would yield a measure of satisfaction on several counts, not least by widening divisions in the rank and file. The government blunted a reversion to obstructionist tactics by proposing to bring forward a bill for intermediate education on condition that time for its passage was not frittered away, and then shrewdly refrained from introducing the legislation until late in the session. The bill was introduced on 21 June 1878 in the House of Lords and received its second reading in the lower chamber on 15 July; it was enacted on 16 August.

By playing its hand skilfully and proposing a measure desired by the Catholic hierarchy, the government showed itself astute in outflanking Parnell: obstruction tactics were substantially averted; where the government miscalculated was on the impact of the legislation for the respective fortunes of Butt and Parnell. Each claimed it as a vindication for his own tactics. Parnell, not Butt, had discovered a key to upholding Irish morale at a time when the party and movement were close to dissolution and the concept of Home Rule was making little impact on British attitudes. Butt lost support because 'he would not strip to fight'.[94] Yet the old chief was by no means finished. A further blockage to more complete clerical adherence to the movement was removed with the death of Cardinal Cullen on 24

October 1878. Butt chose to promote his own approach through a series of letters to constituents. But there were only 15 MPs present at the annual party meeting held on 5 December, a thin turnout that showed the poor morale of the party despite the education measure. Butt attended his last meeting of the Home Rule League on 4 February. The Land Conference which started the next day revealed support for the promotion of parliamentary candidates committed to tenants' rights at the next general election. Meanwhile, a party meeting on 15 February was attended by only twenty-four MPs. Parnell's own position was no less tenuous than Butt's. His attempt to mount another speaking tour in Britain during January 1879 met with a weak response. The by-election result for County Cork on 17 February also showed Parnell's limited appeal among the large tenant farmers who dominated the electorate. Meanwhile, the first major land demonstration was held at Irishtown, County Mayo on 20 April.

In early 1879 Butt continued to argue for his policy, though he never returned to the House of Commons after August 1878. He died on 5 May 1879. Parnell's methods, not to mention his disloyalty to Butt, did not endear him to most of the parliamentarians. Many could not abide him; Butt's demise entrenched their hostility. Parnell's ideas, however, gained a grip on the Home Rulers. When the government failed to accord Ireland satisfactory attention in the 1874 Queen's Speech, Mitchell Henry, acting in Butt's stead, responded:

> [U]nder the circumstances, the government need not expect that any facilities will be given by Irish members for the progress of public business. I, for my part, have never taken any course in this House which could be called obstructive, but I say that the government is putting to a severe test the forbearance, not of the Irish members alone, but of the Irish people.[95]

Conclusion

After Butt's death the party on 22 May chose William Shaw, a Protestant Cork banker and merchant, as chairman. Shaw had presided over the National Conference in November 1873 and, despite being fairly dull, was well regarded in Home Rule circles. Larkin notes that, unlike Butt, Shaw was elected by the whole parliamentary party, though his assertion that the party's constitution was successfully restructured between February and May 1878 is not sustainable.[96] Neither Butt nor Parnell could have foreseen the land crisis which would transform patriotic fortunes. Both asserted that Home Rule could only be pursued successfully when the country as a whole showed a united determination to have it; then a parliamentary party would be able to press a British government into granting autonomy. Each also saw utility in having a party at Westminster for the purposes of influencing opinion, to express Ireland's aspirations, and to gain some practical concessions. Without such boons, they reasoned, middle-class control could be challenged, even threatened, by Fenianism or some other movement supported from below. Where they differed was on the most effective way to press Irish interests. Butt believed, as did Parnell, that reformation of the parliamentary party had to await another general election. The two men shared the premise that real justice would be obtained from a Liberal rather than a Conservative regime and both had a moral vision of Home Rule. In the meantime they shared a wish to entice an existing Ministry to introduce legislation for Ireland. Butt held that the Home Rule quest necessarily required a lengthy period of gestation, an educative process in which the good will of Britain was essential. Real progress on all fronts, he maintained, hinged on patience and on putting Ireland's case with moderation.

Parnell did not so much dispute Butt's diagnosis as establish a separate set of priorities. For him, the emphasis shifted to sustaining morale at home which he held had to be done by a show of strength in the House of Commons. He came to recognise that Ireland lacked training in the niceties of Westminster politics and also had little patience. The experiences of 1874–76 demonstrated to him that without some inducement the party and people could not be held to the mast indefinitely. If impressive achievements were impossible, some other demonstration of activity was mandatory. Parnell observed and then gradually adopted what came to be known as an obstructive policy in the House of Commons. This enabled him and a small band of fellow travellers to stand up for Ireland, to maximise public interest in the party and Home Rule even when little of advantage was likely to result from their endeavours. Parnell spoke for Ireland when Butt appeared to bow and scrape before the imperial lion. It will be recalled that Butt a few years earlier had been emphatic that the Irish should always avoid that very subservience he came to personify.

Obstruction, of course, was never more than a limited tool, best suited to a time when little might be won for Ireland, but it was a tactic that captured public imagination. There was never a possibility of obstruction winning Home Rule and it offered little prospect of being the basis for construction of an organisation capable of marshalling the support of the Catholics of the country over an extended period. British governments had the means to fight back and would do so by curtailing the powers of minorities in the House of Commons. Obstruction had an obvious implication too often overlooked.

It was a parliamentary, a Westminster-based, and fundamentally a Catholic middle-class approach to Ireland's claims; a policy heavily geared towards securing ameliorative measures for Ireland. Parnell's strategy was based on politics from the top down, not mass action. In the late Victorian age, when Parliament was in the ascendant and the House of Commons the engine of reform, it may have been sound to pursue self-government by such means, but there were, as time would show, rocks ahead. In 1879 the Fenian spirit remained alive, but Fenianism was no match for the politics of middle-class Home Rule, even when the latter had so little to show for its efforts. Home Rule had proved a blunt instrument. It captured Catholics' imaginations and bound them to the movement temporarily, but in order to achieve longer-term success it had to be linked to reformism and that always threatened to rent the movement in two. If the outcome of Home Rule politics in the 1870s was limited, important precedents had been set. It was evident that Catholic voters preferred and continued to opt for specific national forms of political representation despite the setbacks to the movement in the 1870s. Between 1874 and the general election in 1880 electoral support for Home Rulers remained remarkable constant: they made three gains at by-elections and lost three more, though in two of these the outcome was a distortion. A Conservative was awarded Tipperary in March 1875 when John Mitchel was returned a second time and disqualified; in May 1876 a seat was lost when the vote was split between two Home Rulers, allowing the third candidate to slip in. Otherwise the vote for Home Rulers held up throughout these years.

Notes

1 Isaac Butt, *Land Tenure in Ireland; A Plea for the Celtic Race* (3rd edn; Dublin, 1866), p. 9.

2 Quoted in Bernard Holland, *The Life of Spencer Compton, Eighth Duke of Devonshire* (London, 1911), I, p. 69.

3 See, E. D. Steele, *Irish Land and British Politics: Tenant-Right and Nationality, 1865–1870* (Cambridge, 1974), p. 30, where he cites Fenian support for land reform.

4 See, R. V. Comerford, 'Patriotism as Pastime: The Appeal of Fenianism in the mid-1860s, *Irish Historical Studies*, XXII (September 1981), pp. 239–50; reprinted in Alan O'Day (ed.), *Reactions to Irish Nationalism, 1865–1914* (London, 1987), pp. 21–32; Tom Garvin, *Nationalist Revolutionaries in Ireland 1858–1928* (Oxford, 1987), pp. 33–7.

5 Quoted in F. S. L. Lyons, *Ireland since the Famine* (4th impression; London, 1976), p. 130.

6 Patrick Corish, 'Cardinal Cullen and the National Association of Ireland', *Reportorium Novum*, 3 (1961–62), pp. 13–61, reprinted in O'Day

(ed.), *Reactions to Irish Nationalism*, pp. 117–65.

7   Quoted in Gerard Moran, *A Radical Priest in Mayo; Fr Patrick Lavelle: The Rise and Fall of an Irish Nationalist, 1825–86* (Dublin, 1994), p. 95.

8   E. D. Steele, 'Cardinal Cullen and Irish Nationality', *Irish Historical Studies*, XIX (March 1975), p. 258.

9   Corish, 'Cardinal Cullen', p. 55.

10   *Ibid.*, p. 57.

11   *The Times*, 6 August 1868.

12   *Annual Register* (1868), pp. 44–5.

13   Quoted in P. M. H. Bell, *Disestablishment in Ireland and Wales* (London, 1969), p. 84.

14   Quoted in H. C. G. Matthew (ed.), *The Gladstone Diaries* (Oxford, 1982), VII, p. 158.

15   See R. V. Comerford, 'Isaac Butt and the Home Rule Party, 1870–77', in W. E. Vaughan (ed.), *A New History of Ireland VI: Ireland Under the Union, II, 1870–1921* (Oxford, 1996), p. 11.

16   R. B. McDowell, *The Church of Ireland 1869–1969* (London, 1975), p. 36.

17   Moran, *A Radical Priest*, p. 96.

18   Quoted in Matthew, *Gladstone Diaries*, pp. 61–2.

19   T. W. Moody, *Davitt and the Irish Revolution, 1846–82* (Oxford, 1981), p. 121.

20   K. T. Hoppen, 'National Politics and Local Realities in Mid-Nineteenth Century Ireland', in Art Cosgrove and Donald McCartney (eds), *Studies in Irish History* (Naas, 1979), p. 218; Ignatius Murphy, *The Diocese of Killaloe* (Dublin, 1995), p. 210; Emmet Larkin, *The Consolidation of the Roman Catholic Church in Ireland, 1860–1870* (Chapel Hill and London, 1987), p. 645; R. V. Comerford, *The Fenians in Context: Irish Politics and Society 1848–82* (Dublin, 1985), p. 174; Moran, *A Radical Priest*, p. 101.

21   Gerard Moran, 'Politics and Electioneering in County Longford, 1868–80', in Raymond Gillespie and Gerard Moran (eds), *Longford: Essays in County History* (Dublin, 1991), p. 182.

22   Quoted in Keith Robbins, *John Bright* (London, 1979), p. 203.

23   *The Nation*, 18 August 1869.

24   Comerford, *Fenians in Context*, p. 176.

25   *The Nation*, 13 November, 10 December 1869.

26   *The Nation*, 20 November 1869.

27   Quoted in Emmet Larkin, *The Roman Catholic Church and the Home Rule Movement in Ireland 1870–1874* (Chapel Hill and London, 1990), p. 84.

28   Isaac Butt to P. J. Smyth, 23 May 1870, P. J. Smyth Papers, National Library of Ireland, MS 8215/2; A. M. Sullivan, *New Ireland: Political Sketches and Personal Reminiscences or Thirty Years of Irish Public Life* (9th edn; Glasgow, 1877), pp. 339–51.

29   Journal, 4 July 1870, William O'Neill Daunt Papers, National Library of Ireland, MS 3041, f. 900.

30　Quotations in this and the next two paragraphs are all from Isaac Butt, *Irish Federalism: Its Meaning, Its Objects and Its Hopes* (4th edn; Dublin, 1874).

31　*The Nation,* 7 January 1871.

32　*Ibid.,* 1 October 1870.

33　*Ibid.,* 17 December 1970.

34　*Ibid.*

35　Quoted in E. R. Norman, *The Roman Catholic Church in the Age of Rebellion* (London, 1965), pp. 417–18.

36　Alfred Webb to John Martin, 25 March 1871, Alfred Webb Papers, National Library of Ireland, MS 1745 (31).

37　*The Nation,* 9, 16 September 1871; for the 15th Earl of Derby's observations on his election, see, John Vincent (ed.), *A Selection from the Diaries of Edward Henry Stanley, 15th Earl of Derby (1826–93) Between September 1869 and March 1878* (London, 1994), p. 90 (23 September).

38　*Ibid.,* 9 September 1871.

39　Quoted in Alan O'Day and John Stevenson (eds), *Irish Historical Documents since 1800* (Dublin, 1992), p. 88; also see the Resolutions of the Archbishops quoted in Larkin, *The Roman Catholic Church,* pp. 165–6.

40　Quoted in J. H. Whyte, 'Bishop Moriarty on Disestablishment and the Union, 1868', *Irish Historical Studies,* X (September 1956), pp. 194–5.

41　Michael Hurst, 'Ireland and the Ballot Act of 1872', *Historical Journal,* VIII (1965), pp. 239–50; reprinted in O'Day (ed.), *Reactions to Irish Nationalism,* pp. 33–59.

42　Quoted in Comerford, *New History,* p. 12.

43　Comerford, *Fenians in Context,* pp. 208 and 222, for maps.

44　Larkin, *The Roman Catholic Church,* p. 182.

45　*Ibid.,* p. 183, where attendance on the first day is cited as some 400; a good account of the proceedings can be found, pp. 183–92.

46　Quotations in this and the next two paragraphs are all from *Proceedings of the Home Rule Conference held at the Rotunda, Dublin on the 18th, 19th, 20th and 21st November 1873* (Dublin, 1874).

47　Isaac Butt to Mitchell Henry, 29 December 1873, Isaac Butt Papers, National Library of Ireland, MS 8695.

48　William L. Feingold, *The Revolt of the Tenantry: The Transformation of Local Government in Ireland, 1872–1886* (Boston, MA, 1984), pp. 82–3, also, p. 15.

49　Larkin, *The Roman Catholic Church,* p. 205; Moran, 'Politics and Electioneering', pp. 187–9; for the influence of the clergy in elections, see, James O'Shea, *Priest, Politics and Society in Post-famine Ireland. A Study of County Tipperary 1850–1891* (Dublin, 1983), p. 44.

50　K. Theodore Hoppen, *Elections, Politics, and Society in Ireland 1832–1885* (Oxford, 1984), p. 249.

51　D. A. Thornley, *Isaac Butt and Home Rule* (London, 1964), p. 203; Lawrence J. McCaffrey, *Irish Federalism in the 1870s: A Study in Conservative Nationalism* (Philadelphia, 1962), p. 22.

52　Quoted in Hoppen, *Elections, Politics, and Society in Ireland,* p. 174.

53　*The Nation,* 31 January 1874.

54 Thornley, *Isaac Butt*, pp. 205–11; Michael MacDonagh, *The Home Rule Movement* (Dublin, 1920), pp. 34–41.

55 Hoppen, *Elections, Politics, and Society in Ireland*, p. 160.

56 Peter Gordon (ed.), *The Red Earl: The Papers of the Fifth Earl Spencer, 1835–1910* (Northampton, 1980), I, p. 118.

57 *The Nation*, 21 February 1874.

58 *Ibid.*

59 Thornley, *Isaac Butt*, p. 213.

60 *Parliamentary Debates [PD]*, 218 (1874), cc. 110–18; see Lady Victoria Hicks Beach, *Life of Sir Michael Hicks Beach* (London, 1932), I, pp. 38–9.

61 *The Nation*, 11 April 1874.

62 *Ibid.*, 28 March 1874.

63 T. A. Jenkins (ed.), *The Parliamentary Diaries of Sir John Trelawny, 1858–1865* (London: Royal Historical Society Camden Series, 1990), entry for 12 July 1860, p. 130.

64 *PD*, 221 (1874), cc. 714–15.

65 Larkin, *The Roman Catholic Church and the Emergence of the Modern Irish Political System, 1874–1878* (Dublin, 1996), p. 382.

66 *Ibid.*, pp. 390, 393–4; Thornley, *Isaac Butt*, pp. 242–50.

67 *The Nation*, 3 July 1875.

68 *Ibid.*, 21 August 1875.

69 Quoted in Larkin, *Irish Political System*, p. 421.

70 *Ibid.*, 8 July 1876.

71 Quoted in Moody, *Davitt and the Irish Revolution*, p. 133.

72 Quoted in MacDonagh, *The Home Rule Movement*, p. 119.

73 Sir Michael Hicks Beach to Sir Stafford Northcote, 1 January 1877, British Library, Earl of Iddesleigh Papers, MS 50021.

74 *Ibid.*, 10 February 1877.

75 *Ibid.*

76 Paul Smith, *Disraelian Conservatism and Social Reform* (London, 1967), p. 266; Richard T. Shannon, *The Age of Disraeli, 1868–1881: The Rise of Tory Democracy* (London and New York, 1992), p. 317, but the Opposition was never able to threaten the government in Divisions, p. 327.

77 *The Nation*, 24 February 1877; See F. H. O'Donnell, *A History of the Irish Parliamentary Party* (London, 1910), I, pp. 171–201.

78 Quoted in Vincent (ed.), *Diaries of Edward Henry Stanley*, p. 390 (14 April).

79 *PD*, 233 (1877), c. 1049.

80 See, Alan O'Day, 'Defining Ireland's Place in Parliamentary Institutions: Isaac Butt and Parnell in the 1870s', in Alan O'Day (ed.), *Government and Institutions in the Post-1832 United Kingdom* (Lewiston, NY/Queenston, Ont/Lampeter, Wales, 1995), pp. 155–90.

81 *The Nation*, 2 June 1877.

82 See, Comerford, *New History*, p. 24.

83 Henry W. Lucy, *A Diary of Two Parliaments: The Disraeli Parliament, 1874–1990* (2nd edn; London, 1885), pp. 300–1.

84 Quoted in F. S. L. Lyons, *John Dillon: A Biography* (London, 1968), p. 21; the three men were O'Connor Power, Biggar and Parnell.

85   Journal, 4 August 1877, O'Neill Daunt Papers, MS 3042, f. 1953; O'Neill Daunt to Butt (copy), 4 August 1877, MS 10508.

86   Richard O'Shaughnessy to Isaac Butt, 29 August 1877, Butt MS 8699 (5).

87   Larkin, *Irish Political System*, p. 513.

88   Quoted in Thornley, *Isaac Butt*, p. 337.

89   Quoted in Larkin, *Irish Political System*, p. 469

90   *Ibid.*, pp. 475–8.

91   *The Nation*, 13 October 1877.

92   *Ibid.*, 20 October 1877.

93   See Butt to Sir Michael Hicks Beach, 5, 19 January, 9 February, 28 May, 17, 18 July 1878, St Aldwyn Papers, Gloucestershire Record Office, PCC/66; also, see, Butt to Sir Stafford Northcote, 12 June 1878, Iddesleigh Papers, British Library, MS 50040; Hicks Beach, *Life of Sir Michael Hicks Beach*, pp. 56–8.

94   Quoted in Feingold, *Revolt of the Tenantry*, p. 96.

95   *PD*, 243 (1878–9), c. 1103.

96   Larkin, *Irish Political System*, p. 557–8.

3

Triumph of parliamentarianism, 1879–84

The land question contains, and the legislative question does not, materials from which victory is manufactured, and that therefore, if you be desperately in earnest and determined on success, it is on the former question, not on the latter, that the battle must of necessity be fought. (James Fintan Lalor)[1]

But large and important as is the class of tenant-farmers, constituting as they do, with their wives and families, the majority of the people of this country, I would not have taken off my coat and gone to work, if I had not known that we were laying the foundations by this movement for the recovery of our legislative independence. (Parnell at Galway, 24 October 1880)[2]

Introduction

Isaac Butt's death coincided with a sea change in the fortunes of Home Rule. However, his departure from the scene did not prove to be the occasion for patching up differences within the movement. The obstruction campaign had been too bitter and some Home Rulers blamed Parnell's intransigence for hastening the old leader's demise. Although Parnell's politics stimulated a good deal of publicity and interest, the Home Rule League was moribund. Obstruction had been an attention-grabbing tactic, but it was not a substitute for constructive reform and showed no sign of evolving into a programme capable of winning self-government or much else. Parliamentarians lacked an issue to mobilise people for a sustained period. James Fintan Lalor in the 1840s noted that only the land issue had the necessary locomotive power to push forward the national question. Parnell soon came to accept Lalor's analysis, though he did so under the pressure of events rather than from intellectual conviction. He saw in the land question a means of promoting Home Rule rather than as an objective to be taken up merely for its own sake in spite of its importance for the mass of the people. Neither Lalor nor Parnell was precisely accurate in their declarations cited above, but there can be no doubt that the land issue offered a unique opportunity to the Home Rule movement. Without it, the self-government campaign, like earlier movements, probably would have withered.

The years from 1879 to 1884 were unprecedented for defining national identity and mobilising the Irish masses, for the development of political discourse and as a catalyst for responses to Parnellism by both British political parties. They conform to the vital transition of the mobilisation phase in Miroslav Hroch's typology (see p. 16). Mobilisation of the multitudes posed challenges and dangers to middle-class control as well. During this period institutions, tactics and the vocabulary underwent vital transitions. Parnell and his colleagues built upon the foundations laid down in the 1870s. After the experience of land agitation there was a determined moderation of mass politics and an emphatic re-emphasis upon electoralism and parliamentarianism.

Emergence of the land question, 1879–80

Between 1877 and 1879 Ireland faced a double agricultural adjustment. Prices for commodities began a precipitous decline and this fall influenced the course of politics beyond the end of the century. By 1879, for example, Irish butter prices fell from 137s to 100s per hundred weight.[3] The value of the potato crop dropped from £12.5 million in 1876 to £7.6 million in 1878. Overall, Ireland's agricultural output by 1879 was worth less than two-thirds its 1876 value. The price fall was not halted, and during the 1880s and 90s agriculture faced profound structural adjustment. That change had unparalleled effects on Anglo-Irish affairs. In the short term this situation was exacerbated by a succession of poor harvests in the late 1870s resulting from cool, wet summers. This development would have occasioned hardship in any event but the poor prices for agricultural commodities deprived farmers of any means to cushion the impact of diminished output.

Most Home Rulers supported greater security of tenure for tenant farmers, but the movement was not founded, and did not principally act, as a land reform organisation. It could not be adapted easily into an instrument to promote that cause. National objects traditionally were pursued through separate, usually single-issue bodies. Many members of the Irish party and Home Rule League were landlords or very moderate advocates of tenants' rights. Prominent obstructionists lacked track records on the land question. Parnell, a landlord, had consistently backed the claims of tenants and supported peasant proprietorship as the ultimate solution, but he seldom addressed the issue. In February 1879 he reaffirmed his position, though he was quick to point out, 'I have never spoken of the land question in the House of Commons.' His interest in the problem arose from a moral self-government conviction that 'if you had the land question settled on a permanent basis you would remove the great reason that now exists to prevent the large and influential class of Irish landlords falling in with the demand for self government'.[4] Parnell's entry into the land arena was tentative. He was not invited to participate in the land demonstration held on 20 April at Irishtown, Mayo. On 27 May he warned the House of Commons that the situation in Ireland was becoming grave but limited his demand to an insistence that something meaningful must be done by the government after the Whitsun recess or 'the question was one which would have to be taken up by the Irish Members in a firm and determined fashion'. As he pointed out, the crisis was one 'which deeply affected their constituencies; and even if they were disposed to hang back a little on the subject, the constituencies would not allow them'.[5] This was scarcely the rhetoric of a man anxious to exploit the land question as the means of igniting a confrontation with the Conservative administration.

In 1878 Parnell had been approached to form an alliance of parliamentarians and land reformers, but he hesitated. He met John Devoy three times (March, April and June 1879) to discuss the linkage of the two elements. At their third meeting Devoy outlined what became known as the 'new departure' which, according to him, Parnell accepted.[6] It consisted of four elements: first, that the open movement should not be detrimental to the interests of Fenianism or its secret preparations for armed rebellion; second, the demand for self-government, though not publicly defined for the present must, nevertheless, be nothing short of a national parliament with full control over all matters of vital Irish interest, and include a responsible Irish executive; third a peasant proprietorship through compulsory land purchase should be defined as the solution to the land question; and fourth, Home Rule MPs should form an absolutely independent party. Whether Parnell formally acceded to this Fenian-instigated package is uncertain. Nothing in it was inimical to his own views. A few days afterwards, on 8 June, he spoke at Westport, where he reiterated his belief in the ultimate goal of a peasant proprietorship, but for the present he supported the pragmatic demand of a fair rent which he defined as that which 'the tenant can reasonably pay according to the times'. Tenants should not, Parnell cautioned, depend upon the MPs; they must rely upon themselves. 'Show the landlords that you intend to hold a firm grip on your homesteads and lands', he urged.[7] On this occasion Parnell did not attempt to outline the means tenants might employ to defend themselves and he made no promise of giving a lead to their efforts. On 26 July he scored his first by-election success with the narrow triumph by James Lysagh Finigan at Ennis. Meanwhile, the government took on board the implications of the crisis not merely in Ireland but throughout the United Kingdom, appointing on 14 August a Commission under the chairmanship of the Duke of Richmond and Gordon to investigate the 'depressed condition of the agricultural interest and the causes to which it is owing; whether those causes are of a permanent character, and how far they have been created or can be remedied by legislation'.[8] The Commission did not report until early January 1881, by which time circumstances were altered. However, Parnell in the short term was cautious about committing himself. On 16 August 1879 the National Land League of Mayo was formed without his involvement.

Until the autumn of that year Parnell kept in touch with the rural agitation, though at a discreet distance.[9] His arena was the House of Commons; he focused steadily on parliamentary business which at that time did not particularly concern Ireland. Following the session, he appeared on public platforms in Ireland with greater frequency than at any time since his campaign on behalf of an active parliamentary approach during autumn 1877. When the Irish National Land League was founded on 21 October 1879 Parnell accepted its Presidency, giving substance to the 'new departure'. The government was alive to this emergent challenge and attempted unsuccessfully to prosecute several of the leaders, including Michael Davitt, a Fenian sentenced to fifteen years' imprisonment in 1870, who had been released from prison at the close of 1877 on a ticket of leave, or parole. On 19 November he, James Daly of Castlebar and James Bryce Killen, a Presbyterian barrister of Belfast were arrested.[10] Altogether twenty-two participants in the campaign were charged. Less than a month later the prosecutions were abandoned. The episode proved to be a propaganda fillip to the agitators and for Parnell who fully identified himself with their case.

As the new body lacked funds, he agreed to head a mission to North America to solicit money for the League's relief effort, departing for the New World on 21 December.[11] He also meant, as he explained in New York shortly after his arrival there on 2 January 1880, to propagate his active parliamentary policy, but this theme slid into the background as the tour progressed.[12] The trip was an outstanding success. It succeeded in raising approximately £72,000 (about £60,000 for relief and £12,000 for the Land League) and confirmed Parnell's reputation, though, in fact, this was much the lowest of the sums raised by the four funds in existence. The Duchess of Marlborough's appeal began on 18 December and netted some £135,00 and the Mansion House Committee, initiated on 2 January 1880, raised about £180,000 This, combined with individual donations sent through the Irish bishops, totalled about £830,000.[13] In Montreal Tim Healy named Parnell the 'uncrowned king of Ireland'. On his return to Ireland *The Freeman's Journal* signalled the esteem Parnell now commanded even from previously sceptical sources, editorialising 'we have no hesitation in rendering to Mr Parnell the praise that is due to him, and which the country accords to him'.[14] The mission subsequently would become a source of controversy and of some embarrassment, especially on account of Parnell's alleged declaration at Cincinnati (20 February) that 'none of us ... will be satisfied until we have destroyed the last link which keeps Ireland bound to England'. Whether he actually uttered this phrase is conjecture, but financial contributions, particularly to the political fund, mushroomed in its aftermath and it was recited against Parnell during the debates on Home Rule in 1886.[15]

Butt had outlined five strands of the nationalist strategy – to educate opinion at home, to express Ireland's demand, to convert the British to Home Rule, to influence world sentiment and to employ the Irish in Britain as a lever on Liberals. Parnell followed much the same course, though with more vigour and greater emphasis on the expressive element. Two major parts of the overall approach were still imperfectly developed. Neither Butt nor Parnell had had firm thoughts about how to sustain mobilisation of the masses. Both lacked any clear notion about financing a large-scale campaign. Butt had been content to appear at large meetings, though he had little appetite for continuous organisation and was no dab hand at fundraising. Parnell's approach was scarcely more sophisticated. He was not a habitué of public platforms, had no plan to create a large-scale popular movement and, in fact, his Presidency of the Home Rule Confederation of Great Britain coincided with its further slide into ineptitude.[16] Because he had scant ambitions to build a huge movement, Parnell entertained few thoughts on how to secure substantial sums of money. The land war fortuitously supplied the means of mobilisation; the tour of North America showed the way to raise funds.

The 1880 general election

On 8 March 1880, while Parnell was in Montreal, the Conservative government called a general election. Polling took place between 31

March and 13 April. He returned home immediately. Parnell's decision to fight the election in person rather than continue the tour was an affirmation of the importance he attached to representation in the House of Commons. His half-formed strategy had several interrelated strands. He needed to do various things: first, to enlarge his basis of support among Irish MPs; second, to assume leadership of the parliamentary party or at least be able to influence decisively the tactics of the leader; third, to crowd out or restrict the power of hostile elements within the parliamentary ranks and movement; fourth, to gain control over constituencies with a majority of Catholic electors; and fifth, to achieve an ascendancy over patriotism generally in order to establish priorities between competing interests. In the wake of the North American tour Parnell was the foremost man in Ireland, but as yet he had not reached the first plateau by establishing his authority in the constituencies. His first by-election success at Ennis had been as recent as the previous July.

Parnell engaged in whirlwind electioneering, aiding a number of young followers to win seats and being returned for three constituencies himself.[17] Riding on a crest of popularity, he remained essentially a parliamentarian not a rabble-rouser, and his strategic insight as to how Irish claims would be advanced differed little from Butt's. Moreover, Parnell's ideas on campaigning and electoral organisation were no more innovative than those employed by Home Rulers earlier. This election relied upon individual initiative and owed scarcely anything to an overarching Home Rule body. While the Home Rule League remained in existence, it was but a shadow of its former self and the Land League was ill-equipped to become an electoral committee. Views on the sort of Home Rule Ireland might seek and declarations on other questions were virtually identical with past platforms, with the partial exception of professed support for parliamentary 'activism' and, of course, the greater emphasis on the land question. Few MPs or candidates since the mid-1870s had attempted to give Home Rule a precise formulation. For Parnell, as with Butt, the object was to muster an Irish force capable of influencing a Liberal regime. While he was abroad the Home Rule Confederation of Great Britain called upon the exiles to vote Liberal.[18] Parnell had not been consulted and expressed displeasure at the decision, but he soon exhibited his own strong preference for a Liberal victory. At Cork City, when it was evident that the Liberals would form the next administration, he affirmed:

> I think Ireland has a far better chance with a large really Liberal and Radical majority in the House of Commons than she would have if there was only a small Liberal majority. If there was only a small Lib-

eral majority, undoubtedly the English, Scotch, and Irish Whigs would turn against opinion, and prevent any measure of real reform; but the Liberal party of England have now no excuse, and as they are strong they will be able to embark on a course of real reform in this country. So let not anybody be of faint heart or suppose that Ireland is not in a position of great power.[19]

Although the Liberals were not universally favourable to Irish 'ideas', they were certainly more inclined to meet these demands than their Conservative counterparts. Only about 16 of the victorious Liberals had supported an inquiry into Home Rule, but nearly all the 130–45 successful Radicals pledged themselves to Irish land reform.[20]

Parnell certainly made a sharp impression on the electorate, but neither he nor his message swept the board. Home Rulers now had 63 seats (Parnell was returned in 3 constituencies, making a total of 61 elected individuals), an increase of 3 on the general election of 1874, but only a minority (27) of the winners fully identified themselves with him and the Land League, while many more persisted in describing themselves as Liberals as well as Home Rulers.[21] The Liberals captured 359 seats to the Conservatives' 238. The 63 Home Rulers (the 2 vacancies created by Parnell's multiple returns were filled after by-elections) could not hold the balance. Yet, the outcome in Ireland was significant for the further polarisation of political alignment.[22] In the southern provinces Conservatives were reduced to 7 seats (2 for Trinity College, plus the soon to be eliminated boroughs of Bandon and Portarlington, 2 for County Dublin and 1 in Leitrim). Few Catholics voted for Tory candidates. But the Irish party was still far short of the 80–90 MPs Butt had postulated as essential to the success of the cause. Moreover, Parnell's status in the party was unsure. His public popularity had been built on opposition – opposition to the staid performance of the party and an aggressive approach to the Conservative government. On 17 May he defeated William Shaw in the annual election of a party chairman, the first occasion when the office had been contested and the last until 1890. The victory, however, was narrow: 23 votes to 18, with several abstentions. Many of the absentees were unenthusiastic about Parnell, and his supporters at this juncture probably totalled only twenty-seven. Whether the eighteen MPs who voted for Shaw or the absentees would acknowledge Parnell's authority, act in unison or submerge their opinions to a dictate of the party majority was unknown, but it seemed improbable. The chairman's powers were ill-defined. Joseph Biggar in May 1880 outlined their scope:

[H]e has the authority, which really amounts to no authority at all, to speak on behalf of the party when he has received authority from a meeting of the party to do so, and he is looked upon by members of the Government, by the House of Commons, and by the English newspaper reading public, as the leader of the party, although in point of fact he has no such authority.[23]

The reality of Biggar's comment was evident when the MPs differed over where to sit in the House of Commons. Colonel Nolan, an obstructionist in the last Parliament, objected to the idea of sitting on the Opposition benches, because 'they would be deserted by their many Liberal friends. Most of them had many good friends on the Liberal side, and for his part he had hardly a friend on the Conservative side.'[24] When a majority opted to sit in Opposition, many Home Rulers chose to ignore the decision and moved across the floor with the Liberals. Members were even treated to the spectacle of the two Irish party whips sitting on different benches. Events soon showed that this was no mere formality. Members sometimes entered opposite division lobbies. On one occasion *The Nation* was moved to observe: 'strange to say, when an adjournment was moved, one of the Home Rule whips canvassed in favour of the motion and the other against, thus sending Irish members of similar opinions into different lobbies and causing confusion in the direction of the party.'[25]

Home Rulers responses to a Liberal regime raised other problems. Many had been lifelong Liberals and looked to Gladstone to remedy Irish grievances. A handful saw no inconsistency between membership of the Home Rule party and exercising Liberal patronage, nor did they consider it to be a bar to seeking personal advancement from the new administration. The venerable politician, The O'Gorman Mahon, MP for County Clare, was incensed in November 1880 when his nomination was not solicited for a Post Office appointment 'after having the upwards of sixty years given unswerving support both in and out of the House to the Liberal party'.[26] When another post became vacant in his constituency the following year he was asked to nominate some fit person.[27] Parnell did not ride to victory on an anti-Liberal ticket; he, too, shared the hope of co-operation with the new government. Advent of a new and seemingly pro-Irish government held out many inducements to schisms in the parliamentary and wider ranks.

The land war, 1880–02

The land war marked an important stage in the development of the Home Rule movement into a vehicle of materialism, acting as a service organisation and becoming a party of social integration. At the same time, at the start of the 1880s the Irish problem had three dimen-

sions – the land, preservation of order (coercion) and local government – each presenting separate difficulties.[28] Gladstone did not
come into office with a set of Irish objectives as he had in 1868. The
Irish portion of the Queen's Speech on 21 May 1880 was limited to a
declaration that the peace preservation legislation would be allowed
to lapse, with the government relying upon the ordinary law. Nevertheless, the Prime Minister was determined to meet Irish claims and
he chose W. E. Forster as Chief Secretary of the Irish Office in the
belief that his past services to the country would make him a popular choice.[29]

The new administration was not well disposed towards Parnell or
his clique and preferred the ideas and advice of the old Butt loyalists.
Three difficulties faced the new Cabinet – coercion, the demand for
land reform and rural distress. Initially, though, the administration
had no plan for dealing with the agrarian crisis, warranting Margaret
O'Callaghan's pithy appraisal that 'the real problem confronting the
Liberal Ministry in 1880 was the problem of deciding what the problem was'.[30] She observes that the problem was twofold: economic and
non-payment of rents. Acting on behalf of the Irish party, O'Connor
Power on 28 May introduced a bill to deal with the situation. It
received a second reading on 4 June. Irish party efforts, though, met
with considerable criticism in Ireland, a portent of the divisions that
would persist within the national coalition over how to deal with the
land question.[31] In view of rural distress the government felt compelled to pay attention, moving Lord Spencer to lament, 'I fear that
we appear in the position of being driven into action by the Parnellites'.[32] The Chief Secretary won Gladstone's agreement to legislate in
order to relieve distress and prevent further deterioration of conditions. On 18 June the government introduced a Compensation for
Disturbances bill, which would allow qualified evicted tenants to
claim redress for any improvements which they had made to the
property if they could prove inability to pay rent because of two successive bad harvests, and if they desired to remain on tenancies on
fair terms that were refused by their landlord. It was to apply to
about half of the country, and the provisions were restricted to tenancies valued at below £30 per annum.[33] This hastily constructed
measure roused intense dissent within the Cabinet and Liberal party.
After being heatedly contested in the House of Commons, where
'sixteen Liberals – "eldest sons", almost entirely – voted against the
bill, and there must have been some 60 or 70 abstentions', it was
passed on 26 July by 304 votes to 237, a smaller than expected majority.[34] In the meantime, three days later the government established
the Bessborough Commission to inquire into the working of the Land
Act of 1870. This was intended to take the heat out of the rural agita-

tion when the Compensation for Disturbances bill looked doomed. In the upper house the bill scarcely had a chance, especially as 'more Liberals voted against the government than with them' in the division on 3 August. It was defeated by 231 to a derisory 51.[35]

Whether this proposed legislation could have defused the crisis is a moot point. The bill was not a palliative to deep-seated agricultural problems.[36] Its rejection, none the less, altered the terms of reference of the Irish problem. Parnell, whatever his predilections, was obliged to take up the cudgel of public agitator, though he sought an understanding with the government: 'provided the approaching land meetings were of an orderly and legal character, the police should not be obtruded upon them in their military capacity'.[37]

After the session, Parnell returned to Ireland to head the campaign. During the autumn the Land League grew rapidly, spreading from the west where it had originated into the south and east, supported in the main by modest-sized tenants who relied upon family labour to work their holdings.[38] It established an estimated 1,000 branches by January 1881 and possibly around 1,800 at some point during the land war, though many of these proved ephemeral.[39] This branch network was based on the parish structure, making it easier as the movement grow, widening its base, for the clergy and 'strong farmers' to influence its character and aims.[40] As analysis of Queen's County shows, the leadership was weighted in favour of larger farmers: by the winter of 1880–01 it was reminiscent of the middle-class members who had dominated the Independent Club, an organisation of substantial tenant farmers formed to defend the interests of the rural bourgeoisie. In Tipperary priests routinely chaired Land League meetings.[41] On 19 September 1880 at Ennis, in one of his most heralded addresses, Parnell outlined the strategy. His declaration was notably lacking in support for agrarian radicalism. He emphasised the value of parliamentarianism, independence from English Ministries, good conduct on the part of tenants, the vitality of public opinion and the need to act constitutionally. At the outset, Parnell set the tone when he called upon those present to avoid signs of drunkenness and to act in a dignified manner, because in that way the government and people of Britain would see that the Irish were fit for self-rule. In spite of divisions within the ranks of the Home Rulers, he defended the party which in the session that had just concluded had been 'on the whole … a good and worthy one'. Nor had the 'uncrowned king' lost confidence in Gladstone. It was the Liberals who must legislate. But he warned tenants:

[D]epend upon it that the measure of the land bill of next session will be the measure of your activity and energy this winter (cheers)

67

– it will be the measure of your determination not to pay unjust rents
– it will be the measure of your determination to keep a firm grip of
your homesteads (cheers). It will be the measure of your determination not to bid for farms from which others have been evicted, and
to use the strong force of public opinion to deter any unjust men
amongst yourselves – and there are many such – from bidding for
such farms (hear, hear). If you refuse to pay unjust rents, if you
refuse to take farms from which others have been evicted, the land
question must be settled, and settled in a way that will be satisfactory to you. It depends, therefore, upon yourselves, and not upon
any commission or any government. When you have made this
question ripe for settlement, then, and not till then, will it be settled
(cheers).[42]

Parnell urged tenants to thwart land-grabbing by placing offenders
in 'moral Coventry', isolating them rather than inflicting violence.
His theme was an affirmation of the virtue of self-help. Throughout
the autumn Parnell and other Leaguers traversed the country gar-
nering support for rent reductions and land reform. On 24 October at
Galway in the speech cited at the beginning of the chapter Parnell
linked the land and national questions saying that he would not have
taken off his coat over the agrarian problem had he not believed it
would lead to Home Rule. Throughout the agitation the land issue
was linked to the national question, though the latter tended to take
a rear seat.[43]

Inevitably, the agitation frightened many respectable people in Ireland and Great Britain. Predictably, also, the campaign was accompanied by violence of the type endemic in agrarian Ireland, usually
orchestrated by tenants against other tenants or attacks on property
and animals.[44] Intimidation was rampant, though many of the acts
were no more than threatening letters, a form much favoured in Ireland (a product of the new literacy – or perhaps semi-literacy judging
from the contents).[45] There was a causal link which the authorities
saw as a connection between Land League branch formation and
rural outrages. With crime on the rise, not least because of an absence
of legal restraint on the ownership and possession of firearms
between June 1880 and March 1881, there was pressure inside the
government and beyond to respond to the breakdown of order. Gladstone was anxious to eschew for the time being at least any special or
coercive measures, but he did agree to the decision of Dublin Castle
to put key Land League figures in the dock for conspiracy to prevent
payment of rent.[46] On 3 November Parnell, Joseph Biggar, John
Dillon, Thomas Sexton, T. D. Sullivan and nine others were charged,
at a trial which began on 28 December 1880. Davitt was confident that
'the jury selected to try Parnell and the rest *is certain to disagree*',[47] a

prophesy that proved correct when on 23 January 1881 it failed to reach a verdict, no doubt because eight of the twelve jurors were Catholics.

By early 1881 the land movement had come to personify national identity. For the moment, remarkably, it forged a unity between regions, classes, urban and rural dwellers and even, to a limited degree, reached across the sectarian divide. In December 1880 Archbishop Thomas Croke observed:

> [W]hatever minor men may aim at, these two [Parnell and Dillon] at least proposed nothing to themselves besides the amelioration of our poor Irish tenants and possibly after that, the repeal of the Union, or what is called Home Rule. ... He [Parnell] is a Protestant, to be sure, but so were Flood and Grattan and Lucas (1st) and Davis and lately Isaac Butt. Anyhow the movement here at least in the south has passed completely into the hands of the priests.[48]

'Tis the leaping to its legs of the whole nation, asking for its rights', was Croke's colourful, if inaccurate, description of the land struggle the following month.[49] Such unanimity would be short-lived, but the land campaign, as Lalor predicted, momentarily tied together diverse strands of the Catholic community. Maintenance of this fragile coalition would depend on the responses of Gladstone's regime in the next session. A Cabinet meeting on 31 December decided to meet the situation by standing on the principles of the Land Act of 1870 and proposing measures for local self-government.[50]

When Parliament convened on 7 January 1881 the Bessborough Commission had just reported in favour of changes in the land law. A week later the Richmond Commission reported; a minority group from this body advocated the three Fs – fair, that is judicially established rents, fixity of tenure so long as the tenant paid rent, and free sale, that is the right of tenants to sell their interest in a property, sometimes known as the 'Ulster custom'.[51] The government announced in the Queen's Speech that it would seek special powers (coercion), land legislation and signalled a wish to take action 'for the establishment of county government in Ireland, founded upon representative principles, and framed with the double aim of confirming popular control over expenditure, and of supplying a yet more serious want by extending the formation of habits of local self-government'.[52] Though not Home Rule in the national sense, the proposal tended in the direction of enlarged self-direction to cultivate experience of popular control. Irish wants would be dealt with in a flexible manner, it seemed, though on Gladstone's not Parnell's terms. This Liberal reform package held dangers for patriotic cohesion, a fact emphasised when on 16 and 17 January William Shaw, along with several of Parnell's critics among the Home Rulers, announced their withdrawal from the Irish party. It also formed a coherent approach to Gladstone's principal preoccupation, the re-establishment of social harmony, enabling the landed order to play its proper role in Irish society.[53] While this certainly jibed with Parnell's own thinking, it held few attractions for the bulk of his followers.

The first order of parliamentary business in the early 1881 session was the introduction of the Protection of Person and Property bill. It was met stoutly by the Irish party which extended one sitting of the House of Commons to forty-one hours (from 31 January to 2 February).[54] On 3 February the Home Secretary, Sir William Harcourt, announced that Davitt's ticket of leave, on which he had been released in December 1877, was suspended. This incensed national MPs, who, if they deplored some of Davitt's activities, saw his imprisonment as vindictive. In the ensuing protest thirty-six Irish party members were suspended from the House of Commons. Resistance to coercion in early 1881 was a landmark in the creation of a Parnellite – as opposed to a Home Rule – party and also led, thereafter, to a much more participatory attitude to parliamentary business than had been characteristic of Irish parties in the past. The Protection of Person and Property Act was enacted on 2 March 1881, and later that month, on 21 March, the Arms Act imposed controls of the ownership of firearms.

The next phase of the Liberal's responses came on 7 April when Gladstone introduced the Land bill without seeking out the views of the Parnellites, a precedent for the Home Rule measure that he put forward in 1886. In both instances certain of the shortcomings were a consequence of not seeking the opinion of Home Rulers.[55] His scheme took account of the recommendations of the Bessborough and the minority report of the Richmond Commissions, and granted the essence of the three Fs. A Land Commission composed of three members supervised the operation of the legislation and had the power to determine the fair rent in each case brought before it. Any individual tenant, tenants and landlords, together or the landlord alone could request the tribunal to adjudicate the rental. Alternatively, the tenant and the property owner could agree on a rent and have it confirmed by the Commission. Rentals were to be fixed for a period of fifteen years. The Ulster custom was codified, the level of compensation for improvements and disturbances a tenant might claim were significantly increased, while the purchase clauses in the Land Act of 1870 were augmented. Tenants who qualified to purchase their holdings were able to secure advances from the Board of Works of up to three-quarters of the sale price at 5 per cent interest, with repayments spread over thirty-five years. Only 731 tenants utilised this portion of the Act. The new or revolutionary principal was legal recognition of tenant interest in the land, usually referred to as the dual ownership of landlord and tenant. Tenants in arrears of rent and leaseholders were excluded from using the new legislation. The former numbered an estimated 250,000, the latter another 125,000. This bill provoked immense controversy. Conservatives and many right-wing Liberals opposed it. Altogether the bill took 58 parliamentary sittings before its passage was secured and even then it succeeded only when the House of Commons refused to accept amendments proposed by the peers. It was read for a third time in the House of Commons on 29 July 1881 and became law on 22 August.

The act was a watershed in attitudes, especially Conservative ideas, about Irish land. In 1880 Lord Beaconsfield had worried that the Compensation for Disturbances bill was merely the lever which would 'lead to other measures'.[56] But even while rejecting the bill of 1880 and the much broader measure in 1881, many Conservatives were reluctant to oppose all forms of Irish land reform. Edward Gibson, the Conservative MP for Trinity College, was anxious that 'we should not shut ourselves up in a "non possumus", but should be ready to deal liberally with the Land Question on its merits, only insisting on proper measures for preserving peace on the one hand, and resisting confiscation on the other'.[57] He was 'inclined to moderate counsels'.[58] In late 1880 Sir Stafford Northcote thought that the Land Act of 1870 should be amended 'for the purpose of giving tenants fuller protection in respect to the improvements they themselves had made; and also for the purpose of removing any hitches which may have been found to occur in the working of the Bright [purchase] clauses'.[59] In April 1881 Beaconsfield's death created a vacuum in the Tory leadership, increasing the tendency for Conservatives to divide on how to treat the land question. After the land legislation had been enacted, Northcote confessed, 'I don't think it will do as much harm as was expected; – that is to say, if the Land League give it a chance'.[60] He quickly discovered that influential Tories were prepared to accept the act but wanted to press for compensation for Irish landlords. Many, in fact, were swiftly being converted to the idea of land purchase.[61] As this was the policy of both Parnell and the Land League, the possibility of some concordance between them and the Conservatives on this question became a distinct possibility. The Land Act forced reconsideration of attitudes in both British parties.

Traumatic though the bill was for British politicians, it had an even larger effect in Ireland. For the Land League, the proposal was a two-edged sword. The cohesion of the movement was shattered. Moderates, 'strong farmers', the clergy and, as was soon evident, Ulster Protestant tenants accepted the legislation. It granted the essence of their immediate demand – security of tenure, rent control and legal recognition of their right of sale of tenant interest. But the bill did not meet the Land League programme of a peasant proprietorship through compulsory purchase and while bolstering the interests of substantial farmers, it provided little comfort for cottiers and none to landless labourers. To many it seemed that the needs of western smallholders, those who had taken the lead in the struggle, had been sacrificed to the avarice of substantial farmers, especially the grazers. Land Leaguers locked horns with one another over their response to the measure. During the spring and summer of 1881 Parnell tried to narrow the gulf. In the division on the bill's second reading, the party, which had earlier aided the measure, opted to abstain. The tactic had been debated hotly at a party meeting, being adopted only when Parnell threatened to resign the chairmanship if his advice were rejected.[62] Nevertheless, several prominent MPs did not adhere to this decision and voted for it. Their course was endorsed by the two leading national newspapers and also by many clergy.

In order to ease the tension after the act became law in August, the tried formula of a conference was invoked. However, before it met a crucial by-election was held in County Tyrone. On 7 September the land-reforming Liberal T. A. Dickson narrowly defeated the Conservative candidate, with the Land League-sponsored aspirant coming a poor third. This confirmed Gladstone's view that the tenant farmers accepted the legislation and certainly indicated that the loose alliance of Ulster Protestant tenant farmers with the Land League had been broken. When the land conference met in Dublin on 15–17 September, Parnell sought to paper over the cracks in the movement with a recommendation that the tenants be counselled to 'test' the act and not to rush en masse into the newly established land courts. The Land League in each district was charged with selecting appropriate cases to place before the tribunals. However this cautious formula broke down immediately, as priests and moderate Home Rulers urged tenants to avail themselves of the act. As soon became visible, very large numbers followed this advice.

The act exposed a deep rift within the hastily constructed national coalition and Gladstone efficiently turned the tables on the radicalised section. Contrary to Lalor's prophesy, the land proved to be a great divider. Agrarian relief, in contrast to Parnell's estimate at Galway the previous year, threatened to scuttle Home Rule, not advance it. Neither Lalor nor Parnell was proved wholly wrong by the Land Act of 1881, but this legislation exposed the fractured possibilities of the land question. It opened a chasm within the Catholic middle class, endangering its political hegemony. The incident was a testimony to the power at the disposal of a flexible British state. Only under the stress of the First World War would Britain's leaders lose the capacity to outflank Home Rulers with timely concessions.

For Gladstone, 1881 had been a decisive year in his re-education on Irish affairs, especially the land problem. His concern for social stability and harmony remained a constant element in the Irish equation, but his notions of how to achieve these mutually reinforcing ends was shifting. The Prime Minister wanted to find a formula to maintain the interdependence of landlord and tenant, something that had broken down under the impact of recent events. There were two distinct but related threads. Landowners had been inclined to seek support from the state to uphold their position, while tenants appeared to lose respect for property rights. Both sides increasingly appealed to Westminster and sought to appropriate public funds for their own purposes. Coercion might aid in pacifying the countryside but it was only a short-term expedient. Land legislation could remove a grievance but on its own could not make the rural community cooperate. Coercive and land acts encouraged an adversarial approach with a corrupting tendency to appeal to central government. Local government, a third part of Gladstone's trilogy, would be a corrective, a way of reconstructing sound social relations and protecting public funds. Even while he was absorbed in making the Land Act work and confronted by what appeared to be Parnellite truculence, Gladstone's mind was turning towards a re-examination of local government. On 13 September, immediately following the land conference in Dublin, he wrote to Lord Granville: 'I am rather advanced as to Home Rule or local rule, not wishing to stipulate excepting for the supremacy of Parliament, and for not excluding Scotland in principle from anything offered or done for Ireland.'[63] Three days later he projected local government as a means of undermining Parnell. To Granville he opened his mind, professing a desire for

> severing him [Parnell] altogether from the Irish people and the mass of the Irish members and by saying that Home Rule has for one of its senses Local Government, an excellent thing to which I should affix no limits except the supremacy of the Imperial Parliament and the right of all parts of the country to claim whatever might be accorded to Ireland. This is only a repetition of what I have often said before, and I have nothing to add or enlarge.[64]

At this time Gladstone viewed Parnellism as an impediment to his aims, but that attitude would undergo revision over the coming months. The Prime Minister's growing attachment to granting Ireland self-governing institutions in the interest of re-establishing the mutual interdependence of the elite and the masses would become a major element in his thinking.

At the beginning of the 1880s both British politicians and Irish leaders were still adapting to each other and learning how to make their relationship function.[65] In the previous Parliament Home Rulers had not posed a sufficient threat and were ignored or, in the case of the obstructionists, denounced; the land war and rise of Parnellism induced a re-evaluation. During autumn 1881 the learning process was in an early, trial and error phase and there was considerable misreading of intent on all sides.[66] Parnell came close to marginalising himself while the government saw him and the Land League as a barrier to the successful operation of the Land Act. Coercion afforded the administration a means, if necessary, of curtailing Land League activity. A number of leaders had been detained in late spring and summer and Parnell's own speeches were subjected to careful scrutiny. As late as 3 October his arrest appeared unlikely, 'having talked mischief but not treason'.[67] However, that soon changed and a few days afterwards at Leeds Gladstone said of Parnell that he desired 'to arrest the operation of the Land Act, to stand there, not as Moses stood, to arrest but to extend the plague'.[68] A long Cabinet meeting on 12 October decided to incarcerate Parnell and leading Land League officials. Between 13 and 15 October Parnell, John Dillon, J. J. O'Kelly and Thomas Sexton were seized and imprisoned in Kilmainham gaol in Dublin as suspects under the Protection of Person and Property Act. Warrants were issued for the arrest of Biggar and Arthur O'Connor, both prominent parliamentarians. Under the act more than a 1,000 Land League 'suspects' were detained without trial.[69] Detention – in moderately comfortable accommodation – revived the popular standing of the 'uncrowned king'. Following his arrest, on 18 October Parnell and the other Land Leaguers issued the 'no rent manifesto', calling upon tenants to refuse to pay rentals as a protest against the detentions. This decree served as justification for the government to suppress the Land League the following day. At the same time the Land Court opened to a massive wave of tenants seeking redress.

O'Callaghan places an interesting, challenging and different construction on this series of events.[70] Adapting a theme earlier expounded by Barbara Solow, she prefers to see the crisis as a set of representations in which the national movement's view of the agrarian crisis was adopted by Gladstone. O'Callaghan suggests that the suspension of habeas corpus and suppression of the Land League together mark the movement's finest hour, providing an easy bridge from the land issue to Home Rule. At the same time Liberal acceptance of the Parnellite representation of Ireland made conversion to Home Rule in 1886 the logical step, though it is less than self-evident why this should be the outcome. While the connection between the

land war and Home Rule is certainly within the conventional interpretative perimeters, her stress upon 'representations', valuable as an
insight, truncates the interaction between Parnellite and British
politicians.

Possibly, Parnell welcomed imprisonment. Certainly, some aspects
of his subsequent behaviour lend credence to O'Callaghan's hypothesis. He wrote to his mistress, Katharine O'Shea; 'politically it is a for-
tunate thing for me that I have been arrested, as the movement is
breaking fast, and all will be quiet in a few months, when I shall be
released'.[71] He certainly had doubts about the land agitation. Its utility was lessened by the Land Act, the organisation was in disarray
and funds were running low. Parnell had never been a genuine agrarian radical; he certainly was not a revolutionary, his taste for public
campaigning remained muted and he preferred reversion to a parliamentary role. In February 1882 he spilled out his feelings on popular
agitation when writing to Mrs O'Shea; 'at least I am very glad that the
days of platform speeches have gone by and are not likely to return.
I cannot describe to you the disgust I always felt with these meetings,
knowing as I did how hollow and wanting in solidarity everything
connected with the movement was.'[72]

The achievement of the land war was to provide an issue capable
of capturing the enthusiasm of a large slice of the Catholic people;
less certain was how this populism could be translated into a sustained political movement. The land movement had several distinct
sections. Local, Dublin and parliamentary elements had been able to
work together, but the relationship was never smooth. Land League
headquarters and the MPs were too often held responsible for the
activities of local leaders over whom they at best had a precarious
influence. Local branches proved incapable of financial restraint,
leaving the central executive beggared for money.[73] Excessive legal-
ism of the Land League, with its policy of 'rent at the point of a bayonet' and fighting the tenants' struggle in the law courts, brought it
close to bankruptcy.

Parnell's period in Kilmainham gave him pause for reflection and
added to his popular stature, but it was unclear what his next step
would be after being released – indeed it was not known when he
would be freed. During his enforced absence, the Irish party deterio-
rated into a rump. Meanwhile, in February Gladstone twice restated
his preference for local government, pointing out on the second occasion his dislike for 'centralisation', and affirming: 'I believe that local
institutions – the institutions of secondary authorities – are a great
source of strength, and that in principle the only necessary limit to
these powers is the adequate and certain provision for the supremacy
of the central authority.'[74] His remarks were welcomed by Home

Rulers though they set off an alarm in some English circles. J. L. Hammond sees these speeches along with Gladstone's letter of 13 February to the Queen, as indicative of a state of mind receptive to self-government.[75]

More immediate difficulties included escalating agrarian disorder and crime, the working of the Land Act and the continued imprisonments. By February it was clear that jailing MPs had not brought about a reduction of agrarian disorder; crime, in fact, had increased. Moreover, certain defects in the land legislation were becoming troublesome and the Conservatives used their advantage in the House of Lords to set up a committee to inquire into its operation. Although the Land Act made provision for tenants to purchase their holdings, that was not its principal intent. Gladstone's measure tended to crystallise a division in British politics between advocates of improved tenure and rental arrangements versus proponents of land purchase. This division was neither absolute nor strictly drawn along party lines. Nevertheless, Gladstone himself was reserved about purchase, while Conservatives were rapidly becoming its foremost advocates. In March the House of Lords committee produced a purchase scheme, which found warm support from a key Tory, W. H. Smith. Gladstone was concerned about the possibility of a Parnellite-Conservative entente based on the scheme. Aside from the political implications of such an alliance, he was anxious that purchase would be effected without sufficient guarantees and carried out at the expense of the imperial exchequer. As a formula to exert proper control over the issue, his own thinking was drawn back inexorably to a local government solution. On 7 April he drafted a proposal to be circulated to the Cabinet concerning the establishment of Provincial Councils (see document 3). On 13 April he justified his scheme to Granville:

> [T]o make the responsibility of the purchasing tenant real, we must have bodies of real weight in Ireland with which to deal and threw upon them the working of the clauses. The Irish are too strong to be governed by agency which has to them a purely English character, and which has its seats Downing Street and Dublin Castle. I am much inclined to believe that the safest course in these arduous circumstances is a bold one, namely calling into existence, as the best form of local government for Ireland, four provincial bodies according to the idea of Lord Russell, which might at once be charged with the management of this question, and which might in a future year take over all the functions of County government.[76]

Even with, or possibly because of the imprisonment of Parnell, Gladstone was increasingly inclined to take up local self-government as the next part of his liberal unionist agenda for Ireland.

Gladstone's ideas could not have much practical effect until the impasse with Parnell was mediated. While the Irish party's position in the House of Commons was attenuated at the outset of 1882, Parnell's influence in Ireland remained paramount. During April a number of emissaries, including William O'Shea, F. H. O'Donnell and Justin McCarthy, let it be known that Parnell desired a resolution of the conflict on the basis of further legislation, allowing tenants in arrears to be brought under the terms of the Land Act of 1881.[77] From mid-April matters matured quickly. On 26 April John Redmond moved the second reading of a bill drafted by Maurice Healy in conjunction with Parnell to deal with arrears. Though William O'Shea, Parnell let the government know that if the arrears difficulty could be resolved, he would use his influence to halt the agrarian campaign, proposing that a satisfactory settlement 'would I feel sure enable us to co-operate cordially for the future with the Liberal party in forwarding Liberal principles and measures of general reform'.[78] On 1 May the Prime Minister explained to an incredulous Irish Viceroy, Lord Cowper;

> [W]e know authentically that Parnell and his friends are ready to abandon No-Rent formally, and to declare against outrage energetically intimidation included, if and when the government announce a satisfactory plan for declaring with arrears. We had already as good as decided upon a plan and we do not know an absolute reason why the form of it should not be 'satisfactory'.[79]

Parnell and his parliamentary colleagues were released on 2 May 1882 in what has since been known as the Kilmainham Treaty, an understanding rather than a formal compact in which the land war would be brought to an end in exchange for legislation permitting tenants in arrears of rent to make use of the Land Act of 1881. W. E. Forster, in protest, resigned the same day. The Treaty soon became the subject of bitter recriminations due in no small part to the assassinations in Phoenix Park on 6 May of the newly appointed Chief Secretary of the Irish Office, Lord Frederick Cavendish, younger brother of Lord Hartington and husband to Gladstone's favourite niece, and of Thomas Burke, the permanent Under-Secretary. This event placed Anglo-Irish relations in a predicament. The murders probably shielded Parnell from internal criticism over the compact, but the government's friendlier intentions towards Ireland were dealt a setback. Whether the tragedy pushed Parnell more quickly towards moderation is possible, though doubtful, as the logic of the Kilmainham Treaty suggested this course already, but it surely re-enforced movement along this trajectory. Public and private sentiment dictated imposition of a further dose of coercion – the Prevention of

Crime bill – which became law on 12 July 1882. During that summer the Irish party was able to revive its self-confidence and establish cohesion in the debates on special legislation. Agrarian radicals were left to seethe beneath the surface at the turn of events. On 18 August the arrears legislation was enacted, allowing tenants on holdings valued at less than £30 to seek relief. Qualifying tenants would be liable for one year's arrears, with the government paying half the balance and landlords having to suffer the loss on the rest.[80]

As summer advanced, parliamentarianism largely supplanted radical agitation. Parnell dissolved the Ladies' Land League in August and in October Land League funds were removed from the hands of its Treasurer, Patrick Egan, thereafter being under the direct control of the party leader.[81] The land had proved a source of Irish division. Parnellism had initially gained a wider audience through obstruction and then via the land struggle, but both issues had exhausted much of their capacity to induce unity. The challenge was to find a cause capable of bonding them together, one that would be acceptable to Catholic middle-class opinion and at the same time ensure its political dominance.

Parliamentarianism, 1882–84

By summer 1882 the Home Rule movement had succeeded in mustering Catholics, however briefly, and secured credit for a major piece of legislation. It still lacked a number of things – money, organisation and a programme. The platform of the past two years – land – was now threadbare. Parnell was a charismatic leader – a figure capable of transfixing followers – but he had no aptitude for organisation. Max Weber theorised that history tends to alternate between the spell of the charismatic leader and his disciples' efforts to routinise and institutionalise this authority. The Home Rule movement fits this hypothesis.

During May, June and July 1882 Parnell was chiefly involved in parliamentary affairs. The debates on the new crime bill and the arrears legislation absorbed his and many in the party's energies; it forced a 28-hour sitting between 30 June and 1 July. The Prevention of Crime bill was passed on 12 July, the Arrears bill on 18 August. Despite some souring of relations between the Parnellites and Liberals in the aftermath of the Phoenix Park murders and the new coercion measure, many of the Irish, and especially Parnell, were intent upon improved co-operation in the future. The Irish party long complained that they were not consulted and the new Chief Secretary, George Otto Trevelyan, set about correcting this omission.[82] A good deal of the subsequent barbs exchanged between Liberals and Parnellites were play-acting, though some figures on both sides took their roles to heart. During the summer Parnell tried to get Gladstone to commit the government to further reforms. Certainly, the Prime Minister's view of Parnell had undergone a remarkable transition over the past months. On 19 September he concluded, 'that since his liberation he has acted … with as much consistency as he could, and has endeavoured to influence his friends in the same direction'.[83] In essence, this remained Gladstone's view until the close of the decade.

After the experience of the past three years, Parnell was slow to consent to the resurrection of a national organ, especially one patterned on the Land League. He had much cause to distrust formal organisations both before and during the land war; his own preference was for parliamentary rather than mass activity. His great skill in manipulating popular sentiment enhanced Parnell's suspicion of structures. Davitt later described him as being very reluctant to revive a national organisation.[84] Parnell agreed in September 1882 to the establishment of a new national body. Notice was given of a national conference called

> for the purpose of discussing a programme of reform for Ireland, which will be submitted for adoption by us. The chief feature of this programme will be the uniting together on one central platform of the various movements and interests that are now appealing to the country for separate sanction and support.[85]

Shortly before the conference met, Parnell – via Mrs O'Shea on 6 October – sought to engage Gladstone in another attempt at devolving legislation, a formula for local influence without dismantling the authority of Parliament. He advocated that Irish bills should be referred to a grand committee made up of the Chief Secretary, law officers and all Irish MPs. This idea had surfaced previously and its effect for exclusively Irish business would be to create a national subcommittee within the House of Commons. The Prime Minister was restrained by his colleagues who were more guarded about the proposal, though he did inform Mrs O'Shea:

> it is certainly my personal opinion that, in any plan of devolution which Parliament ought or is likely to adopt, regard should be had to the local principle, and a reasonable scope be given to it. One of the powerful arguments in favour of such plans is their tendency to promote the passing of measures in which particular parts of the United Kingdom are particularly interested.[86]

Parnell and Gladstone were on a parallel course with respect to the need for decentralisation of purely Irish business. Parnell's notion is of more than passing interest. It encouraged Gladstone to develop his thinking and showed Parnell's concern to find a formula that allowed popular feeling to be expressed within a framework that maintained effective checks and balances. For him, it was part and parcel of the rationale behind the earlier federalist programme. Parnell was eager to elicit a response from Gladstone prior to the national conference. A favourable reception from the Prime Minister would give Parnell additional scope for manoeuvre at the conference.

When the conference met in Dublin on 17 October the delegates established the National League. Its purposes and outlook differed from previous national organisations by sponsoring a range of causes. The first plank of the platform was the pursuit of national self-government. Parnell set the tone:

> [U]ntil we obtain for the majority of the people of the country the right of making their own laws, we shall never be able, and we can never hope to see the laws of Ireland in accordance with the wishes of the people of Ireland, or calculated as they ought to bring about the permanent prosperity of our country.[87]

Other aims were land reform, local self-government, extension of the parliamentary and municipal franchises, encouragement of Irish industrial development and a bettering of conditions for the industrial labourer. The goal of the Land League – a peasant proprietorship – was reaffirmed, though without insisting on compulsory purchase. However, the programme did advocate compulsory purchase by county boards of land that owners did not cultivate themselves and which was unoccupied by tenants, enabling its resale or letting to agricultural labourers and small farmers. The conference endorsed the demand that tenants be protected from rental increases resulting from their own improvements and the admission of leaseholders to the provisions of the Land Act. It advocated rate-supported housing for agricultural labourers along with abolition of poor rates on these dwellings, the removal of the quarter-acre clause as a qualification for poor relief during spells of illness and the creation of representative county boards to wield the financial and administrative authority presently vested in grand juries or other bodies.

Although this platform contained little new, for the first time it brought under one organisation far-reaching objectives that previously had been the domain of many bodies, each sponsoring a single cause. It was the fruition of a multi-faceted movement capable, in theory, of ordering priorities and pushing the whole slate of reforms forward in a cogent fashion. Although it was not yet apparent what the order of priorities would be, this was certainly a significant increment in the conversion of the movement from individual representation to a party of social integration catering for, and encompassing, the needs of its members. The League was to have local branches spread throughout the country. These branches were to send delegates to county conventions while at the apex of the pyramid stood a central council of forty-eight members. Only sixteen of these were to be nominated by the party with the rest elected by county conventions. Until the completed structure of the League was up and running the central council was to be directed by the parliamentary party. The National League was the confluence of people, priests and party united under a common banner to advance the accepted aspirations of the country's majority. In practice, it remained a centrally dominated body controlled by a Dublin and London clique loyal to Parnell.[88] In the short term this made little difference as the League remained a small eastern organisation until early 1885. Parnell did not revive for a further year the defunct Irish organisation in Great Britain, with its embarrassing Fenian undercurrent. When it was reorganised in autumn 1883 the British organ, like the National League in Ireland, was kept firmly under the thumb of the parliamentarians, its President, T. P. O'Connor, being a close associate of Parnell.

Gladstone's response had a further dimension in the autumn session (lasting from 24 October to 2 December 1882) of the House of Commons – alteration of its rules aimed at limiting the ability of minorities to thwart business. His approach had been foreshadowed in the previous Parliament. The proposals were intended to curtail unlimited prolongation of debates by small minorities and especially to halt the repeated use of delaying procedures such as adjournment. Gladstone also sought to introduce his earlier idea of grand committees to deal with specific areas of business, though for the time being this did not include one dedicated to Irish affairs. At the close of December he expressed his hope that the idea could soon be applied to Ireland, stating that 'the subject of local government eclipses all the rest in importance'.[89] He wanted it to be introduced soon and constructed along the lines of his earlier plan of bodies for the four provinces. Gladstone, who went to Cannes in mid-January 1883, where he was to remain until early March, had wanted to announce the government's support for local government in Ireland at the outset of the parliamentary session in 1883.[90] His colleagues prevented such a declaration. However, Gladstone's correspondence shows that the institutional question was maturating and becoming 'ripe' for settlement.

From the time of his release from Kilmainham, the House of Commons was the centre of Parnell's and the Home Rule movement's creative influence. This was partly a matter of preference, but it also reflected the constraints on political activity in Ireland under the

Coercion Act. Parnell's public appearances in Ireland were infrequent.[91] In 1882 he spoke in Dublin four times in rapid succession in August, attended the conference for the establishment of the National League in the Irish capital in October, and gave two speeches in his constituency, Cork City, in mid-December. He did not reappear on a platform in Ireland until the Monaghan by-election in June 1883, which was won by Healy and during the remainder of that year he delivered only four further speeches in the country, though one delivered at the National League Convention on 30 August pointed to the reformist direction he now took (see document 4). His activity in Ireland was even more measured the following year. He addressed meetings in Drogheda and Dublin in April at Tuam in late May (his first venture to the west since 1881), speaking again in Dublin at the beginning of September.

Several of Parnell's colleagues served short terms of imprisonment for offences under the Prevention of Crime Act, but this did not detract from the parliamentary thrust of party activity. The National League was no more than a shadow of the old Land League. In many parts of the country, notably in Ulster, it hardly existed,[92] or was found only on a limited scale, while it remained scarce on the ground in other places such as in Westmeath. There it was reported in September 1884 that 'the weekly meetings of the National League are wonderfully small and if they reflect the spirit of Mullingar that spirit must be nationally weak'.[93] During 1883 the party developed a tighter organisational apparatus in the House of Commons and members now were much more apt to sit, act and vote together. This was achieved by a greater degree of unity due to a further shake-out of nominal Home Rulers. Parnellism became more cohesive by crowding out hostile elements within the party and movement. The decline in real party numbers did not weaken Home Rule as it had in previous times; it was apparent that the opponents' days were numbered. By autumn 1883 Gladstone saw the opposition to Parnell in Catholic portions of the country as 'so weak that we are threatened with almost their entire extinction at the next election', while the nominal Home Rulers' indifferent attendance at the House of Commons made them negligible assets.[94] Until the split of the Irish party over the Parnell divorce scandal in December 1890 it was thereafter impossible for anyone but a Parnellite to be successful in a constituency with a majority of Catholic voters.

During 1883 the parliamentary party, like the movement in Ireland, ran at a lower ebb. The apparent contradiction of a movement based on aggressive militancy and the reality of a muted performance was disguised by a compliant and vigorous journalism which sent forth the message of a party slavishly attentive to the country's needs. To the National League in Dublin in late August 1883 Parnell defended his reluctance to formulate specific legislative schemes: 'I have always held that it was most undesirable for the Irish people to make proposals on such questions as Irish land and Irish self-government; but that we should, rather by agitation and organisation, set our English rulers and governors to work to consider these matters, and to make their own propositions.' He went on to offer his conception of Home Rule and its likely extent with the observation: 'I have every hope that before long a measure in the direction of local self-government will be laid before Parliament; and though it may not go the whole distance that we go, yet, undoubtedly, it will give considerable further powers to the Irish people'. He observed that this reform would 'train them in those habits of self-government and self-reliance which are of so much advantage and of such vital importance in forming a nation'. Even when Ireland became self-governing he foresaw 'the Queen would be our Queen' and Irishmen would continue to be British subjects.[95] What he, and the movement, anticipated at this point was something akin to local elective institutions with an introduction, probably by gradual stages, of some overarching Dublin assembly. His far from utopian prospectus was as close as he came to a definition of Home Rule until 1885.

Loyalty to Home Rule after 1882 owed much to lingering gratitude resulting from the land campaign, an absence of creditable alternatives and Parnell's charismatic qualities; it owed little to any specific plan, an efficient organisation or pronounced expectations. As one bishop observed at the end of May 1883: 'right or wrong, the people are under the impression that it is owing to Parnell's action they have been rescued from the direst tyranny ever endured by a people from the landlord class.'[96] Coercion, too, gave the party a cause round which it could rally opinion while providing a convenient excuse for its relative inactivity. Coercion was the spur to Home Rulers' takeover of the elective element of Poor Law Boards.[97] William Feingold points to this local manifestation as an effective means of giving the National League a function during a time of Parnellite inactivity. The party was well advanced along the path towards becoming an institution of social integration and the fulcrum of national identity; it had a rich materialist programme but the priorities were not established and Home Rule jostled for space among these. In 1883 the parliamentarians projected themselves on issues such as coercion, the Corrupt Practices bill and a few other major topics. By lowering the expenses of parliamentary elections, The Corrupt and Illegal Practices Act enacted on 25 August, abetted the party's ambition to monopolise the representation of constituencies with Catholic majorities. Also, the Labourers' Act (passed on 25 August 1883) provided the legislative framework for the provision of housing of a large rural group mainly ignored in the land acts.

Another significant change in the party was apparent as well. Unlike in the past, MPs carefully applied themselves to all public business.[98] Questions like financial assistance for river drainage, harbour development and the fishing interest in Ireland, along with matters ranging from Sunday closing and pension provisions, were pursued vigorously. Useful concessions were won. After successfully defeating government plans on one proposal, Herbert Gladstone gave credit to Irish members diligence:

> [T]he Parnellite members have been very fair in their tone about the bill, both in public and in private and I believe that most of them wish it to pass. At the same time they refuse to agree to the withdrawal of all discretion from the guardians by which the Local Government Board is left absolute master of the situation.[99]

No matter seemed too trivial; Parnellism normally aided progressive causes. J. J. O'Kelly, for instance, attacked a private member's bill enabling a railway to take possession of additional land in north London. In his opinion it was 'almost indecent that railway directors should come down to that House, in order to support a railway company in taking possession of every plot of land that belonged to the people'.[100] The party supported the Agricultural Holdings bills for Scotland and England, with members urging that tenants in other parts of Britain be given all the rights so recently granted to Irish farmers.[101] Furthermore, Irish MPs made aggressive use of Question Time, typically exposing an injustice to, or a complaint of, a constituent. The majority of questions pertained directly to constituency concerns, a new departure in Irish parliamentary behaviour, and one remarkable in a party with so notable a carpetbagger element, whose members professed to be national rather than simply local representatives.

Attention to mundane topics, the routine of committees, ponderous involvement in Question Time and nightly vigilance in the corridors of Westminster were unexciting activities except when depicted in the pages of a tame national press, but they presaged a different sort of Irish representation. Adaptation of Parnellism from an issue to a service organisation had wide-ranging implications. Perhaps as Sinn Féin later asserted, intimacy with the culture of Westminster emasculated them but it also made Parnellites conversant with the British political elite and practised in the ways of getting things done. Active Irish representation made it seem less sinister, enhancing its value as a parliamentary ally. After all, MPs like the nominal Home Rulers who seldom attended were no use to British politicians; Parnellites who sat up nightly and could be counted upon to make themselves heard and felt in the division lobby were altogether more potent as allies or opponents.

During 1884 the integration of Parnellism into the fabric of British politics was substantially completed. Gladstone and now, increasingly, Conservatives saw Parnellism as a permanent feature of the political landscape; one which, if not exactly welcome, was nevertheless a force less full of malice than it had appeared two or three years earlier. The Irish party for its part became progressively more enmeshed in parliamentary affairs. In February 1884 the annual party meeting determined to present twelve bills concerning country government, extension of the municipal franchise, election of Poor Law Guardians, voter registration, revision of the land laws and similar matters.[102] As the year worn on, the party even elected to speak on behalf of clerical education interests, something most members undertook informally already. The process culminated when on 1 October 1884 the Irish Catholic hierarchy passed a resolution asking the party to act as parliamentary spokesmen for its education demands.[103] The no doubt inevitable decision to act as the clerical mouthpiece was a further step towards the party being remoulded into a service institution, and largely completed its transition into a party of social integration. Church, party and people were rapidly being bonded into a mutually reinforcing socio-political culture. In April Parnell maintained that the party was the only 'efficient means for securing beneficial reform in Ireland'.[104] At Drogheda a few days later he appeared to relegate the Home Rule demand to a back burner, stating 'in [his] judgement the Irish land question, if it is to be settled by constitutional means, will have to be settled before the national question can be settled by constitutional means'.[105] Institutional innovation, though, was not completely neglected. Parnell and another MP, Bernard Molloy, reverted to the Irish grand committee idea, stressing its beneficial effects:

> [I]f the government would agree to this ... they would, in all probability, find that much of the energy now devoted by Irish Members to outside matters – to matters of a negative kind ... would be applied to their own affairs, and that the experiment would be so successful and beneficial that it would be repeated.[106]

Reformism faithfully replicated the mood of the country; it certainly gelled with middle-class Catholic interests. National MPs were able to conceal the transition by the judicious mixture of highly charged rhetoric with pedestrian ambitions. This approach could be made to work so long as the movement had an obedient press and no persuasive critic emerged to draw attention to the emasculation of the Home Rule demand. Parnell was helped by the bulk of Irish radicals giving precedence to agrarian issues rather than to Home Rule. When after 1883 Davitt began making troublesome noises about land nationalisation, the middle-class leadership quickly moved to discredit his ideas. The position was abetted by a determination to build a party and movement compliant with the views of the national leadership. Ireland's clergy had a pivotal part to play. Only the Church had an organisational apparatus that reached throughout Catholic Ireland; it alone had the resources to be truly national in character. After 1882 the Church turned towards Parnellism, thus opening the possibility of political mobilisation without the necessity of establishing, maintaining and funding a vast free-standing network. A clerical-dominated movement was not prone to the radicalism and the undiluted localism that plagued the operations of the Land League.

Conclusion

The land war was a sobering experience. In the aftermath Parnellism grew into a conventional political institution, multifaceted and reformist. It was aided in this by developments in British politics and shifts in the attitudes of the Catholic Church. The consequence was a rhetoric, with a vagueness of meaning, about what Parnellism sought, especially on the question of self-government. Progressive Liberals could subscribe to one type of home government – local representative institutions – without taking on board the full traditional national programme. Parnellism responded by either relegating Home Rule to a distant horizon with other matters receiving priority, or by appearing to define the demand in such a way as to be consistent with the reforming zeal of Gladstonians. By 1883 it was apparent as well that a wing of the Conservative party was ready to take up some Irish demands and was notably flexible on the issue of land purchase and denominational education. But whatever the actual programme of Parnellism, the cement that held together the loyalty of rival Irish factions was the self-government aspiration. A major difficulty continued to beset the movement. Though very popular in the short term, Parnell had not made it clear whether it was a reformist or a self-government association. There was an underlying tension between notions of a service institution and one dedicated to a single all-encompassing goal: self-government. Furthermore, there was a dysfunction between local and national politics which in time would rear its head as well. William Feingold notes that the national and local movements had a different set of enemies.[107] For the national party it was the British government, whereas the local organisation was more concerned about the Local Government Board and landlord influence on the Boards of Poor Law Guardians. Confirmation of this division comes from another source. In Westmeath after 1882 a chasm opened between the young educated townspeople who dominated the National League or the Land League before it, the Poor Law Boards and the Mullingar Town Council, and the farmers and shopkeepers who wished to revert to the a political co-operation with the landlords of the 1870s, not least because the League appeared ready to emphasise the claims of the agricultural labourers.[108] Precedent suggested that no national coalition would hold together as essentially a service movement, but would require a single great purpose to glue together the disparate elements.

The years up to 1884 were crucial in the development of the forms, rhetoric, organisation and strategy of Home Rule. Also, they were important for constructing the liberal unionist responses of British politicians. Parnell and his colleagues built upon the foundations laid down in the 1870s. After the chastening experience of the land agitation, there was a rejection of the mass politics and a concentration upon electoralism and parliamentarianism.

Notes

1   Liam Fogarty (ed.), *James Fintan Lalor* (Dublin, 1947), p. xxiv.

2   *The Freeman's Journal*, 25 October 1880.

3   T. W. Moody, *Davitt and the Irish Revolution, 1846–82* (Oxford, 1981), p. 209.

4   *The Freeman's Journal*, 4 February 1879.

5   *Parliamentary Debates [PD]*, 234 (1879), c. 1397.

6   T. W. Moody, 'The New Departure in Irish Politics, 1878–9', in H. A. Croone, T. W. Moody and D. B. Quinn (eds), *Essays in British and Irish History* (London, 1951), p. 329.

7   *The Freeman's Journal*, 9 June 1879.

8   Quoted in Margaret O'Callaghan, *British High Politics and a Nationalist Ireland: Criminality, Land and the Law Under Forster and Balfour* (Cork, 1994), p. 12.

9   See, Michael Davitt to John Devoy, 23 August 1879, in William O'Brien and Desmond Ryan (eds), *Devoy's Post Bag 1871–1928* (Dublin, 1948), I, p. 453.

10   Moody, *Davitt and the Irish Revolution*, pp. 351–4.

11   See, *ibid.*, pp. 475–99.

12   *New York Times*, 3 January 1880.

13   Moody, *Davitt and the Irish Revolution*, p. 356; for the fullest account, see, Norman Dunbar Palmer, *The Irish Land League Crisis* (New Haven, CT, 1940), pp. 83–105.

14   *The Freeman's Journal*, 22 March 1880.

15 See, Sir Henry James, *The Work of the Irish Leagues* (London, 1890), pp. 164–7, 173–4.

16 Alan O'Day, 'The Political Organization of the Irish in Britain, 1867–90', in Roger Swift and Sheridan Gilley (eds), *The Irish in Britain 1815–1939* (London, 1989), pp. 199–203.

17 Alan O'Day, *The English Face of Irish Nationalism: Parnellite Involvement in British Politics, 1880–86* (Dublin, 1977; revised edn, Aldershot, 1994), p. 11.

18 *The Nation*, 13 March, 24 April 1880.

19 *The Freeman's Journal*, 15 April 1880.

20 Thomas William Heyck, *The Dimensions of British Radicalism: The Case of Ireland 1874–95* (Urbana and Chicago, 1974), pp. 50–1, appendix B, pp. 242–4.

21 R. V. Comerford, 'The Land War and the Politics of Distress, 1877–82', in W. E. Vaughan (ed.), *A New History of Ireland, VI, Ireland Under the Union, II, 1870–1921* (Oxford, 1996), p. 40, but provides no substantiation for this larger figure.

22 K. Theodore Hoppen, *Elections, Politics, and Society in Ireland 1832–1885* (Oxford, 1984), pp. 329–30.

23 *The Freeman's Journal*, 18 May 1880.

24 *The Nation*, 29 May 1880.

25 *Ibid.*

26 The O'Gorman Mahon to Lord Richard Grosvenor (copy), 28 November 1880, the O'Gorman Mahon Papers, University of Chicago.

27 Grosvenor to The O'Gorman Mahon, 4 August 1881, *ibid.*

28 Jonathan Parry, *The Rise and Fall of Liberal Government in Victorian Britain* (New Haven and London, 1993), p. 292.

29 T. W. Moody and R. A. Hawkins with Margaret Moody (eds), *Florence Arnold-Foster's Irish Journal* (Oxford, 1988), p. 3.

30 O'Callaghan, *British High Politics*, p. 19.

31 Comerford, 'The Land War', p. 41.

32 Earl Spencer to Earl Cowper, 17 June 1880, quoted in Katherine, Countess Cowper, *Earl Cowper, K.G.: A Memoir* (London, 1913), p. 367.

33 Lord Eversley [G. J. Shaw-Lefevre], *Gladstone and Ireland. The Irish Policy of Parliament From 1850–1894* (London, 1912), p. 115.

34 Dudley W. R. Bahlman (ed.), *The Diary of Sir Edward Walter Hamilton, 1880–1885* (Oxford, 1972), I, p. 28 (27 July 1880).

35 Lord Selborne to A. Hamilton, 11 August 1880, Selborne Papers, Lambeth Palace Library; see, Moody, Hawkins with Moody (eds), *Florence Arnold-Foster's Irish Journal*, p. 9 (7 August).

36 See, Barbara Lewis Solow, *The Land Question and the Irish Economy* (Cambridge, MA, 1971).

37 Moody, Hawkins with Moody (eds), *Florence Arnold-Foster's Irish Journal.*, p. 16 (4 November).

38 Andrew W. Orridge, 'Who Supported the Land War? An Aggregate-Date Analysis of Irish Discontent, 1879–1882', *Economic and Social Review*, 12 (April 1981), pp. 223, 226; see, W. E. Vaughan, *Landlords and Tenants in Mid-Victorian Ireland* (Oxford, 1994), pp. 208–26.

39   Palmer, *Irish Land League Crisis*, p. 280; Moody, *Davitt and the Irish Revolution*, p. 458; for the social composition, see, Samuel Clark, *Social Origins of the Irish Land War* (Princeton, NJ, 1979), pp. 246–76.

40   See, Paul Bew, *Land and the National Question in Ireland 1859–82* (Dublin, 1979); J. W. H. Carter, *The Land War and its Leaders in Queen's County, 1879–82* (Portaoise: Leinster, 1994), p. 77; James O'Shea, *Priest, Politics and Society in Post-Famine Ireland: A Study of County Tipperary, 1850–1891* (Dublin, 1983), pp. 72–3.

41   O'Shea, *Priest, Politics and Society*, pp. 74, 82.

42   *The Times*, 20 September 1880.

43   See, Donald E. Jordan jun., *Land and Popular Politics in Ireland. County Mayo from the Plantation to the Land War* (Cambridge, 1994), p. 231, Table 7.1, also, pp. 230–63.

44   For a table of evictions and outrages, quarterly, by province, 1878–83, see, Moody, *Davitt and the Irish Revolution*, p. 567.

45   Vaughan, *Landlords and Tenants*, p. 209.

46   For a good account see, O'Callaghan, *British High Politics*, pp. 62–70.

47   Michael Davitt to John Devoy, 16 December 1880, in O'Brien and Ryan (eds), *Devoy's Post Bag*, II, p.24.

48   Quoted in Mark Tierney, *Croke of Cashel: The Life of Archbishop Thomas William Croke, 1823–1902* (Dublin, 1976), p. 106.

49   *Ibid.*, p. 110.

50   O'Callaghan, *British High Politics*, p. 71.

51   Palmer, *Irish Land League Crisis*, pp. 248–50; Elizabeth R. Hooker, *Readjustments of Agricultural Tenure in Ireland* (Chapel Hill, NC, 1938), pp. 60–1.

52   Quoted in J. L. Hammond, *Gladstone and the Irish Nation* (New impression; London, 1964), p. 210.

53   Allen Warren, 'Gladstone, Land and Social Reconstruction in Ireland 1881–1887', *Parliamentary History*, 2 (1983), pp. 155–6, 171.

54   See, Thomas Wemyss Reid, *Memoirs and Correspondence of Lyon Playfair* (reprint; Jeminaville, Scotland, 1976), pp. 292–3.

55   Eversley, *Gladstone and Ireland*, p. 151.

56   Beaconsfield to Lord Cairns, 20 July 1880, Cairns Papers, Public Record Office, London, 30/51/67.

57   Sir Stafford Northcote to Lord Sandon, 20 November 1880, Viscount Harrowby Papers, used at Sandon Hall.

58   Sir Stafford Northcote to R. A. Cross, 29 November 1880, R. A. Cross Papers, British Library, Add. MS 51265.

59   Sir Stafford Northcote to Lord Cairns, 18 December 1880, Cairns Papers, 30/51/43.

60   Sir Stafford Northcote to Alice Northcote, 28 August 1881, Earl of Iddesleigh Papers, British Library, Add. MS 50032.

61   See, Viscount Chilston, *W. H. Smith* (London, 1965), p. 171.

62   *The Freeman's Journal*, 6 May 1881.

63   Quoted in Agatha Ramm (ed.), *The Political Correspondence of Mr Gladstone and Lord Granville 1876–1886* (Oxford, 1962), I, p. 291.

64   Quoted in *ibid.*, p. 293.

65   See, O'Day, *English Face of Irish Nationalism*, pp. 51–9, 95–100; Allen Warren, 'Foster, the Liberals and New Directions in Irish Policy 1880–1882', *Parliamentary History*, 6 (1987), pp. 95–126.

66   See, Eversley, *Gladstone and Ireland*, pp. 164–74.

67   Moody, Hawkins and Moody (eds), *Florence Arnold-Foster's Irish Journal*, p. 257 (3 October).

68   Quoted in John Morley, *The Life of William Ewart Gladstone* (London, 1903), III, p. 61.

69   Richard Hawkins, 'Gladstone, Forster, and the Release of Parnell, 1882–8', *Irish Historical Studies*, XVI (September 1969), pp. 417–45.

70   O'Callaghan, *British High Politics* pp. 4, 80; also, see, p. 107.

71   Katharine O'Shea, *Charles Stewart Parnell: His Love Story and Political Life* (London, 1914), I, p. 207. For a discussion of the construction of this biography, see, R. F. Foster, *Paddy and Mr Punch: Connections in Irish and English History* (London, 1993), pp. 123–38.

72   *Ibid.*, pp. 235–6.

73   See, Bew, *Land and the National Question*, passim.

74   Hammond, *Gladstone and The Irish Nation*, p. 255.

75   *Ibid.*, pp. 256–7.

76   *Ibid.*, pp. 259–62.

77   See, F. H. O'Donnell, *A History of the Irish Parliamentary Party* (London, 1910), II, pp. 121–5.

78   Quoted in Hammond, *Gladstone and the Irish Nation*, p. 277.

79   Cowper, *Earl Cowper*, pp. 577–8.

80   See, Comerford, 'The Land War' p. 50.

81   *Ibid.*

82   O'Day, *English Face of Irish Nationalism*, pp. 61–78.

83   Quoted in Hammond, *Gladstone and the Irish Nation*, p. 308.

84   Michael Davitt, *The Fall of Feudalism in Ireland* (London, 1904), p. 371.

85   *The Nation*, 30 September 1882.

86   Quoted in Hammond, *Gladstone and the Irish Nation*, p. 311, also see, pp. 309–14.

87   *The Freeman's Journal*, 18 October 1882.

88   C. C. O'Brien, *Parnell and his Party, 1880–90* (Corrected impression; Oxford, 1964), pp. 126–33.

89   Quoted in Hammond, *Gladstone and the Irish Nation*, p. 330.

90   See, *ibid.*, pp. 334–7.

91   See, Alan O'Day, 'Parnell: Orator and Speaker' in D. George Boyce and Alan O'Day (eds), *Parnell in Perspective* (London, 1991), p. 210.

92   B. M. Walker, *Ulster Politics: The Formative Years, 1868–86* (Belfast, 1989), pp. 205–8.

93   Quoted in A. C. Murray, 'Nationality and Local Politics in Late Nineteenth-Century Ireland: The Case of County Westmeath', *Irish Historical Studies*, XXV (November, 1986), p. 146; also see, pp. 144–5.

94   Gladstone to Lord Spencer, 20 October 1883, Fifth Earl Spencer Papers, Althorp.

95 *The Freeman's Journal*, 30 August 1883.

96 Quoted in Emmet Larkin, *The Roman Catholic Church and the Creation of the Modern Irish State, 1878–1886* (Dublin, 1975), p. 188.

97 William L. Feingold, *The Revolt of the Tenantry: The Transformation of Local Government in Ireland, 1872–1886* (Boston, MA, 1984), pp. 158, 239. Patriotic preponderance increased sharply in the 1883 elections to the Dublin Corporation Council as well. See, Mary Daly, *Dublin, the Deposed Capital* (Cork, 1984), p. 215.

98 See, O'Day, *English Face of Irish Nationalism*, pp. 131–8.

99 Herbert Gladstone to J. D. Cape, 7 August 1883, Viscount Gladstone Papers, British Library, MS 46050.

100 *Parliamentary Debates* [PD], 279 (1883), c. 217.

101 *Ibid.*, 282 (1883), c. 199.

102 *The Freeman's Journal*, 9 February 1884.

103 Larkin, *Roman Catholic Church*, p. 244.

104 *The Freeman's Journal*, 7 April 1884.

105 *United Ireland*, 19 April 1884.

106 *PD*, 284 (1884), cc. 1905–33.

107 Feingold, *Revolt of the Tenantry*, p. 181.

108 Murray, 'Nationality and Local Politics', pp. 144–5.

4

First Home Rule crisis, 1884–86

The great day of the Home Rule statement will be remembered in history as long as Ireland is in existence. (Lewis Harcourt, 8 April 1886)[1]

Home Rule does not mean National Independence. This proposition needs no elaboration. Any plan of Home Rule whatever implies that there are spheres of national life in which Ireland is not to act with the freedom of an independent State. Mr Parnell and his followers accept for Ireland restrictions on her political liberty absolutely inconsistent with the principle of nationality. ... A *bona fide* Home Ruler cannot be a *bona fide* Nationalist. (A. V. Dicey, 1886)[2]

Introduction

Irish parliamentarianism reached its apogee in 1885 and 1886 when both major British parties courted it. Parnell's success was capped when in April 1886 the first comprehensive self-government scheme was proposed by Gladstone. This initial foray into Home Rule had extensive ramifications. It closed a period of fluidity in politics, giving the Conservatives and their allies, the Liberal Unionists, a long-term grip on power at Westminster. The incident sped up the realignment of the Liberal party.[3] Gladstone's conversion further entrenched the predominance of the Irish party in Ireland, at the same time boosting electoralism. Thereafter Irish self-government had a fairly exact meaning. Gladstone's proposal was the standard by which subsequent self-government schemes were measured. Why did Home Rule become the foremost issue at this moment in time? There are several explanations – the personalities of the era, the minutiae of day-to-day politics, concern about the state of Ireland

and the empire, recognition of democratic rights and notions of justice to Ireland.

Franchise reform fostered a climate conducive to Home Rule. In 1884 Liberals sought to implement enfranchisement on its own, but at Lord Salisbury's instigation Conservatives blocked the bill in the House of Lords until the Gladstone Cabinet agreed to a redistribution of constituencies.[4] The complete package of reforms was not passed until summer 1885, but the outline of the new system began to fall into place by late autumn 1884. In Ireland the main impact was twofold: first, it was placed on an identical electoral footing with the rest of the United Kingdom, a step towards the equality promised by the Act of Union, and second, elimination of the small borough seats erased a stumbling-block to a Parnellite advance, also reinforcing the rural orientation of the party. In total, twenty-two boroughs were disenfranchised and three other boroughs were reduced from two to a single member, with twenty-one of these seats reallocated to the counties. Belfast and Dublin, which were also divided into single-member constituencies, each now had four MPs. The Irish electorate was increased from approximately 222,018 to 737,965. About one in every two adult males possessed the ballot in Ireland, a slightly lower proportion than in the United Kingdom as a whole. The effect was to create a vastly enlarged Catholic electorate comprising not just the better-off classes but also a substratum of cottiers and agricultural labourers. A reduction in borough constituencies and enfranchisement virtually ended Conservative and Protestant influence outside Trinity College and south Dublin in the southern provinces. Catholics had considerable electoral possibilities in Ulster.[5] Overall, Ireland escaped without any reduction in seats and was slightly over-represented in relation to population. Gladstone's refusal to tinker with 'fancy' franchises or try proportional representation ensured that the minority in Ireland outside parts of Ulster must be submerged in a sea of Catholic voters. Isaac Butt's prognosis of eighty to ninety Home Rule MPs came of age; Parnellism reaped the reward. The country was polarised along a confessional and now a geographical axis.

Reform had an impact for Home Rule in Great Britain as well. An Irish population variously estimated at 750,000–2,000,000 was scattered across the land, and a number of constituencies contained substantial Hibernian electors. Butt and then Parnell had contended that this vote could be mustered to pressurise Liberals into responding to Irish wants. Prior to the electoral changes the Irish did not exert great force in British constituencies; after 1885 it appeared that another strand of Home Rule strategy was in place.

Local government and coercion, autumn 1884–June 1885

As 1884 drew to a close, Ireland become prominent on the political docket. The Prevention of Crime Act was due to expire in July 1885. At all points between November 1884 and June 1885 discussion of Irish affairs was connected with coercion. In September 1884 Chamberlain thought: 'we shall have an awful business over the renewal of the crimes act. I wish Spencer could see his way to let it drop but I imagine there is no hope of this.'[6] Reform of local government was an obvious bargaining chip in a fresh round of negotiations; Gladstone and Parnell already agreed on it. Chamberlain's influence had grown over the past years and since 1879 he had wanted to see 'a modified form of Home Rule'.[7] In late November William O'Shea left him 'a short note of Mr Parnell's views respecting the renewal of the crimes act and Irish local government'.[8] Parnell's own limited expectations were expressed to Archbishop Croke shortly thereafter when he wrote of the importance he assigned to franchise legislation and his 'hope that we may be able to follow this up next session by laying the foundations of a wide and comprehensive scheme of local government'.[9] Chamberlain opposed 'separation' but could accept 'Home Rule' though 'anxious to find out exactly what it means'. He was clear that he did not find Butt's version of Home Rule acceptable, for it 'would infallibly lead to a demand for entire separation'. He added:

> [O]n the other hand I consider that Ireland has a right to a local government more complete, more popular, more thoroughly representative and more far-reaching than anything that has hitherto been suggested; and I hope that the first session of a reformed Parliament will settle this question, so far at least as what is generally called county government is concerned.[10]

While welcoming Chamberlain's overture, Parnell was anxious for him understand that:

> [W]e do not propose this local self-government plank as a substitute for the restitution of our Irish Parliament but solely as an improvement of the present system of local government in Ireland. The claim for restitution of Parliament would still remain. Some people think it would be weakened, others, strengthened by the concession. I myself think that this improvement of local government in Ireland, if carried out, would have very little effect one way or other upon the larger question.[11]

As 1885 began Parnell was conscious of growing criticism that the Irish party had become reformist rather than the vanguard of Home Rule. Even the party's reform agenda disappointed agrarian radicals who thought its objectives excessively modest. A brief rebellion at the Tipperary by-election in early January underlined the potential vulnerability of the movement when the votes of newly enfranchised electors were thrown onto the scales. Parnell knew that his movement stood accused of doing too little for small farmers, labourers and urban dwellers. He had no intention of jettisoning reform, but to pursue it in a way which did not fragment the national coalition. At Clonmel, when receiving the Freedom of the Borough, he reminded his countrymen that while supporting the improvement in local government provision 'this question was of course, distinct from their right to have their own independent Parliament. Local government was a question that should be developed even under an Irish Parliament but they could never and would never claim anything less than the Parliament of Grattan.' Parnell's actual expectations still remained limited, for as he pointed out:

> [N]o country in the world was governed in such an absolutely unrepresentative fashion as they were by the grand juries, and their powers must go to the elected bodies who represent the ratepayers. The public boards controlling Irish developments were also unrepresentative being nominated by the Lord Lieutenant. The education system, too, was unsatisfactory.[12]

To those who wanted to pursue Home Rule alone, the quest for ameliorative legislation threatened the integrity of the movement. Parnell appreciated the inherent contradiction between national and reform ambitions and sought to run them in tandem. Some Home Rulers were contemptuous of his supposed intellectual mediocrity and, confident of their own powers, looked forwarded to his displacement. His habitual palliative for factionalism was to stress the single great plank, Home Rule. In the face of mounting dissension, Parnell reverted to his traditional formula, pointing to the primacy of the national demand. At Cork on 21 January he sought to assuage doubts among his own followers about the party's intent in the next Parliament. Standard paraphrases of this speech often neglect to note that his ringing patriotic testament came towards the close of extended remarks best called hectoring and moderate. Even the declaration of national faith carried a note of *déjà vu* when Parnell pointed to an extended time span for the realisation of full self-government, a distant day when neither he nor the current movement might be in existence:

> I am convinced that when the reckoning up comes, after the general election of 1886, that we shall have cause to congratulate ourselves in the possession of a strong party, which will bear down all opposition, and which aided by the organisation in our country behind

us will enable us to gain for our country those rights which have been stolen from us.[13]

After considering some of the grievances which the party would seek to rectify through Parliament he went on to declare:

[B]ut I go back from the consideration of these questions to the consideration of the great question of national self-government for Ireland. I do not know how this great question will be eventually settled. I do not know whether England will be wise in time and concede to constitutional arguments and methods the restitution of that which was stolen from us towards the close of the last century. It is given to none of us to forecast the future, and just as it is impossible for us to say in what way or by what means the national question may be settled, in what way full justice may be done to Ireland, so it is impossible for us to say to what extent that justice shall be done. We cannot ask for less than the restitution of Grattan's Parliament, with its important privileges and wide and far-reaching constitution. We can not, under the British Constitution, ask for more than the restitution of Grattan's Parliament. But no man has the right to fix the boundary to the march of a nation; no man has a right to say to his country: 'Thus far shalt thou go and no further', and we have never attempted to fix the *ne plus ultra* to the progress of Ireland's nationhood, and we never shall. But, while we leave these things to time, circumstances, and the future, we must each one of us resolve in our own hearts that we shall at all times do everything which within us lies to obtain for Ireland the fullest measure of her rights. In this way we shall not give up anything which the future may put in favour of our country; and while we struggle today for that which may seem possible for us with our combination that we shall not do anything to hinder or prevent better men who may come after us from gaining better things than those for which we now contend.[14]

Besides being an affirmation of national identity, Parnell's speech was tactically astute, managing the near impossible task of satisfying almost everyone while giving no clue as to any specific reform priorities, or clarification of what he meant by Home Rule other than citing Grattan's Parliament as the limit of the demand possible under the British Constitution. The speech was a matchless case of Parnell's infinite capacity to mix mundane realism with uplifting sentiments. It also showed that he kept his powder dry for seeing off the overambitious lieutenants around him. On 11 February the death of Cardinal Edward McCabe removed an obstacle to Parnell's advance.

The notion of trading local government for the renewal of some provisions of the Crime Act circulated through the government until the beginning of May when the Cabinet declined to support the introduction of local government. By that date the bloom of local government wilted for Parnell, in part, because it became embedded in many Liberal minds, in spite of his warnings, as a substitute for a Dublin Parliament while important elements in the national coalition pounced on it as too meagre. To Chamberlain it was 'the kind of Home Rule we can safely grant'.[15] More ominously, Cardinal Manning, the Catholic Archbishop of Westminster, intruded into the picture. Through his intimate contacts with Irish MPs , the Cardinal learned of the negotiations in progress. He soon began to collude with Chamberlain's friend and Cabinet colleague, Sir Charles Dilke, President of the Local Government Board. Manning, Dilke was led to believe, had the Irish bishops in tow and, jointly, they were prepared to accept Chamberlain's plan and 'denounce, not only separation but also an Irish Parliament'.[16] During an interview with Manning, Chamberlain was informed that the local government scheme would be adequate for 'satisfying all just and reasonable demands'.[17] Local government, as it was proffered in spring 1885, increasingly spelled a grave danger. As Parnell had explained, the ultimate goal had to be legislative independence or his coalition would suffer internal haemorrhaging. Gladstone, too, developed doubts about the local government option as a lasting response to Ireland's aspirations. According to Edward Hamilton, Gladstone's private secretary, the Prime Minister believed 'there is much to be said against a half-measure, and in favour of some bold scheme which would strike the imagination of the Irishmen. We have had too much experience of the failure of half-measures in Ireland.'[18]

The burst of activity during the early months of 1885 spurred formation of the Irish Loyal and Patriotic Union on 1 May. Local government did not disappear after the Cabinet rejected the plan in early May, but took on a lease of life. The episode embodied pointers for the Home Rule crisis. Irish local government negotiations moved through several overlapping stages, but there was an almost resplendent ambiguity throughout over what precisely was meant by the term and a very wide gap in the expectations held by key participants. Nearly everyone in the Home Rule camp welcomed the idea, but the mode of its introduction profoundly affected Irish receptivity then, as it would do later in 1906–07 when it was resurrected. From a Parnellite point of view, no scheme at all was preferable to one which, if useful in the abstract, nevertheless threatened to disrupt the movement.

The Parnellite–Tory alliance, summer 1885

During the first five months of 1885 events gradually pushed the Irish party and Tories together. Important Conservative leaders were alarmed by what they saw as Gladstone's incompetence, especially in foreign and imperial policy. News of General Gordon's death at Khartoum in February confirmed Conservative apprehensions. They were not content with Liberal conduct of Irish affairs either. Leading Conservatives mostly accepted the need for land purchase, supported denominational education and, though less universally, were prepared to take up local government. Underpinning Tory attitudes was the impact of franchise reform and an abiding fear of unrestrained radicalism. Chamberlain had been stumping the country making menacing noises about the 'ransom' that those who neither 'spin' nor 'toil' must pay.[19] Parnellism was not a natural ally for Conservatives – just the reverse. But Irish MPs had shown themselves to be effective critics of Gladstonian government, they attended the House of Commons regularly, and on some topics such as blocking the atheist Charles Bradlaugh's admission to Parliament, co-operation with them brought satisfying results.[20] Surfacing in some minds as well was a feeling that the Irish vote in British boroughs might be thrown onto the scales against the Radicals. In later February the Irish and Conservative party whips conferred over the question of electoral boundaries in Ireland, but no further contact seems to have taken place before May.[21] At the same time as the Cabinet rejected the local government plan, it also determined to renew the prevention of crime legislation. The Irish party was anxious to discomfiture the administration. But how could it do this?

For several years the patriotic press had argued that an Irish vote was worth two in a Division. More frequent Parnellite attendance and the augmentation of party numbers at by-elections in 1883 and 1884 gave substance to the claim, though Liberals continued to enjoy a working majority. The road to an understanding between Irish MPs and Tories was opened up over the coercion issue. In early May Hicks Beach wrote to Salisbury: 'I do not think we ought to *turn* them out, unless we feel that we, if in office, could do without a renewal of the Irish Coercion Bill.' He did 'not like Spencer's system, & do not believe it necessary'.[22] On 20 May Lord Randolph Churchill announced that there was

> an absolute and unimpeachable constitutional doctrine, that while any British government may reasonably, and with perfect confidence apply to Parliament, in times of great popular disorder, for exceptional and unconstitutional powers, at the same time, when that popular disorder has passed away, the government is bound by the highest considerations of public and of constitutional doctrine to return to and to rely on the ordinary law. We had every reason to hope, and I think every reason ultimately to believe that the time of great popular disorder in Ireland has passed away, or, at any rate, had been largely mitigated.[23]

If ready to dispense with special powers, Churchill reminded his audience that the party was guided by the binding principle of 'the maintenance of the connexion between Ireland and Great Britain'.[24] Conservative willingness to govern through the ordinary law formed the basis of the unlikely revolution. In the early hours of 9 June a combination of Tories and Irish abetted by Liberal absentees defeated the government on a budget amendment. Though not obliged to resign, demoralised Gladstonians gladly surrendered office in order to avert the looming struggle to renew the Prevention of Crime Act, inspiring Henry Lucy's remark: 'if there had been no coercion bill lying in the pathway there would have been no government defeat on Tuesday morning'.[25]

Gladstone's resignation created an extraordinary situation. Because an election could not be called until the reform legislation had been passed and a fresh electoral register compiled, Salisbury was obliged to head a minority government. He accepted office on the condition of not being overthrown by a capricious Liberal vote, but at the same time Conservatives could not put forward controversial questions. An old friend, Lord Carnarvon, was entrusted by Salisbury with the Lord Lieutenancy. Carnarvon accepted on the grounds of satisfying 'myself as clearly as I can of the general feeling and state of Ireland and that my colleagues in conjunction with me consider the whole future policy to, and government of, Ireland'.[26] His vague outlook soon became the working brief for important innovations.

Prior to departing for Dublin the new Viceroy met Manning who assured him that the Irish bishops 'all agree in favour of the Union with England'.[27] According to the prelate, they wanted significant local government but not a central parliament. He offered to put Carnarvon in touch with the Irish archbishops. From his contacts with ecclesiastics Carnarvon believed that a programme which granted social, institutional and education demands would meet Home Rulers' claims. During the summer he pushed forward his project: land legislation (the Ashbourne Act provided £5 million for tenants to purchase holdings over 49 years at 4 per cent interest) and the Education Endowments Act (benefiting Catholic education to the tune of £140,000). While in Ireland the Viceroy made friendly gestures to Catholics; in late summer he toured the west in order to inform himself about conditions. Most interestingly, on 1 August he held a secret interview with Parnell at which he learned how restrained the Irish chieftain's ambitions seemed to be. Parnell told Carnarvon of his desire for a 'central Parliament' but left the Viceroy with the impression that he was flexible about its form. The Irishman spoke of the need for a 'gradual growth' of self-government in order to 'accustom the people' to the exercise of responsibility. He did not wish to have an Irish Parliament to be responsible for resolving the land question; he saw its functions as being mainly concerned with education, railway traffic, arterial drainage, fisheries, manufacturing and similar matters. Additionally, the Irish leader stressed the importance of land purchase and emphasised that he was 'anxious to find a common ground. He said that it must be a matter of compromise'.[28] Later a public controversy erupted over what actually transpired at this meeting. Based on Parnell's attitude Carnarvon was persuaded to press on with his ideas for the amelioration of Irish grievances and even came to support the idea of, as yet undefined, self-government. Conservative liberal unionism consisted of friendly gestures, appeasing the clergy, promoting a peasant proprietorship and increasing responsible self-government. This frame of reference left them close to the Liberal and moderate Irish perspectives. Receiving local government or attenuated Home Rule from a Conservative regime appealed to Parnell because it could be pushed through the House of Lords and recommended to Ireland without appearing that the larger ambition was forsaken.

While the Tories made much of the running during summer 1885, Gladstone and other Liberals were not idle bystanders. Chamberlain and Dilke were frustrated in their intention to visit Ireland, though not before the former revealed his desire to find that 'a complete and effectual system of local government may be, and I hope it would be, found sufficient to satisfy the Irish national sentiment and to relieve the irritation that now prevails'.[29] On 14 July Herbert Gladstone uttered what was taken to be a declaration for Home Rule, suggesting that the 'proper policy was to throw to the winds all coercive legislation, at the same time proving their trust of the Irish people by allowing them to manage their own affairs … giving to them what would be a free and constitutional government'.[30] His remarks were received with interest in Ireland; *The Nation* observed: 'Mr Gladstone goes straight to the point, and, of course, when we consider whose son he is, his words must carry double weight.'[31] On 14 July, via the mediums of Lord Richard Grosvenor and Mrs O'Shea, Gladstone sought out Parnell's views on local government. The reply when it came on 21 July proclaimed: 'I believe that nothing less than a scheme based on the lines of Mr Herbert Gladstone's last speech at Leeds would be acceptable now, or, considered calculated to settle the Irish question.'[32] Grosvenor wrote twice more (23 and 28 July) to Mrs O'Shea to elicit Parnell's views before Gladstone wrote to her directly on 4 August, by which time the Irish leader had had the secret interview with Carnarvon. She responded the following day suggesting that local government reform would be like 'putting the cart before the horse', also pointing out:

[I]n view of recent events, however, and of the present attitude of both the great English parties towards Ireland, it is now felt that leaders of English public opinion may fairly be asked to consider the question of granting to Ireland a constitution of a similar nature to that of one of the larger colonies with such modifications as may be necessary to secure practically certain guarantees, first for the maintenance of the supremacy and authority of the Crown, secondly for the equitable treatment of landowning interests and thirdly for the security of freedom of conscience and the fair treatment of the minority by the majority.[33]

Gladstone found this letter 'too interesting, almost, to be addressed to a person of my age and too weakened sight since it substitutes for a limited field one almost without bounds'. He advised also 'that into any counterbidding of any sort against Lord R. Churchill I for one cannot enter'.[34]

Gladstone's contacts with Parnell were not a singular effort. Other Liberals kept in touch with various Irish figures. From these private contacts and through public statements it was clear that Liberals, like Conservatives, were prepared to accede to a significant granting of local control over Ireland's affairs, even if the degree and nature of this concession remained in doubt.

The 1885 general election

Following the close of Parliament on 14 August 1885 politicians prepared for the general election. Throughout the year the National League had experienced remarkable growth. From a modest base up to the end of 1884 (371 branches in April 1883) it expanded to 818 in July 1885, possibly reaching 1,261 at the end of the year.[35] Of this total, 287 (70 in April 1883) were located in Ulster, only 5 fewer than in Connaught, and northern contributions to party funds exceeded those from the western province by £300. James Loughlin suggests that the mushrooming membership was less a popular endorsement of Home Rule than a reflection of the desire to be part of the process of nominating men to stand for Parliament, local branches being the avenue to participation at National League county conventions formed to choose candidates.[36] On 15 August Davitt planted the standard of agrarian Radicals. He denounced the recently passed Ashbourne Act that had been praised by Parnell at the meeting with Carnarvon, as a 'landlord relief bill', criticising in the next breath the power and organisation of the National League.[37] He demanded that the full democratic apparatus of the League's constitution be implemented. Others soon took up Davitt's cry against land purchase: Parnell was not going to be given a clear field.[38] William O'Brien poured fuel on the flames, suggesting that the National League branches in each district set the 'fair price' that might be paid by tenants and impose a boycott on anyone who offered more.[39] The maximum price, he thought, should never exceed fifteen years rental. O'Brien's idea would turn the National League into a land adjudication body, much like the old Land League, and would certainly cause it to fall foul of a British government of any complexion. The 'uncrowned king' reacted to the danger in the time-honoured fashion. On 24 August he reminded the people of Ireland:

> [A]lthough during this Parliament which has just expired we may have said very little about Home Rule, very little about legislative independence, very little about the repeal of the union, yet I know well that through each of our hearts the thought of how these good things might be best forwarded was never for a moment absent, and that no body of Irishmen ever met together who have more consistently worked, and worked with greater effect, for that which always must be the hope of our nation until its realisation arrives.[40]

He stated that the party now stood before the country on 'a platform with one plank only and that one the plank of national independence'. Resolution of other questions, he said, must await the establishment of self-government. When Home Rule arrived other grievances would be remedied by the Irish Parliament. 'We have, therefore, a great work before us, both in the English House of Commons for a while, and also in the Irish chamber', he declared.[41] Parnell's speech contained nothing new but showed a determination to focus eyes on the big unifying ideal which stood unimpaired at the expense of divisive claims.

Parnell's next major address elaborated the Home Rule theme, asserting that Britain 'will have to grant to Ireland the complete right to rule herself or they will have to take away from us the share – the sham share – in the English constitutional system which they extended to us at the Union and govern us as a crown colony without any parliamentary representation whatever'. After laying out this unlikely eventuality, he claimed that what Ireland wanted was 'a constitution similar to that which is enjoyed by each and all of the larger colonies and that is practically what we are asking for'. His deeper motive soon spilled out when he warned of 'a very sore and cruel winter [ahead] for the agricultural community', counselling restraint in all quarters, for 'while I hope all of you, coming as you do from the many different localities of Ireland, will each in your own station preach moderation, I think we ought to expect moderation from the other side'.[42] Home Rule, then, was also a cry aimed at containing an ominous rural situation. Parnell realised that the movement could not sit by indefinitely. For the benefit of the landlords and the government he cautioned:

> [W]e should be untrue to ourselves, as we should undoubtedly be untrue to our suffering fellow-countrymen, if we did not endeavour to do what in us lay to shield the helpless tiller of the soil from extermination and from banishment during the coming winter. The outlook in all other respects is hopeful for Ireland, but undoubtedly the great depression of prices, the agricultural depression, introduces a new and very great difficulty.

In Parnell's estimation the 'land question ... is the real question of Ireland at present'.[43] Davitt shortly afterwards concurred, though in a different sense, saying the 'rent question would be the question of the coming winter'.[44]

Neither Parnell nor his colleagues were consistent about whether the campaign was being fought mainly on self-government or land. Gladstone soon contributed his voice to the mêlée though primarily for Liberal reasons. In his manifesto to Liberals he once more focused attention on the institutional issue:

> [T]he limit is clear within which any desires of Ireland, constitutionally ascertained, may, and beyond which they cannot, receive the assent of Parliament. To maintain the supremacy of the Crown, the unity of the empire, and all the authority of Parliament necessary for the conservation of that unity, is the first duty of every representative of the people. Subject to this governing principle, every grant to portions of the country of enlarged powers for the management of their own affairs is, in my view, not a source of danger, but a means of averting it, and is in the nature of a new guarantee for increased cohesion, happiness, and strength.[45]

His statement has been characterised as one which all Liberals might accept and constrained by an inability to get an indication from Parnell of what the Irish actually wanted. Yet, even so bland a decree had a swift impact. In its wake, national figures in contradictory ways reverted to the self-government claim. Justin Huntly McCarthy exemplified the confusion of ideas. He asserted: 'they would have Grattan's Parliament. They would be as free as a state in the great American union – free to make their own laws for their own people in their own way', while his father, Justin McCarthy, 'was for taking all instalments of justice'.[46] A majority of Parnellites, to judge from their declarations, seem to visualise the Home Rule they expected in the foreseeable future as extended local government. Perhaps more interesting (or from a Protestant point of view worrying) was what Parnellism and its grassroots supporters expected a home government to do. Some clue is available in statements such as those of the younger McCarthy, who said: 'they did not want Grattan's Parliament. They wanted something much more. Grattan's Parliament would never satisfy the lost aspirations of an awakened Nationality. ... They would have a Parliament suited for a free Catholic country'.[47] To his primarily Catholic audience this meant self-government designed to reverse the English Conquest and promote specifically sectarian interests.

The rapid growth of the newly formed House League showed up the growing subterranean divisions within the Catholic community. Originating in County Longford in the summer of 1885, with the objectives of reducing 'rack-rents' in town residential accommodation, improving of dwellings, fostering sanitation and encouraging home industry and legislation to boost the ownership of houses by their occupiers, this movement quickly gained a following. Some radicalised sections of the Home Rule coalition sympathised with the programme, though, like the labourers' demands, it found little support among the clergy and bourgeois elements, perhaps because urban housing was controlled by middle-class landlords who were often members of the National League.[48] The House League disappeared in mid-1886, a casualty of Gladstone's adoption of Home Rule, but like the labourers' question the issues it raised remained a potential time-bomb. Just as the main grievances of labourers were directed at an exploiting Catholic tenant farmer class, the urban dwellers often found themselves at odds with a rentier caste of Catholic shopkeepers and clergy. This was a foretaste of the *fin de siècle* attack upon graziers. The House League might, if it thrived, redress the rural bias of the Irish party, though at the cost of further complicating the ordering of priorities.[49] It is a matter of speculation about how politics might have developed if groups such as the labourers or the urban under class had established their agendas. It is unlikely that an all-class and still theoretically all-creed national movement could have accommodated a further widening of the platform. Parnell was aware of the difficulties and attempted once more to restore order in the movement by insisting at the first National League convention at Wicklow on 5 October 1885 that the party stood on the platform 'of a single plank, that plank being legislative independence'.[50]

Home Rule was not ignored by Conservatives. At Newport on 7 October Salisbury stated:

> Our first principle on which we have always gone is to extend to Ireland, as far as we can, all the institutions in this country ... [We look] upon the integrity of the Empire as a matter more important than almost any other political consideration that you can imagine, and

we could not regard with favour any proposal which directly or indirectly menaced that which is the first condition of England's position among the nations of the world.[51]

For him, the popular analogy of Austria-Hungary offered nothing which could form 'any substantial solution of the difficulties of the problem'. To ensure that his positive comments on institutional change were not misconstrued, he went on to reaffirm that 'to maintain the integrity of the Empire must undoubtedly be our first policy with regard to Ireland'.[52]

During the autumn there was no scarcity of palm-readers to decipher the ambiguities of political rhetoric, or a shortage of emissaries between Irish and British politicians. Healy's contacts with Henry Labouchere aimed at appropriating Parnell's role to a coterie of the Irish leader's lieutenants. Parnell, well aware of the pitfalls of too many cooks spoiling the stew, reopened his correspondence with Gladstone through Mrs O'Shea. She offered Gladstone a paper containing the Irish leader's ideas on self-government.[53] Entitled, 'A Proposed Constitution for Ireland', Parnell's scheme was the fullest Irish contribution on the topic for some years (see document 5). It bore similarities to earlier proposals and called for an Irish Parliament with virtually full control over domestic matters. Protestants were to be guaranteed representation in proportion to their numbers but denied anything amounting to a veto. This scheme would abolish the Lord Lieutenancy, but no law passed by the Irish Parliament would take effect without the assent of the Crown. Parnell did not resolve the question of Ireland's future representation at Westminster. While this was more of an early draft than a carefully structured constitution, it laid down effectively the division of powers and Ireland's financial liability. But it was more than any Liberal or Conservative leader was prepared to endorse. Gladstone's response, conveyed through the Liberal Chief Whip, was noncommittal. However, Parnell's suggestions contributed to the evolution of Gladstone's own ideas which he set down on paper on 14 November. This sketch of Irish self-government contained more safeguards than Parnell's scheme or those which could be found in the Government of Ireland bill in 1886, but it revealed how far Gladstone had moved beyond mere local government. There was an growing consensus that significant Irish self-government would be conceded by the new Parliament. That expectation, however, was something quite different from a concession of a full Dublin Parliament on the model outlined by Parnell. Irish ambitions continued to have a key place in campaign speeches; Home Rule in some form took on more definite shape in the mind of the electorate than at any earlier moment. Assertions in

1886 that the issue had not been aired during the general election were not wholly accurate. Few Liberals and scarcely any Conservatives openly supported what became known as Home Rule. Successful Liberal election addresses reveal that approximately a hundred made no reference to the Irish question and only fourteen stated a readiness to concede the country legislative independence.[54] Many candidates from both British parties, though, offered a broad endorsement of extended responsible institutions of an undefined nature.

Much hinged on the outcome of the general election. On 21 November Parnell issued a manifesto calling upon the Irish in Britain to vote against all but a handful of Liberal and Radical candidates.[55] Three days later polling commenced. When balloting ended on 9 December, Liberals had amassed 335 seats, Conservatives 249 and Home Rulers 86. Efforts by the Irish Loyal and Patriotic Union to undermine Parnellism in Ireland were in vain. Parnellites won 85 of 103 constituencies, including 17 – a majority of one – in Ulster. In the whole of the southern provinces the 2 seats allotted to Trinity College eluded them. T. P. O'Connor's victory in the Scotland Division of Liverpool brought the Parnellite total to 86. Ireland's party preferences had been heard at the polls. Impressive though the triumph was, it was yet more meaningful as a measure of how completely Parnellism had become a party of social integration and confirmed the pattern of political alignment along a confessional axis. This picture had been evident since the early 1870s, but expansion of the electorate and the elimination of small boroughs etched it in stone. Priests played a major role in the selection of candidates. Archbishop Walsh reported of the men selected in his diocese: 'all are Catholics, I asked to have this so', despite Dublin being one of the few places with a substantial Protestant presence.[56] In Ulster the party deliberately sought to gain a monopoly of the Catholic vote irrespective of the impact this had for winning the adhesion of Protestants.[57] Important though the election was, Brian Walker's useful analysis exaggerates its impact on polarisation which pre-dates this time.[58] The effect of the Irish vote on British constituencies was less clear. Some alleged that between twenty-five and forty Tory seats were held at Parnell's behest, but such estimates came almost entirely from Liberals and Parnellites. Few Conservatives shared this opinion and it is doubtful whether outside the constituency won by O'Connor Liberals were defeated in more half a dozen places because of the Irish vote.[59] At the conclusion of the balloting no party had an outright majority. Tory and Irish numbers exactly equalled the Liberal total but this combination could not hope to govern without Liberal complicity. Parnell's capacity to act as kingmaker depended on the rigidity of party allegiance.

The Home Rule bill, December 1885–June 1886

When the outcome of voting became clear Parnell let it be known that he expected 'the settlement to come from the Liberals'.[60] Cranbrook spoke for most Tories when he observed: 'Parnellite dictation is for us out of the question.'[61] Without much hesitation Salisbury decided against entering into negotiations to retain power, though Conservatives agreed not to resign before the new Parliament met. Gladstone, in private, had 'Ireland on the brain'.[62] On 17 December, via his son Herbert, the wider world had an inkling of his Home Rule disposition. As Arthur Balfour perceptively noted, though Gladstone was not 'committed publicly to Home Rule' he had 'corresponded with so many persons' in a self-government sense that 'it will be difficult for him now to withdraw, even if it were consistent with his character to do so'.[63] Once again there was no shortage of volunteer go-betweens. Parnell privately sought to commit Gladstone to some programme.[64] In the end, although there was much speculation, no compact was struck between the Liberals and Irish prior to the opening of Parliament on 12 January and nothing resembling a definitive notion of Home Rule emerged. Spencer's papers afford a revealing glimpse of the tangled web of rumours that abounded even within Gladstone's circle.[65]

On 26 January the government announced an intention to reintroduce coercion legislation to replace that which had lapsed the previous summer. Following defeat on a non-Irish vote, Salisbury resigned on 28 January and Gladstone returned to office. He was summoned by the Queen on 29 January and formally assumed office on 3 February on the very restricted pledge 'to examine whether it is or is not practicable to comply with the desire ... for the establishment ... of a legislative body, to sit in Dublin, and to deal with Irish as distinguished from imperial affairs'.[66] Few people doubted that some concession to Ireland was in the pipeline, but it was widely believed that this would probably result in extended local government.[67] Indeed, by threatening a fully empowered Dublin Parliament – a sort of political bomb – Gladstone ensured that colleagues and opponents would happily accept advanced local government with perhaps a central board or some other 'national' organ at its apex. He linked the land and institutional questions, determining to treat them simultaneously. Before the situation evolved, however, the crisis of the Galway by-election interrupted. The vacancy arose from T. P. O'Connor's double election in Liverpool and Galway, and his decision to sit for the English constituency. Parnell made the Irish party accept Captain O'Shea as its candidate, and he was elected on 10 February. Throughout that month Gladstone worked on his proposals alone or in conjunction with a handful of advisors. He had given careful attention to colonial, especially the Canadian, models, but he did not consult either the Cabinet or the Irish party. On 22 February Lord Randolph Churchill addressed 10,000 Unionists in Belfast, using the phrase 'Ulster will fight; Ulster will be right'. Only on 25 February did Harcourt, whose support was critical, see 'a draft of the new Irish Land Bill he [Gladstone] has invented under a solemn promise that it shall not be shown to anyone, even to any of the Cabinet'.[68] On 7 March he received the first paper on Home Rule, which he greeted with derision. Harcourt, his son related, 'tells me that Gladstone's Home Rule Bill is utterly impracticable and keeps on calling him (G) "criminal lunatic"'.[69]

Relations inside the Cabinet did not improve. On 13 March the question of Ireland was raised by Chamberlain rather than Gladstone, who, apparently would have preferred to pass over it once again. From that time onwards the Cabinet was absorbed in heated disputes about the Irish proposals. On 15 March Chamberlain and Sir George Otto Trevelyan, a former Chief Secretary, submitted their resignations, but these were suspended for the time being. Between then and the introduction of the Home Rule bill on 8 April the government was in a continuous state of chaos, with threatened resignations and bitter recriminations. The Cabinet meeting of 26 March was for Harcourt 'by far the most disagreeable he had ever seen'.[70] Chamberlain and Trevelyan afterwards put their resignations into effect; two other Ministers threatened to join them.[71] Atavistic tribal loyalty, rather than shared beliefs, now kept Gladstone's reluctant crew together. Throughout the crisis Harcourt's position remained decisive. Had he resigned, Home Rule could not have proceeded, yet he was well known to be sceptical about it. Opponents had difficulty mobilising against the issue right up to the introduction of the bill because, as Derby noted, 'no one knows what the Ministerial scheme in its latest development is to be'.[72] Parnell was not privy to the bill's contents before early April.

Despite the inclement weather, huge crowds assembled outside the Palace of Westminster hours before the introduction of the bill on 8 April in hopes of catching a glimpse of chief participants. Reputedly as much as £1,000 was offered for the privilege of a spot in the visitors' gallery. The chamber itself 'was crammed to suffocation from floor to ceiling'.[73] Nothing detracted from the rapt attention Gladstone commanded through the whole of his 3-hour 25-minute speech outlining the scheme (see document 6). A Land Purchase bill followed on 16 April. The two proposals were intended to be taken as a package capable of bringing Irish grievances to an end. Certainly, the Home Rule proposal stood as a huge triumph, an unmistakable recognition of the Parnellite case; it also gave form to the moral vision of self-government. It was fashioned to achieve the reconciliation and co-operation visualised by the early federalists, then later by Butt and Parnell, though not, of course, by the bulk of Irish members or Catholics generally.[74]

The bill was not, in Gladstone's words, a finished proposal, but only relatively minor details were left open.[75] It would create an assembly in Dublin with 307 or 309 members, depending on whether the new organ decided to confer upon the Royal University two seats giving it parity with Trinity College. The new body was unicameral but divided into two orders which could choose to sit and vote separately. The first order would be made up of the 28 representative Irish peers currently in the House of Lords plus 75 members elected for ten years by voters who met the £25 franchise condition (a very restricted group in nineteenth-century Ireland). Membership would be restricted to men of considerable substance – they were required to have an income or to own property that brought in at least £200 a year, or to have capital of £4,000. The 28 peers would ultimately be replaced by members elected on the £25 franchise. A second order would have 204 or 206 members elected on the present parliamentary franchise. The Irish assembly's life would be a maximum of five years. If the orders decided to sit separately and disagreed over legislation, a disputed bill could not be passed before a dissolution or until three years had elapsed, whichever was the longer. The Irish body would be obliged to respect the prerogatives of the Crown. An Irish executive was to be responsible to the domestic legislature. The Viceroyalty was retained, but Catholics were no longer to be barred from the office. This assembly was to have authority over all areas not specifically excluded: 'Everything which is not excepted is confessed.'[76] Exclusions fell under three main headings: the powers of the Crown, defence, and foreign and colonial affairs. An Irish chamber could not unilaterally amend the Government of Ireland Act. No religion could be endowed or restraint placed upon confessional practices. Other prohibitions included legislating on the law of trade and navigation, coinage and legal tender, weights and measures, copyright and similar matters. The Royal Irish Constabulary would remain under imperial control for the time being. With minor limitations intended to protect current office-holders, the civil service and judiciary were to come under Irish authority immediately. Domestic revenue would be levied and collected by the new body, but custom duties were to be retained in imperial hands. Irish representation at Westminster was to cease.

The scheme was constructed in a way that was to enforce co-operation between the two Irelands, at least between a predominantly

Catholic rural bourgeoisie and a southern Protestant propertied class. In a constitutional sense the proposal had three important defects.[77] It failed to deal with the question of Irish representation at Westminster after Home Rule was implemented, taxation powers were not dealt with adequately and the bill did not establish a satisfactory justification for the continued supremacy of Westminster. In spite of these limitations it was the most satisfactory of the schemes proposed between then and 1912. Parnell's response on behalf of the Irish party endorsed the principle but he expressed reservations about four aspects: the Irish party was unhappy with, first, imperial retention of custom duties; second, the level of Ireland's financial contribution, third, the failure to turn over control of the constabulary; and fourth, separate voting by the two orders. 'Whatever maybe the fate of the measure', he told the House of Commons, 'the cause of Irish autonomy will have gained enormously in a way it never could otherwise have gained by the genius of the right hon. gentleman.'[78] Further deficiencies and omissions were highlighted during the debates. The most important of these were enumerated by Chamberlain who cited four conditions essential to modify his opposition to the measure. He demanded retention of Irish representation at Westminster, creation of a separate Ulster assembly, modification of the organisation and power of the first order and abandonment of the Land Purchase bill that had been introduced on 16 April.[79] In the plans of 1893 and 1912 all but the Ulster demand were met.

Arguments about the proposal took place at three fronts – in the House of Commons, through the press and opinion journals and at a series of public meetings mainly held during and after the Easter recess. It was quickly apparent that none of the principal groups had been carefully groomed for the debate. The Irish party had assembled an arsenal of points in favour of Irish autonomy but their exclusion from Gladstone's counsels did not allow them to construct a defence of this specific scheme. Liberals who opposed it were reluctant to mobilise against Gladstone or Home Rule while hope of reconciliation remained.[80] Conservatives, too, were not prepared for an effective attack upon the plan. Gladstonians, likewise, were not drilled to defend the measure, though in the early running they benefited from having a concrete proposal to put forward.

Although Irish institutional reform had been ventilated for some years, Gladstone's initiative went far beyond what anyone anticipated from a sitting government. Public discussion was important, especially after the bill's defeat in the House of Commons. *The Times* instigated a campaign against it and two volumes of anti-Home Rule correspondence were published.[81] W. E. H. Lecky's input took on considerable significance. Both Gladstone and the Parnellites were fond of referring to Lecky's historical studies of the late eighteenth century. But Lecky was an early recruit to the anti-Home Rule camp. He saw Home Rule and the Land League as inextricable linked. Establishment of an Irish Parliament, in his view, would establish a reign of terror where the forces of both democracy and communism would be rampant.[82] His letter to *The Times* published on 6 January contended that the liberty of the individual was more vital than representative institutions, setting the anti-Home Rule counter-attack on a firm intellectual plain. Lecky's intervention ensured that the argument could not be solely about the virtue of elective representative institutions and majoritarianism, but must take account of how these were employed. Lecky reflected the popular temper, observing in a letter published on 5 May:

> I do not believe – and I do not think the people of Great Britain will believe – that the government of Ireland can be safely entrusted to the National League – to priests and Fenians and Professional agitators supported by the votes of an ignorant peasantry, whose passions it has been for many years their main object to inflame.[83]

Nevertheless, between 8 April and 7 June the heart of the battle was waged in the House of Commons.

Discussions in the House of Commons can be broken into two segments. Before the Easter recess Liberal and Irish Unionists speakers occupied a considerable amount of parliamentary time. After the break other figures entered the debates, though overall the numbers of speakers was comparatively small, with individual addresses often being lengthy. During the first phase, participants, including Gladstone's opponents, paid tribute to his eloquence and most speeches were delivered in a moderate tone. This tone persisted, in part, in the second stage, but there was a tendency for Ulster Conservatives to be ill-tempered. However, in general, the dispute was conducted with decorum and without remarkably bad feeling, perhaps a surprise given the emotional temperature. Parnellites were much more active after the recess, focusing on refuting anti-Home Rule arguments. The second reading consumed fourteen nights and was a tutorial on the history of Ireland, recent political developments there, the nature of the British Constitution, concepts of liberty and representation, and the relative rights of minorities. Additionally, considerable attention was given to the forms of government elsewhere, including Norway–Sweden, Austria–Hungary, Canada and the United States. Home Rule's advocates laid out a case, the main lines of which were:

1. The Irish were a historic nationality aspiring to self-determina-

tion and this want was confirmed at the general election. Recognition of Ireland's nationality was felt to be deeply desired; granting it would solidify the connection with Britain presently based on force rather than consent.

2. Respect for the rule of law currently undermined in Ireland was contingent not merely upon good legislation but upon it being enacted by the appropriate persons. Westminster-made laws for purely Irish matters had failed and now it was essential to engage the people of Ireland in their own governance.

3. The menace of social disorder necessitated immediate action. Coercion was discredited and the only alternative was self-rule.

4. Alternatives like national councils or the central board scheme were not suitable because the Irish did not want them.

5. Questions such as education and, more urgently, land reform required an intermediate body in Ireland to protect the financial interest of the British taxpayer and Exchequer.

6. Removal of purely Irish business and Ireland's representatives from Westminster would enable Parliament to proceed efficiently with its proper functions.

7. This bill contained adequate safeguards for minority interests and ensured the supremacy of Parliament.

8. Intermediate concessions could not cure the disease infecting Anglo-Irish relations; Home Rule promised 'finality'.

Added to this list, Jonathan Parry offers the interesting observation that the Liberal party in 1886 was bound together by the recognition of the dignity and virtue of the common people. Support for Home Rule was a way of indicating that recognition.[84]

Opponents attempted to counter these points, making other arguments at the same time. Speakers objected to all or part of the Liberal–Parnellite version of Irish history and, while frequently accepting that Ireland had been misgoverned in the past, they held that this had now been corrected. Most also rejected the utility of foreign analogies. Some denied that the Irish were of a different nationality, or, if they were, that the proposed form of self-government was suitable or could be granted without injuring British and imperial interests. Others contended that as Ireland was represented – indeed over-represented – at Westminster in relation to population and especially with respect to wealth, London-made laws were not alien. Nearly all rejected the contention that there was a stark choice between coercion and Home Rule, some urging the eradication of social disorder by a more thoroughgoing application of the law. A number of speakers concentrated on the principle of taxation without representation if Ireland ceased to send Members to the Westminster

Parliament. Other themes included fears of separation, concerns about turning Ireland over to the National League and the threat to property. Only sometimes enunciated but always present was the commonly held belief that 'Home Rule meant Rome Rule', a slogan expressive of the idea that Irish Catholics were obedient to the dictates of their Church. A few extreme opponents suggested that the Irish were unfit for self-rule.

The bill's specifics, notably the financial provisions and the future authority of Parliament, drew anti-Home Rule fire. Opponents insisted that a constitutional measure of this complexity and significance required the verdict of the electorate, observing that nothing of the sort proposed had been before the voters in 1885. Most speakers declared themselves in favour of reform in Ireland and stated a willingness to extend responsible self-government by way of elective local institutions. Strengths in the anti-Home Rule case included the suddenness of the proposal, doubts about so large a constitutional change and refusal to accept the polarity of Gladstonian self-government or coercion. The primary weakness rested on the reluctance to recognise the force of national identity or the legitimacy of the electoral mandate for Home Rule. According to the opposition, the electoral verdict lacked validity because of the inflated Parnellite numbers and widespread intimidation.

There was one very large consideration – the future position of the loyal Protestant minority.[85] Increasingly, this question dominated discussions. In the estimation of some speakers guarantees in the bill were inadequate and requirements specified for the first order were so low that in practice it too would be dominated by Parnellites. Gladstone pronounced himself willing to listen to ideas concerning Ulster, though in private he had not been sympathetic to arguments for giving the province or part of it special status. During his introductory speech he stated: 'I cannot allow it to be said that a Protestant minority in Ulster or elsewhere, is to rule the question at large for Ireland. ... But I think that the Protestant minority should have its wishes considered to the utmost practicable extent in any form which they may assume.' He then called for an 'unprejudiced discussion of Ulster options'.[86] Those who demanded the exclusion of Ulster based their arguments on four propositions: its different history, the existence of a localised Protestant plurality, the wishes of the people there and the region's greater economic vitality and integration into the British and Atlantic markets. Home Rulers effectively refuted the first three points and tried to ease fears that a Dublin regime would discriminate against any portion of the people or their economic interests. They argued that it was impossible to define a Protestant Ulster; a majority of seats were held by Home Rulers and respective numbers of Protestants and Catholics were nearly equal. Parnellites showed that Ulster was not even the most prosperous province.

On the other side, William Johnson, MP for Belfast South, pleaded that the 'Protestants of Ulster would be dominated and tyrannised' and pledged that 'the dictates of that Irish Parliament would be resisted by the people of Ulster at the point of the bayonet'.[87] A fundamental difficulty about an Ulster solution was the novelty of the demand and an absence of enthusiasm for one by Irish Unionists. Doubts were cast on the idea by Irish anti-Home Rulers themselves. On 9 April David Plunkett, MP for the University of Dublin, stated: 'the position of Ulster … is a matter of so little importance that it may be thrown over altogether.'[88] Colonel Edward Saunderson, MP for Armagh North, declared on 12 April against Ulster exclusion, stating: 'we are prepared and determined to stand and fall, for weal or woe, with every loyal man who lives in Ireland.'[89] The principal advocates of an 'Ulster solution' were British, not Irish Unionists.

While opposing special status for Ulster, some Parnellites were alive to the bill's utility to Protestants. William O'Brien saw in Gladstone's proposal 'a most marvellous plan for re-creating society out of the ruins almost in Ireland – aye, and of giving to a caste that is fallen and helpless such a chance as it never had before, and never could have anticipated, and, I must say as it scarcely deserves'.[90] John Redmond three days later observed that that 'if any Protestants wanted protection, they were not those in Ulster, but those in the South and West who were in such a miserable minority'.[91] William Abraham, a Methodist sitting for County Limerick, saw in the present religious balance sufficient power 'to prevent any one of them from being tyrannical or illiberal' and, by implication, that the loss of Ulster Protestants would disturb this equilibrium.[92] On 7 June Parnell addressed the question, citing the need for Ulster Protestants to be included in order to defend minority and Liberal Catholic educational interests, to secure the protection of the 400,000 Protestants in the other provinces and because 'we cannot give up a single Irishman'.[93] Parnell, of course, had a different beginning point for his national sentiment; his sprang from what George Boyce, as noted in chapter 1, describes as a colonial identity (see p. 16). By 1885 he was the sole Protestant left in the parliamentary party, though a handful were selected to sit in the new House of Commons in order to reduce the appearance of being a Catholic political group. National identity had become an ethnic rather than a Western European-type nationalist movement. For Parnell, the Home Rule proposal with the inclusion of Ulster held a promise of driving it back onto a course congenial to Protestants such as Butt and himself.

In the long term Gladstone's myopia about Ulster haunted a settlement, but in 1886 this was a minor stumbling block to the passage of his measure. It would have been difficult then to formulate an 'Ulster solution' in the face of Irish party opposition and an absence of a concerted demand for one from Irish Unionists. The Home Rule measure was a vital stage in the development of an Ulster conscious-ness, but the bill could not be expected to anticipate this develop-ment. Nor could Gladstone – who, like Parnell, viewed Home Rule as a means of enforcing intra-communal co-operation – have spon-sored an Ulster exclusion that must defeat his purpose. Paradoxi-cally, Home Rule in 1886 widened the ethnic division.

The second strand of Gladstone's package – the Land Purchase bill – roused greater dissatisfaction and was soon withdrawn. Abandon-ment of the scheme weakened the logic of Gladstone's position, though it was not the reason for the failure of the Government of Ire-land bill. From at least March 1885 it was evident that Home Rule would have immense difficulty surviving. Gladstone held the initial advantage of surprise and his opponents required time to coalesce against the proposal. Gladstone's tactical advantage was ephemeral. His burden was to persuade MPs to accept his plan and neither a majority in the House of Commons nor public opinion was won over. Opposition came from four major centres – Conservatives, dissident Liberals, Irish Unionists and Nonconformists. They were linked by fears of Catholicism, concern for the impact of Home Rule on the empire, mistrust of Parnellites and dislike of the specifics of Glad-stone's bill. L. P. Curtis, jun. suggests that the episode marked a divi-sion between Anglo-Saxonist's who accepted a view of inherent Irish racial inferiority and environmentalists who adopted the position that the failings of the people were attributable to specific conditions and, if these were improved, Catholics would behave much like Eng-lishmen. He sees the outcome of the debate as a triumph of the Anglo-Saxonist view prevalent among the middle and upper classes who were active participants in politics.[94] The speeches of Chamber-lain, Hartington and Salisbury do not suggest that Ireland should permanently be denied self-governing institutions on racial or any other grounds, but that these should be constructed along different lines from Gladstone's plan. Chamberlain and others strongly advo-cated local self-government which from a racist perspective was as objectionable as Home Rule.

Conservative and Liberal dissidents were careful to link opposi-tion to Home Rule with acceptance of other types of Irish reform. Sal-isbury, in an important speech during the crisis, stated that he had no wish to disparage Catholicism: 'I offer no opposition in principle to the idea of that local government being extended to Ireland, if only you are careful first that it is not a step to something very different, and secondly, that the interests of minorities are protected.' Yet he cautioned:

> confidence depends upon the people in whom you are to confide. You would not confide free representative institutions to the Hottentots, for instance ... my alternative policy is that Parliament should enable the government of England to govern Ireland. Apply that recipe honestly, consistently, and resolutely for 20 years and at the end of that time you will find that Ireland will be fit to accept any gifts in the way of local government or repeal of coercion laws that you may wish to give her.[95]

Lord Hartington, speaking for right-wing Liberals, followed a conciliatory course:

> [I can] see no reason why they should limit themselves to opposition to Mr Gladstone's bills, or refuse to indicate their willingness to support safe and well-considered measures for the satisfaction of what is reasonable in the Irish demand. All Liberals have, I think, pledged themselves to support an extension of local self-government in Ireland on lines similar to those which may be adopted for the rest of the United Kingdom.[96]

Parry points out that those Liberals who opposed Home Rule saw Gladstone's measure as a contravention of the Liberal myth of 'national and imperial integration under the rule of law, and the responsibility of the propertied for the maintenance of order and extension of morality'.[97] On 27 May at a special meeting of his supporters Gladstone stated that no major alterations would be offered but that the second reading was only to be a test of opinion.[98] Defeat by only 341 to 311 in the early hours of 8 June could be counted a moral triumph. Even those who wanted Home Rule, dismissed many of its specifics as unworkable.

The loose drafting of the measure along with the presumed veto of the House of Lords has led to speculation concerning Gladstone's motives. What the peers might have done was not put to the test: because they rejected the bill of 1893 does not demonstrate that they would have done the same in 1886, though this may well have been the case. In 1886 the capacity of the Upper House to resist the popular assembly was less finely developed. Gladstone made crucial errors in the handling of Home Rule. James Bryce, in retrospect, distinguished four major mistakes: first, Gladstone's failure to allow the country and even most of his Cabinet colleagues to know his intentions, laying himself open to the charge of changing his principles; second, Herbert Gladstone's injudicious flying of the 'Hawarden Kite'; third, introducing the proposal too early in the new Parliament instead of preparing the ground; and fourth, when it became apparent that the bill was in trouble, he should have admitted that the country required more time to consider the subject.[99]

Conclusion

Why did Gladstone opt for a large measure in 1886? Opponents said he was an old man in a hurry. No doubt age was a factor, though Gladstone was influenced by two realisations – the democratically expressed opinion of Ireland and the need to do something that would appeal to the imagination of the Irish. At the same time he seems according to T. A. Jenkins, to have needed a great 'national' problem requiring resolution in order to justify retention of the Liberal leadership.[100] Richard Shannon points out Gladstone's conviction of the moral superiority of the masses against the selfish classes. Mixed into this was his 'distinction between lower opportunism which follows public opinion and a "higher insight" which is providentially derived and accredits its bearer with the ways and means of forming and directing the public mind'.[101] He had developed an appreciation of Parnellite moderation and came to see advantages in making the Irish shoulder the burden of running the country. They, he reasoned, should carry the odium for administration now falling upon Great Britain. In 1886 only two of the eight groups outlined in chapter 1 (see p. 13) concurred in the Home Rule scheme – Catholics in Ireland and, more incompletely, a major political group in Great Britain: the Liberal party. Gladstone's action set the perimeters for all subsequent discussion of Irish matters. At the same time his proposal solidified the position of both the Irish party and Parnell. By first initiating the bill and then sticking with it he cut the ground from under Parnell's rivals.

There was another frequently neglected dimension to the episode. Parnellites in the session up to 8 April continued to perform in the House of Commons much as they had left off in 1885. They were vigorous participants in parliamentary affairs, often demanding concessions to Ireland or equalisation of treatment between the two countries which seemed to contradict the principle of Home Rule.[102] Parnellite MPs were divided internally on only sixteen, mainly minor, divisions.[103] Usually the Irish party could be found affirming Radical or progressive measures. Detailed analysis of voting patterns in the House of Commons reveals a congruence of outlook between Home Rulers and progressive Liberals. The crisis polarised the political nation along ideological rather than class lines.[104] The impact of the episode was important for crystallising anti-Irish and anti-Catholic prejudice in Britain, though, of course, it did not create this sentiment.[105]

Notes

1   Lewis Harcourt's Journal, 8 April 1886, Harcourt Papers, Bodleian Library, Oxford, MS 378.

2   A. V. Dicey, *England's Case Against Home Rule* (new impression; Richmond, Surrey, 1973), p. 32.

3   See, Thomas William Heyck, *The Dimensions of British Radicalism: The Case of Ireland 1874–95* (Urbana, Chicago and London, 1974), pp. 151–77.

4   See, John D. Fair, *British Interparty Conferences: A Study of the Procedure of Conciliation in British Politics, 1867–1921* (Oxford, 1979), pp. 51–5.

5   Andrew Jones, *The Politics of Reform, 1884* (Cambridge, 1971), p. 25; see, B. M. Walker, *Ulster Politics: The Formative Years, 1868–86* (Belfast, 1989), p. 177.

6   Joseph Chamberlain to Sir Charles Dilke, 12 September 1884, Sir Charles Dilke Papers, British Library, MS 43875

7   Quoted in T. A. Jenkins, *Gladstone, Whiggery and the Liberal Party 1874–1886* (Oxford, 1988), p. 116.

8   C. H. D. Howard (ed.), *Joseph Chamberlain: A Political Memoir* (London, 1953), pp. 136–7.

9   Quoted in Mark Tierney, *Croke of Cashel: The Life of Archbishop Thomas William Croke 1821–1902* (Dublin, 1976), p. 172.

10   C. H. D. Howard (ed.), 'Documents Relating to the Irish "Central Board" Scheme, 1884–5', *Irish Historical Studies*, VII (March 1955), p. 240.

11   *Ibid.*, p. 242.

12   *The Times*, 10 January 1885.

13   *Ibid.*, 22 January 1885.

14   *Ibid.*

15   Quoted in Peter Gordon (ed.), *The Red Earl: The Papers of the Fifth Earl Spencer, 1835–1910* (Northampton, 1981), I, pp. 301–3.

16   Quoted in Stephen Gwynn and Gertrude Tuckwell, *The Life of the Rt. Hon. Sir Charles Dilke* (London, 1917), II, p. 129; A. B. Cooke and J. R. Vincent (eds), *Lord Carlingford's Journal: Reflections of a Cabinet Minister 1885* (Oxford, 1971), pp. 97–8 (1 May); see, also, David Nicholls, *The Lost Prime Minister: A Life of Sir Charles Dilke* (London, 1995), pp. 167–8.

17   Quoted in C. H. D. Howard, 'Joseph Chamberlain, Parnell and the Irish "Central Board" Scheme, 1884–5, *Irish Historical Studies*, VII (September 1953), p. 344.

18   Dudley Bahlman (ed.), *The Diary of Sir Edward Walter Hamilton* (Oxford, 1972), II, p. 852.

19   For the controversy see, J. L. Garvin, *The Life of Joseph Chamberlain* (London, 1932), I, pp. 545–65.

20   See, Walter L. Arnstein, *The Bradlaugh Case. A Study in Late Victorian Opinion and Politics* (Oxford, 1965), pp. 201–24.

21   Sir Rowland Winn's Memorandum, 2 March 1885, Salisbury Papers, Hatfield House.

22   Sir Michael Hicks Beach to Lord Salisbury, 7 May 1885, *ibid.*: (copy), St Aldwyn Papers, Gloucestershire Record Office, PCC/30.

23 *The Times*, 21 May 1885.

24 *Ibid.*

25 Henry W. Lucy, *A Diary of Two Parliaments: The Gladstone Parliament 1880–1885* (London, 1886), p. 481.

26 Lord Carnarvon to Lord Salisbury, 16 June 1885, Carnarvon Papers, British Library, MS 60825.

27 Cardinal Manning to Carnarvon, 19 June 1885, *ibid.*, MS 60829.

28 'Memorandum of Interview with Parnell', *ibid.*; Sir Andrew Hardinage, *The Life of Henry Howard Molyneux Herbert, Fourth Earl of Carnarvon, 1831–1890* (London, 1925), III, pp. 178–81.

29 Quoted in Howard (ed.), *Political Memoir*, pp. 154–6.

30 *Leeds Mercury*, 15 July 1885.

31 *The Nation*, 18 July 1885.

32 Katharine O'Shea to Grosvenor 21 July 1885, W. E. Gladstone Papers, British Library, MS 44316.

33 Katharine O'Shea to Gladstone, 5 August 1885, *ibid.* MS 56446.

34 Gladstone to Katharine O'Shea (copy), 8 August 1885, *ibid.* MS 44269.

35 C. C. O'Brien, *Parnell and his Party, 1880–90* (corrected impression; Oxford, 1964), p. 133; James Loughlin, *Gladstone, Home Rule and the Ulster Question 1882–93* (Dublin, 1987), p. 30; Walker, *Ulster Politics*, p. 206.

36 Loughlin, *Gladstone*, p. 31.

37 *The Freeman's Journal*, 17 August 1885.

38 Healy defended the Ashbourne Act against its critics. See Frank Callanan, *T. M. Healy* (Cork, 1996), p. 109.

39 *The Freeman's Journal*, 24 August 1885.

40 *The Times*, 25 August 1885.

41 *Ibid.*

42 *Ibid.*, 2 September 1885.

43 *Ibid.*

44 *The Freeman's Journal*, 9 September 1885.

45 *The Times*, 19 September 1885.

46 *Ibid.*, 29 September 1885; *The Freeman's Journal*, 1 October 1885.

47 *Newry Reporter*, 26 November 1885.

48 James O'Shea, *Priest, Politics and Society in Post-Famine Ireland: A Study of County Tipperary 1850–1891* (Dublin, 1983), pp. 124, 132.

49 A brief consideration of the House League can be found in Loughlin, *Gladstone*, pp. 44–6.

50 *The Times*, 6 October 1885.

51 *Ibid.*, 8 October 1885.

52 *Ibid.*

53 J. L. Hammond, *Gladstone and the Irish Nation* (new impression; London, 1964), pp. 422–3.

54 Lord Edrington, 'Liberal Election Addresses', *Nineteenth Century*, XIX (April 1886), pp. 606–19.

55 Quoted in full in Alan O'Day and John Stevenson (eds), *Irish Historical Documents since 1800* (Dublin, 1992), pp. 106–8.

56 Quoted in Emmet Larkin, *The Roman Catholic Church and the*

Creation of the Modern Irish State, 1878–1886 (Dublin, 1975), p. 341.

57   Walker, *Ulster Politics*, p. 224.

58   *Ibid.*, p. 266; B. M. Walker, *Dancing to History's Tune, History, Myth and Politics in Ireland* (Belfast, 1996), pp. 15–33.

59   See, Alan O'Day, 'The Political Representation of the Irish in Great Britain, 1850–1940', in Geoffrey Alderman, John Leslie and Klaus Pollmann (eds), *Comparative Studies on Governments and Non-Dominant Ethnic Groups in Europe, 1850–1940: Governments, Ethnic Groups and Political Representation*, IV (Aldershot and New York, 1993), pp. 56–8.

60   *The Freeman's Journal*, 7 December 1885.

61   Nancy E. Johnson (ed.), *The Diary of Gathorne Hardy, later Lord Cranbrook, 1866–1892: Political Selections* (Oxford, 1981), p. 584 (20 December).

62   Diary, 12 December 1885, Sir Edward Hamilton Papers, British Library, MS 48643.

63   Arthur Balfour to Lord Salisbury, 23 December 1885, quoted in Robin Harcourt Williams (ed.), *Salisbury–Balfour Correspondence: Letters Exchanged Between the Third Marquess of Salisbury and his Nephew Arthur James Balfour 1869–1892* (Hertford, 1988), p. 127.

64   Alan O'Day, *Parnell and the First Home Rule Episode, 1884–87* (Dublin, 1986), pp. 125–35.

65   Peter Gordon (ed.), *The Red Earl: The Papers of the Fifth Earl Spencer 1835–1910* (Northampton, 1986), II, pp. 79–104.

66   Quoted in John Morley, *The Life of William Ewart Gladstone* (London, 1903), III, p. 292.

67   See, A. B. Cooke and J. R. Vincent, 'Ireland and Party Politics, 1885–7 (II)', *Irish Historical Studies*, XVI (March 1969), pp. 321–2.

68   Lewis Harcourt's Journal, 25 February 1886, Harcourt Papers, MS 377.

69   *Ibid.*, 8 March 1886.

70   *Ibid.*, 26 March 1886.

71   *Ibid.*, 29, 30 March 1886.

72   Diary, 7 April 1886, John Vincent (ed.), *The Later Derby Diaries. Home Rule, Liberal Unionism, and Aristocratic Life in Late Victorian England* (Bristol, 1981), p. 66.

73   Harcourt Journal, 8 April 1886.

74   See, Terence Denman, *A Lonely Grave: The Life and Death of William Redmond* (Dublin, 1995), pp. 35–6; for a version of this point phrased slightly differently, see, Callanan, *T. M. Healy*, p. 113.

75   *Parliamentary Debates [PD]*, 304 (1886), cc. 1036–85.

76   *Ibid.*, c. 1065.

77   Vernon Bogdanor, *Devolution* (Oxford, 1979), pp. 19–24.

78   *PD*, 304 (1886), cc. 1124–34.

79   *Ibid.*, cc. 1190–1.

80   See, Vincent (ed.), *Later Derby Diaries*, pp. 66–9, especially entry for 29 May 1886.

81   *Home Rule. A Reprint from* The Times *of Recent Articles and Letters* and *Home Rule. A Reprint from* The Times *of Articles and Letters, in Continuation of the Previous Volume* (London, 1886).

82 Lecky's stance can be traced in Donal McCartney, *W. E. H. Lecky Historian and Politician 1838–1903* (Dublin, 1994), pp. 96, 114–36.

83 Quoted in *ibid.*, p. 121.

84 Jonathan Parry, *Democracy and Religion: Gladstone and the Liberal Party, 1867–1874* (Cambridge, 1986), p. 446.

85 For an important treatment of this dimension see, Loughlin, *Gladstone*, pp. 123–71.

86 *PD*, 304 (1886), cc. 1053–4.

87 *Ibid.*, cc. 1231–2.

88 *Ibid.*, cc. 1334–5.

89 *Ibid.*, cc. 1335–6.

90 *Ibid.*, 305, cc. 631–2.

91 *Ibid.*, c. 970.

92 *Ibid.*, c. 1247.

93 *Ibid.*, cc. 1175, 1179–80.

94 L. P. Curtis, jun, *Anglo-Saxons and Celts: A Study of Anti-Irish Prejudice in Victorian England* (Bridgeport, CT, 1968), pp. 98–103.

95 *The Times*, 17 May 1886.

96 Quoted in Bernard Holland, *The Life of Spencer Compton, 8th Duke of Devonshire* (London, 1911), II, pp. 157–8.

97 Jonathan Parry, *The Rise and Fall of Liberal Government in Victorian Britain* (New Haven and London, 1993), p. 297.

98 Hammond, *Gladstone*, p. 488.

99 H. A. L. Fisher, *James Bryce* (New York, 1927), I, pp. 216–17.

100 Jenkins, *Gladstone*, pp. 247–9.

101 Richard Shannon, 'Gladstone and Home Rule', in Lord Blake, *Ireland After the Union* (Oxford, 1989), pp. 50–1.

102 O'Day, *Parnell and the First Home Rule Episode*, pp. 157–66, 170–7.

103 William C. Lubenow, *Parliamentary Politics and the Home Rule Crisis: The British House of Commons in 1886* (Oxford, 1988), p. 155.

104 *Ibid.*, p. 319.

105 See, James Loughlin, *Ulster Unionism and British National Identity since 1885* (London and New York, 1995), pp. 23, 28.

5

Unionist counter-offensive, 1886–92

The phrase Home Rule will be used invariably in these pages to denote any scheme or policy which involves the establishment of a Parliament in Ireland, together with an Executive Government responsible to that Parliament. ... The question of Home Rule has no relation whatever to the question of Local Government. ... This distinction is most important, for it at once enables a speaker to put an end to the use of 'ambiguous phrases'. People write and talk of letting Ireland 'manage her own affairs', or speak of 'Irish autonomy', whenever they do, it is a sure sign either that they possess no clear ideas on the subject, or that they wish to confuse the minds of their hearers. (*The* [Liberal Unionist] *Speaker's Handbook on the Irish Question*)[1]

Introduction

Following the defeat of the Home Rule bill, the Cabinet decided to appeal to the country. It was an intense general election marred by vituperation. Parnell devoted his entire efforts to the British constituencies, seeking to reassure voters on Home Rule. His lieutenants also attempted to persuade British electors of Home Rule's virtues. Parliament was dissolved on 26 June with polling taking place between 1 and 17 July. Conservatives won 317 seats, Liberal Unionists 77, while the Gladstonians were reduced to 191 and the Irish party held 85. The swing against the Liberals was 5.7 per cent. Unionism won the parliamentary contest, but the position at Westminster was exaggerated; the popular vote was less lopsided and evidence suggested that many Liberal voters had abstained. There was ample reason for Home Rulers to hope the verdict would be reversed at the next general election. By-elections between 1886 and 1892 lent credence to optimism; the Unionist majority fell from 116 to 66. The Liberals, however, had to overcome a weakness of newspaper support. The events of 1886 caused a shift of editorial backing, especially in Scotland.[2]

The Unionist coalition was a marriage of convenience, its future problematic. Events in 1886 settled several matters. Parnellism had no realistic alternative to co-operation with the Gladstonians; the semblance of Irish party independence evaporated when the GOM took up Home Rule. Home Rule now possessed a firm definition, though the specifics of any later plan were not necessarily etched in stone. Alternatives to a Dublin Parliament – local government, denominational education and land reform – remained plausible Irish policies but the likelihood of Ireland's Catholics being satisfied with these alone lessened immeasurably. Ulster's status had been raised, albeit tentatively, threatening to complicate a future self-government settlement. The Irish party could count on the backing of the Catholic multitudes who were firmly in the grip of middle-class leaders. Alternative versions of the self-government ideal would have to await another day. But, Catholic politics by 1886 reached the outer limits of its appeal in Ireland and the Irish party could not enlarge its numbers in the House of Commons. The Butt–Parnell strategy of massing Irish forces to put pressure on Liberals was inverted. Liberals now insisted that the Parnellite infantry fall in line and augment its own thinned ranks. Another strand of the old approach was threadbare as well. The electoral power of the Irish in Britain was shown to be hollow. After 1886 four interrelated questions arose: what did Home Rule mean? were there attractive alternatives to a Dublin Parliament? to what extent were political alignments capable of being revised? and how decisive was the role of particular personalities?

The 1886 general election

British leaders' statements about Home Rule and Irish reform during the electoral campaign were indicative of their understanding of the issues and of their future intentions. Liberals, Conservatives and even the Parnellites in the post-1882 period agreed on the need for change in Ireland. Gladstone's Home Rule bill split the political world into two ideological camps, but it did not break the consensus on Irish reform. Tory spokesmen condemned Gladstone's plan, but key figures were insistent that Irish change would proceed. W. H. Smith's election address was typical. He opposed Home Rule but pointed out the necessity of transformation in the pattern of land ownership, the need for local government and the desirability of government aid to relieve Irish poverty.[3] Similarly, Salisbury observed that Conservatives had no wish to govern Ireland by coercion, stressing his desire for good relations with Catholics. He reiterated the Tories' favoured remedy, local government. The Conservative leader believed 'that the extension of local government to Ireland would be a great advantage ... and would have the effect, though I fear the time would be a long one of training the Irish gradually into those habits of material forbearance which are necessary for a civilised community'.[4] Although Salisbury's words were not identical to Parnell's statements the previous year, their respective outlooks were not irreconcilable. Hicks Beach's election address underlined the Conservative view that 'it should be our guiding principle to equalise as far as possible political privileges or disabilities throughout the United Kingdom'.[5] Lord John Manners urged: 'what is wanted is peace, repose, and the development of industries other than that of agriculture; and those boons can only be obtained through a just and impartial administration of the law by a government prepared to avail itself of every opportunity to foster nascent native enterprise.[6] Tory opinions were sufficiently similar to Parnell's to reduce the gap between what the Irish demanded and what Conservatives might deliver.

Liberal Unionists, too, decried the Home Rule proposal but were at pains to emphasise loyalty to the ideas of liberalism, supporting the now standard panacea: responsible local government. There were distinctions within the Unionist camp, but overlaying these was a generally shared acceptance of change. Unionism differed from Gladstone (numerous Liberals were sympathetic to the reformism of their opponents) on the precise remedies that should be tried and also on the timing of their introduction. Most were anxious to concede a measure of land purchase. They were not hostile to institutional changes and something like a Dublin assembly might even be tried at a future time. Unionists, however, rejected Gladstone's scheme. At the same time most had grave misgivings about Parnellism, pointing out the current disturbed state of the country. Unionists characteristically accepted the need for reform but wanted it administered in dosages prescribed by themselves. They shared a view that reform must not be seen as the consequence of giving way to Parnellite pressure either in the House of Commons or in Ireland.

Gladstonians, in contrast, took less interest in alternative Irish reforms, indeed, frequently spoke out against land purchase, but shared a common adherence to some measure of Home Rule. Enthusiasm for Home Rule often ran in inverse proportion to dislike of land purchase. Liberals were not uniform about what they meant by Home Rule or the powers an Irish regime might exercise. Gladstone's bill gave Home Rule a shape, but by the time of the second reading he insisted that the specifics were open to further consideration. Early in the campaign Gladstone asserted that 'our plan is that Ireland should under well-considered conditions, transact her own affairs'.[7] Among Home Rule's benefits, he stressed, first, the consolidation of the unity of the empire, and a great addition to its strength; second, the stoppage of a heavy, constant, and demoralising waste of the public treasury; third, the abatement and gradual extinction of ignoble feuds in Ireland, and the development of her resources which experience shows to be the natural consequence of free orderly government; fourth, the redemption of the honour of Great Britain from a stigma fastened upon her, almost from time immemorial, in respect to Ireland, by the judgement of the whole civilised world; and lastly, the restoration of Parliament to its dignity and efficiency, and the regular progress of the business of the country. His purposes reflected a mixture of moral and pragmatic outcomes that were gauged, mainly by British interests. He pointed out that the principle only, not the specifics of his bill, was the issue before electors. Gladstone initially linked Home Rule and land purchase but in the face of the unpopularity of the latter among Liberals he announced 'only one survival is, I think certain, that is the survival of the principle and policy of self-government for Ireland'.[8] His views on the Ulster difficulty also showed development. Whereas he had firmly rejected any sub-species of Home Rule within Ireland, he now concluded that he had an open mind on proposals to resolve the problem, though he could not countenance separation of the province from the rest of the country.

Orthodox Liberals remained loyal to the principle of Home Rule but expressed reservations about the provisions of the recent scheme. Sir Henry Campbell-Bannerman's address observed that the plan before Parliament had been 'imperfect and open to criticism in some of its details ... Her Majesty's Government, if called upon to deal with the question, will have perfect freedom in determining the particular methods by which they should seek the attainment of the main object of their policy'.[9] Lord Rosebery, the Foreign Secretary, supported the principle only, insisting that Ulster's position required careful consideration, promising that 'the government will take into their utmost consideration the claims of Ulster and will endeavour to make such arrangements as will satisfy Ulster'.[10] The Chancellor, Hugh Childers, was more guarded yet, stating that Ireland's representation at Westminster must be retained for all business and that he supported 'only a limited form of local legislature'.[11] During the campaign Childers further elaborated his view that 'the legislative body to be constituted in Ireland would not be a Parliament, and to that he adhered distinctly'.[12] According to him, the Westminster Parliament would be able to repeal any legislation creating an Irish assembly. Childers demanded that there must be adequate protection for property. George Shaw-Lefevre declared: 'on some details, particularly the question of excluding the Irish members from Westminster … he had not altogether agreed with the proposals of the government',[13] while John Morley entertained 'grave doubts whether any scheme will be found for introducing that principle of full and continuous representation for all purposes into any satisfactory settlement of the Irish difficulty'.[14] Divergence among Liberals was considerable and beneath the surface many did not like it in any form. Stuart Rendel thought: 'we must go to the country on the Gladstone ticket, say as little as we can about Ireland and as much about the Church and land.'[15]

Differences over land purchase were even wider. Lord Spencer was 'certain the Irish land question cannot be settled without giving Home Rule. I am equally certain that Home Rule will not pacify Ireland unless some solution is found on the land question.'[16] Childers initially wanted to use the whole of Irish revenue as security for land purchase.[17] Soon afterwards, he opposed the issue altogether.[18] Shaw-Lefevre spoke 'in favour of a more limited application of land purchase'.[19] Dilke opposed the issue and declared that it would never be carried by the Liberal party.[20] In the aftermath of the election Harcourt concluded: 'you never can or will have Home Rule *with* a Land Bill. You may perhaps have it without. The Land Bill did, and always will, kill the Home Rule measure.'[21]

Parnellites had a simpler task, but they were inconsistent about what they meant by Home Rule as well. Some gave unqualified support to Gladstone's scheme, others only to the idea of Home Rule. At Portsmouth Parnell attempted to distinguish Gladstone's plan from Grattan's Parliament, conveniently overlooking his earlier pledge never to ask for less than its restitution. 'The statutory legislature which we have accepted is not', he explained, 'like Grattan's Parliament, a supreme co-ordinated Parliament, but it is a subordinate one … if the Irish legislature did pass enactment's in the slightest degree oppressive of the Protestants of Ireland, I should say that Ireland would justly deserve to lose her privilege.'[22] A few days later he admitted that the bill 'is not everything that we asked for, but we recognise in it a fair offer, and one which, taken in connexion with the friendly feeling between the two democracies, would lead to a final settlement of this question'.[23] It seemed that the scheme was not, after all, the final solution but only a milepost. Parnell's pledge during the second reading had been a source of irritation among his followers. According to Parnell, Gladstone's bill was actually superior to Grattan's Parliament.[24] In the previous year Parnell had been plagued by colleagues' conflicting interpretations of what might constitute Home Rule – that problem though less obtrusive now, did not wholly disappear. Dissension was more on details and the possibilities of resolving other matters, notably the land question. Davitt could scarcely conceal his dislike of land purchase and Dillon's hostility to it also popped up at embarrassing moments.[25]

Voting in the general election began on 1 July and it was apparent immediately that Unionism was triumphant. By 7 July Sir Edward Hamilton noted the ineffectual impact of the Irish in Britain, observing: 'it is clear, I think, that the power of the Irish vote has been greatly overrated.'[26] Two days later he recorded: 'so much for all the absurd apprehension expressed a year ago that with the extended franchise the Conservative party would be swept off the board.'[27] As the returns poured in, Henry Labouchere jibed: 'justice to Ireland is not very enticing to the English, and ought to have been part of a general programme containing sops to the city and to the agricultural labourers, who like most other people have a keen eye to number one.'[28] When balloting finished on 17 July Unionism had a clear majority, but the Conservatives could not govern without aid from Liberal Unionists. Under Hartington's leadership the latter declined office, but were prepared to give a Tory Ministry general support. As in mid-1885, no one in summer 1886 was sure what lay ahead. If the coalition held firm, a new general election could be postponed for as long as seven years, by which time different issues might have emerged to supersede Home Rule. Everyone was conscious that Home Rule's fortunes rode on Gladstone's shoulders and he seemed unlikely to be around indefinitely. W. H. Smith opined: 'the G.O.M. seems to me to have become something very like a dangerous lunatic. Of him probably there is an end. But he has loosened avalanches which will roll when he is gone.'[29]

The intellectual debate

Political scheming and concrete plans of devolved government were one part of the Home Rule equation, but intellectual and constitutional arguments contributed other dimensions, spurring a critical discussion about the nature of the United Kingdom and what did and should constitute 'Britishness'. Great Britain was a random unsystematic creation which, if it had a geographical logic, was none the less more of an afterthought than a carefully devised design. This entity or 'nation' underwent extensive evolution during the nineteenth century. Its earlier foundations of Crown, Aristocracy and Church had been modified even in Conservative thinking, as different national and religious groups where incorporated into the community. Walter Bagehot identified the chemistry of the modern nation through its institutional fabric, focusing on the Constitution with its dignified and efficient elements. Bagehot's analysis assumed a relatively unified organic state: minorities existed but were subsumed into the larger community. Dignified parts of the Constitution offered an umbrella enabling diverse interests within the United Kingdom to identify with the nation as a whole, while conflicting ambitions were moderated through efficient institutions. Even before 1886 Parnellism was testing this construct, and Gladstone's advocacy of devolved government took this challenge a stage further. Disintegration of the organic state idea was a threat to British and Irish Unionists, though each approached the dilemma from separate standpoints.

Historians have explored the reasons for the intelligentsia's disenchantment with Gladstonianism.[30] Intellectuals, Tom Dunne suggests, were motivated by a linked set of concerns revolving around the questions of democratic and imperial government. Opponents of Home Rule, he suggests, fall into seven main categories – those disillusioned with liberal policies and fearful of democracy; those convinced of the doctrine of classical liberal imperialism and its emphasis upon colonial self-government; academics whose professional work was conservative; those with a particular enthusiasm for India; so-called 'Irish experts'; 'failed' politicians; and those who stressed the moral basis of politics and tended to see it in terms of the defence of the status quo.[31] The common ground between proponents and critics of Home Rule was how best to cope with democratic pressure and Irish threats to the empire. A. V. Dicey, Goldwin Smith and W. E. H. Lecky were all critics, while James Bryce was an advocate of Home Rule; all four were central figures in the debate.

Dicey was a cogent critic of Home Rule. His impressive tome, presaged by a series of articles earlier in the year, *England's Case Against Home Rule*, was published in November 1886, stating the argument against Gladstone's proposal. His rejection of Home Rule is portrayed as a radical response, reflective of a concern that it would fail the needs of both Great Britain and Ireland. Bryce, paradoxically, is alleged to have supported Home Rule as a conservative remedy, for 'democracy will not coerce, and therefore we must come to this end; so we had better to be it at once quickly'.[32] Bryce saw Ireland's disaffection as an impediment to improved relations with the United States. The ideological struggle was Anglocentric; participants perception of Home Rule was principally in terms of its impact upon Great Britain. An important result of the debate was the crystallisation of conceptions of 'Britishness' and what constituted the United Kingdom.

The cleavage is expressed by the terms 'pluralist' and 'organicist'. The first preferred to accept that the United Kingdom was an amalgam of four nationalities and various religions within which provision for 'distinctive' traditions would strengthen the nation. The organic view typified by Dicey argued that the forces of history were in the direction of consolidation of a syncretic state. To reverse this 'evolution' endangered the integrity of the nation and was out of step with European and Great Britain's national development. As Salisbury said in December 1887, it was 'necessary that the generations, as they grow up, should believe that the consolidation [of the British Isles] is inevitable. It is necessary that they should have faith in the fibre and the resolution of the state that desires to weld them into a common whole.'[33] Such ideas are characterised as conservative and anti-democratic; in reality they stemmed from a positive and liberal Western European conception of the state. Unionists were sensitive to individual rights; Parnellites emphasised collective responsibilities. For Chamberlain, Home Rule, especially the Ulster dimension, sharpened his thinking about what constituted Great Britain, playing a crucial part in his transition from a radical to an aggressive patriotism, from being an advocate of the rights of majorities to a protector of minority interests, from scourge to a defender of established institutions.[34]

If the driving force behind Dicey's and Bryce's opposing views was the implication of Home Rule for Britain, it also had ramifications for Irish Protestants. George Boyce observes that the impact was to create unbearable stresses within both communities in Ireland.[35] For Catholics, there was the enticement that while being a minority in the United Kingdom, they might achieve majority status within Ireland; Protestants saw it reducing them from a United Kingdom majority to an impotent Irish minority. As the debate progressed, both groups found themselves marginalised as 'outsiders' in the increasingly redefined British national community. Like many 'national' or ethnic groups in nineteenth-century Europe, Protestants were forced to make a previously unthinkable choice of allegiance. Earlier, they had no difficulty being Irish and at the same time part of the United Kingdom; in the face of Home Rule, they opted to be British. Boyce observes: 'the conflict between Great Britain and Ireland was not one between an "emergent" colonial people with its masters, but between Irish and English nationalism, with Irish, and especially Ulster Protestants, forced to decide for themselves where their best chances of survival lay.'[36] Absorption into an Eastern European-type ethnic nation-state held no attraction. If holding multiply loyalties ceased to be viable, becoming 'British' was a more certain protection for the Irish Protestants, particularly those in Ulster, even if in the process they became merely marginal Britons. Intellectuals and politicians in the mid-1880s found in Home Rule an ideal issue on which to hone their ideas on the nature of the modern state, especially concerning the historical evolution of a Western European model of a multi-ethnic, multi-religious pluralist society built on notions of common citizenship and the rule of law. In spite of some excesses of anti-Irish and anti-Catholic expressions, Home Rulers and their opponents essentially were agreed that Ireland's Catholics ultimately had the capacity to be merged fully into the greater British community though they differed on the best means of achieving it.

A period of flux, June 1886–March 1887

In Salisbury's estimation, Conservatives 'were returned with one mandate – to maintain the Union'.[37] The new administration had to deal with three problems: the land question, public order and the power of Parnellism, which had established an iron grip on Catholic districts. There was no realistic prospect of breaking it by conventional means such as elections – Catholic Ireland was demonstrably a one-party region where priests enforced loyalty. To preserve the Union the government had to find a way to contain and then roll back Parnellism without crushing it, leaving the door ajar to something worse. In 1886 Home Rule was effectively defeated at the ballot box in Britain. Voting preferences left untended could prove fickle. Unionists had a respite, but safety lay with weakening Parnellite power. Before Unionism levelled its sights on the enemy, however, it went through a transitional stage.

In 1885 Salisbury's intentions to implement Irish reform had been signalled by the appointment of Carnarvon; in 1886 this was made implicit again by the restoration of Hicks Beach to the Irish Office. Hicks Beach had a reputation as a moderate reformer, accepting the position of Chief Secretary for Ireland on the basis that he might be able to do good there.[38] His aim, he said, was to effect 'a policy which has for its great object the social and the material welfare of Ireland'. He hoped 'that our tenure of office may show that we shall leave Ireland in a more peaceful, more prosperous, and more orderly condition than that in which, unfortunately, we now find it'.[39] Salisbury recognised that a flexible approach, such as Hicks Beach adumbrated, was essential to keep Liberal Unionists on board.

The largest immediate problem facing the new administration was a resumption of rural discontent. Continued falls in commodity prices had pressed hard on farmers; judicial rents fixed under the 1881 legislation proved burdensome and these could not be amended for fifteen years. In the first six months of 1886 the Irish party used the prospect of Home Rule to keep the lid on agrarian agitation. By mid-summer patience was wearing thin. The national coalition was deeply divided over land purchase. On 3 July *The Nation* repudiated it.[40] The pre-session meeting of the Irish meeting party on 4 August reaffirmed 'the right of the Irish people to self-government and declare that no measure offering less legislative or executive control over Irish affairs can be accepted as a settlement of the Irish national question'. It attempted to bridge the growing differences over the land question:

> [W]e deem it our duty to warn the government that the great depreciation in the price of agricultural produce since the period when the bulk of the judicial rents were fixed renders it impossible that these rates can be paid; and we would suggest immediate revision of such rates, the re-modelling of the rent-fixing clauses, so as to secure protection for the improvements of the tenant … together with such a suspension of evictions and wiping out of arrears as will enable the occupiers of the soil to live and pay their rent.[41]

The Catholic hierarchy added its voice to the demand for land legislation. Throughout the country, meetings were held to devise means of protecting tenant farmers.

When Parliament opened on 19 August (it had been convened formally on 5 August), the government outlined the possible need to improve methods of enforcing public order, but concentrated on local government reform, land legislation and measures to assist Ireland's economy.[42] Speaking on 21 August, Churchill, now leader of the House, announced the appointment of a commission headed by Lord Cowper, a former Liberal Viceroy, to investigate the operation of the Land Act of 1881 and the Purchase of Land Act, 1885. In his response to the Queen's Speech, Parnell pointed to the depth of the crisis and called for the suspension of tenant evictions. After his amendment to the Address had been defeated on 27 August, Parnell warned: 'neither the Irish members nor the government had any control over the events which might occur in Ireland during the months of the winter'. Yet he 'desired that it should not be supposed that because he had done so, he was going again to lead such an agitation as took place in the winter of 1880'.[43] After the defeat of the amendment, Parnell introduced the Tenants' Relief bill, aimed at suspending evictions where a tenant had paid one-half of the rent. This proposal also would admit leaseholders to the Land Act of 1881 and give Land Courts the power to reduce judicial rents. On 20 September the bill was defeated in the House of Commons; Parliament was prorogued four days later. If Parnell was reluctant to recommence the land struggle, the prospect was relished by many of his followers. William

131

O'Brien had already warned that should the Tenants Relief bill fail, '[we should] put it in force ourselves in Ireland, and give as good as we get to every landlord and official who blocks the way'.[44] For those who wanted to renew the land war, Parnell's double defeat in the House of Commons offered the necessary excuse.

Resumption of the land campaign raised doubts among Liberals about the utility of Home Rule and the alliance with Parnellism. It also posed a threat to Parnell's leadership. Many Liberals were unenthusiastic about both Home Rule and land legislation. They had no alternative programme for dealing with the agrarian crisis. Tory purchase schemes raised the spectre that they could undermine Home Rule and perhaps even Parnellism. Irish spokesmen hastened to reassure Liberals of their fidelity, though they did not rule out acceptance of Conservative concessions. 'Mr G may be assured that our party will never desert him', promised Justin McCarthy.[45] Archbishop Walsh added to Parnell's dilemma. Though he advocated land legislation and Home Rule, his stance deviated from the Irish leader's on important points, dissenting publicly from the pledge Parnell offered on the second reading of the bill: 'I must say that I was a little surprised at the readiness with which that pledge was given. ... Personally I could not have been a party to the giving of it.'[46]

While not indifferent to the looming agrarian crisis, the government resisted being pushed into premature action. Until the commission reported, Hicks Beach hoped that serious disruption could be averted by a combination of additional policing in the most troubled districts and Ministerial pressure on landlords to exercise restraint. Sir Henry Redvers Buller was dispatched to Kerry, an exceptionally disturbed area, to deal with intimidation. He was soon struck by the enormity of the job and by the obstinacy of landlords. Before long he and Hicks Beach were adopting a vigorously anti-landlord outlook. The Chief Secretary saw them preferring 'to lie on their backs and howl to the government'.[47]

In an attempt to improve the Irish situation from another angle Hicks Beach, in early November, resumed contacts with Walsh. The Archbishop, though happy to enter negotiations, wanted to dispel concern that the Church might be lured into a separate compact, making 'it plain that we insist on a settlement of the Education Question, so far as an English Parliament can settle it, but at the same time we make no "bargain" of any kind on the question of Home Rule'. However, on 8 November, he confessed privately:

I am a good deal engaged in the Education Question – trying a little diplomacy! I have even confidence that the present government will do a good deal for us in this most important matter. Perhaps indeed on this account, as on some others already mentioned by your Grace, it is no harm that the establishment of our Home Rule system was a little delayed.[48]

Conservative concessions on education were hampered by fear of a Protestant backlash in Britain and also by the Catholic hierarchy's escalating appetite. After meeting with Hicks Beach, Walsh wrote to him on 16 December:

[A]s for the university I can only say what I have said from the beginning. So long as Trinity College is allowed to stand, as it does, in the most prominent public building perhaps in Dublin, representing the highest favour of the state in the matter of University Education exclusively reserved for the central stronghold of the non-Catholic education of this mainly Catholic country, so long we must continue to protest against the policy which withholds from us all that we ask for – equality.[49]

Equity had an elastic meaning. Walsh earlier had defined it as implying equality based on the respective numbers of each confession.[50] Archbishop Croke soon reverted to this position:

I am not sure, indeed, at the same time, that *'equality'* in that sense is not rather low ground for us Catholics to take, in as much as being the vast majority of the inhabitants of this country, we have a right to have state support and privilege extended to us in some proportion as would fairly represent, and recognise our numerical superiority.[51]

Hicks Beach's intentions began to be knocked off course by the rapid escalation of agrarian troubles. In August Timothy Harrington had suggested that 'the time had come when all the branches of the National League in the country should reorganise themselves and get ready to fight the battle of the tenants'.[52] On 17 October Dillon outlined the Plan of Campaign which was then published in *United Ireland* six days later. The government tried to take legal action against O'Brien and Dillon in November; they were charged with criminal conspiracy on 16 December, with the jury disagreeing on a verdict on 24 February 1887. On 18 December the Plan of Campaign was declared 'an unlawful and criminal conspiracy'.[53]

Liberals looked warily upon developments in Ireland. Lord Rosebery was anxious 'to give Tories a chance' and 'avoid appearance of complicity with Irish agitation as connected with the crime which might spring up'.[54] Morley and Harcourt wanted to avert a 'rush through the land with a Fiery Cross'.[55] In November an attempt to bring the party together on an 'intermediate measure' of self-government was floated, but Parnell declined any such suggestion on the grounds that 'such a course would be repudiated by the active men in his party'.[56] With compromise ruled out, Liberals became anxious that they would be linked to the agitation in Ireland. Harcourt was avid 'that we must have nothing to do with the present agrarian tactics of Dillon & Co'.[57] Hamilton believed Gladstone's position was 'getting more and more difficult on account of automatic association with "Plan of Campaign"'.[58] In this charged atmosphere schemes for a Liberal reunion matured. Hamilton speculated at the close of the year that fusion with Chamberlain might be brought about by some endeavour to settle the land question in Ireland. 'A settlement would put to the test the not uncommon contention that it is not Home Rule but the land which the Nationalists want.'[59] Liberal circles were awash with a slate of Irish reforms intended as substitutes for Home Rule.

Irish entanglements were proving a stumbling block not just between parties but within them. Even Parnell was feeling the pressures of his agrarian and clerical supporters who were jostling for their own ends. Home Rule alone was proving a less than sure cement. There was, fortunately, a solution nicely tailored to all parties' difficulties peeping up over the horizon – coercion. In November Morley thought: 'the first business next January, as it was last, will be Coercion. That blessed word will give a new shake to the kaleidoscope, and all the present talk will prove to be perfectly idle.'[60] Notice in the Queen's Speech on 28 January 1887 of the intention to seek additional powers drew to a close the period of uncertainty which had lasted since the general election. Hicks Beach resigned at the beginning of March because of ill health; on 7 March Arthur Balfour was appointed the Chief Secretary. As Salisbury's nephew, he carried weight with the Prime Minister and had already had the experience of dealing with the agrarian revolt in Scotland. Home Rule's brief life at the top of the agenda drew to a close.

Unionist offensive, March 1887–autumn 1889

Balfour brought a new touch to the Irish Office. He soon proved both determined and successful in halting the Parnellite onslaught, thereby instilling Unionism with fresh self-confidence.[61] Margaret O'Callaghan suggests that his administration marks a difference of kind, not just of degree. Balfour's approach, she maintains, by refusing to distinguish between different kinds of patriot, effectively stymied the Home Rule movement.[62] Curtis catalogues measures designed to combat rural disorder, such as: the revival of morale and procedures of the Irish administration; encouragement of landlord resistance by the development of the 'syndicate' of owners, along with attempts to make the more unreasonable of them see sense;

suppression of the Plan of Campaign; proclamation of meetings; prosecution of agitators, subjecting political prisoners to the ordinary prison rules; the arrest of participating clergy; enforcement of the law against the press; resort to the courts in order to impose financial strains on Plan funds; the use of channels to the papacy to gain its intervention; and the creation of a Special Commission intended to discredit Parnellism by establishing its connection with crime.[63] Virginia Crossman observes that Balfour's achievement lay in allowing anti-Home Rulers to justify their refusal to countenance Irish party demands because they emanated from a small group of self-serving and power-hungry individuals prepared to use any means to attain their ends.[64] He subscribed to his uncle's perception: 'the severity must come first. They must "take a licking" before conciliation will do them any good.'[65]

The Cowper Commission made its report at the beginning of March, recommending admission of leaseholders – farmers who held their land for a specified term or lease – to coverage under the 1881 Land Act, reduction in the length of judicially fixed rents and, where appropriate, adjustment of existing rentals. Salisbury saw in the revision of rents 'the price we have to pay for the Union and it is a heavy one'.[66] Meanwhile, the government proceeded with the Criminal Law and Procedure bill introduced on 28 March 1887, giving the Irish Executive permanent emergency authority, subject to parliamentary review, over designated or proclaimed disaffected districts, and the right to deal summarily with conspiracies for withholding rents, acts of boycotting and intimidation, resistance to evictions and similar specified activities. The government thus could avoid having to return to Parliament to have special powers renewed, blunting one weapon in the Irish party's armoury.

On 7 March *The Times* began publication of a series of articles titled 'Parnellism and Crime', reproducing on 18 April what purported to be a facsimile letter from Parnell condoning the murder of Thomas Burke in Phoenix Park nearly five years earlier. Parnell allegedly confessed: 'I cannot refuse to admit that Burke got no more than his deserts.'[67] To this, the newspaper taunted:

[W]e have publicly stated, and we repeat the statement, that the present allies of the Gladstonians, the men whom MR GLADSTONE and his colleagues are assisting to paralyse law and to render government impossible in Ireland, have been, and are, associated, closely and continuously, with the worst of criminals, with agents and instruments of murder-conspiracies, with the planners and paymasters of cowardly and inhuman outrage, with preachers of the 'gospel of 'dynamite', who are at the same time the financiers that furnish the funds on which the 'parliamentary party' subsist. ... MR

PARNELL must understand the gravity of the question raised by the accusations we have formulated and supported with evidence, but he cannot expect that his simple repudiation of the letter we publish this morning will have any weight with public opinion. He must be prepared with some more solid proofs, if he is to annul the effect of a disclosure which reduces the passionate denials with which his party encounter unpleasant truths.[68]

The prevailing mood was captured in Tom Merry's cartoon captioned 'Guilty, or Not Guilty'. Parnell immediately denounced the letters as forgeries, a claim dramatically upheld almost three years later when Richard Pigott was exposed as their nefarious author. Spencer spoke for many Liberals, noting 'Parnell's letter is a great sensation. It may be a forgery. We don't know. If it is not it is very ugly but it really is not much worse than before.'[69] Balfour encouraged *The Times* exposé. The facsimiles were an important ingredient in this offensive. Merry again captured the atmosphere in another of his wickedly incisive cartoons, 'Clean Bowled', depicting the Irish leader as caught out holding a cricket bat labelled 'treason'. The Unionist assault left Justin McCarthy to surmise, 'it is plain to me that the attacks in *The Times* will render social life rather a terrifying thing to me just now'.[70]

Balfour proceeded with his determined throttling of the Plan of Campaign. On 15 and 17 April 1887 William O'Brien and John Dillon were arrested. The government's arm was strengthened when the Criminal Law and Procedure Act came into force on 19 July. Within the first month proceedings were taken out against 659 persons.[71] Prosecutions by the close of the year bit into the agitation's operations. Parnell had already sought to limit the extension of the Plan. One of the features of the struggle was the participation of the clergy, a manifestation of the now close alliance of priests and party. Through intermediaries, the government began to lobby at Rome, and in mid-1887 the Vatican sent a personal emissary to Ireland to investigate conditions. On 23 August a fresh Land Act was passed, admitting about 100,000 leaseholders to the benefits of the previous legislation and allowing tenants who were threatened with eviction because they were unable to pay excessive rents to apply to the courts for reductions in proportion to the decline of commodity prices. The court could fix the repayment of arrears so as to spread it over a reasonable period of time. Rentals that had been set between 1881 and 1885 could be reviewed once, and these and other rents were to be fixed thereafter for three years only. Thus, the main recommendations of the Cowper Commission were rapidly implemented. This was not meant as a comprehensive measure. Balfour believed that the 'only final solution is *purchase*'.[72] His quarrel with leaders of the

Plan of Campaign is described as having less to do with their objective than the means employed.[73] When the legislation had initially been introduced in the spring of 1887 Balfour had reminded sceptical colleagues: 'the landlords must not consider it a solution. They must take it in connection with the whole policy of the government; and they must feel that the sacrifice asked of them (if sacrifice it be) is absolutely required if the Union and all the Union means to them, is to be maintained.'[74] In the wake of the new Land Act, Archbishop Walsh spent the next few months attempting to arrange a conference between tenants and landlords to settle the issue. Croke, who opposed the idea, feared that 'its success just now would be little short of a National disaster'.[75] In early August the National League had been proclaimed an unlawful conspiracy; by the end of the year the numbers of local branches began to nosedive. Additionally, the Cabinet dealt with the Irish party nemesis in the House of Commons by restricting the power of minorities to obstruct government proposals and by reducing the scope of Question Time, a favoured means to harass Ministers.

Coercion was proving effective but it was the one part of Balfour's approach which united the opposition. Opponents were aided by well-publicised incidents. At Mitchelstown, Tipperary on 9 September 1887 the constabulary fired into a crowd that had just been addressed by Dillon. Imprisonment of agitators – especially MPs – and their prison conditions, as in the case of O'Brien the following year, offered useful *cause célèbres*. Coercion cemented the Parnellite–Liberal accord, though Michael Barker's contention that it was more instrumental in keeping the alliance together than a common commitment to Home Rule is excessive.[76] Spencer's papers reveal the extent of Liberal's belief in Irish self-government through these years.[77]

During 1888 Balfour's administration persisted in applying pressure, receiving a bonus when the Vatican issued a rescript on 20 April condemning the Plan of Campaign. Parnell in response finally supported the Plan publicly, though he still declined to take an active role. On 5 May Archbishop Walsh encouraged leaders of the Plan to drop the agitation:

> I am strongly of opinion that, as a matter of *politics* or *tactics*, an opportunity should be taken just now to drop the Plan of Campaign as quietly as possible. It did splendid work for the tenants. But there is no doubt it led recently to much embarrassment. Mr Parnell never liked it. Of course the same must be said of Gladstone and the other Liberal leaders who have given such splendid help for the last year or two. As regards its justification from a moral point of view a great deal could be said about the Plan in the abstract, which could not be said of its actual operation. At all events waiving the theology of the

137

matter, and looking at it as an affair of *practical politics*, I can see no room for doubt in the matter.[78]

Soon it was noticed that 'the priests go much less to [Plan] meetings than they did'.[79]

On 8 May in his speech at the '80 Club' Parnell once more distanced himself from the Plan, reaffirming the central importance of Home Rule and the Liberal alliance.[80] The Land Purchase Act of 1888 increased by £5 millions the sums available under the Ashbourne Act. Altogether, the legislation of 1885 and 1888 enabled 25,376 tenants to purchase their holdings, transferring 942,625 acres to them.[81] This fresh initiative further heightened dissension in Irish ranks. Dillon and Davitt were quick to oppose the principle of the legislation.[82] Some branches of the National League, following this line, imposed a boycott on tenants who indicated a wish to buy their holdings. Parnell, meanwhile, supported purchase and cast a wary eye on the activities of his erstwhile associates. O'Callaghan observes that Dillon and O'Brien 'were men with fixed goals but no strategy', failings that would be replicated several times again in the coming years.[83] Their management of the Plan contained a staggering flaw – a disregard of fiscal prudence. By the close of 1888 the agitation was running desperately short of money. It was costing some £20,000 per year and its leaders were under pressure to confine the Plan to those estates where it was already in operation. On 24 July 1889 O'Brien wrote to Dillon: 'on my return I found things in a very deplorable condition – not a kick in the country and deep depression among the Campaigners'.[84]

The government had ample reason to be encouraged. Several members of the Catholic hierarchy were making friendly noises, Parnellites were increasingly demoralised, Parnell himself was subjected to criticism from his own supporters and the Liberals remained in disarray. At the same time, the Plan of Campaign was deteriorating. Parnell never successfully lifted the cloud which hung over him as a result of *The Times* allegations. Several times he demanded a parliamentary inquiry, but the Ministry resisted. Salisbury's government, after all, had nothing to gain by alleviating Parnell's discomfort. In July 1888, however, it relented, insisting that an official commission be invested with the wide remit of investigating crime in Ireland. Parnell reluctantly agreed. At this stage the government supposed that it had the means to deal both Parnellism and Gladstone a crippling blow. The Commission began sessions on 17 September 1888, meeting 128 times between then and 22 November 1889.[85] The proceedings attracted immense interest. Undoubtedly the key moment came between 20 and 22 February 1889 when Pigott was unmasked as the forger.[86] From 30 April until 8 May Parnell gave evidence. Reflecting on his testimony Archbishop Croke wrote: 'the truth is so far as I am a judge, having in view all I know of the doings of the Party for the past ten years, that there is a great deal that Parnell will find difficult to explain.'[87] Despite a hesitant performance Parnell was spared the scrutiny he would have faced without Pigott's unmasking. His and the movement's prestige leapt to a new high. An opponent conceded: 'there is no doubt of the complicity of the Parnellite leaders in the crimes of the agitation, but the question has been confused by the letters & the Pigott forgeries, & the truth thereby obscured.'[88] Another Unionist remarked: 'there is something extremely entertaining in the present posture of affairs with regard to the Parnellite Commission. That *The Times* has been stupid beyond all that history tells us of stupidity is surprising enough. It is perhaps even more surprising that the results of their stupidity should have spread such dismay among our own people.'[89] The Commission report that was issued on 13 February 1890 underlined the involvement of Parnellism in the agrarian conspiracy and concluded that certain participants – Davitt, Dillon and O'Brien – had joined in order to further Irish independence. O'Callaghan maintains that the Commission effectively destroyed Parnellism by equating it with crime. According to her, by recasting the debate in terms of defeating crime the viability of the Irish party at Westminster was ended. Thus, she argues, Parnell's inactivity after 1887 can be ascribed to the dismantling of his achievement: Parnell's version of constitutionalism was effectively dead before the divorce crisis.[90] She is no doubt correct to counsel caution before dismissing the impact of Balfour's policy and the work of the Special Commission. Her suggestion that the Irish party lost some of its appearance of influence after 1886 is on safe ground, though her thesis that the effective basis of Parnellism had been eroded before the split is less persuasive and Crossman points out that Parnell's stature with Liberals was actually enhanced.[91] O'Callaghan's observation is more convincing – that the Irish national movement between 1879 and 1886 evolved from a crude agrarian base to a sophisticated political strategy, but that Balfour negated this development, remoulding the nature of the challenge to a parody of the confused conspiracy of 1879–81. She notes that he was 'facilitated by the personal enmities that existed within the [Irish] parliamentary party'.[92]

Reformism and counter-attack, 1889–90

Parnell's renewed ascendancy allowed him more freedom of manoeuvre than he had had for some time, but as events would soon show national unity was a façade. In March at the '80 Club' and again in July when receiving the Freedom of Edinburgh, Parnell pointedly restated the primacy of Home Rule and the value of the Liberal alliance.[93] In summer 1889 he finally gave public support to the failing land movement. Nevertheless, O'Brien on 14 August complained that 'having started the new Tenants' Defence League … he now flatly refuses to take any effective steps to put life in it'.[94] When the new body was formally launched in Dublin on 25 October Parnell did not attend, but he wrote to the Lord Mayor outlining its limited objects. Its purposes were 'to protect tenants against the landlord conspiracy, uphold civil liberties, [and] assert basic trade union rights of combination'.[95] Parnell's status allowed him to speak out more favourably on Tory-sponsored plans. In June he supported the government's Shannon drainage scheme though he wanted it brought under popular control, but this plan was soon withdrawn. Opponents characterised it as a blatant bribe. Government plans to promote light railways opened a further rift. Some supported the idea, others were opposed.

Conservative education schemes predictably stirred up trouble between the Irish and Liberals, though they also caused discord within the Unionist coalition. In June 1889 Walsh explained to Parnell that should government responses prove unsatisfactory, 'you would press this matter on the attention of the Ministry, and of the House of Commons by every means at the disposal of the Irish Parliamentary Party'.[96] At the close of the parliamentary session, Balfour outlined proposals for the creation of a state-endowed Catholic college. T. D. Sullivan hailed the announcement, albeit with reservations:

> [U]nless I am mistaken the English Home Rule ranks will be divided over it, and there may be a row in the Tory camp. The English Nonconformists and Radicals are almost to a man secularists in education matters, and after what happened in the Royal Grants question [Parnellites had voted with the government], the arising of a new cause of difference between them and us may, I fear, impair to some degree their sympathy with us in the Home Rule question.[97]

Gladstone gave Parnell the same message when he warned that the mention of religious endowments in Ireland would sever them from the Nonconformists. *The Freeman's Journal* tried to bridge the growing rift:

> [T]he Liberals of Great Britain may rest assured that there is an end of overtures to the Tories. Broken promises and deluded hopes – these have been the fruits of every Tory and Irish alliance. … Every tie of gratitude, of mutual goodwill and mutual interest, binds us irrevocably to the Liberal party, so long as they remain firm upon the principle of Home Rule.[98]

Whatever Liberals or Irish Catholics felt, the idea quickly ran up hard against resistance within the Conservative party. Ulster Protestant opinion took umbrage at Balfour's plan.[99] By mid-September the Chief Secretary conceded to his uncle that the proposal might have to be dropped and soon afterwards Chamberlain counselled him to abandon it.[100]

Signs of restiveness among Liberals, even on Home Rule, were evident. One noted that the Parnellites 'could never be counted on, and on all questions which are Liberal touchstones, such as unsectarian education and protection they would vote against us to a certainty'.[101] R. B. Haldane, a rising young Liberal, complained that the leadership was 'apt to regard the establishment of a Parliament and Executive in Dublin as the be-all and end-all of Liberal policy' and while he accepted this as legitimate for Gladstone, he argued that 'his colleagues are hardly justified in adopting substantially the same course'.[102] Rosebery was anxious to open a dialogue on the shape of the future Home Rule plan. In summer 1889 he urged Gladstone to appoint a party committee to examine the 1886 bill and formulate ideas for discussion. Gladstone side-tracked this suggestion at the expense of angering some senior colleagues, insisting 'as regards any scheme of the future so much would depend on the exigencies of the moment'. Of his refusal, Sir Edward Hamilton opined: 'Mr G Has too much parental love for his own child', a view he recorded more strongly in late September, when he noted: 'there seems to be a slight and not unnatural tinge of jealousy about letting the Irish measure slip out of his hands. He takes no account of the possibility, if not the probability, that it will fall to others to shape the next Home Rule scheme.'[103] He did elicit Parnell's opinions on the prospective plan, discussing it with him in London in March 1888 and then more fully at their Hawarden meeting in December 1889.[104]

The prospect of further purchase legislation augured fresh divisions. Gladstone thought that Parnell could, when it suited his purposes, 'cut a somewhat Tory figure'.[105] Nevertheless, Parnell and Gladstone were intent upon taking advantage of the Irishman's new stature. Re-emphasising Home Rule would enable Parnell to contain the growing wave of critics within his coalition. In December he made several addresses at Liberal rallies in English towns on his way to stay with Gladstone at Hawarden. For both, the meeting offered a welcome opportunity to turn the attention of their own respective supporters back towards the Home Rule commitment. In Gladstone's case the Home Rule question was a means of pulling Parnellites away from overly enthusiastic acceptance of Tory reforms. Balfour exposed a gaping hole within Parnellism and between it and the Gladstonians, laying bare differences. Even an enervated Tory administration was not short of options.

On 24 December 1889 Captain O'Shea filed a petition for divorce naming Parnell as co-respondent. Katharine O'Shea had been Parnell's mistress since the beginning of the decade and the relationship was well known in political circles. Considerable resentment had been building up against Parnell. But although there was a concern that Parnell's public standing might be damaged, O'Shea's allegation drew only limited attention until the case came before the court the following November.[106] It was confidently expected that it would be withdrawn or that Parnell would be able to defend himself successfully. In the meantime, Conservatives, despite the setback of the forgeries, did not lose all momentum. On 24 March Balfour introduced a large-scale Purchase bill which Parnell viewed with guarded favour. When Walsh criticised party absenteeism and, implicitly, the leadership in June, Parnell retorted sharply that 'they had stood by their posts during the last five years as a body like men ... they had done their duty without complaint – a laborious and a fatiguing and a disagreeable duty; that they have fought an uphill battle, and that as a party and as a body our countrymen are proud of them.'[107] Conservative policy had worked sufficiently well so that by later 1890 Balfour 'has been driving about the west of Ireland without any escort, and has been received everywhere with the greatest civility and respect', though Crossman disputes whether his policy had the success attributed to it.[108]

On the eve of the divorce court hearing there was a replication of the 1883–85 circumstances. Although Parnellites could no longer align with anyone but Gladstone, they none the less found areas of agreement with Unionists and functioned on a day-by-day basis as a reformist rather than an ideological party. However, when the party performed principally as a service organisation, it roused immense internal tensions. Additionally, as Frank Callanan argues, there was an inherent contradiction between Parnell's attempt to restrain Catholic agrarian nationalism and the forces working to foster it.[109] Gladstone, for Liberal party reasons, and Parnell, at times, because of Irish needs, coalesced to reassert the primacy of Home Rule. The new political system did not work perfectly, but on the whole it was well calculated to meet the exigencies of high politics, linking these to local opinions. For the short term it allowed the Irish middle classes to maintain an effective grip on politics at home, while permitting English politicians to contain Parnellism. Whether so inherently unstable a construct would be viable over an extended period was unsure. Then on 17 November, after two days of uncontested testimony, Captain O'Shea was granted a decree nisi, turning the political world on its head. During the following days rumblings over Parnell's conduct – particularly among English Nonconformists –

become commonplace. The verdict quickly led to a major crisis in Liberal and Irish politics. Following a well-orchestrated campaign, on 25 November Parnell was re-elected party chairman for the coming session, but dissatisfaction with his retention of the leadership swiftly materialised. Gladstone responded the same day, releasing the text of his letter to Morley containing the phrase that in the event of Parnell remaining chairman his own leadership would be 'almost a nullity'.[110] On 29 November, in the face of rising criticism, Parnell's 'Manifesto to the Irish People' was published. Critics requisitioned a party meeting which convened on 1 December in Committee Room 15 of the House of Commons. On 3 December the Catholic Episcopal Standing Committee condemned Parnell. The party's fraught deliberations lasted for three days, after which Justin McCarthy and forty-four other Irish MPs withdrew, leaving Parnell at the head of twenty-eight loyalists. The probable distribution between the two sides was fifty-four against his continued leadership, with thirty-two continuing to stand behind him. On 10 December Parnell went to Dublin where he received a hero's welcome. However, in the first trial of political strength at the Kilkenny North by-election on 22 December an anti-Parnellite triumphed. The split had become a reality. Conservatives unexpectedly found their situation transformed. Instead of being at the sharp end of Liberal and Irish attacks, they enjoyed the luxury of retreating to the sidelines while Home Rulers tore themselves apart. Once more Tom Merry encapsulated the moment in his cartoon 'Exit the Uncrowned King' published on 22 November, followed in the next issue by the caustic, 'O Romeo, Romeo!', depicting Parnell driving his carriage to Mrs O'Shea's residence at Eltham.[111]

The death of Parnell

The bitter contest emanating from the divorce engulfed Parnell, pitting the remnants of his movement against a far larger number of Home Rulers who were backed by the overwhelming might of the priesthood. Both sides necessarily had to manufacture organisations and a rhetoric to spell out their respective positions.[112] The struggle went through several phases up to Parnell's death on 6 October 1891.[113] In the initial sequence all sides attempted to lay claim to the Home Rule mantle. Parnell gained some success as a consequence of the Boulogne negotiations, which ran from 30 December to 11 February, when Gladstone was obliged to give assurances about the future Home Rule bill. After February 1891 Parnell never abandoned his claim to be the authentic protector of Home Rule – indeed, maintained that only he could ensure the implementation of a sound scheme – but Parnell increasingly slipped away from stressing the purity of the self-government question. His shift was not unambiguous. He began with greater frequency to search out support on other matters such as the land, labour and social questions. In particular he emphasised his wish to aid the peasantry, expressing also a willingness to co-operate with the Conservatives on land purchase. He sought to portray himself as the defender of party 'independence', standing against Liberal 'dictation'. By the time of his death Parnell was losing numerical strength but he had discovered a constituency.[114] His candidate lost the Sligo North by-election on 2 April and another defeat was suffered in Carlow on 8 July. However, Radicals, portions of the urban working classes, Fenians and assorted outsiders began to flock to his standard. Advocates of orthodox Home Rule and alliance with Liberalism – Parnell's own earlier touchstones – carried the day against his more wide-ranging platform.

Because Parnellism ultimately depended upon Parnell himself, it is impossible to be certain of the final outcome had he not died. Many people, including his opponents, believed that he would triumph in the end.[115] His dismay at the movement's drift into an ethnic nationalism, coupled with his own attempt to find a new basis for national identity, might have borne fruit had he lived. Frank Callanan suggests that the struggle between Parnell and Healy, at root embodied the former's desire to contain an assertive Catholic agrarianism and the latter's wish to exploit a proprietorial nationalism.[116] Parnell's rediscovery of social or class-based questions opened a path to Irish Protestants, whereas, as Callanan, observes, Healy's rhetoric pointed to the evolution of a modern chauvinistic nationalism.[117] Following Parnell's death on 6 October (he was buried in Glasnevin Cemetery on 11 December, rather than in the more appropriate Mount Jerome), the fate of Home Rule hung in the balance. The Unionists' strategy of resistance, together with social and economic reform, was vindicated by events. Their conclusion that given time the national coalition would crack was correct, if not in the way anticipated. For many Home Rulers, 'Tis not that we loved our leader less, / But we love our country more.'[118]

The end of Salisbury's second government

Parnell's death did not heal Irish schisms. The movement was torn in two; McCarthy's larger section remained tied to Liberalism. A smaller section under John Redmond was not less attached to Home Rule, but professed to have a more flexible approach to alignments in the House of Commons. In practice, it, too, had to look to the Liberals.

The relationship between Home Rulers and Liberalism became increasingly unequal. Isaac Butt had urged, and Parnell had perfected, a strategy of applying Irish pressure on Liberals. But Parnell's ability to enforce concessions from them waned after 1886, though the theoretical potential remained intact. After 1891 this pretence vanished. In January 1891 Gladstone gave voice to this change, maintaining: 'I think it is time that the relative position of Home Rule will for platforms and candidates undergo some change, but this will best be done by emphasising other matters.'[119] The Newcastle Programme adopted at the National Liberal Federation conference in early October 1891 endorsed a string of social and other reforms to be promoted by Liberals. This reflected the party's need to broaden its appeal and ended the narrow focus on Home Rule. Liberals now advocated church disestablishment for Wales and Scotland, local option for the sale of drink, abolition of the plural franchise, triennial parliaments, reform of the land laws in Great Britain and the creation of district and parish councils along with powers to acquire land for allotments and other public purposes. This programme endorsed the maximum hours of work for certain categories of labourers and supported the payment of MPs. Parnell in 1891 took up some of these causes, advocating a socially conscious platform that anticipated progressive Liberalism.

Meanwhile, the Conservatives pressed forward their Irish remedies. On 24 March 1890 Balfour introduced a new Land Purchase bill which finally became law on 5 August 1891. This legislation, containing novel features, was meant to increase the rate of tenant purchases.[120] Instead of landlords being paid in cash, as was done earlier, they were issued with guaranteed stock bearing 2.75 per cent interest. At the same time the sum repaid by purchasers could vary from year to year and counties were made to bear the cost of defaults. The maximum sum made available under the measure was £33 million, making it larger in monetary terms than all previous land acts combined, but it was less effective than expected. Applications for loans declined immediately. More money was loaned during the next five years, but dismay at the confusing financial provisions, concern over the variance of annual repayments and landlord objections to the method of compensation militated against effectiveness.

The Land Purchase Act of 1891 created the Congested Districts Board to stimulate the economy in the poorest regions.[121] This section was directed at improving the material situation of western cottiers, thereby addressing the main thesis of Conservatism, the belief that the want of Ireland was prosperity. Originally, the Congested Districts Board covered parts of Donegal, Leitrim, Sligo, Mayo, Roscommon, Galway, Kerry and Cork, taking in some 3,608,569 acres with a population of approximately half a million. The powers conferred included purchase and development of estates, encouragement of improved farming, promotion of fishing and local industries while it also supervised the construction of bridges, piers and roads – exactly the sort of state interventionism in Ireland demanded by Home Rulers, though, predictably, many were critical of Balfour's initiative. Balfour observed of his handiwork: 'I have really some hope now that it will succeed, not indeed in entirely removing the evils with which it was intended to deal, but in mitigating their severity.'[122]

Several years would pass before the effects and deficiencies of the Congested Districts Board were realised. In the meantime, Balfour and his successor as Chief Secretary of the Irish Office from October 1891, W. L. Jackson, sought to moderate distress with temporary relief measures. During the short parliamentary session of 1892 the government considered two other pieces of legislation. The Local Government bill of 1892 had been adumbrated in 1888 when analogous legislation for Britain was passed; application to Ireland had formed part of Conservative policy since 1885. In October 1890 Balfour had promised that the measure would follow *mutatis mutandis*, the system adopted for Britain. A bill was introduced in February 1892 and had its second reading on 24 May, being dropped on 13 June as the government's term of office neared its close. This bill, which had wide support from Ulster Unionist MPs, proposed to establish county and district councils elected on a franchise of all cesspayers.[123] Cumulative voting was meant to protect minorities in all parts of the country. These bodies would be constrained by limitations on spending authority and relatively easy impeachment of members. Though a failure in the short term, the projected extension of local government was a vital ingredient of measured increments of democratic control and equalisation of conditions throughout the United Kingdom. More successfully, the government brought in the National Education bill which was enacted just before Parliament was prorogued. This measure increased funding for primary schools, in principle ending the payment of fees, improved teachers' pensions and introduced compulsory attendance. Like other Conservative reforms, this formed part of a materialist liberal unionist prescription, demonstrating that Unionists, haltingly, could bring to Irish affairs precisely the degree of attention Home Rulers claimed was beyond the capacity of London-based government.

Conclusion

The first Home Rule incident raised vital practical and theoretical questions. Liberal and Irish proponents of Home Rule developed and reiterated a pluralist concept of the United Kingdom as a remedy for Ireland's disaffection. To support this hypothesis they cited history, recent actions and the conduct of the post-1886 Salisbury regime. Prior to 1886 the Irish case for institutional reform had not gone unchallenged but seemed unlikely to be adopted by a major British party and was dismissed often without careful enunciation of an alternative prescription. Liberal unionism had been practised since Sir Robert Peel's administration and was not the property of any political creed. When it became a serious option Home Rule forced Unionists to develop a closely reasoned approach to counter it. Accretion of Liberal Unionists and the progressive instincts of certain Conservatives, notably Arthur Balfour, married to the intellectual thrust of Dicey, Lecky, Goldwin Smith and others, allowed for the emergence of a cogent doctrine of firmness and impartiality in administration of the law along with positive efforts to meet Ireland's material wants, exemplifying a Unionist concept of an organic state.

There is a facile assumption that this Unionist programme was doomed to failure; despite defeat at the general election of 1892, it was a remarkable success. Ireland had been partly pacified, the agrarian agitation quelled, the Home Rulers divided, the Catholic Hierarchy reached out for an accommodation, landownership was considerably extended and other reforms met specific Irish requirements. At the same time the balance sheet shows failures: Home Rulers still commanded the loyalty of Catholics in Ireland, and although Conservative blunders on law enforcement and the taint of association with the Pigott forgeries handed them easy propaganda victories, the never deeply submerged anti-Irish sentiment behind Unionism further undermined its nobler intentions. Yet, at the end of the day, the Salisbury administration displayed impressive flexibility and its thesis concerning how to counter Home Rule was neither fully proved nor disproved by 1892. As a doctrine it was not *ipso facto* less appropriate than Gladstone's pluralism.

Notes

1   *The Speaker's Handbook on the Irish Question* (2nd edn; London, 1887) pp. 1–2.

2   Stephen Koss, *The Rise and Fall of the Political Press in Britain: Volume One: The Nineteenth Century* (London, 1981), pp. 286–9.

3   *The Times*, 18 June 1886.

4   *Ibid.*, 19 June 1886.

5   *Ibid.*, 21 June 1886.

6   *Ibid.*

7   W. E. Gladstone, *Speeches on the Irish Question in 1886* (Edinburgh,

1886), pp. 179–83.

8 *Ibid.*, pp. 222–3, 242.

9 *The Times*, 17 June 1886.

10 *Ibid.*, 22 June 1886.

11 *Ibid.*, 21 June 1886.

12 *Ibid.*, 22 June 1886.

13 *Ibid.*, 17 June 1886.

14 *Ibid.*, 21, 22 June 1886.

15 Quoted in Kenneth O. Morgan, 'Lloyd George and the Irish', in Lord Blake, *Ireland under the Union* (Oxford, 1989), p. 84.

16 *The Times.*, 21 June 1886.

17 *Ibid.*, 22 June 1886.

18 *Ibid.*, 26 June 1886.

19 *Ibid.*, 30 June 1886.

20 *Ibid.*, 26 June 1886.

21 Quoted in A. G. Gardiner, *The Life of Sir William Harcourt* (London, 1293), II, p. 8.

22 *The Times*, 26 June 1886.

23 *Ibid.*, 30 June 1886.

24 *Ibid.*

25 Diary, 7 July 1886, Sir Edward Hamilton Papers, British Library, MS 48634.

26 *Ibid.*

27 *Ibid.*, 9 July.

28 Henry Labouchere to Sir William Harcourt, 11 July 1886, Sir William Harcourt Papers, Bodleian Library, Oxford, MS 57.

29 Quoted in A. B. Cooke and A. P. W. Malcolmson (compl.), *The Ashbourne Papers, 1869–1918* (Belfast, 1974), p. 174.

30 J. L. Hammond, *Gladstone and the Irish Nation* (new impression; London, 1964), pp. 532–54; Christopher Harvie, *The Lights of Liberalism: University Liberals and the Challenge of Democracy 1860–86* (London, 1976), pp. 218–42; Richard A. Cosgrove, *The Rule of Law: Albert Venn Dicey, Victorian Jurist* (Chapel Hill, 1980), pp. 115–36; Donal McCartney, *W. E. H. Lecky: Historian and Politician 1838–1903* (Dublin, 1994), pp. 114–36; Tom Dunne, '*La Trahison des Clerics*: British Intellectuals and the First Home-Rule Crisis', *Irish Historical Studies*, XXIII (November, 1982), pp. 134–73.

31 Dunne, '*La Trahison des Clerics*', pp. 140–1.

32 Quoted in Harvie, *Lights of Liberalism*, p. 226.

33 Quoted in D. George Boyce, '"The Marginal Britons" The Irish', in Robert Colls and Philip Dodd (eds), *Englishness: Politics and Culture 1880–1929* (London, 1986), p. 234.

34 James Loughlin, 'Joseph Chamberlain, English Nationalism and the Ulster Question', *History*, 77 (June 1992), p. 219.

35 Boyce 'Marginal Britons', pp. 230–53.

36 *Ibid.*, pp. 248–9.

37 Quoted in Lady Victoria Hicks Beach, *The Life of Sir Michael Hicks Beach* (London, 1932), I, p. 280.

38 Sir Michael Hicks Beach to Lord Salisbury, 25 July 1886, St

Aldwyn Papers, Gloucestershire Record Office, PCC/31.

39 *Parliamentary Debates [PD]*, 303 (1886), c. 291.

40 *The Nation*, 3 July 1886.

41 *Ibid.*, 7 August 1886.

42 *PD*, 308 (1886), cc. 59–70.

43 Quoted in C. C. O'Brien, *Parnell and His Party, 1880–90* (corrected impression; Oxford, 1964), p. 200.

44 Quoted in Sally Warwick-Haller, *William O'Brien and the Irish Land War* (Dublin, 1990), p. 82.

45 Justin McCarthy to Henry Labouchere, 1 August 1886, Viscount Gladstone Papers, British Library, MS 46016.

46 *The Freeman's Journal*, 16 August 1886.

47 Quoted in Hicks Beach, *Sir Michael Hicks Beach*, I, p. 299.

48 Quoted in Emmet Larkin, *The Roman Catholic Church and the Plan of Campaign in Ireland 1886–1888* (Cork, 1978), pp. 27, 28.

49 Archbishop Walsh to Sir Michael Hicks Beach, 16 December, St Aldwyn Papers, PCC/53.

50 See, *The Freeman's Journal*, 15 January 1886.

51 Quoted in Larkin, *The Roman Catholic Church*, p. 39.

52 Quoted in O'Brien, *Parnell and His Party*, p. 200, n. 3.

53 Hicks Beach, *Sir Michael Hicks Beach*, I, p. 299.

54 Quoted in Michael Barker, *Gladstone and Radicalism: The Reconstruction of Liberal Policy in Britain 1885–94* (Hassocks, Sussex, 1975), p. 77.

55 Quoted in *ibid.*

56 Quoted in Michael Hurst, *Joseph Chamberlain and the Liberal Reunion* (London, 1967), p. 83.

57 Quoted in *ibid.*

58 Quoted in *ibid.*, p. 94.

59 Quoted in *ibid.*, pp. 97, n. 4, 125, n. 2.

60 Quoted in Barker, *Gladstone and Radicalism*, p. 78.

61 Balfour's strategy of containment is credited by Margaret O'Callaghan with 'killing' Parnellism. See, Margaret O'Callaghan, *British High Politics and a Nationalist Ireland: Criminality, Land and the Law Under Forster and Balfour* (Cork, 1994), p. 120. Also, see, L. P. Curtis, jun., *Coercion and Conciliation In Ireland 1880–1892: A Study in Conservative Unionism* (Princeton, 1963), p. 174.

62 O'Callaghan, *British High Politics*, pp. 114, 118.

63 Curtis, *Coercion and Conciliation*, pp. 174–300.

64 Virginia Crossman, *Politics, Law and Order in Nineteenth-Century Ireland* (Dublin, 1996), p. 154.

65 Quoted in Curtis, *Coercion and Conciliation*, p. 169.

66 Quoted in *ibid.*, p. 341.

67 Quoted in Alan O'Day and John Stevenson (eds), *Irish Historical Documents since 1800* (Dublin, 1992), p. 114.

68 *Ibid.*

69 Spencer to his wife, 18 April 1887, in Peter Gordon (ed.), *The Red Earl: The Papers of the Fifth Earl Spencer 1835–1910* (Northampton, 1986), II, p. 146.

70 Justin McCarthy and Mrs Campbell Praed, *Our Book of Memories: Letters of Justin McCarthy to Mrs Campbell Praed* (London, 1912), p. 91.

71 Crossman, *Politics, Law and Order*, p. 174.

72 Quoted in Curtis, *Coercion and Conciliation*, p. 337.

73 Crossman, *Politics, Law and Order*, p. 166.

74 Quoted in Catherine B. Shannon, *Arthur J. Balfour and Ireland 1874–1922* (Washington, DC, 1988), p. 46.

75 Quoted in Larkin, *The Roman Catholic Church*, p. 129.

76 Barker, *Gladstone and Radicalism*, p. 78.

77 See, Gordon (ed.), *The Red Earl*, II, pp. 132–80.

78 Quoted in Larkin, *The Roman Catholic Church*, p. 211.

79 Quoted in *ibid.*, p. 291.

80 *The Freeman's Journal*, 9 May 1888.

81 Elizabeth R. Hooker, *Readjustments of Agricultural Tenure in Ireland* (Chapel Hill, NC, 1938), p. 65; for the rate of purchase in Cork, see, James S. Donnelly, jun., *The Land and the People of Nineteenth-Century Cork: The Rural Economy and the Land Question* (London, 1975), p. 368.

82 Donnelly, *The Land and the People*, pp. 368–71.

83 O'Callaghan, *British High Politics*, p. 118.

84 Quoted in Warwick-Haller, *William O'Brien*, p. 115. Laurence M. Geary, *The Plan of Campaign 1886–1891* (Cork, 1986), p. 122.

85 R. V. Comerford, 'The Parnell Era, 1883–91', in W. E. Vaughan (ed.), *A New History of Ireland VI: Ireland Under the Union, II, 1870–1921* (Oxford, 1996), p.75.

86 See the description by Henry W. Lucy, *A Diary of the Salisbury Parliament, 1886–1892* (London, Paris and Melbourne, 1892), pp. 157–8.

87 Quoted in Mark Tierney, *Croke of Cashel: The Life of Archbishop Thomas William Croke 1821–1902* (Dublin, 1976), p. 231.

88 Quoted in Emmet Larkin, *The Roman Catholic Church and the Fall of Parnell, 1888–1891* (Liverpool, 1979), p. 26.

89 Quoted in *ibid.*, pp. 26–7.

90 O'Callaghan, *British High Politics*, pp. 112–21.

91 Crossman, *Politics, Law and Order*, p. 173.

92 O'Callaghan, *British High Politics*, p. 118.

93 *The Times*, 9 March, 20 July 1889.

94 Quoted in Warwick-Haller, *William O'Brien*, p. 120.

95 *The Freeman's Journal*, 7 October 1889.

96 Quoted in Larkin, *Fall of Parnell*, p. 108.

97 Quoted in *ibid.*, pp. 110–11.

98 *The Freeman's Journal*, 6 September 1889.

99 Alvin Jackson, *The Ulster Party: Irish Unionists in the House of Commons, 1884–1922* (Oxford, 1989), pp. 178–81.

100 Blanche E. C. Dugdale, *Arthur James Balfour* (London, 1936), I, pp. 168–9; see also, pp. 170–1.

101 Quoted in Barker, *Gladstone and Radicalism*, p. 99.

102 Quoted in H. C. G. Matthew, *The Liberal Imperialists* (Oxford, 1973), p. 266.

103 Dudley W. R. Bahlman (ed.), *The Diary of Sir Edward Walter*

Hamilton 1885–1908 (Hull, 1993), pp. 200, 102–3.

104   H. C. G. Matthew (ed.), *The Gladstone Diaries with Cabinet Minutes and Prime-Ministerial Correspondence, 1887–1891* (Oxford, 1994), XII, pp. xxxvii, 252–4, 256.

105   Quoted in Barker, *Gladstone and Radicalism*, p. 99.

106   Bahlman (ed.), *Sir Edward Walter Hamilton*, p. 112 (21 March 1890).

107   *The Times*, 30 June 1890.

108   Quoted in Larkin, *Fall of Parnell*, p. 205; see, Crossman, *Politics, Law and Order*, pp. 179–80.

109   Frank Callanan, *T. M. Healy* (Cork, 1996), p. 113.

110   Quoted in John Morley, *The Life of William Ewart Gladstone* (London, 1903), III, p. 437.

111   *St Stephen's Review*, 29 November 1890.

112   Callanan, *The Parnell Split 1890–91* (Cork, 1992), p. 65.

113   Information derived from F. S. L. Lyons, *The Fall of Parnell 1890–91* (London, 1960); and Callanan, *The Parnell Split*, though the events are interpreted differently here than in either of these accounts.

114   Callanan, *The Parnell Split*, p. 278.

115   Tierney, *Croke of Cashel*, p. 246.

116   Callanan, *The Parnell Split*, p. 279; *T. M. Healy*, p. 113.

117   Callanan, *T. M. Healy*, p. 344.

118   Quoted in George-Denis Zimmermann, *Songs of Irish Rebellion: Political Street Ballads and Rebel Songs 1780–1900* (Dublin, 1967), p. 64.

119   Quoted in Barker, *Gladstone and Radicalism*, p. 205.

120   See, Hooker, *Readjustments*, pp. 68–70.

121   Curtis, *Coercion and Conciliation*, pp. 355–62; for the other proposals, see, pp. 362–92.

122   Quoted in *ibid.*, p. 362.

123   Jackson, *The Ulster Party*, pp. 170–1.

6

Second Home Rule episode, 1892–95

There was a perfect union of hearts between the Irish Protestants and the Irish Roman Catholics, and there was a perfect harmony of sentiment between England and Ireland from the year 1782 to the year 1795. This was no dream. It has happened before. Why should it not happen again? Gifted with the power of self-government, why should they not exhibit, on the one hand, that strong fraternal concord among themselves, and on the other hand, that harmonious sentiment towards England which characterised the period I have named? (Gladstone, 6 April 1893)[1]

For many years the House of Commons had been trying to accommodate the feelings of the Protestant and Catholic Parties to each other. The Government had now brought forward a Bill, which irrevocably ranged nine out of 10 Protestants on one side, and nine out of 10 Catholics on the other. (Sir John Brodrick, 7 April 1893)[2]

Introduction

Neither the Liberal government of 1893–95 nor the second Home Rule bill have attracted extensive interest. Reasons for this oversight are easily discerned. In spite of Gladstone's efforts the bill was rejected by the House of Lords; Liberals, like Home Rulers, were soon in disarray, with national self-government firmly sidelined for nearly two decades. The second Home Rule incident is treated as a repetition of 1886. The year of its defeat – 1893 – in Irish national mythology is accorded immense importance, though not because of the self-government struggle. Instead, it is honoured as a beginning of the turning away from old-style politics and towards the resurrection of the nation's culture and soul under the early tutelage of Douglas Hyde and the Gaelic revival. Developments in Irish policy in these years had long-term consequences. As in 1886 and again in 1912, the bill was constructed as a parliamentary device; many particulars of the 1893 scheme were repeated in 1912. Gladstone departed from the political scene shortly after of the bill's rejection; the experience soured many Liberals on the Home Rule formula and the dispute heralded the vibrant assertion of the veto powers of the House of Lords.

Home Rule had a further significance for Irish political alignment. By the time of the general election in July 1892 a second bill had become an imperative for anti-Parnellites, who saw it as means of preserving themselves in Ireland. In late July, when it appeared that the Liberals might postpone introducing such a measure, Dillon believed:

> [U]nless we had a distinct declaration from Mr G that the Home Rule Bill would be introduced the first thing next session and kept to the front as the foremost gov. measure till passed thro' the Commons, we could not hold our own in Ireland. That we did not require them to state what they would do if the Lords rejected it, but gave my view of what would be best.[3]

Home Rule consumed more House of Commons time than any other bill in the nineteenth century. Discussions required eighty-two days. Nearly a thousand speeches were delivered against the bill and approximately half that number made in its favour. A bevy of pertinent issues were articulated.

The July 1892 general election

By late winter of 1892 Salisbury's government was on its last legs. Liberal managers began to collude with Irish leaders to firm up their alliance for the anticipated general election. Similarly, Irish loyalists, particularly those in Ulster, began charting their response in case Liberals formed the next administration and introduced another Home Rule proposal. On 17 June 1892 some 12,000 delegates attend a huge convention at Belfast to express loyalty to the Union and oppose Home Rule. They pledged not to accept Home Rule and, if it was enacted, to pursue a policy of passive non-cooperation with a Dublin regime. This demonstration received substantial attention in Britain, *The Times* devoting two pages to it. A similar protest meeting of southern Unionists was held in Dublin. Predictably, Liberals and Home Rulers tried to minimise the importance of this resistance. Many Unionists, while opposing Gladstonian Home Rule, were ready to reaffirm their commitment to other reforms, notable democratic local government.

National factions prepared for a showdown. Parnellism entered the fray terminally ill. In December 1890 the Parnellite rump numbered thirty-three MPs, or nearly 39 per cent of Home Rulers, and still claimed the allegiance of thirty members on the eve of the general election. Their anti-Parnellite rivals captured six of the seven by-elections held in constituencies with Catholic majorities between December 1890 and the general election of 1892. At the general election, held between 4 and 18 July, Parnellites contested 44 of the country's 103 seats, facing an anti-Parnellite candidate in every case.[4] Substantial portions of the country – Cork, the midlands and Ulster – were without a candidate upholding 'the principles and policies of our lost leader'.[5] Anti-Parnellites put up candidates in a further 41 constituencies, 18 of which (16 in Ulster and the 2 for Trinity College) were uncontested. Parnellites won only 9 seats (5 in the counties and 4 borough constituencies, 3 of which were in Dublin). In the 43 constituencies where rival factions met head-to-head, anti-Parnellites out-polled Parnellites on average by 100,000 votes to 70,000. Parnellism did much less well in rural than in urban seats where sections of the lower middle class, especially the petite bourgeoisie and artisans, gave it support. Without its leader, Parnellism was gravely weakened, lacking even a compelling ideology. In Ulster, where Parnellism hardly existed, Catholic voters coalesced behind the anti-Parnellites, in part, as the best option to face Unionism. The National League in the north had virtually collapsed, with the anti-Parnellite, National Federation membership outnumbering it thirty to one.[6] Elsewhere, the Parnellites had little organisational apparatus and scarcely any funds. Adding to their liabilities, the priesthood was staunchly anti-Parnellite. Combined Home Rule numbers were slightly reduced to eighty-one MPs (eighty in Ireland plus T. P. O'Connor, the incumbent in Scotland Division of Liverpool); these garnered 78.1 per cent of ballots cast in Ireland. In Ulster the outcome of polling damaged the Home Rule case, for instead of holding a majority of seats in the province, the numbers now stood at eighteen Unionists and fifteen Home Rulers, defying Gladstone's assertion in 1886 that a majority in the province supported self-government.

The Parnellite rump had a degree of internal cohesion, though its attitude towards Home Rule and material reforms scarcely differed from its opponents, who had the advantage of numbers but were torn asunder by internal rifts and found themselves at the mercy of their Liberal allies. Already there were strains arising from disputes between Dillon and Healy over *The Freeman's Journal*.[7] Justin McCarthy lacked the qualities to lead so motley a crew. F. S. L. Lyons describes Home Rulers as 'disunited, ill-disciplined, and with no outstanding leader, the very antithesis of the party which had assumed a role of such importance in 1886'.[8]

Home Rulers' patience was rewarded by the swing to the Liberals in Great Britain. Unionist numbers were trimmed to 315, with the Liberals and Home Rulers combined returning 355 MPs. But the Gladstonians were less successful than they had forecast, capturing 48 per cent of the vote in England, 62.8 per cent in Wales and 53.9 per cent in Scotland. On learning the outcome, Gladstone bemoaned: 'the burden on me personally is serious: a small Liberal majority being the heaviest weight I can well be called to bear.'[9] In these circumstances Gladstone worried about the implications of trying to pass another Home Rule bill.

The limitations of the Home Rulers' position did not elude the anti-Parnellites. Shortly after the election they began carping about Liberal neglect; Healy, who had faithfully supported the Gladstonian alliance during the O'Shea divorce crisis, now complained about the retention in Dublin Castle of so many Unionist sympathisers.[10] The Parnellite rump called for an autumn session in 1892 to deal with the problems of the evicted tenants.

Making the second Home Rule bill, July 1892–January 1893

The second Home Rule episode differed from 1886 in significant ways. First, the idea of Irish self-government and the cases for and against had been fully aired. Second, both national factions had been consulted about the plan. Third, Gladstone took account of defects in the 1886 measure. Fourth, Gladstonians and the opposition had time to hone their respective strategies.

Although Gladstone and the Liberals were committed to Home Rule, the timing of its introduction and the specifics of any scheme were not settled matters. On learning of the inauspicious parliamentary arithmetic, Gladstone preferred to postpone introduction of a measure for a year; alternatively, he was inclined to bring forward a resolution or short bill meant to secure endorsement of the principle.[11] William Harcourt wanted to begin the session of 1893 with a series of other measures.[12] Morley, who recognised that for many Liberals 'the temperature of feeling for the Irish task was not by any means uniform or equable', was alarmed by Gladstone's equivocation.[13] Their slender margin in the House of Commons rendered rejection of Home Rule in the House of Lords more likely, though it was impossible to forecast exactly what action the peers might take. The decision to proceed with a full-blown bill was taken only on 28 July after Gladstone met with Spencer and Morley. This course had a firm rationale. It would keep faith with the anti-Parnellites, Liberal promises could be seen to be upheld, and the principle if not the actual implementation of self-government would be secured in the House of Commons. If Unionists resorted to the Lords' veto, this might be overridden, or at least the opposition's dependence on a hereditary body laid bare. As a consequence of the narrow Liberal majority and the divisions within the Gladstonian ranks, Salisbury decided to meet Parliament.

The Conservative government was defeated on a vote of no confidence and on 15 August Gladstone was invited to form a Liberal government. The Liberals and Home Rulers won by a margin of 350 votes to 310, a portent of the large turnouts for divisions throughout this parliamentary session. Discussion of the Queen's Speech concentrated on Irish policy and prefigured the Home Rule debates. G. J. Goschen on 8 August had developed a theme that would be given prominence in the later attack upon Gladstone's plan: 'the policy of the government as regards Home Rule was not condemned. ... The majority has been achieved ... not by the language of Home Rule, but it has been gained by other language and other promises.'[14] He asserted that 'we have a majority in Great Britain'. Home Rule, as Goschen observed, could only be carried with Irish votes. Unionist speakers aired other important arguments. The position of Ulster was given greater prominence in 1893 than in 1886. T. W. Russell, an Ulster Liberal Unionist, showed that the general election refuted the claim that the northern province preferred Home Rule, for a majority of its MPs now opposed the doctrine:

> [B]ut, whatever may be the nature of that measure, it can have only one meaning for the people of Ulster. It means their degradation as citizens. It will place their religious freedom, purchased at a great price, at the mercy of Archbishop Walsh. It will place their civil rights wrung from Kings, at the disposal of the most unscrupulous body of politicians that Ireland has ever produced. It will place the commerce of Ulster at the mercy of men, some of whom have converted the smiles, and the prosperous town of Tipperary into a howling wilderness, and who, to carry out the basest of ends, have not scrupled to lay waste and bare great tracts of country, and to turn smiling fields into waste and deserted plains. This, and much more, any form of Home Rule will mean to Ulster.[15]

Home Rulers wanted to know what Liberals had in mind. McCarthy, anxious to forge a safe middle ground, hoped that the government would carry out the administration of Ireland in accord with the spirit of public opinion. His party wished something to be done about amnesty for those still imprisoned as a consequence of being convicted during the dynamite campaign of the mid-1880s, wanted to see coercion suspended and an inquiry into the cases of the tenants evicted during the Plan of Campaign.[16] John Redmond struck a more extracting tone, though his actual demands were virtually identical to those of the anti-Parnellites. He objected that since 1886 the government of Ireland 'has been based upon principles diametrically opposed to those which are dear to the hearts of all Irish Nationalists. It has been based on the idea that Ireland is simply a province of Great Britain, whereas we claim, on the other hand, that Ireland is a nation and that it has the rights of a nation.'[17] The Parnellite leader unintentionally gave credence to Goschen's complaint that Home Rule had not been properly brought before the nation. While he absolved Gladstone of ambiguity, Redmond noted that 'the Liberal party has been speaking through many mouths, and through the columns of the leading Liberal papers in different parts of the country, and doubts have been raised as to whether the Liberal policy is the same as it was in June 1886'. Furthermore, he demanded that if Home Rule were rejected by the House of Lords, 'it should not be dropped or hung up in favour of any other portion of the Newcastle programme'. He made plain his concern about not knowing what sort of scheme Liberals would introduce:

> [T]herefore we say we are in absolute ignorance with respect to the scheme that is to be proposed, and apparently we may continue in ignorance until a cut-and-dried proposal is brought down to that Table, and then, we shall be, as in 1886, in a position of most terrible difficulty – the difficulty of being forced either to accept this cut-and-dried scheme in all its main features, as it is proposed, or else to take the enormous responsibility of rejecting it.[18]

Redmond spoke in support of the evicted tenants and amnesty as well. Towards the conclusion of the debate T. C. Harrington reiterated the pleas for amnesty and the evicted tenants.[19] Home Rulers attempted to dispel the case for Ulster, suggesting that when northern Protestants experienced self-government they would appreciate the virtues and fairness to themselves, becoming its strongest proponents.

Gladstone, as in January 1886, signalled the Liberal intent without giving away details. The GOM took issue with many Unionist arguments, particularly those alleging that the dependence on Irish votes to pass the measure would amount to an illegitimate majority, maintaining that Ireland's case had been before the country at the general election. He denied that Ulster occupied an exceptional place. Declining to give a pledge about amnesty on the one hand, Gladstone on the other announced that he hoped that landlords and evicted tenants would reach an informal settlement during the autumn, making legislation unnecessary. What most interested his audience was any foretaste of the Home Rule bill. Gladstone did not provide specifics, but stated that the principles of Home Rule were well-known; these were 'limited, on the one hand by the full and effectual maintenance of the imperial supremacy which pervades the whole of the Empire, and, on the other by the equally full and effectual transference to Ireland of the management of her local concerns'. This he followed with a reminder that 'the question of Ireland is almost, if not altogether, my sole link with public life'. On the question of what might be done if the House of Lords rejected the bill, Gladstone was non-committal though he warned that it would be a grave step for the peers to act against the will of the House of Commons, affirming that it is 'impossible for such a government to regard the rejection of such a bill as terminating its duty'.[20]

During late summer and autumn 1892 the new Prime Minister began preparation of the Home Rule proposal. It could not be introduced before the parliamentary session of 1893; in the meantime Dillon persuaded Morley to do something about the evicted tenants. Morley set up a judicial inquiry which reported the following year, resulting in the Evicted Tenants bill of 1894, another measure destined to stumble in the House of Lords.[21] Gladstone looked at various sources to guide his Home Rule ideas: the earlier bill of 1886, the plan of Sir Charles Gavan Duffy published in 1887, the discussions with Parnell when he visited Hawarden at the end of 1889, along with numerous solicited and volunteered contributions. In March 1892 Redmond endorsed of the contents of the 1886 bill, suggesting only a few modifications. Redmond had a meeting with Morley in early October when the Chief Secretary assured him that the new bill would be one that a Parnellite could freely accept. Gladstone conferred with leading anti-Parnellites in March and June to discuss a future plan. In July 1892 he and Morley had met Dillon, McCarthy and Sexton. Thereafter, Gladstone – via Morley – stayed in touch with anti-Parnellites, including Healy, with whom he had a frosty relationship.[22]

In October, through James Bryce, Gladstone received the views of Edward Blake, the experienced Canadian leader, who had been recruited to the anti-Parnellite ranks because of his constitutional expertise. Blake's suggestions weighed heavily with Gladstone. On 19 November Bryce drafted a memorandum with further suggestions of his own, and on 21 November a Cabinet committee, consisting of Gladstone, Morley, Spencer, Lord Herschell, Sir Henry Campbell-Bannerman and Bryce, was established to consider the bill. The Chancellor of the Exchequer, Harcourt, was not included probably because Gladstone 'dreaded the well-known opposition which was sure to be given to the measure, in whatever shape it was produced, from the most prominent person in the Cabinet'.[23] Liberals paid dearly for Harcourt's exclusion when the financial clauses proved faulty and a hastily contrived fiscal arrangement had to be substituted. On 24 November Gladstone circulated a memorandum with ideas on how Home Rule might be financed;[24] this part of the work was reinforced by a paper drawn up on 14 December by Lord Welby, Edward Hamilton and Alfred Milner. On behalf of the anti-Parnellites Sexton drew up his own financial proposals; this paper was passed on to Morley on 13 January. It did not find favour with Gladstone but, in contrast to 1886, this showed that Irish leaders ideas at least were considered. Gladstone's bill was informed by a wealth of information and opinion.

Parliamentary discussion, January–September 1993

Chronological analysis of the Home Rule contest in 1886 provides an unusual snapshot of events; similar treatment of 1893 is also revealing. In 1893 the lengthy process worked to the benefit of the Unionists by exposing weaknesses in the bill, legitimising deployment of the peers' veto. In the Queen's Speech on 31 January the government announced:

> [T]he Irish question stands foremost in the scheme of legislative labour proposed for the ensuing Session. ... Two alternatives are before us: There is the present system which I may describe as democracy, tempered or qualified by coercion, and there is the alternative of concession within the limits of prudence to the demand of Ireland for local self-government.[25]

Introduction of Home Rule ensured that this would be a lively parliamentary session. On 3 February Henry Lucy recorded:

> [T]he House of Commons since it met, for what prophets are agreed in forecasting as a momentous Session, has been busied with many things. Egypt, Uganda, and Ireland have severally passed in review. But Ireland has, in its familiar manner, been the lean kine that swallowed up the rest. All Parliamentary roads lead to Ireland. With whatever object or prospect, a sitting may commence, some Irish question is safe to interpose. Publicists are used to speak of 'the' Irish Question as if it existed in the singular number. There is, truly, only one Irish Question, as the earth has only one atmosphere. But it is everywhere, varying as the atmosphere varies, yet ever present.[26]

When Gladstone introduced the bill on 13 February 1893 it bore the hallmark of the 1886 plan with emendations and new features (see document 7). As in 1886, the occasion stimulated huge public and parliamentary interest. In the House of Commons every seat was taken, some being keenly contested. Lucy amusingly reported:

> [A]mong the personal encounters that took place in various parts of the battlefield the fight between Colonel Saunderson and Mr Wallace, member for Limehouse, attracted exceptional attention. The Colonel had, Mr Wallace said, dropped into his seat. Certainly he had dropped on to his hat, which chanced to be on the seat. Mr Wallace, though representing a London constituency is, like the Colonel, an Ulster man. When under provocative circumstances Ulster meets Ulster there is naturally a fight, and this incident supplied no exception to the rule. Mr Wallace tried to pull the Colonel out of the seat. The Colonel stands six feet high, is all bone and muscle, and was born fighting. He gently but firmly laid Mr Wallace on his back and resumed his seat.[27]

Gladstone's introduction lasted two and a quarter hours and, according to Lucy, 'the explanation of the intricate measure was a model of lucidity; the opening passages of the speech soared on lofty heights of eloquence; the stately peroration that closed it will take rank with its most famous predecessors.'[28]

Supporters and opponents girded themselves for battle. Advocates of Home Rule still needed to make the case for a major constitutional change, but they had the advantages of time, several years of educating public opinion and a more united Liberal party. The opposition, unlike in early 1886, knew what lay ahead and was organised for the coming trial. Home Rule's opponents had a six-strand approach – to capture public opinion in the event of an election on the issue; to legitimise the use of the House of Lords veto should the measure pass in the House of Commons; to expose the risks of Irish self-government; to open and exploit differences known to exist among Liberals; to discover and emphasise defects in the specifics of the scheme; and to enlist sympathy for the minority in Ireland, especially Ulster Protestants. It proved an absorbing task, demanding Unionist MPs' continuous attention.

The Prime Minister began in introduction, stating that 'in 1886 there were five propositions laid down as cardinal principles from which there ought to be no departure'. He then announced:

> [C]hanges there have been – far from unimportant changes, but not I think, in any manner trenching upon any of those declared principles of 1886. The object of the Bill was stated – and that remains the object of the Bill, with regard to which everything else is secondary and conditional – the object of the Bill was to establish a Legislative Body sitting in Dublin for the conduct of both legislation and administration in Irish as distinct from Imperial affairs. First then, Imperial unity was to be observed; secondly, the equality of all

Kingdoms was to be borne in mind; thirdly, there was to be an equitable re-partition of Imperial charges; fourthly, any and every practicable provision for the protection of minorities was to be adopted; and, fifthly, the plan that was to be proposed ought to be as, at least in the judgement of its promoters, to present the necessary characteristics of I will not say finality, because that is a discredited word, but a real and a continuing settlement.[29]

An attempt to counter concerns about the relationship between the Westminster Parliament and the proposed assembly came in the preamble which affirmed the supremacy of the United Kingdom Parliament. The proposal allowed for a Dublin legislature with two houses, an elected upper council of 48 members returned for eight years by those possessing a high property qualification and a lower assembly of 103 elected for five years on the existing parliamentary franchise.[30] Gladstone estimated that approximately 170,000 people would be qualified to vote for members of the upper council. If a bill were rejected by either chamber, it could then be passed by a joint majority vote of the two sitting together or should that fail to resolve the difference the proposed legislation might then be re-introduced after a lapse of two years or a dissolution and be carried by the popular assembly alone. Exclusions and the extent of the council's jurisdiction were much the same as in 1886. A reduced Irish representation of eighty MPs would remain at Westminster, but there would be 'limitations on their voting powers'.[31] No separate provision was made for Ulster. The Prime Minister's brief flirtation with an Ulster dimension in 1886 disappeared. In 1892 he had dismissed demands for any concessions, asserting that Ulster's 'claim to be exempted from the control of an Irish legislature was preposterous. "Ulster forsooth!" – Ulster that returned to Parliament as many Nationalists as Unionists. Ulster whose record was the bloodiest record of all the 4 Provinces.'[32] For Gladstone, 'the object of this Bill is autonomy and self-government for Ireland in matters properly Irish'.[33]

John Kendle outlines the seven major differences between this and the earlier bill.[34] First, the Irish legislature was to have two component parts that would sit separately. Second, the supremacy of the imperial Parliament was clearly stated in the preamble. Third, the viceroy's term was fixed at six years and Catholics were eligible to hold this post. Fourth, special provision was made for the appointment of an executive committee of the Privy Council in Ireland (an Irish Cabinet). Fifth, future appeals would be to the Privy Council alone and not to the Privy Council and House of Lords. Sixth, Irish numbers in the Westminster House of Commons were reduced to eighty and these had limited rights, being barred from voting on any bill or motion expressly confined to Great Britain or to one of its parts

(England, Scotland and Wales), on any motion or resolution relating to a tax not raised in Ireland, on any vote or appropriation of money otherwise than for imperial services, and on any motion or resolution affecting Great Britain or person or persons therein. Seventh, all Irish customs duties were to be collected by the United Kingdom exchequer and treated as Ireland's contribution to imperial expenditure. Colin Matthew suggests that this second bill had the virtues of not mixing Ireland with grander ideas of Home Rule-all-round – that is, for Scotland, Wales and England, as well as for Ireland – and that the powers of an Irish legislature would be assumed gradually.[35] However, it did not fulfil the principles laid down by Gavan Duffy, who suggested that the country be carved up into thirty-five three-member constituencies which he believed would ensure a proportionate level of minority representation.[36] As a further backstop for the minority he urged that a Senate consisting of fifty-four members should be a nominated body. In his opinion, Gladstone's measure failed to ensure an appropriate level of minority representation in the popular chamber, while it limited the functions of a Dublin legislature and executive rather than creating an authority where neither contending party could be 'suppressed nor overborne'.[37]

Immediate reactions to the scheme were predictable. Sir Edward Clarke, responding for the opposition, objected to the absence of arrangements for Ulster. For the anti-Parnellites, Sexton said that the Irish accepted the proposal as a settlement of the constitutional question.[38] John Redmond, speaking for the Parnellites, was more tentative, stating 'the bill is a compromise between the full demands which Ireland has made in the past and that which you are willing to concede. The institution offered is a compromise and is accepted as a compromise.'[39] He wanted full Irish representation at Westminster retained so long as Ireland's Parliament did not have complete control over internal affairs, including the police. He conceded that 'your Parliament in England will have the dual power to take away our Parliament from us and to pass laws for Ireland over our heads in contravention of the wishes of the Irish Legislature', suggesting that the autonomy granted would be less than total even in domestic matters.[40]

Gladstone commended Home Rule again as the democratic desire of Ireland, an instalment of justice owed to the neighbour island. As in 1886, his argument was based on his interpretation of history. Home Rule was intended to erase the alienation of the two countries, strengthening the necessary connection between them. According to him, adequate arrangements protected both the supremacy of Parliament and the minority in Ireland. The opposition denied his claim. They were abetted by a number of weaknesses in the bill. Gladstone's refusal to consider separate treatment for Ulster was an obvious target. But there were others. Reducing Ireland's representation to eighty affirmed the well-known over-representation of the country, giving substance to opposition arguments that Home Rule was being pressed by an illegitimate parliamentary majority. This eventually brought forth Chamberlain's demand for a referendum on Home Rule if it were passed by the House of Commons. Allowing Irish MPs to vote only on some questions was exposed as unworkable in practice. Additionally, the opposition cleverly struck at the inadequacy of the statement confirming the supremacy of Parliament, another feature requiring modification. Finally, the financial provisions were based on erroneous calculations; in late May a new scheme was introduced. Defects in the plan helped compensate Unionists for their weakness of parliamentary numbers.

From the beginning the opposition contested the bill tooth and nail. On 11 March 1893 Gladstone announced that he would proceed with it on a day-by-day basis in order to make better progress. He was 'faced by the most resolute and reckless party of obstruction unknown since Mr Parnell was in the height of his power and in the thick of the fight'.[41] The government position was made worse by the Speaker's decision limiting the use of the closure to occasions when it commanded a large majority, thereby placing an additional burden on the parliamentary timetable. This was not modified until late June. Furthermore, the government's small majority of forty-two faced a constant danger of snap defeats on amendments. Throughout the many months of debate, even in August, attendance reached remarkable heights, with divisions sometimes attracting more than 600 MPs. Liberals soon became restive about the neglect of their own interests.

During the Easter break Balfour made an important interjection. In his uncle's stead he went to Belfast where he addressed a rally at the Ulster Hall.[42] His visit heartened the Ulster stand against Home Rule, but his words, if imprecise about what form of resistance would be sustainable, hinted, as Churchill did in 1886 and Andrew Bonar Law would do in 1912, at Conservative support for refusal to recognise a Dublin regime. Introduction of the bill spurred the formation of Unionist organisations. The Ulster Defence Union was founded in March. Soon some 200 Unionist clubs were in operation.[43]

After the Easter recess, Lucy remarked, 'both sides mean business, the business of the opposition being obstruction', noting that he could not 'call to mind any epoch of obstruction exceeding in deliberation, and pertinacity that which clogged the wheels of Parliament during the past eight weeks'.[44] Yet the arguments, if prolonged, raised matters of importance. On 6 April Gladstone, in the statement quoted at the head of the chapter, enunciated a fundamental objective of Home Rule – reconciliation of conflicting traditions in Ireland in the interest of establishing a stronger connection with Great Britain. His reaffirmation of the moral purpose of Home Rule was a reminder that the establishment of self-government in Ireland was never meant to satisfy Catholic ambitions for an ethnic state. Gladstone also reiterated his well-worn theme that the present method of ruling Ireland was economically wasteful, costing twice as much per head as in the rest of the United Kingdom. In his opinion the present system was a blot on Parliament without even pacifying Ireland. Home Rule would improve administrative efficiency and reduce its cost.[45] Home Rulers, in contrast, were intent upon control over the administration, not its reduction. For them the plums of patronage were a rich pudding not to be cast aside lightly.

Gladstone's arguments were based on the notion of one Irish nation which had been artificially divided; Home Rule, he believed, would induce a reconciliation between these. Unionists began with a different proposition, accepting the existence of two Irelands and seeing maintenance of the Union as essential to harmony. This position allowed them to focus attention on Ulster and reject Home Rule for any part of Ireland at the same time. An Ulster MP, for instance, rejected Gladstone's case, stating that his party 'would not accept, any separate Parliament. The loyalists of Ulster had declared their intention of making common cause with their fellow Unionists in the rest of Ireland.'[46] The demand for separate treatment for Ulster did not disappear but was pursued mainly by British MPs. On 7 April Sir John Brodrick, in the citation at the beginning of the chapter, refuted Gladstone's contention that self-government would unify Irishmen, suggesting, moreover, that the proposed bill exacerbated divisions. On 10 April A. H. Smith denied that this or any similar bill might forge 'Ireland a nation, for there was no single nationality within her shores, the people being sharply divided'.[47] Ulster MPs took a prominent part in debates but they were by no means of a single mind among themselves or with their British Unionist colleagues. Alvin Jackson notes that while loyalist representatives posed as imperialists they were actually not concerned with the empire but with Ireland.[48] Some Ulster MPs and most British Unionists distanced themselves from the extreme statements of colleagues such as Saunderson.[49]

Home Rule and Liberal MPs adopted a self-denying ordinance, eschewing frequent participation, but this began to fray as the discussion proceeded. There was growing doubt in national circles that the Home Rule proposal met Irish wants. W. H. K. Redmond on 10 April expressed his dissatisfaction, declaring, however, that they would support the bill in the division lobby, although it was a poor measure. He warned that 'no settlement would be produced by the passage of the bill in its present shape'.[50] On 22 April, after twelve nights of debate, the second reading passed by 347 votes to 304, and the bill went into committee. Sir Edward Hamilton observed:

[T]here was nothing like the same excitement after the division as there was in 1886. The result was a foregone conclusion on this occasion. The principle of Home Rule has accordingly been affirmed; but there is an absence of all real enthusiasm even among Irishmen! English Liberals accept the Bill because they believe it is inevitable and they are heartily sick of the Irish Question. Irishmen take it, because it is the best they can get.[51]

Despite the fierce contest to date, the struggle had only just begun, for in committee the opposition scrutinised the bill even more closely.

Committee discussions commenced on 8 May and extended until the early hours of 28 July. On 27 June, after sixty-three sittings, the government introduced the guillotine. Clauses thereafter were voted upon in batches, some receiving little or no consideration. In committee the government was forced to accept a number of amendments, one of which, on 16 May, made more explicit the declaration of imperial supremacy; on 1 June Unionists succeeded with an amendment preventing the Irish Assembly from creating a centralised force to replace the Royal Irish Constabulary.[52] In late May the government admitted that it had made a major miscalculation of Irish revenue and substituted a new fiscal settlement. The revised plan closely followed Harcourt's earlier paper, proposing that two-thirds of Ireland's revenue would be reserved for local charges and the remaining portion was to be the contribution to the imperial exchequer. Imposition and collection of all Irish taxes was to be retained for six years by the Westminster government. Home Rulers, particularly the Parnellites, greeted this new plan coolly. Under it an increase in Irish revenue automatically resulted in a proportionately larger imperial contribution, which was likely to cause friction between Dublin and London. This plan led to two further developments. First, in June Gladstone dropped the idea of retaining eighty Irish MPs in the House of Commons for limited purposes, in favour of their being able to debate and vote on all questions.[53] Second, Home Rulers' concern about the fiscal aspects provided the germ for what became the Royal Commission on the Financial Relations Between Great Britain and Ireland, formed in 1894.

On 4 August the bill was reported, though not before a near riot in the House of Commons at the close of the committee stage on 27 July, and finally passed on 2 September by 307 votes to 276. Despite many

Liberals' doubts about the issue, the majority in the division lobby remained steady throughout the long parliamentary process. John Redmond acknowledged that the bill had a 'full and largely fair discussion', though he deplored the amendments that, in his opinion, weakened it. According to him:

> [N]o man in his senses can any longer regard it either as a full, a final, or a satisfactory settlement of the Irish Nationalist question. The word 'provisional' has, so to speak, been stamped in red ink across every page of the Bill. No man can claim that such partial and restricted powers as are conferred by this Bill can by any human ingenuity be invested with any element of finality.[54]

On 1 September Saunderson warned: 'before Home Rule can be shoved down our throats the forces of the Crown must be employed [against Ulster]'.[55] After the bill passed, Chamberlain, who had been the driving force behind the Unionist opposition, wrote to the Duchess of St Albans: 'we have done with the Home Rule Bill in the House of Commons at last. ... I sincerely believe we have killed it. ... It has been so knocked about that there is no strength in it.'[56]

Debates began in the House of Lords on 4 September. On the following day the Duke of Devonshire (the Marquess of Hartington) in moving rejection of the bill stated the Unionist case. He considered the weaknesses of the proposal. The crux of his argument centred on the right, indeed the obligation, of the Lords to vote down the bill. While recognising the limits of the peers' legitimate powers when faced with a popular mandate, he argued that the Home Rule measure lacked this essential quality:

> I shall be told that the House of Commons approved of this Bill, and that the General Election gave to the House of Commons the necessary mandate and authority to work out the organic details of the measure. I traverse that argument at every step. ... I deny that the House of Commons received any mandate upon Home Rule at all at the last election; and I say further that, if there were a mandate, it was a conditional mandate, and that the conditions were not within the knowledge of the country. Before this measure is passed into law, we have a right to demand that the judgement of the country shall be given, not upon a cry, not upon an aspiration, not upon an impatient impulse, but upon a completed work; and that this measure, the result of the collective wisdom of the government and Parliament shall be submitted to the country for its approval, aye or no.[57]

Thus, he, like Chamberlain, stated the conditions under which a major constitutional change should be endorsed by Parliament – after a verdict by the nation – and challenged the government to submit the proposal to the country. Devonshire's position was that the peers did not posses an unrestricted but only a conditional veto. The Home Rule question in 1893 opened the gate to a wider and less restrained application of this limited right. When the division came during the sitting on 8 September, Lucy commented: 'four days had sufficed for an ungagged House of Lords to dispose of a matter the gagged House of Commons had talked round for more than fourscore'.[58] Bringing 'together the largest muster of peers on record', the House of Lords rejected the bill by 419 to 41.[59] Given the full ventilation of the cases in the House of Commons and in public, longer consideration by the Lords would have been superfluous.

Gladstone was not in London when the peers voted and he remained away until 1 November. The Cabinet did not convene to discuss the bill's rejection and when it next met neither Home Rule nor the action of the House of Lords was considered. H. W. McCready pinpoints this refusal as the first step of the Liberal party's retreat from Home Rule.[60] McCready's sequence for Liberal disengagement from Home Rule is seen as an evolutionary development between 1893 and 1905. He identifies the Cabinet refusal to appeal to the country against the veto of the House of Lords as the first increment, followed by the review of Liberal policy in 1899, the step by step and clean slate approaches of 1901–02 and, finally, Campbell-Bannerman's advocacy of the step by step approach in November 1905. Here, McCready's format is adopted, but extended to eight increments signposted in the text over the years 1893–1910. Gladstone wished to revive the bill in the next session, but this was turned down by his colleagues. Liberals tacitly accepted that the peers, not themselves, spoke for the nation. When the Cabinet assembled at the beginning of November Ireland was not ignored, but now an Evicted Tenants' bill had priority. Home Rule entered upon a new phase.

Colin Matthew makes four points about the episode.[61] First, he sees it as a stand-off; second, he points out that events of the summer played into Unionist hands; third, that there was no overwhelming case for a dissolution based on the abuse of power by the House of Lords; and finally, that the incident was a remarkable exercise in representative politics. The first three observations can be endorsed, though the last is more contentious, illustrating better the rigidity of post-1886 party allegiance. Liberals were inclined to let the peers do their dirty work.[62] Possibly, a majority of Liberals had little enthusiasm for the scheme and supported it in hope of Home Rule's defeat without, as in 1886, breaking up the party. It was widely assumed that the Home Rule obsession was peculiar to Gladstone; when he disappeared it would be downgraded. Given Gladstone's age, the temptation to wait out the situation was irresistible. Could the bill have been constructed in ways satisfying a sufficient portion of the opposition, allowing it to be implemented? James Loughlin argues that if Gladstone had made an offer to treat Ulster separately, this could have divided the Unionists, while Home Rulers must have accepted control over three-quarters of the country.[63] In light of the subsequent history this is a seductive hypothesis. However, it involves *ex post facto* reasoning. Certainly, there was some sympathy for an Ulster solution in both British parties, but Gladstone would have had to revise his entire concept of Ireland's history and laid himself open to a charge of gross inconsistency in order to tender such an offer. No less pertinently, most British and southern Irish Unionists did not want Home Rule in any guise, while the bulk of northern loyalists rejected an Ulster solution. Ulstermen wanted to remain part of the British state and not be relegated, as they saw it, to colonial status.[64] Unionists were opposed to Home Rule in any form; erection of two rather than one ethnic state offered no attraction. Had such a partition solution been canvassed, the problems of Home Rule finance would surely have come to the fore.

The parliamentary struggle, of course, was only one aspect. On the ground in Britain and Ireland the battle was fought fiercely as well. A majority of newspapers and opinion journals once more opened their pages to Home Rule's critics. The opposition followed much the same line of argument developed in the House of Commons. W. E. H. Lecky, once again, played a prominent role in this extra-parliamentary campaign.[65] His view that the national leadership could not be entrusted with the fate of Ireland chimed with popular perceptions. He made clear that this absence of trust was more decisive in rejecting Home Rule than defects in the structure. Lecky caught Home Rule advocates on the soft underbelly with his insistence that the material progress of the country was unlikely to advance under Gladstone's proposal. Much national rhetoric emphasised the materialist purpose of self-government. If British governments could remedy the grievances of the country, self-government would be redundant. Perhaps, however, nothing caught the opposition mood more neatly than a popular Belfast loyalist song (for the full text, see Document 16):

> I'm an Irishman – born in loyal Belfast,
> And many bright years, boys, in it I have passed.
> In my boyhood days, when I first went to school,
> That's the place where I heard of this subject, Home Rule.
> On that Irish Question some topics I'll state,
> It concerns dear Old Ireland, my country's fate
> Would be ruined for ever if Home Rule was passed –
> A desperate struggle would commence in Belfast.[66]

Rosebery's Premiership, 5 March 1894–23 June 1895

Home Rule had kept Gladstone in politics. Its defeat marked the end of an era, though he retained office until March 1894, when Parliament was prorogued. In the meantime there remained much work on the parliamentary timetable. The Parish Councils bill required thirty-eight days, becoming law only after extensive amendment in the House of Lords. Similar fates befell the Employers' Liability and the Scotch Sea Fisheries bills. Gladstone's retirement had been rumoured for several months; he finally resigned on 3 March. Even before his exit a storm was brewing in national circles. The tenants' campaign had been left unresolved at the onset of the Home Rule debate. In 1892 the Parnellite rump had defended the tenants' interest and for many of their anti-Parnellite opponents the land problem was paramount. Dillon considered that the tenant struggle took second place only to Home Rule. When Parliament adjourned in 1893 an agitation under the auspices of the Redmonites was begun on the estate of Lord de Freyne. In November Healy admonished the Chief Secretary: 'where it will lead you to, if the Parnellites press their advantage, God only knows. You have delivered yourself and us in the hands of our enemies.'[67] Still, at this juncture, the implications of the relative weighting given to Home Rule, the Liberal alliance and the demand for other Irish reforms was not precise. It was implicit, though, that if Home Rule was not going to be implemented, Catholics in Ireland would demand other concessions.

Throughout the history of the Home Rule movement there had been a division between self-government purists and reformers. These ideological currents ran through all the Home Rule groups, but each competing faction blurred the distinction between these aims. All had become primarily material Home Rulers. In the absence of doctrinal purity the question of whether parliamentarians were advocates of self-government or constituted a service organisation was left conveniently ambiguous. Debates in the House of Commons during February and early March 1894 revealed the service orientation of every faction. MPs articulated similar themes, though Parnellites were able to take a more critical view of the Liberal regime. Many MPs gave attention to the needs of their constituencies. In February Donal Sullivan enquired about the hours of employment and retirement prospects for some categories of Irish civil servants. Bernard Molloy and P. J. Kennedy reiterated the long-standing objection to the removal of Irish paupers to Ireland. Captain Donelan argued that harbour and dock improvements were necessary at Haulibowline, Cork, while Dr Ambrose and T. B. Curran pointed to the delays in postal deliveries in their constituencies.[68] Irishmen moved a large number of private members bills as well. In early March a newly elected Parnellite informed the House that 'there was a lamentable want of employment over the length and breadth of the country. In this matter the policy of the government seemed to be that of masterly inactivity.' He objected to unfair foreign competition, to the unsatisfactory protection afforded by the Merchandise Marks Act and to the neglect of appropriate technical education, and he observed that there was a need to transfer labour between regions, as was done in some continental countries. This MP believed: 'whether the government was Liberal or Conservative the time was coming when it would have to consider these matters that were exercising the brains of working men'.[69] These and other comments revealed the breadth of the Catholic national programme beyond Home Rule; much of it could be offered by the Conservatives.

Lord Rosebery's accession to the Premiership marked a change in the fortunes of Home Rule and of Irish politicians' influence. Rosebery advocated some degree of Irish autonomy, but he had also shown sympathy for Ulster's position, never being an unreserved exponent of Home Rule. When the new parliamentary session opened on 12 March the Queen's Speech promised legislation to deal with the question of evicted tenants. That same day Rosebery assured supporters that Home Rule 'will be pressed to the forefront, and, as far as in me lies, pressed to a definite and successful conclusion'.[70] Later in the day in the House of Lords he responded to Salisbury with the declaration:

> [T]he Noble Marquess made one remark on Irish Home Rule with which I confess myself in entire accord. He said that before Irish Home Rule is concluded by the Imperial Parliament, England as the pre-dominant member of the Three Kingdoms will have to be convinced of its justice and equity. That may seem to be a considerable admission to make, because your Lordships well know that the majority of Members of Parliament elected from England proper are hostile to Home Rule.[71]

Lucy observed: 'it is long since so brief a remark was followed by such swift upheaval'.[72] Subsequently, this has been known as the 'pre-dominant partner' speech. In the House of Commons the following day Redmond denounced Rosebery's remarks as 'preposterous and insulting to the Irish people'.[73] Efforts at damage limitation were only partly successful. Dillon, who was present at the Prime Minister's major attempt at rectification in Edinburgh shortly afterwards, said he was

> firmly convinced that in Lord Rosebery the cause of Ireland had an honest and an honourable champion who would be false to no

pledge which was given by the government to which he belonged as Foreign Secretary and to no pledge given to the people of Ireland by the statesman of England into whose place he had stepped courageously.[74]

The incident aggravated the tensions among both Home Rulers and Liberals as well as between them. Morley agreed that Rosebery's statement was an accurate account of what they had privately agreed, but that it was 'not to be said at this delicate moment'.[75] Healy thereafter no longer gave automatic support to the Liberals. His position became analogous to that of the Redmondites; they now were prepared in theory to treat Irish reforms on their merits whether offered by a Liberal or Conservative regime. Rosebery's accession added to existing confusion in national circles. On 8 April Redmond proclaimed that the movement 'was face to face with the ruin of the Home Rule cause, and was in a position of disunion, squalid and humiliating personal altercations, and petty vanities. So that any measure of national autonomy must be hung up till the English cared to give it.'[76] None of the Irish factions knew quite what to do; neither were they well suited to respond to this challenge by advocating Home Rule exclusively, nor to accept reform as the immediate priority. Irishmen were hamstrung now by the inherent implications of material Home Rule and other internal divisions. This malaise infected the Liberals as well. Edward Hamilton on 5 May noted:

> There is no denying that a general feeling of disappointment & lukewarmness pervades the Liberal party and many sections which split it up. And why? What did people expect? Did they think that Rosebery could work wonders which Mr G could not even himself work? That all the wolves and lambs of the party would lie down peacefully together under a new & untried leader? that Home Rule would be discarded and the Irishmen remain happy? or that some new scheme of Home Rule would be produced which everybody including the Irishmen themselves would accept? ... The fact is, there has been for a long time no enthusiasm for any measure. There was enthusiasm for an individual; & now that that individual has retired from the scene, there is no enthusiasm at all. It is not due to defects of leading, but to apathy on the part of the constituencies.[77]

But the anti-Parnellites did not bolt from the Liberal alliance. When the session closed on 21 August Lucy recorded that contrary to expectations the Irish stayed faithful to the 'Ministers who brought in the Home Rule Bill'. During an almost wholly British session, he noted that the Irish 'on the two occasions when the Budget Bill was in sore jeopardy every one of Mr McCarthy's men was either polled or paired'.[78]

Following the O'Shea divorce scandal, chronic financial shortfalls plagued all factions. It was difficult to sustain patriotic organisations at the best of times and the task was now nearly impossible. Provision of finance for needy MPs burdened already lean coffers. Parnellism in the 1880s enjoyed comparative financial independence though it conserved resources from the mid-1880s by ceding to the clergy and its allies, the strong tenant farmers and shopkeepers, who had effective control over local organisation. Surrendering local operations came at a cost. When the priests and provincial middle classes deserted Parnell after the divorce scandal, he found himself bereft of constituency organisation. During the 1890s national leaders were even less masters in their own house. A financially impoverished movement was a weathercock in Ireland, leaving it at the same time dependent upon the Liberals at Westminster. Embarrassing revelations resulted. In 1894 the anti-Parnellites were accused of bartering four Irish seats to the Liberals for £800 per year, a charge only partly dispelled, undermining morale.[79]

Financial problems were matched by internal dissension within the majority section. Disputes between Dillon and Healy by 1894 weakened the coalition. In September Dillon prophesied: 'we are very close to a final struggle with Healy and his gang, and I dare say this would be as good a time to have it fought out as any that could be selected.'[80] He thought the confrontation could strengthen the party and revive contributions to the parliamentary fund. There seemed little prospect of averting further clashes. In addition, Liberal reluctance to set a timetable for another attempt at Home Rule dampened Irish spirits.

With the departure of Gladstone, Liberals now preferred a programme of modest administrative and economic reform. Home Rule's defeat in 1893 opened the door to land reform once more. The land question might solve the chief Irish need, but it threatened the cohesion of both the national ranks and of Unionism. T. W. Russell, the Ulster Unionist MP, observed in late April 1894 that the land question would predominate because 'rightly or wrongly, men consider Home Rule to be dead'.[81] Tenants in both the north and south still had a number of grievances. These included the exclusion of leaseholders and holders of fee farms from judicial rental reductions, while there was also a demand for an extension of purchase facilities. In March 1894 Morley announced the government's intention to introduce legislation for the reinstatement of evicted tenants. He also established a select committee to inquire into the working of the land acts. The Evicted Tenants' bill, introduced in April, contained provision of the compulsory purchase of some lands. Initially, the government hoped it would prove relatively uncontroversial, but the opposite proved true. Unionists held that Morley underestimated the cost to public funds and looked askance at the creation of a further land court.[82] On 26 May he established the Royal Commission on the Financial Relations Between Great Britain and Ireland. After being cross-examined Edward Hamilton confessed: 'there is no doubt that relatively to Great Britain Ireland is taxed more heavily, but how the inequality can be adjusted I confess I do not see.'[83] The Royal Commission was a representative body which did not report until 1896. Meanwhile, Russell sought to muster popular support in Ulster for land reform and thereby put pressure on Ulster Unionists and Conservatives. However, on 14 August the Evicted Tenants' bill was defeated in the Lords.

In 1895 the Chief Secretary responded to the thirst for land legislation with a bill to advance land purchase. This was introduced on 5 March 1895, but was abandoned in June as the government stumbled towards extinction. During his tenure at the Irish Office Morley instituted administrative reforms and gave Catholics a larger slice of appointments. All Home Rule factions were consulted about vacant posts. Morley subsequently claimed to have nominated 554 Catholics out of a total of 637 appointments to the Commission of the Peace and also to have reduced Protestant predominance from three or four to one to approximately two to one among holders of posts in the local administration.[84] In the political sphere, though, his Chief Secretaryship gave little satisfaction. Redmond believed Morley to be the weakest Chief Secretary the country had known, while Dillon in 1895 expressed relief at the Liberal defeat in the general election.[85] Elizabeth Matthew recorded:

> John Dillon says he is truly thankful that the last three years are over for the Liberals had neither the power nor the courage to do anything and the alliance made it often necessary to tolerate or condone conduct on the part of the Irish Government which ought properly to have been objected to, while John Morley was a disappointment from beginning to end.[86]

On 21 June 1895 the government lost a vote on the Army estimates. The defeat was a surprise in a House of Commons in which fewer than half the MPs were present. Rosebery resigned two days later and Salisbury accepted office on 25 June. On 8 July Parliament was dissolved. The parties prepared once more to face the electorate.

Conclusion

The second Home Rule bill narrowed the Irish political landscape. This time, three of the eight groups defined in chapter 1 (see p. 3) supported it – Catholics in Ireland, the Liberal party and the House of

Commons, but other major groups remained firmly opposed. The defeat of Home Rule and Gladstone's departure marked the close of the Liberal party's pre-occupation with Home Rule, allowing other issues to come to the fore. Because Home Rule no longer seemed an imminent threat, a section of northern Unionism was able to adopt views similar to those of national leaders. Management of the national coalition became tenuous in the aftermath of the Home Rule episode, its *raison d'être* more amorphous. The situation was not comparable to 1886. Then, Home Rule seemed only a matter of time, a question of converting more groups and Gladstone's restoration to power. In contrast, the prospects after 1893 were scarcely encouraging. Return of a future Liberal government no longer automatically assured another attempt at Home Rule. John Redmond in 1894 conceded that 'we recognise, of course, the fact that as the Home Rule Question stands at the moment we cannot, in Ireland, hope to have it carried into law without another General Election, and without a verdict being given in its favour by the people of these Kingdoms.'[87]

There was a growing sense that Ireland lacked its previous zest for Home Rule. According to Archbishop Croke in early 1895, 'the country is notoriously and indeed shamefully apathetic. There is no desire for Home Rule.'[88] Liberals left two legacies that soon would bear fruit – the Royal Commission on the Financial Relations Between Great Britain and Ireland and Morley's abandoned land purchase proposal. Morley's efforts to increase Catholic numbers in the Irish administration and on the Commission of the Peace addressed another chronic grievance. He continued the momentum towards what would become known as the 'step by step' approach to Irish wants. Liberal and Conservative outlooks were on a compatible course. Since 1886 Irish self-government had been at the apex of British political life – alliances, coalitions of interests and party programmes had been dominated by the question. Afterwards, instead of Home Rulers seeming to determine the agenda and set the pace of reform, they were sidelined, being supplicants of boons in the gift of others. Liberal unionism had weathered the elements and stormed back with renewed vigour, staking out its claim to the future course of the self-government question.

Notes

1 *Parliamentary Debates [PD]*, 4th series, 10 (1893), cc. 1603–4.
2 *Ibid.*, c. 1749.
3 Quoted in F. S. L. Lyons, *John Dillon: A Biography* (London, 1968), p. 156.
4 Material derived from C. J. Woods, 'The General Election of 1892:

The Catholic Clergy and the Defeat of the Parnellites', in F. S. L. Lyons and R. A. J. Hawkins (eds), *Ireland Under the Union: Varieties of Tension* (Oxford, 1980), pp. 289–319.

5   Quoted in *ibid.*, p. 308.

6   James Loughlin, *Gladstone, Home Rule and the Ulster Question 1882–93* (Dublin, 1987), pp. 245–7.

7   See, Frank Callanan, T. M. Healy (Cork, 1996), p. 412.

8   F. S. L. Lyons, *The Irish Parliamentary Party 1890–1910* (London, 1951), p. 38.

9   Quoted in H. C. G. Matthew, *Gladstone 1875–1898* (Oxford, 1995), p. 327.

10   See, Lawrence W. McBride, *The Greening of Dublin Castle: The Transformation of Bureaucratic and Judicial Personnel in Ireland 1892–1922* (Washington, DC, 1991), p. 48.

11   Matthew, *Gladstone*, p. 330; D. A. Hamer, *Liberal Politics in the Age of Gladstone and Rosebery: A Study in Leadership and Policy* (Oxford, 1972), p. 282.

12   A. G. Gardiner, *The Life of Sir William Harcourt* (London, 1923), II, p. 179.

13   Viscount Morley, *Recollections* (London, 1918), II, p. 322.

14   *PD*, 4th Series, 7 (1892), cc. 116–17.

15   *Ibid.*, c. 253.

16   *Ibid.*, cc. 124–5.

17   *Ibid.*, cc. 164–75.

18   *Ibid.*

19   *Ibid.*, cc. 281–2.

20   *Ibid.*, cc. 210–14.

21   Lyons, *John Dillon*, pp. 156–7.

22   T. M. Healy, *Letters and Leaders of My Day* (London, 1928), II, pp. 382–6; Callanan, *T. M. Healy*, p. 419–20.

23   Quoted in Gardiner, *Sir William Harcourt*, II, p. 219.

24   See, Loughlin, *Gladstone*, pp. 257–64.

25   *PD*, 4th Series, 8 (1893), cc. 1250–1.

26   See, Henry W. Lucy, *A Diary of the Home Rule Parliament 1892–1895* (London, 1896), p. 38.

27   *Ibid.*, p. 47.

28   *Ibid.*, p. 55.

29   PD, 8 (1893), cc. 1250–1.

30   *Ibid.*, c. 1255.

31   *Ibid.*, c. 1263.

32   Dudley W. R. Bahlman (ed.), *The Diary of Sir Edward Walter Hamilton 1885–1908* (Hull, 1993), p. 157 (15 June 1892).

33   *PD*, 8 (1893), c. 1267.

34   See, John Kendle, *Ireland and the Federal Solution: The Debate Over the United Kingdom Constitution, 1870–1921* (Kingston and Montreal, 1989), pp. 75–9.

35   Matthew, *Gladstone*, p. 336.

36   Sir Charles Gavan Duffy, *A Fair Constitution for Ireland* (2nd edn;

Dublin and London, 1892), pp. 12–16.

37 *Ibid.*, pp. 7–8.

38 *PD*, 4th series (1893), c. 1279; *ibid.*, c. 1316.

39 R. Barry O'Brien (ed.), *Home Rule Speeches of John Redmond, M.P.* (London, 1910), p. 43.

40 *PD*, 4th series, 9 (1893), cc. 163–80

41 Lucy, *Home Rule Parliament*, p. 80.

42 See, Blanche E. C. Dugdale, *Arthur James Balfour* (London, 1936), I, pp. 215–16.

43 Patrick Buckland, *Irish Unionism: Two: Ulster Unionism and the Origins of Northern Ireland 1886–1922* (Dublin, 1973), pp. 15–16.

44 Lucy, *Home Rule Parliament*, p. 93.

45 *PD*, 4th series, 10 (1893), cc. 1604–5.

46 *Ibid.*, cc. 1690–1.

47 *Ibid.*, c. 1899.

48 Alvin Jackson, *The Ulster Party: Irish Unionists in the House of Commons, 1884–1911* (Oxford, 1989), p. 120.

49 *Ibid.*, pp. 124–9.

50 *PD*. 10 (1893), c. 1896.

51 Bahlman (ed.), *Sir Edward Walter Hamilton*, p. 199 (21 April).

52 Loughlin, *Gladstone*, pp. 267–73.

53 Matthew, *Gladstone*, p. 338.

54 *PD*, 4th series, 14 (1893), cc. 1168–70.

55 *Ibid.*, c. 1781.

56 Quoted in J. L. Garvin, *The Life of Joseph Chamberlain, 1885–1895* (London, 1933), II, p. 577.

57 Quoted in Bernard Holland, *The Life of Spencer Compton, Eighth Duke of Devonshire* (London, 1911), II, pp. 254–5.

58 Lucy, *Home Rule Parliament*, p. 251.

59 Matthew, *Gladstone*, p. 211 (9 September).

60 H. W. McCready, 'Home Rule and the Liberal Party, 1899–1906', *Irish Historical Studies*, XIII (September, 1963), p. 317.

61 Matthew, *Gladstone*, pp. 338–40.

62 Peter Fraser, *Lord Esher: A Political Biography* (London, 1973), p. 67.

63 Loughlin, *Gladstone*, pp. 274–83.

64 Jackson, *The Ulster Party*, pp. 122–4.

65 Donal McCartney, *W. E. H. Lecky: Historian and Politician 1838–1903* (Dublin, 1994), pp. 124–9.

66 Quoted in Georges-Denis Zimmermann, *Songs of Irish Rebellion: Political Street Ballads and Rebel Songs 1780–1900* (Dublin, 1967), p. 310.

67 Quoted in Healy, *Letters*, II, p. 401.

68 *PD*, 4th series, 21 (1894), cc. 389–90, 456, 719, 1023, 1047–8; 22 (1894), c. 560.

69 *Ibid.*, cc. 92–3.

70 Quoted in Robert Rhodes James, *Rosebery: A Biography of Archibald Philip, Fifth Earl of Rosebery* (London, 1963), p. 337.

71 Quoted in The Marquess of Crewe, *Lord Rosebery* (London, 1931), II, pp. 444–5.

72 Lucy, *Home Rule Parliament*, p. 320.

73 Quoted in James, *Rosebery*, p. 338.

74 Quoted in Lyons, *John Dillon*, p. 162.

75 Fraser, *Lord Esher*, p. 67.

76 Quoted in Gwynn, *The Life of John Redmond* (London, 1932), p. 84.

77 Quoted in David Brooks (ed.), *The Destruction of Lord Rosebery, From the Diary of Sir Edward Hamilton, 1894–1895* (London, 1986), p. 138.

78 Lucy, *Home Rule Parliament*, p. 409.

79 Lyons, *John Dillon*, p. 166.

80 Quoted in *ibid.*, p. 164.

81 Quoted in Alvin Jackson, 'Irish Unionism and the Russellite Threat, 1894–1906', *Irish Historical Studies*, XXV (November, 1987), p. 383; many points in this paragraph are derived from pp. 376–404

82 Brooks (ed.), *Destruction of Lord Rosebery*, pp. 38–40.

83 Quoted in *ibid.*, p. 250 (24 May).

84 Morley, *Recollections*, I, pp. 339–40.

85 Quoted in Wilfrid Scawen Blunt, *My Diaries: Being a Personal Narrative of Events 1888–1914* (facsimile edition; New York, 1980), Part II, p. 197.

86 Quoted in Lyons, *John Dillon*, p. 174.

87 *PD*, 4th Series, 22 (1894), c. 181.

88 Quoted in Mark Tierney, *Croke of Cashel: The Life of Archbishop Thomas William Croke 1832–1902* (Dublin, 1976), p. 255.

7

'Killing Home Rule with kindness': alternatives, 1895–1905

What is going on is talk about the past, and inactivity regarding the present. We went to war for Home Rule and should continue that war each in his own way as best we may ... we have the evicted with us and we are letting them starve ... in fact horse racing, cycling and other amusements is what the country is most eager about at present. (Alfred Webb, 1897)[1]

No sane person, least of all the sane community of persons which is known to be the predominant partner, would ever consent to hand over the destinies of Ireland and the very heart of the Empire to a Parliament which would be guided and controlled and composed of those who have expressed their earnest wish that we might be overthrown on this southern field of battle. (Lord Rosebery at Liverpool, 14 February 1902)[2]

Introduction

Unionist reformism and Liberal reluctance to give priority to Home Rule were key factors after 1895. From 1877 until 1893, Anglo-Irish affairs often appeared to be driven by Home Rule and Liberal imperatives. British Conservatives and Irish Unionists for a long decade after the second Home Rule bill reversed this position. Unionists set the agenda; Liberals and Home Rulers were left responding to these initiatives. The shift away from Home Rule opened a fresh field. By 1905 these made a mark.

An alternative policy, 1895–99

'Killing Home Rule with kindness' has a chequered reputation, described variously as an experiment which benefited Ireland but failed to wean the Irish away from Home Rule, as a formula unlikely to distract people from patriotic ambitions and as having a dubious impact on the Irish economy. Recently, it has been denied that a coherent policy existed at all. Andrew Gailey sees Irish reforms as tactical responses to Westminster politics. Legislation, he alleges, was concocted to meet British needs. Nevertheless, Conservative legislation presented a challenge to Home Rulers and Liberals, fraying the bonds binding them together.[3]

The new government had to deal with five interrelated problems: land holding; general economic development, including deeply entrenched poverty, particularly in the west; administrative institutions; the need for greater responsible government; and, towards the close of the 1890s, containment of political agitation. More secure in 1895 than during his previous administration, Salisbury had an enviable asset. All Irish groupings were now in a minority; none could dictate or even appear to set the pace of events as they had done for many years, though the Prime Minister was receptive to the ideas of T. W. Russell in the early years of this administration. Henry Lucy quipped: 'to begin with, the compact, well-led, Irish party that faced the Treasury Bench up to the opening of the Session of 1886 is rent in bewildering wealth of factions. All the Irish Secretary of today has to do is to "lie low, say nuffin", and the Irish members opposite will rend each other in pieces.'[4] With the inclusion of 71 Liberal Unionists, Salisbury's coalition held 411 seats in the new Parliament, resulting from the general election held between 12 and 26 July. An opposition of 259 MPs was made up of 177 Liberals and 82 Home Rulers (including 12 Parnellites). Dillon's and Healy's estrangement opened a further division among Irish Members. Controversy marred over half of the conventions summoned to select anti-Parnellite candidates.[5] By the close of 1895 Healy had been expelled from the executives of the Irish National League of Great Britain (7 November) and the National Federation (13 November). Dillon completed the triumph over his adversary on 18 February 1896 when he succeeded Justin McCarthy as party chairman, winning by a margin of 38 to 21. This was a pyrrhic victory. Healy and his supporters remained a factor in the House of Commons; he still commanded a sizeable following in Ireland, and British leaders continued to treat him as a central figure in Irish affairs. Clerical support gave Healy a power base. The absence of national unity was cruelly exposed once again when the Convention of the Irish Race, which met in Dublin between 1 and 3 September was boycotted by the Parnellite and Healy factions with all but one member of the Catholic hierarchy also choosing to stay away.

Salisbury's regime was the beneficiary of a general political malaise and an absence of widespread agrarian unrest in Ireland. In September 1895 Gerald Balfour reported that Home Rule is 'sleeping very soundly'.[6] Liberal disarray after the election defeat and the personal vendetta between Rosebery and Harcourt deflated the opposition. Morley, the chief exponent of Home Rule, lost his seat in the general election and was soon immersed in writing Gladstone's biography. One of the few areas of agreement between Rosebery and Harcourt was their lack of enthusiasm for Home Rule. Following his embarrassment in March 1894, Rosebery began a measured retreat from Home Rule using as his justification the need to bring Liberalism up to date.[7] After his resignation as Liberal leader on 6 October 1896, Rosebery continued to put distance between himself and Home Rule, marking the second increment in Liberal disengagement (see p. 167). Haldane's article in December, titled 'The Future of Liberalism', offered the initial suggestion of the 'step by step' approach to Irish self-government.[8] When Harcourt succeeded to the leadership he held true to disengagement from Home Rule. In 1898 a Liberal organ, *The Westminster Gazette*, declared: 'there is no further benefit to be got by repeating the processes which failed in 1886 and 1893.'[9] The next year *The Times* approvingly observed that the Liberals were anxious 'to run away from Home Rule as fast as decency would permit them'.[10] On the other side of the ledger, Irish Unionists and especially the Irish peers kept the policies of the new government under surveillance but fortunately for Salisbury the bonds of loyalty and the size of his majority allowed him to hold this truculent element in check.[11] The very existence of a vigilant Irish Unionism was a useful counterweight when the Prime Minister wanted to dampen down the excesses of Conservative reforming enthusiasm.

The 'union of hearts' that had actually existed in the post-1886 years was between Liberal Unionists and Conservatives. It had been boosted by the electoral defeat in 1892 and the second Home Rule bill. Following the general election in 1895 Liberal Unionists consummated their match when members accepted Cabinet posts. In 1895 Salisbury's choice as Chief Secretary of the Irish Office was another nephew, Gerald Balfour, Arthur's younger brother. Gerald's selection, without a seat in the Cabinet, ensured that Balfourian ideas would continue to exert a major influence on Irish policy. Reformism was augmented by the labour, vigour and growing stature of Sir Horace Plunkett (a contemporary and member of the same house at Eton as Gerald Balfour). Having won the marginal South Dublin constituency in 1892 and been re-elected in 1895, Plunkett pressed forward his belief that Ireland suffered from agricultural and technical retardation as a result of poor specialist knowledge and an absence of appropriate training. He was not obedient to the rigidities of political orthodoxy. For him, the key to a vibrant Irish economy lay in improved agricultural practices, better technical knowledge and efficient marketing. Observation of co-operation in Wyoming gave Plunkett a model for rural vitality. He believed that adoption of similar practices would advance Ireland. To achieve Irish development he harnessed enthusiasm for reform to a Conservative emphasis on self-reliance. As his ideas did not neatly fit into the polarised framework of Irish politics, Plunkett, not surprisingly, attracted hostility from both camps.

T. W. Russell contributed to the reformist impulse of the new administration. Russell, an Ulster MP, was a Liberal Unionist, a Presbyterian and a temperance advocate, who represented the Protestant farmer interest.[12] Like Plunkett, he was unconventional and often found himself at odds with landlord-dominated Ulster Unionism. Russell had a substantial following among rural Presbyterians, attracting support from some Catholic farmers in Ulster as well. Because Home Rule was moribund after 1893, figures like Plunkett and Russell had wider scope for their reforming zeal. Russell supported Morley's land programme; when he found the Ulster landlord faction unresponsive, he resorted to organising a mass movement to secure his aims. Like Plunkett, he was regarded with suspicion by orthodox Unionists, but in the mid-1890s Russell exercised considerable influence and accepted a junior office in the new ministry on condition it adopted land reform.

Plunkett's notion was superficially similar to Parnell's. Parnell believed that if the land question was resolved Irishmen could reach across sectarian and class boundaries, allowing the Protestant Ascendancy to assume its place at the head of the nation. Parnell's project vanished when the land war completed the process of converting national identity into an agrarian Catholic middle-class preserve, though from time to time he still reverted to this theme.[13] Despite a rhetoric which, in part, spoke of an all-creed nation, few seriously wanted it on terms enticing to Irish Unionists. Plunkett sought to apply Parnell's prescription shed of its overt political overtones, getting Irishmen to co-operate on economic and social questions. His underlying goal was to preserve the Union by making it agreeable. Both men were unconventional among their class. But there was a vital difference between them. Fundamentally, Parnell was a moral Home Ruler; Plunkett, in contrast, was a materialist. Whereas Plunkett advocated co-operation between all sectors of society, Parnell in 1891 groped towards a class-based political realignment. Russell, like Plunkett, sought material prescription to make Home Rule redundant, but he shared Parnell's late conversion to class-based politics.

In 1895, as in 1886, the Unionist regime entered office not as an agent of resistance but as one sponsoring measured reform. In his election address, Arthur Balfour set the tone, maintaining: 'land purchase is the key to the land question in Ireland and if the land question … were once settled, there would be no other Irish question at all.'[14] Gerald Balfour enunciated the idea of 'killing Home Rule with kindness' in his first major policy declaration at Leeds in October.[15] Plunkett's analysis differed in emphasis but had the same end in view. In August 1895 he published a 'proposal affecting the general welfare of Ireland', suggesting that representatives from all sides meet with him during the parliamentary recess with a view to promoting a diet of mutually desired reforms.[16] Orthodox Unionists and anti-Parnellites declined his invitation. Justin McCarthy, chairman of the majority, refused on the grounds that he could not participate in any association that aimed at seeking a substitute for Home Rule. Healy and Redmond expressed sympathy for the initiative and the latter, after some arm twisting, agreed to participate. Colonel Edward Saunderson, leader of the Ulster Unionists, stated that he would not sit on any committee with Redmond, declining also because it had too great a tinge of Irish independence. Plunkett persevered and assembled a representative group, including Lords Mayo and Monteagle (Unionist peers), Redmond and Timothy Harrington (Parnellites), Fr Finlay and Sir John Arnott (representing southern commerce), Thomas Andrews and Thomas Sinclair (Liberal Unionists) and T. P. Gill (anti-Parnellite) who acted as secretary. This Recess Committee under Plunkett's inspiration emerged as an energetic pressure group, producing a report of 418 pages on 1 August 1896. The report analysed all aspects of the Irish economy under forty-three different categories. Among the measures advocated were co-operative banking, technical education and the creation of a consultative council for agriculture. Not everyone was enamoured with the Recess Committee's labours, though it attracted wide interest and received encouraging support. To Gladstone, whose ambition was to entice the two sides to work together, Gill promoted the work of the Committee as 'reaching a turning point when Unionism and nationalism will cease to be antagonistic in Irish minds and when … a genuine synthesis between these two principles will be worked out'.[17] However, *The Freeman's Journal* saw the recommendations as a 'burlesque substitute for Home Rule' and from this time as well the influential Unionist Lord Ardilaun began a vitriolic campaign against Plunkett.[18] Plunkett's critical attitude towards the powerful Royal Dublin Society provoked hostility.

Before the Recess Committee's work had time to mature, Gerald Balfour began to put his own plans into place. In February 1896 Irish

MPs raised the issue of amnesty for the remaining prisoners convicted for dynamite offences in Liverpool, Glasgow and London in
the mid-1880s. Plunkett and W. E. H. Lecky, the Unionist MP for the
University of Dublin, supported their release.[19] Their stance was
sharply condemned as apostasy by many Unionists, including Saunderson. The remaining prisoners were granted their freedom a few
months later, with the last, Thomas Clarke, one of the signatories to
the Proclamation of 1916, set free in September 1898. This removed
another patriotic bone of contention. Also, in April 1896 Balfour
introduced a fresh Land Purchase bill based on Morley's earlier draft
which also replicated Russell's earlier proposals.[20] All sides agreed
that new legislation was essential. Tenant applications to purchase
had slipped alarmingly; new legislation was need to revive sales.
When enacted on 14 August it made available a further £36 million,
while lowering interest rates and extending the repayment period. At
the same time it altered provisions of the law of tenure and amended
the procedures of the Land Commission. Applications for purchase
under the act swiftly rose from £50,000 in value in 1895 to £750,000 in
1897 and then to £2 million in 1898.[21] Provision for the compulsory
sale of bankrupt estates angered many Unionists, an indication of the
potentially divisive nature of the land question for Salisbury's government.

Interest in a common platform for Ireland accelerated following
publication in 1896 of the Report of the Royal Commission on the
Financial Relations Between Great Britain and Ireland. The majority
report alleged that the country was being overtaxed by £2,750,000
annually. Home Rulers had long carped about over-taxation; at last
they had the satisfaction of seeing their contention verified. The
report, though, did not win universal acceptance. It embarrassed the
government. Arthur Balfour, Salisbury and the Chancellor of the
Exchequer, Sir Michael Hicks Beach, denied the veracity of Ireland's
over-taxation, a position held by some Liberals as well. In Ireland a
series of protest meetings drew support from all classes. This was an
ideal platform to launch a non-partisan Irish coalition. In December
1896 the Lord Lieutenant informed Salisbury:

> [T]he agitation which has now commenced throughout Ireland is
> not a lawless one – it is hardly less hostile to the government. Men
> of all parties, religions and classes are acting in concert. Meetings are
> being convened in all parts of the country and I doubt whether so
> strong and unanimous a movement has ever set foot in Ireland in
> our time.[22]

Early in 1897 this movement crystallised into the All-Ireland Committee, which this time had support from the Unionist leader,

Colonel Saunderson, along with that of Redmond and Healy.

The Convention of the Irish Race held between 1 and 3 September 1896 was a signal for progress towards a wide materialist platform. The Irish in Canada and the United States, dismayed at the bickering in Ireland and concerned with the impact of feuding on Home Rule's prospects, were the driving force behind this conclave. Hopes of using the Convention to resurrect unity soon evaporated, although, predictably, much of the rhetoric was directed at the need for unity and Home Rule. However, the Convention advocated other reforms, also. Resolutions endorsed a traditional list of demands, including land reform, legislation for labourers, satisfaction of Catholic education claims, along with newer issues like the introduction of local self-government, relief from over-taxation and government support for the teaching of Gaelic.[23] Most of the programme could be gained from Conservatives as easily as Liberals and predicated a Westminster strategy. Meanwhile, Healy's dispute with Dillon continued to intrude on the public scene. From late 1896 his popular forum was what in January 1897 became the People's Rights Association. When it met for the first time on 12 January this new organ adopted a twelve-point programme. Some sections reiterated Healy's own views on the conduct of the parliamentary party and movement, while the remainder proposed a gaggle of the usual reforms.[24] The various platforms entreated Irish representatives to press a broad materialist programme at the Westminster Parliament, and to seek reforms from whatever government held office. As only Home Rule was clearly outside the remit of Salisbury's government, a Conservative ministry had the potential to satisfy the country's wants in the immediate future. This was analogous to the situation in 1884–85 but with an all-important difference. In 1885 Parnellites had been, or seemed to be, part of a partnership but now Irish MPs were supplicants, not so much for Home Rule but for pragmatic legislation.

Reformism had become the chief means by which to redeem Home Rule fortunes in the later 1890s. Demoralised by disputes, the poor state of the movement's finances, differing objectives and diminished Liberal interest in the issue, MPs did not overlook the importance of service to their constituencies. This work provided a crucial link between local communities and Westminster politics. During 1896 and 1897 MPs made their presence felt in the House of Commons. In April 1896, for example, Captain Donelan pleaded that the army should purchase more of its meat locally for troops garrisoned in Ireland. A few days later both he and J. P. Farrell complained about postal delays in their respective constituencies. At the beginning of May J. C. Flynn and R. McGhee reverted to the long-standing grievance of discrimination against Catholics seeking promotions in the

Royal Irish Constabulary. Farrell also criticised the reduction of the salaries for collectors of income tax in Ireland.[25] These were little-known MPs and their participation frequently took up mundane matters. Many times they and other members expressed concerns or argued for government intervention inconsistent with national pro-fessions. Such labours received attention in the local press and at the grass roots constituents were well aware of the 'activity' or its absence on their behalf.[26] This side of parliamentarianism compen-sated for the sagging umbrella of Home Rule and helped preserve an otherwise ineffectual dispute-riddled movement, also qualifying William O'Brien's much cited acid judgement, 'eighty men power-less', or F. S. L. Lyons's verdict of this era as 'the waste land'.[27]

During Salisbury's ministry the Catholic hierarchy predictably reverted to the education question. In May 1896 Home Rulers tem-porarily aligned behind the Education bill which would strengthen the financing of denominational institutions in England and Wales; in early 1897 Archbishop Walsh tried to engage all factions in a joint effort to advance the Catholic university claim. He saw this as 'the basis upon which co-operation could take place'.[28] Redmond soon proposed an eight-point platform as the common formula for a reunified party.[29] This called for national self-government, but he also advanced a slate of other demands including specifically Parnellite themes like independence from all parties as well as advocating man-hood suffrage, land reform and the development of Irish resources. Timothy Harrington hoped that social issues would enable the Irish National League to attract American funds once more.[30] Co-opera-tion in the House of Commons, he thought, might be restored by establishing a jointly sponsored evicted tenants' fund and co-ordina-tion of efforts on other measures. Meanwhile, the government con-tinued to press ahead with its Irish programme, though at an uneven pace and over the objections of some of its own supporters. In 1897, in response to the extremely wet summer, Gerald Balfour enabled Boards of Poor Law Guardians to extend loans for spraying and pur-chasing seed potatoes. An attempt at legislating for agriculture more generally, however, had to be dropped. Still, in the opinion of observers the sting had been drawn from Home Rule, a verdict attested to in the comment of Alfred Webb cited at the head of the chapter. By July 1898 Dillon was complaining of many MPs that 'an increasing number are prepared to throw themselves into oceans of whiskey & into nothing else'.[31]

The largest reform, however, was the Local Government bill intro-duced in the House of Commons on 21 February 1898 (enacted on 12 August). It established democratically elected county and urban councils throughout Ireland. This legislation had been long foreshadowed; its main features were derived from the act passed in 1888 for the rest of the United Kingdom. It established county councils along with urban and rural district councils elected for three years on a wide franchise, including, for the first time, peers and eligible women. The new councils had the fiscal and administrative functions, though not the judicial responsibilities, of the old landlord-dominated and much maligned grand juries. They were able to receive grants from the Treasury and were empowered to impose their own local rates. Tenants had their rates lightened while the government agreed to pay half the county cess and half of the landlords' poor rates, thereby offering the rural elite a financial inducement to compensate for the loss of political power. The legislation contained a number of checks to mollify Unionists. District councils' financial autonomy was limited: county councils could veto district council budgets, no district council could exceed by more than 25 per cent in any year the average of the three previous years' expenditure on roads and the clergy of all denominations were barred from membership. The Ulster MP, William Johnson, known for his anti-Catholic rhetoric, confided that the reform was 'approved all round'.[32] Saunderson praised the measure as a means of enlarging sectarian and class conciliation.

National opinion was friendly to the bill. Redmond termed it 'a far better measure than could be conferred upon Ireland by any Liberal administration'.[33] O'Brien was yet more euphoric, claiming: 'for the first time since the Norman invasion, it places vast departments of local government in the hands of the native race, with certainty that the powers at present given can be made the means of winning still wider ones.'[34] He saw the councils as a multitude of local Home Rule parliaments which will 'sooner or later inevitably develop into one National Parliament'. Though more cautious, Dillon welcomed it as well. In conjunction with the earlier takeover of the Boards of Poor Law Guardians, the legislation effectively allowed middle-class Catholics to take possession of local institutions. On the existing grand juries Unionists held 704 seats and Home Rulers a mere 47, but in the elections of 1899 they seized 551 places on the county councils, leaving Unionists with only 124, 86 of which were in Ulster.[35] They also were highly successful in the elections for the urban councils and held 78 per cent (a slight excess on their proportion of the population) of the representation on Boards of Guardians. Elective organs fulfilled O'Brien's expectation of there being a myriad of local parliaments, in important respects providing Ireland not simply with responsible government but with a framework that reflected the realities of parochial pluralities. In Catholic regions, Home Rulers predominated; in the Protestant parts of Ulster or elsewhere, Unionists held power. Perhaps this arrangement was not a triumph for mutual tolerance, but it did result in a meaningful democratic self-government reflective of Ireland's profound divisions.

Another impact of the act was to affirm Liberal feeling that Gladstonian Home Rule had outlived its usefulness. Setting in motion the third increment in Liberal withdrawal from Gladstonian Home Rule (see p. 167), Rosebery argued in July 1898 that 'this great experiment must be allowed time for development, and that it cannot soon or hastily be encumbered or overshadowed by an Irish parliament or any analogous body. ... British constituencies would not permit such a course.' A re-focus on Irish economic issues was, in Rosebery's estimation, essential and while he did not insist upon 'the permanent exclusion of Home Rule in some form or another from the contemplation of Liberals', the former Prime Minister insisted: 'it does imply perfect freedom of action, great caution in legislation, and ... a dramatically different method of approach.'[36]

Arthur Balfour wanted to follow up local government reform with a Catholic university measure. The idea was debated in the House of Commons in January 1897. Balfour prepared a draft bill that was circulated to the Cabinet in November 1898 and published the following January.[37] When the question was discussed in Parliament in February it soon became evident that Balfour had miscalculated. Opposition to the measure was immense and it was withdrawn. However, Conservatives had not exhausted their Irish programme. Under Plunkett's prodding, the Department of Agriculture and Technical Instruction was established in 1899. Faced with Tory legislation, Liberals progressively lost confidence in the Home Rule panacea. David Lloyd George, a rising Welsh Radical, said in late 1898:

[I]n 1886 there were special circumstances in existence which are absent now. Since then sweeping reductions have been made in rents. British capital has been pledged to the extent of several millions to convert peasants into freeholders – construct harbours and light railways and otherwise to develop the resources of the country. Above all and this one most – the population of the country has been so depleted by constant emigration that the pressure which produced symptoms of unrest in the past has now been relieved. There is an absence of that excitement and disturbance so painfully evident in 1886.[38]

Irish responses to the changing environment were not uniform but one stream represented by William O'Brien saw little to be gained by not recognising the opportunity and pressing for reform at the expense of the narrow focus on national self-government. In the autumn of 1898 he tried to convince Dillon to drop the Home Rule stance for the time being, arguing 'that any one who asked the Liberal leaders to make Home Rule the first plank in their platform would be an idiot; that they ought to be set free of this dead weight … and that whatever party came in next time the most they could do would be to carry a good land bill'.[39]

Tory success was achieved at a price, one that some among the faithful found too dear. Balfourian reforms never appealed to a significant sector of the Cabinet, the Land Act alienated many landlords, education schemes frightened Protestant opinion and the Local Government Bill incensed Irish Unionists in the southern provinces. Southern Unionists, though a small minority, had disproportionate influence with Conservatives though family, social and educational links.[40] Hostility to Conservative legislation was summed up by one Irish Unionist when he declaimed angrily that 'he would not meet a thief, therefore he would not meet Gerald Balfour'.[41] Salisbury took note of Irish Unionist sentiment and began to favour the landlord interest during 1899 and 1900. Also, after a period of rural quiescence, the agrarian problem in Ireland, notably in the west, began to flare up. Smallholdings, widespread poverty in the region covered by the Congested Districts Board and antagonism to the increase of cattle-ranching in the west gave a fresh launching pad to William O'Brien, now settled in Mayo. The United Irish League was founded on 23 January 1898.

Commemoration in March of the centenary of the 1798 rising and O'Brien's new land campaign spurred interest in the national movement, though it was still a largely unfocused revival.[42] From the beginning O'Brien's demand that grazing farms be broken up raised difficulties. The land question had ceased to present a simple division between mainly Protestant landlords and Catholic tenants. This new phase more often pitted Catholic tenants, shopkeepers and even priests who held grazing land against other Catholics – poor cottiers and landless labourers – who coveted their property.[43] For O'Brien, the campaign had the vital object of directing patriotic energy towards a common cause and thereby ending internal bickering. He believed that 'peace can be most effectively brought about by paying less attention to the differences among leaders and concentrating the energies of the people upon a united and practical struggle in which these petty matters cease to have very much importance'.[44] During 1898 the movement began to spread. By October it had fifty-three branches, mainly in Mayo, but it had made inroads in six other counties.[45] In January 1899 O'Brien posited the no doubt exaggerated claim to 180 branches with more than 35,000 members in Connaught, though the actual totals probably were closer to 94 branches and 8,853 subscribers. Still, it was evident that the movement was gaining ground. The convention at Claremorris at the end of January adopted a platform containing the traditional nostrums. The movement sought the break up of grazing land and demanded full national self-government along with the endowment of a Catholic university.[46] Other aims included the restriction of the Crown's right to challenge jurors in political cases, preservation of the Gaelic language, encouragement of Irish manufactures, provision of decent dwellings for artisans and town labourers and securing the election of true patriots to the newly created councils. Ten months later the United Irish League's Constitution promulgated a nearly identical list of aims at Cashel.[47] The locus of interest of the new agrarian movement remained practical reforms. Re-emergence of difficulties in Southern Africa in the spring of 1899, culminating in war on 11 October, diverted the attention of the Cabinet from Irish affairs and marked another shift in the fortunes of the movement, though not of the Home Rule question.

The Boer war and land purchase, 1899–1904

The Boers' struggle (11 October 1899 to 31 May 1902) offered a focus for Irish unity, if only on the basis of antipathy to English imperialism. Healy, for instance, said he had 'no imperial soul'.[48] Many people in Ireland did favour Britain's stance. A fierce battle broke out in the Dublin Corporation Council in March 1900 over resolutions supporting and condemning British efforts in the conflict.[49] Irish leaders doubted the wisdom of excessive attacks upon the military campaign. Dillon in the autumn was privately critical when the Irish members offered an address congratulating President Paul Kruger of the Transvaal Republic. To his confidant, Edward Blake, he wrote: 'I dislike the whole business exceedingly and am disposed to believe that if evidence could be produced … it would certainly offer grounds for the government proceeding against us in the House of Commons.' Yet he counselled Edward Blake to affix his name to the address because the present need 'is to create & maintain a united … party & the means by which that is done is, a fighting policy on the Transvaal Question'.[50]

The new land struggle and the Boer War rejuvenated anti-British feeling among a section of middle-class Catholics. Following the setback to the Conservative educational initiative in 1899 Cardinal Logue expressed this frustration: it is 'useless to seek the redress of a Catholic grievance from the English Parliament', insisting as well 'there is therefore only one hope left and one course open to us, that is to cease agitation for particular remedies and to go in with all the energy the country can command for Home Rule'.[51] On 30 January

1900 the Irish party was reunited, but the deep wounds lacerating it remained visible. This party was not the same as Parnell's in spirit, confidence or effectiveness. It differed in another way, also: this party was ostentatiously reformist. When Dillon and Edward Blake drew up a plan for reunion it included independence from all English parties, Home Rule, and the need to rectify grievances on land, the labourers, taxation and education.[52] Following his election as party chairman on 6 February Redmond recited the usual dismal picture of the past decade, stating that the object of the united party 'is to secure for Ireland a measure of Home Rule at least as ample as that embodied in the Bills of 1886 and 1893', but as well proclaiming that 'the party also [is] to fight on the old lines for the redress of all Irish grievances, notably those connected with land, labour, taxation and education'.[53] In the Irish Parliamentary Party Manifesto, issued on 10 February 1900, reunion was heralded as 'an event which will if the Irish people so choose mark a turning point in the history of the national movement'. It declared:

> [T]he supreme question of national self-government must be restored to its rightful position as the greatest of all political issues; but apart from the question of Home Rule, Ireland stands in immediate need of several reforms of the first importance. The land question is still unresolved. It can never be solved till the industry of agriculture – the main industry of our country – is freed, by the universal establishment of compulsory purchase of an occupying proprietary, from the burden which still weighs it down, and by some great scheme replacing the land in the poverty-stricken districts of the west in the possession of the people.[54]

This emphasis upon a broad, primarily reform agenda, was reiterated at the Irish National Convention held on 19 and 20 June. Resolutions adopted included the usual demands, along with calls for the reform of tenants' rights in towns, the abolition of the right of the Crown to challenge jurors in political cases and the encouragement of the Gaelic language as a means to enhance national identity.[55] The United Irish League was recognised by the convention as the official organisation of the national movement.

Convergence around reform facilitated reunion and was in no small part an outcome of the work of the Balfour brothers. 'Killing Home Rule with kindness' obliged both Liberals and national supporters to re-evaluate their positions. Without a clear objective, lacking funds, in the absence of towering leadership, and faced by growing divisions among the rural Catholic middle classes, the national coalition had few options but to respond to Conservative policies. The Irish party functioned as a service organisation which along with an absence of serious domestic competition facilitated its survival. By keeping the Home Rule banner aloft, if only symbolically, the party was able to retain the allegiance of those who assigned primacy to self-government.

Conservatism, by championing reform, left the divided Liberals with restricted options. Between 1896 and 1899, despite Rosebery's intervention in 1898, there had been an absence of clarity in Liberal thinking on Home Rule.[56] In 1899, shortly after Campbell-Bannerman had assumed the party leadership, Herbert Gladstone pleaded for a reappraisal of Irish policy, marking a fourth stage of Liberal disengagement from Home Rule (see p. 167). This was not an attempt to define a new policy but an effort to evade having one. Gladstone wrote to the new leader, revealing not merely an absence of a serious Liberal programme but even a reluctance to devise one until the Irish again held the balance of power in the House of Commons. After speculating that the effect of the elective local government would be to give them 'great power of leverage', he noted that, 'sooner or later the Home Rulers will hold the balance in the House of Commons'.[57] Soon after, Haldane reiterated the 'step by step' formula. However, so long as Conservatives enacted beneficial Irish legislation, they held a tactical advantage. Home Rule, Conservatives believed, was an electoral liability for the Liberals, leaving themselves the luxury of little to fear from the opposition. True safety, though, lay in satisfying an Irish public whose appetite was seemingly insatiable.

Home Rule's prospects were not altered by the general election held in the autumn. Liberals declined to make Home Rule a campaign theme. T. P. O'Connor, who was instrumental in rallying the support of the Irish in Britain, 'wanted to make it as easy as possible for our people to vote for the Liberals' and inveighed against 'pressing the Liberal candidate too close on the question of Home Rule'.[58] To those who were dismayed by his moderation, O'Connor retorted by denouncing the insistence on 'demanding the Home Rule pledge in season and out of season'. Polling took place between 29 September and 12 October; at its conclusion Conservative's were returned to Westminster with 402 seats, including 68 Liberal Unionists, while Liberals, Labour and others equalled 186; in addition, 82 Home Rulers were elected, creating a combined total of 268 to face Salisbury's ministry. Ireland's over-representation, especially of the southern provinces, became a source of controversy. In April 1900 Lord James of Hereford observed that Ireland, instead of having 103 members, was entitled to only 73.[59] George Wyndham, a Balfour protégé, became Chief Secretary of the Irish Office; his arrival did not herald a different approach to Irish affairs.

Irish party opposition to the Boer War proved a two-edged sword.

Between 1900 and 1902 they criticised its conduct, raising questions about the cost to Ireland, the treatment of wounded soldiers on their repatriation home, the promotion of Catholics and the inferior status of Catholic chaplains, yet they were quick to laud the bravery of Irish regiments. At the same time they complained about the low levels of military procurement in Ireland. *The Freeman's Journal* suggested that the absence of contracts for Irish goods was a 'boycott' and saw this practice as the distribution of patronage 'by England for England's advantage'.[60] There was also the constant reality that Irish soldiers served the colours with conspicuous bravery, something William Redmond, for instance, was always ready to salute.[61] In 1899 28,352, or 13.2 per cent of British soldiers were Irish-born; during the conflict thirteen Irish infantry battalions and three cavalry regiments saw service.[62] Erskine Childers observed: [it is] impossible to believe these are the men whom Irish patriots incite to mutiny. They are keen, simple soldiers, as proud of the flag as an Britisher.'[63] In recognition of this contribution, the Queen awarded Irish regiments the right to wear the shamrock on St Patrick's Day. Redmond, speaking for the party and to the dismay of Dillon, gushed: 'the Irish people will receive with gratification that her Majesty has directed that for the future the shamrock shall be worn by Irish regiments on March 17 to commemorate the gallantry of Irish soldiers in South Africa.'[64]

Debates on the Boer War afforded an opportunity to re-educate Irish opinion on the rationale of the national movement. Davitt in January 1902 went so far as to declare that not even Home Rule was worth the price of 'partaking in England's wicked and sordid outrage upon another Christian nation's country and freedom'.[65] Irishmen were not the only critics of the conflict but their voices were shrill, their participation out of proportion to their numbers, prompting Salisbury in 1902 to cite this as evidence that the Irish were unready for self-government.[66] The war had an invigorating effect similar to the obstructionism of the 1870s, directing attention to the party, uniting a significant numbers of Catholics. Revived party morale was accompanied by greater parliamentary activity. In May 1901 *The Times* bore witness to this renewed vigour:

> The Irish Nationalist Members, who boasted at the beginning of the session that they would shake the Government in the saddle have not yet done much to give effect to their threats but they have indemnified themselves by frequent debates, long speeches, and sweeping claims. The ingenuity with which they make use of the machinery of the ballot in the House of Commons secures them far more opportunities of raising debates than the regular opposition.[67]

Redmond early the following year repeated the old Parnell pledge: 'if we cannot govern ourselves, we can take good care not to allow them to govern themselves'.[68] In 1902 the government met this challenge, reducing the scope for employing procedural delays of business.

During 1899 and 1900 the land question re-emerged and the United Irish League expanded rapidly. According to constabulary estimates it had 865 branches with 86,119 members by the close of 1900.[69] Its agrarian platform reinforced the party's reformist tendency. In March 1900 Redmond defined the purposes of the League:

> The United Irish League from its origin and its provincial constitution, seems specially adapted to the prosecution of an agrarian reform, which, in my judgement, has become a question of the most pressing importance. Next to Home Rule itself the most important reform which is needed today in Ireland is a scheme of land purchase which (due regard being had to the claims of the labouring classes) will make the tenant farmers proprietors of their holdings, and bring the land question at last to the stage of finality. I believe such a scheme can be carried out on a basis which will do no injustice to the landlords, and will root the tenants in the soil.[70]

At the beginning of 1902, in response to violence and intimidation, the government decided to bring in coercion. Coercion, as always, united Catholic Ireland and gave the party a fighting posture. In January Redmond told the House of Commons that 'the Irish people, being united and strong, will not allow themselves to be driven out of their privileges and rights ... it is not possible ... by methods of coercion to break the spirit of the people of Ireland.'[71] Thereafter, it would be difficult to escape Irish party wrath. In March the counties of Cavan, Clare, Cork, Leitrim, Mayo, Roscommon, Sligo, Tipperary and Waterford, along with Waterford and Cork cities, were proclaimed disturbed areas and brought under the provisions of the Coercion Act passed during 1902. By September over half the country plus Dublin had been proclaimed and forty prominent Leaguers were imprisoned. The Irish Chief Secretary was vilified by *The Freeman's Journal*, and denounced as 'the newspaper destroying tyrant',[72] though T. P. O'Connor pointed out a short while later that 'the Irish had in Wyndham a man who tried to be impartial'.[73]

Between 1900 and 1902 the Conservatives made few fresh attempts to introduce ameliorative reforms, though Wyndham had wanted to legislate on the education and land questions. In December 1901 he wanted 'to smash the agitation, introduce a Land Bill, get money for a Harbour-fishing Policy in the West and float a Catholic University'.[74] On 26 January 1902 he mused, 'nobody knows better than I do the risk of doing anything in that country. But I know that the risk of doing nothing is far greater and that to take the advice of extremists at either pole is not a risk but a certainty of disaster.'[75]

Despite an apparent decline in Conservative initiatives, Liberals did not respond by drawing closer to the Irish party. Its sympathy for the Boers, the more aggressive behaviour of MPs in the House of Commons since reunion and Redmond's apparent readiness to disassociate himself from the Liberals marked a start to the fifth stage in Liberal party disengagement from Home Rule (see p. 167). In July 1901 Rosebery enunciated what soon became known as the 'clean slate'. At the beginning of September Wemyss Reid wrote to Rosebery: 'the Liberal party got its charter of freedom when Dillon & Redmond made their speeches demanding an independent Parliament in Dublin'.[76] On 28 September at Ladybank Asquith pointed out that based on population Ireland was entitled to seventy-one MPs, but he objected to a redistribution of seats that would affect it alone, demanding instead a scheme for the whole of the United Kingdom. He went on to state that a grant of self-government to Ireland was governed by two guiding principles: 'the necessity of maintaining the universal, absolute, and unimpaired supremacy of the Imperial Parliament, and, subject to that condition the policy of giving as large and as liberal a devolution of local powers and local responsibilities as statesmanship can from time to time devise'.[77] His theme was quickly endorsed by Haldane, who on 3 October stated that he gave Gerald Balfour credit for his

> Local Government Act and as that experiment had succeeded he thought the time had come when they might safely go a little further; but the extension of Local Government must entail a diminution of Irish representation in Parliament, and the supremacy of the Imperial Parliament must be maintained in its integrity both constitutionally and in practice. The Liberal party ... should set its mind to the reconsideration of its policy in regard to Ireland.[78]

Sir Edward Grey speaking in Newcastle on 11 October supported Asquith's position:

> [A]fter all that had been said during the war it would be impossible for Liberal members to enter upon a crusade to convert the British electors to grant the Irish demand. Nevertheless, he believed that towards Home Rule in Ireland things must move. Things could not stay as they were. They could not rest with the present measure of local self-government. If Irish demands did not force it upon this country the necessities of the case, our own needs, and the trouble in the House of Commons would force it upon us. He believed that progress in that direction must be made, not in one great measure, but step by step.[79]

There were three routes, according to Grey, to fulfilling Ireland's need – by informal association of county councils which might be given 'legal recognition and some administrative powers', by provincial councils, or through the creation of 'one council for the whole of Ireland'.[80] The purpose of reform, in Grey's estimation, was to increase the 'efficiency' of Irish institutions, underlying the traditional Liberal view that self-government was meant to improve the quality and responsibility of people, not promote a separate national existence The Asquith/Haldane/Grey policy did not repudiate Home Rule, but Rosebery, in effect, did when in December he reverted more explicitly to the 'clean slate' in Irish affairs.[81] At Liverpool on 14 February 1902 he stated that as a consequence of the Local Government Act 'the conditions of the problem of Irish government have fundamentally changed', suggesting, as cited at the head of the chapter, that 'no sane community of persons' would turn over Ireland's destinies to those who eagerly sought Great Britain's defeat in South Africa.[82] In place of Home Rule Rosebery proposed to substitute a fresh Liberal approach, centring on the extension of county government, devolution and the reform of Dublin Castle. Conceding that it might be possible to grant Ireland a local subordinate legislature as part of a scheme of imperial federation, he emphasised this would not be an independent parliament. Significantly, Rosebery maintained that Liberals 'must give up any hope of satisfying the sentiment of Irish leaders in this matter'. Ireland, he proclaimed, would have to be governed 'without the hope of Irish gratitude'.[83] Views insistent upon a reformulation of post-Gladstonian ideas on Ireland found an outlet with the formation of the Liberal League on 24 February 1902, but it did not attempt to resolve the differences between the 'step by step' and 'clean slate' alternatives.

An English bill, Arthur Balfour's education measure, caused a rift between the Irish party and Liberals. It dissolved the school boards in England and Wales while, in what became the most contentious aspect, rate support was given to denominational schools. In May 1902 most Irish party MPs expressed support for the measure. By mid-summer Balfour's bill was under attack from Nonconformists, who coined it 'Rome on the Rates'. Both the English and Irish Catholic hierarchies impressed on Redmond the importance they attached to the legislation. The party chairman worried that abandonment of resistance to the government would 'destroy the influence of the representatives of Ireland upon the Government of England and expose them to contempt and powerlessness in every opportunity that may offer for extorting favourable terms for our fellow-countrymen either in England or in Ireland'.[84] The dilemma was resolved by absenteeism from the House of Commons, but the

MPs reappeared en masse in December to provide the bill with its margin of victory in the division lobby.

In 1902 Wyndham wanted to introduce further land legislation prior to the coercion measure.[85] But his bill, Wilfrid Blunt noted, was 'makeshift',[86] and in June he was forced to withdraw it. Rural violence and agitation increased sharply over the next few months. On 3 September Captain John Shawe-Taylor published a letter in *The Times* suggesting a conference of landlord and tenant representatives to hammer out a formula for land purchase. Wyndham grasped this straw. Shawe-Taylor's proposal was greeted enthusiastically by William O'Brien, though not by Dillon who opposed negotiations, believing the tenants would gain little. His view was that the Irish should continue to put pressure the government; the state should be held accountable for whatever unsatisfactory clauses any land legislation might contain.

O'Brien's view prevailed. His and Shawe-Taylor's initiative led to a conference, attended by representatives of landowners and tenants. When it convened on 20 December, the landlord plenipotentiaries Earls of Dunraven, Mayo and Meath, plus Viscount Powerscourt, met Redmond, O'Brien, Harrington and T. W. Russell acting as the tenants' spokesmen. It reported on 3 January 1903. The conference managed to work out an agreement and reported in favour of Treasury loans to fund tenant purchase; this formed the basis of Wyndham's bill introduced on 25 March 1903, the largest single piece of land purchase legislation. The Chief Secretary had ensured the support of Irish landowners in advance.[87] This measure encouraged the sale of entire estates, which could proceed when three-quarters of the tenants on any estate opted to purchase their holdings. The price to be paid varied according to the value of the holdings and the money required was to be advanced by the state to be repaid over 68½ years by annuities at 3.25 per cent.[88] In order to bridge the difference between what the landlords demanded and tenants could afford to pay, a 12 per cent bonus on the selling price was to be paid out of the Irish revenues to landowners for each sale. A sum of £12 million was appropriated for bonus payments. As a further sweetener, landlords were granted the right to sell their demesnes, the portion of the estate reserved for their private use, to the Estates Commissioners for a sum up to £20,000 and repurchase these on the same terms offered to the tenants. Landowners were to be paid in cash, not stock. An upper limit of £150 million was sanctioned for land purchase.

The land question always held dangers for national unity and this occasion proved no exception. Dillon had never liked the initiative, Michael Davitt soon denounced the act and *The Freeman's Journal* threw its weight on the scales against it. In the short term the outcome of collaboration was a success. Wyndham was so encouraged that at the beginning of February 1903 he withdrew the imposition of coercion. The land scheme – the Wyndham Act – came into force on 14 August. Redmond hailed it as 'the most substantial victory gained for centuries by the Irish race for the reconquest of the soil of Ireland by the people'.[89] More accurately, the affluent tenant farmers were its beneficiaries. At this stage O'Brien's and Redmond's conception of conciliation and reformism was in the ascendant though many in the patriotic ranks remained sceptical. Still, the Wyndham Act, as well as abetting land purchase, led to an immediate lessening of agrarian disorder. During 1903 there was a 33 per cent drop in reports of intimidation, a 70 per cent decline in boycotting, 60 per cent fewer people required police protection and there was a 50 per cent decrease in the numbers and acreage of grazing farms that had not been let or stocked.[90]

The spirit of conciliation encouraged some people, notably certain Unionists, along with O'Brien to explore further avenues of potential co-operation. For O'Brien, this was 'conference plus business', by which he meant negotiations between Unionists and nationalists, resulting in concrete results. Dunraven spearheaded an emergent progressive Irish Unionism based on the ideals championed by Plunkett. He envisaged fresh co-operation that would provide 'a fair chance for labourers, a just readjustment of taxation, higher education, the obtaining for Ireland of such an extension of self-governing power as would give the Irish people full control of all purely Irish affairs'.[91] Self-rule meant forms of local government that spelt no danger to the constitution, not a Dublin Parliament on the Gladstonian model, though his language was deliberately vague so as not to wound patriotic susceptibilities. Dunraven found in O'Brien a willing accomplice. O'Brien had chaffed at the constraints of post-Parnell national politics. Moreover, he was piqued at the criticism and backsliding of members of the Irish party over the Land Act. While he did not abandon Home Rule as a long-term aim, he assured Dunraven: 'I am not more than you, at the present moment, in a position to give, in an actual scheme a definition of Home Rule ... all that is necessary is to try to discover as many points of contact as possible.'[92] To redefine the objective of Gladstonian Home Rule held out pregnant possibilities, and, equally, grave dangers for the unity of the national coalition.

In the spring of 1903 the Royal Commission on Education, despite many caveats and disagreements, broadly supported the establishment of a Catholic college in Dublin. It received a very chilly reception from Irish Unionists. Wyndham, however, was undaunted. In September he proposed a variant of the Royal Commission plan, but soon adopted another scheme that would amalgamate the Queen's College, Belfast, Trinity College and the new Catholic institution into the University of Dublin.[93] Shawe-Taylor canvassed for a new conference on education. By late September this resulted in 'a general sketch of Irish policy' including suggestions for improvements in drainage, housing, education at all levels, the poor law and communications.[94] Dillon saw in this a threat to the dominance of the Irish party and restated his opposition to fresh conferences. To Redmond he warned: 'I, as you know, have all along been opposed to the policy of allowing the initiative on the direction of large Irish questions to be taken out of the hands of the Irish party and handed over to conferences summoned by outsiders.'[95] Redmond was more guarded this time around, especially about the idea of a conference to settle the university question. He had seen how divisive the land conference had been. Disgruntled at criticism of the Land Act and resistance to further reforms through conferences provoked O'Brien's resigned from the party on 6 November 1903. His departure injured but did not destroy the reform orientation of the party. Education as a avenue of co-operation traversed along a bumpy course and in January 1904 it ground to a halt.

During the following year Dunraven began thinking of a bold step that could link Irishmen of good will more securely and lay Gladstonian Home Rule to rest. This spirit was given expression in the formation of the Irish Reform Association founded on 25 August 1904. Dunraven approached the Lord Lieutenant and Under-Secretary with his idea on devolved government. He believed they concurred with him. The Under-Secretary, Sir Anthony MacDonnell, who had been appointed in 1902, assisted in drafting the plan which Dunraven published on 31 August. Through September MacDonnell became increasingly involved in the proposal, apparently believing that it enjoyed the blessing of Wyndham. Its cornerstone was a financial council which would have twelve elected and twelve nominated members to prepare and submit estimates to Parliament for Irish services. The Lord Lieutenant would be its President with the Irish Chief Secretary an *ex officio* member. The council was to have the power to distribute money but not to determine the level of spending or taxation. There was to be a second legislative council consisting of all Irish MPs and representative peers along with the non-parliamentary members of the financial council. This body would promote bills of purely Irish content. The initiative, however, was abruptly terminated when in a letter to *The Times* on 27 September Wyndham declared 'without reserve or qualification that the Unionist Government is opposed to the multiplication of legislative bodies within the United Kingdom'.[96]

Redmond welcomed the Dunraven scheme as 'a declaration for Home Rule. ... quite a wonderful thing'.[97] Soon, though, he could not detect sufficient merit in the plan to lend his name to it. Dillon, as usual, was deeply opposed, believing 'any vote of confidence in Lord Dunraven, or any declaration of satisfaction at the foundation of the Irish Reform Association would tear the ranks of the Nationalists of Ireland to pieces. ... Conciliation, so far as landlords are concerned, was another name for swindling the people.'[98] More cautiously, Redmond in the aftermath of the incident directed his objections to the specifics of the plan not the principle of co-operation, calling it a blatant attempt 'to get rid of us'.[99] Lord Castledown touched on the real difficulty when he noted that devolution was '*too advanced* for the party of Unionists and not sufficiently so for the other side'.[100]

Decline of Conservative 'kindness'

After the devolution crisis, there was no substantial attempt to restore 'Constructive Unionism'; Wyndham himself became the object of scorn within his own party. In February 1905 Colonel Saunderson observed that relations with the government were 'strained almost to breaking point'.[101] Henry Lucy observed after the debate on MacDonnell's role in the devolution plan: 'if any other Province of the Kingdom than Ulster had been concerned in the matter the affair might have been hushed up last September ... but Ulster is a sleuth-hound which having once got its nose on the trail, does not uplift it except to spring on the fugitive.'[102] One outcome was the formation of the Ulster Unionist Council which held its first meeting on 3 March 1905, three days before Wyndham resigned. By exciting Protestant suspicions, the devolution crisis marked a sharp turnback toward sectarian politics.[103] Balfour, though, in one final gasp, in April after Wyndham's departure, reaffirmed his commitment to setting up a Catholic university, but had to concede that the opposition within his own ranks was too strong to proceed for the present.

Wyndham's successor, Walter Long, changed the emphasis of the Irish Administration. He was anxious to re-establish Conservative policies and thereby restore Unionist confidence. In his view, 'what the country wants now is rest and peace, steady quiet but firm administration, wholesome food & drink. She had had too much quack medicine lately! ... I am convinced patience and firmness will put things right.'[104] Long gave directions for the vigorous prosecution of agrarian offences and issued instructions that land sales should not proceed where intimidation had been employed against landowners. He ensured that sound Unionists were appointed to official positions. Long's brief spell in Ireland did not mark a complete reversal of his predecessors' ideas.[105] He was prepared to spend money in the country and at Belfast in April he outlined his belief that 'the government should be administered justly, impartially, and fairly as between all creeds',[106] a philosophy that had characterised Conservative outlook, if not always practice, since the 1870s. Crucially, though, the Conservative government was weakened by disputes over tariff reform. That plus the Education Act were a tonic for Liberals. From 1903 Liberals scored a succession of by-election victories. Irish party interest in co-operation with Unionists diminished. Events after 1900 showed once again the attractions and dangers of reformism. Ultimately, Home Rule and reformism only worked in a symbiotic relationship.

If the Achilles heal of 'constructive Unionism' had been exposed, the Liberals and Irish party did not retrench under the Home Rule umbrella. By 1904 a gap had opened between Rosebery and those who favoured a 'step by step' approach along the lines developed by the Conservatives. A sixth increment in Liberal disengagement (see p. 167) can be discerned in the progression towards general acceptance and then adoption by the party of the 'step by step' approach. Devolution discarded by the Tories made a powerful impression on Liberals. In late November 1904 Thomas Lough prepared a memorandum advocating a version of it.[107] 'Step by step' Home Rule was a natural extension. James Bryce, a mainstream Home Rule Liberal, thought that the Irish situation would be transformed under the impact of land purchase. On 26 January 1905 he wrote to Goldwin Smith: 'as to Home Rule, no one thinks it possible to bring into the next Parliament a bill like that of 1893. But probably there may be some further steps towards granting local powers and removing topics from the British Parliament, while retaining its ultimate control.'[108] On 3 February he speculated: 'when they have got the land much of the steam will have gone out of the boiler.'[109] Asquith on 24 February at Birmingham confirmed the impress of devolutionary ideas, praising the abortive scheme of the previous year.[110] Grey on 15 March stated that his policy would be 'to go on with the sympathetic policy [devolution] where the Government dropped it'.[111] In a Home Rule debate in the House of Commons on 12 April Campbell-Bannerman lauded the necessity of pursuing a programme of good government in Ireland as a means of healing the country's current divisions.[112] As the year progressed and the Conservatives became visibly weaker, Home Rule did not find an enlarged place in Liberal plans. At the beginning of autumn the Liberal approach lacked clear definition. Asquith in the face of heckling at Earlsferry on 11 October stated that the 'gradual association of the Irish people with the management of their own affairs step by step should be the aim and ideal of the Liberal policy in regard to Ireland'.[113] On 20 October Morley, speaking for orthodox Gladstonians, retorted, emphasising the Liberal commitment to Home Rule, but admitted he did not 'expect to see reform of the Irish Government the first measure of the new Parliament'.[114] Objecting to Morley's remarks, Asquith wrote to Herbert Gladstone: 'if we are to get a real majority in the next House of Commons, it can only be by making it perfectly clear to the electorate that … it will be no part of the policy of the Liberal Government to introduce a Home Rule bill in the next Parliament.'[115] Rosebery joined the debate at Stourbridge on 25 October supporting 'large administrative reforms' along the lines laid down by Balfour and Wyndham.[116] Campbell-Bannerman sidestepped the controversy, but it was increasingly obvious that he had to find means to ease internal Liberal differences. Writing on 19 November Lord Crewe reminded Campbell-Bannerman: 'probably there are fewer British Home Rulers than there were in 1886 and 1893'.[117] After clearing the path with Irish leaders, Campbell-Bannerman on 23 November at Stirling advocated the middle or Asquithian position:

> [I]f I were asked for advice – which is not likely, perhaps – by an ardent Irish Nationalist I would say, 'your desire is, as mine is, to see the effective management of Irish affairs in the hands of a representative Irish Parliament. If I were you I would take it in any way I can get it, and if an instalment of representative control was offered to you, or any administrative improvements. I would advise you thankfully to accept it, provided it was consistent with and led up to your larger policy'. I think that would be good advice. But I lay stress on the proviso – it must be consistent with and lead up to the larger policy. To secure good administration is one thing, and a good thing in itself, but good government can never be a substitute for government by the people themselves.[118]

He predicted that the next Parliament would be absorbed mainly in social questions. This satisfied the Liberal rank and file, insuring that the party would not sponsor anything more drastic than devolution in the next Parliament, though Rosebery mistakenly read his remarks as a declaration for Home Rule. Asquith, Grey and Haldane repudiated this interpretation. Balfour resigned on 4 December and Campbell-Bannerman took office the following day. Several members of the new Cabinet stipulated that there should be no Home Rule bill.

By and large the Irish leadership was prepared to accept Liberal imperatives. Few were so naive as to think the Liberals would readily restore the primacy of Gladstonian Home Rule. In February 1905 Herbert Gladstone reported that Redmond 'has to maintain Home Rule as a minimum … but fully realises the difficulties of the Liberal position. Thinks Home Rule will come by degrees, and not unreasonable.'[119] In early November 1905 Bryce worried that Redmond might 'think he must play strong' in order to avert divisions within his own camp. Prior to his Stirling address Campbell-Bannerman had a secret interview with Redmond and T. P. O'Connor when he was assured that the Irish party would be accommodating on the Home Rule question.[120] Following his tentative affirmation of Home Rule at Stirling, *The Freeman's Journal* pronounced that the Liberal leader's stance was satisfactory.[121] A compact on the basis of limited reform was cemented. Liberals, with the tacit understanding of the Irish party, strengthened rather than repudiated Conservative reformism, while a 'step by step' approach and devolutionary ideas were at the heart of those institutional innovations likely to see the light of day. Both the purposes and nature of Home Rule had undergone an implicit reformulation.

Conclusion

The years between 1893 and 1905 were critical for Home Rule. They marked not a wasteland but a series of bold attempts to explore Irish ailments and strategically target trouble spots while also consolidating the triumph of liberal unionist ideas. The national movement underwent an unacknowledged reorientation during this period. Ultimately the experiment seemed forlorn, therefore commanding comparatively little attention. However, in late 1905 there was no reason to anticipate that it had not laid the foundation for a different and dynamic Anglo-Irish relationship, one that rendered obsolete the polarities of the past. The fresh developments owed little to patriotic ideas, organisation or pressure. Whereas earlier British leaders responded to Irish ferment, national party leaders now found themselves largely reacting to Conservative plans, relegated to the fringes and seemingly incapable of applying Parnell's formula of using the Home Rule cry to extract concessions from Westminster or regain the moral initiative. Still, during this time Ireland gained more than at any comparable earlier period. There was a further flaw which spelt trouble for the future. Except for a brief spell and including only a few people, neither side in Ireland showed much evidence of being able to work together. Both found adversarial techniques more reassuring.

Notes

1 Alfred Webb to J. F. X. O'Brien [1897], J. F. X. O'Brien Papers, National Library of Ireland, MS 13418–477 (13).
2 *The Times*, 15 February 1902.

3   See, F. S. L. Lyons, *Ireland since the Famine* (4th revised impression; London, 1976), pp. 202–23; Joseph Lee, *The Modernisation of Irish Society 1848–1918* (Dublin, 1973), pp. 122–9; Andrew Gailey, *Ireland and the Death of Kindness: The Experience of Constructive Unionism 1890–1905* (Cork, 1987).

4   Henry W. Lucy, *A Diary of the Unionist Parliament 1895–1900* (Bristol and London, 1901), pp. 91–2.

5   F. S. L. Lyons, *John Dillon: A Biography* (London, 1968), p. 165.

6   Quoted in Catherine B. Shannon, *Arthur J. Balfour and Ireland 1874–1922* (Washington, DC, 1988), p. 87.

7   Peter Stansky, *Ambitions and Strategies: The Struggle for the Leadership of the Liberal Party in the 1890s* (Oxford, 1964), pp. 201–2.

8   H. C. G. Matthew, *The Liberal Imperialists: The Ideas and Politics of a Post-Gladstonian Élite* (Oxford, 1973), p. 268.

9   Quoted in David W. Gutzke, 'Rosebery and Ireland, 1898–1903: A Reappraisal', *Bulletin of the Institute of Historical Research*, LIII (May, 1989), p. 89; reprinted in Alan O'Day (ed.), *Reactions to Irish Nationalism, 1865–1914* (London, 1987), p. 286.

10   *The Times*, 4 February 1899.

11   Andrew Adonis, *Making Aristocracy Work: The Peerage and the Political System in Britain 1884–1914* (Oxford, 1993), p. 79.

12   See, Alvin Jackson, 'Irish Unionism and the Russellite Threat, 1894–1906', *Irish Historical Studies*, XXV (November 1987), pp. 376–404.

13   See, *PD*, 3rd Series, 393 (1890), c. 988.

14   *The Times*, 11 July 1895.

15   Quoted in Gailey, *Ireland and the Death of Kindness*, p. 26.

16   Trevor West, *Horace Plunkett, Co-Operation and Politics: An Irish Biography* (Gerrards Cross, Bucks, 1986), pp. 44–9.

17   T. P. Gill to Gladstone, 25 August 1896, T. P. Gill Papers, National Library of Ireland, MS 13509 (5).

18   West, *Horace Plunkett*, pp. 48–9.

19   *Ibid.*, p. 50.

20   Jackson, *The Ulster Party: Irish Unionists in the House of Commons, 1884–1922* (Oxford, 1989), p. 146.

21   Gailey, *Ireland and the Death of Kindness*, p. 91.

22   Quoted in *ibid.*, p. 102.

23   Margaret A. Banks, *Edward Blake, Irish Nationalist: A Canadian Statesman in Irish Politics 1892–1907* (Toronto, 1957), p. 171.

24   F. S. L. Lyons, *The Irish Parliamentary Party 1890–1910* (London, 1951), p. 63.

25   See, *PD*, 4th series, 49 (1896), cc, 9–10, 205, 338–39, 432, 448, 1142–3, 1460–1, 1597–8.

26   For examples, see, Jackson, *The Ulster Party*, p. 87, 196–242; *Colonel Edward Saunderson: Land and Loyalty in Victorian Ireland* (Oxford, 1995), pp. 135–41. Also, Terence Denman, *A Lonely Grave: The Life and Death of William Redmond* (Dublin, 1995), pp. 60–1.

27   William O'Brien, *An Olive Branch in Ireland and its History* (London, 1910), p. 67; Lyons, *John Dillon*, pp. 144–78, 80.

28   Archbishop William Walsh to T. C. Harrington, 17 January 1897, T. C. Harrington Papers, National Library of Ireland, MS 8576 (51).

29   Denis R. Gwynn, *Life of John Redmond* (London, 1932), p. 90.

30   Lyons, *Irish Party*, p. 79.

31   John Dillon to William O'Brien, 8 July 1898, William O'Brien Papers, National Library of Ireland, MS 8555 (13).

32   Quoted in Jackson, *The Ulster Party*, p. 173; see, p. 175.

33   *PD*, 4th series, 55 (1898), c. 448.

34   Quoted in Philip J. Bull, *Land, Politics and Nationalism: A Study of the Irish Land Question* (Dublin, 1996), p 134.

35   Shannon, *Arthur J. Balfour*, pp. 103–4.

36   Quoted in John Kendle, *Ireland and the Federal Solution: The Debate over the United Kingdom Constitution, 1870–1921* (Kingston and Montreal, 1989), p. 84.

37   Jackson, *The Ulster Party*, pp. 178–86.

38   *South Wales Daily News*, 3 November 1898.

39   Quoted in Joseph V. O'Brien, *William O'Brien and the Course of Irish Politics, 1881–1918* (Berkeley and Los Angeles, 1976), p. 142.

40   See, Patrick Buckland, *Irish Unionism: One: The Anglo-Irish and the New Ireland 1885–1922* (Dublin, 1972).

41   Quoted in Elizabeth, Countess of Fingall, *Seventy Years Young* (London, 1937), p. 232.

42   Timothy J. O'Keefe, '"Who Fears to Speak of '98?"': The Rhetoric and Rituals of the United Irishmen Centennial, 1898', *Eire-Ireland*, XXVII (Fall, 1992), pp. 67–91.

43   See, Paul Bew, *Conflict and Conciliation in Ireland 1890–1910: Parnellites and Radical Agrarians* (Oxford, 1987), p. 41.

44   Quoted in Bull, *Land, Politics and Nationalism*, p. 113.

45   O'Brien, *William O'Brien*, p. 112.

46   Sally Warwick-Haller, *William O'Brien and the Irish Land War* (Dublin, 1990), p. 193.

47   *The Freeman's Journal*, 19 November 1899.

48   *PD*, 4th series, 78 (1900), cc. 857–9.

49   G. Walpole, *Extra-Parliamentary Hansard* (London, 1901), I, p. 477.

50   John Dillon to Edward Blake, 31 October 1900, Edward Blake Papers, National Library of Ireland, MS 4682 (458).

51   Quoted in Gailey, *Ireland and the Death of Kindness*, p. 131.

52   Banks, *Edward Blake*, pp. 213–14.

53   Quoted in Walpole, *Extra-Parliamentary Hansard*, I, p. 422; John Redmond to T. C. Harrington, J. Jordan and T. M. Healy (copy), 3 January 1900, John Redmond Papers, National Library of Ireland, MS 8576.

54   Quoted in Walpole, *Extra-Parliamentary Hansard*, I, p. 433–5.

55   *Ibid.*, I, pp. 769–74.

56   Matthew, *The Liberal Imperialists*, p. 289.

57   Herbert Gladstone to Sir Henry Campbell-Bannerman, 8 December 1899, Sir Henry Campbell-Bannerman Papers, British Library, MS 41215.

58   Quoted in L. W. Brady, *T. P. O'Connor and the Liverpool Irish*

(London, 1983), p. 154.

59 Walpole, *Extra-Parliamentary Hansard*, I, pp. 769–74.

60 *The Freeman's Journal*, 20 June 1901.

61 Denman, *A Lonely Grave*, p. 58.

62 Arthur Davey, *The British Pro-Boers 1877–1902* (Tafelberg, SA, 1978), p. 144; also, see, Terence Denman, '"The Red Livery of Shame": The Campaign Against Army Recruitment in Ireland, 1899–1914', *Irish Historical Studies*, XXIX (November, 1994), pp. 208–33.

63 Quoted in Andrew Boyle, *The Riddle of Erskine Childers: A Biography* (London, 1977), p. 94.

64 O'Brien, *William O'Brien.*, pp. 120–1.

65 *The Freeman's Journal*, 9 January 1902.

66 Alan Ward, *Ireland and Anglo-American Relations, 1899–1921* (London, 1969), pp. 265–6.

67 *The Times*, 23 May 1901.

68 *Ibid.*, 23 May 1901.

69 Shannon, *Arthur J. Balfour*, p. 116; P. J. Bull, 'The United Irish League and the Reunion of the Irish Parliamentary Party, 1898–1900', *Irish Historical Studies*, XXVI (May 1988), p. 76.

70 Quoted in Walpole, *Extra-Parliamentary Hansard*, I, p. 481.

71 *PD*, 4th series, 101 (1902), c. 124.

72 *The Freeman's Journal*, 27 May 1901.

73 *PD*, 4th series, 99 (1901), c. 1320.

74 Quoted in J. W. Mackail and Guy Wyndham, *Life and Letters of George Wyndham* (London, 1924), II, p. 434.

75 *Ibid.*, p. 436.

76 Quoted in Gutzke, 'Rosebery and Ireland', p. 95 (reprint, p. 292).

77 *The Times*, 30 September 1901.

78 *Ibid.*, 4 October 1901.

79 *Ibid.*, 12 October 1901.

80 *The Times* report is not explicit on these alternatives. See, Matthew, *The Liberal Imperialists*, p. 275.

81 Robert Rhodes James, *Rosebery: A Biography of Archibald Philip, Fifth Earl of Rosebery* (London, 1963), pp. 430–1.

82 *The Times*, 15 February 1902.

83 *Ibid.*

84 *The Freeman's Journal*, 28 November 1902.

85 For the rural agitation that precipitated the bill, see, Bew, *Conflict and Conciliation*, pp. 70–95.

86 Wilfrid Scawen Blunt, *My Diaries Being a Personal Narrative of Events 1888–1914* (reprint; New York, 1980), II, p. 20.

87 Jackson, *The Ulster Party*, p. 164.

88 See, Elizabeth R. Hooker, *Readjustments of Agricultural Tenure in Ireland* (Chapel Hill, NC, 1938), pp. 79–89.

89 Quoted in Gwynn, *John Redmond*, p. 102.

90 O'Brien, *William O'Brien*, p. 166.

91 Earl of Dunraven, *Past Times and Pastimes* (London, 1922), II, p. 2.

92 Quoted in O'Brien, *William O'Brien*, p. 159.

93 Jackson, *The Irish Party*, pp. 188–90.

94 Gailey, *Ireland and the Death of Kindness*, p. 197.

95 Quoted in William O'Brien, *An Olive Branch*, p. 258.

96 *The Times*, 27 September 1904; see, Kendle, *Ireland and the Federal Solution*, pp. 90–4; Eunan O'Halpin, *The Decline of the Union: British Government in Ireland 1892–1920* (Dublin, 1987), p. 45.

97 Quoted in Gwynn, *John Redmond*, p. 106.

98 Quoted in William O'Brien, *An Olive Branch*, pp. 326, 339.

99 *The Freeman's Journal*, 27 October 1904.

100 Quoted in Gailey, *Ireland and the Death of Kindness*, p. 300.

101 Quoted in *ibid.*, p. 258; for a bitter-sweet appraisal see, Henry W. Lucy, *The Balfourian Parliament 1900–1905* (London, 1906), pp. 366–8.

102 Lucy, *Balfourian Parliament*, p. 364.

103 Jackson, *The Ulster Party*, pp. 243–83.

104 Quoted in John Kendle, *Walter Long, Ireland, and the Union, 1905–1920* (Kingston and Montreal, 1992), p. 26.

105 *Ibid.*, pp. 25–8; O'Halpin, *Decline of the Union*, pp. 53–7.

106 Quoted in Kendle, *Walter Long*, p. 29.

107 H. W. McCready, 'Home Rule and the Liberal Party, 1899–1906', *Irish Historical Studies*, XIII (September 1963), p. 339.

108 James Bryce to Goldwin Smith (copy), 26 January 1905, Bryce Papers, Bodleian Library, University of Oxford, Vol. 17.

109 James Bryce to A. V. Dicey, 3 February 1905, James Bryce Papers, National Library of Ireland, MS 11011.

110 *The Times*, 25 February 1905.

111 *Ibid.* 16 March 1905.

112 *PD*, 194 (1905), c. 1506

113 *The Times*, 12 October 1905.

114 *Ibid.*, 21 October 1905.

115 H. H. Asquith to Herbert Gladstone, 22 October 1905, Viscount Gladstone Papers, British Library, MS 45995.

116 *The Times*, 26 October 1905.

117 Marquess of Crewe to Sir Henry Campbell-Bannerman, 19 November 1905, Campbell-Bannerman Papers, MS 41213.

118 *The Times*, 23 November 1905.

119 Quoted in McCready, 'Home Rule', p. 341.

120 Sir Henry Campbell-Bannerman to Herbert Gladstone, 20 November 1905, Campbell-Bannerman Papers, MS 41217.

121 *The Freeman's Journal*, 24 November 1905.

8

Liberal unionism,
1905–10

The land agitation was largely yoked to the national question to draw it. It now appears to have come about that the national question be used eternally to draw every other question. That is what I object to. (Alfred Webb to John Redmond, 4 June 1907)[1]

I feel we are in for Home Rule in some form, but it makes the whole difference, whether it is provincial Home Rule – i.e. Ireland to the United Kingdom like Quebec to the rest of Canada – or National Home Rule, i.e. Ireland like Canada, virtually quite independent of the rest of the United Kingdom. I don't suppose the Unionist party can go in for Home Rule in any form, but if it comes in spite of us, not much harm would be done by Provincial Home Rule. It is Ireland like Canada, which would be so dangerous and disintegrating. (Alfred Milner to Arthur Balfour, 7 April 1910)[2]

Introduction

Balfour resigned on 4 December 1905 and Campbell-Bannerman took office as Prime Minister on the following day. A change of government did not transform the prospects for Home Rule or bode a shift in Irish policy. At the general election held between 13 and 27 January 1906 Liberals gained their largest parliamentary electoral victory, capturing 399 seats to merely 156 for the Conservatives and Liberal Unionists. The new Labour party returned 29 MPs and Home Rulers went to the new Parliament with a further 83. Three 'others' completed the picture. Observers noted that this independent majority allowed the Liberals to shelve Home Rule until the two general elections of 1910 made them once again dependent on Irish votes in the House of Commons. If chronologically satisfactory, this view does not allow for Liberal determination to evade another Home Rule measure which pre-dates the formation of the new government. Campbell-Bannerman's administration stood ready to give Ireland attention within a liberal unionist framework. Two dilemmas afflicted the Irish party – the problem of functioning as both a service and an ideological organ; and whether it was completely independent or aligned with Liberalism. In two respects Liberalism from 1906 to 1910 differed from its previous position with regard to Ireland: it had an independent majority for the first time since the second Gladstone ministry; and this was the only time since 1868 when Liberals either did not come into office or soon afterwards attempt to pass a major Irish measure.

Devolution, December 1905–mid-1907

Installation of the Liberal government reinforced liberal unionism. Campbell-Bannerman had ruled out an attempt at a Gladstonian scheme for the next Parliament. Liberals had already disengaged from Home Rule as an active policy. The new administration began what can be identified as a seventh step in this process (see p. 167). In the absence of clear electoral support for Home Rule they backed away from offering a bill certain to invoke the peers' veto. Between 1899 and 1902 further detachment had taken place when the Liberals were out of office and needed to find a programme capable of reviving the party's electoral prospects. Now the new government operated in another environment – apart from anything else, it enjoyed a huge parliamentary majority. But Liberals did not want to dissipate energies on something that was by now so contentious within the party, and, anyway, the foremost priority was British questions. Liberal attitudes in office exacerbated Irish party problems.

If Liberals entered office with few Irish plans, they recognised that Ireland could not be left untended. James Bryce's appointment as Chief Secretary in the Irish Office was meant as a gesture of good will. But Healy predicted: 'Bryce will cut no figure here, or in the House. He is a speaker with an unpleasant Belfast voice, and for all his learning commands no weight.'[3] It soon became apparent to Irish MPs that Bryce's feelings toward them were equivocal.

The election campaign had underlined Liberal reluctance to touch Home Rule. Winston Churchill's election address proclaimed:

> I shall support no Irish legislation which I regard as likely to injure the effective integrity of the United Kingdom or to lead, however indirectly to separation. I am persuaded that considerable administrative reforms are required in the government of Ireland and I

would gladly see the Irish people accorded the power to manage their own expenditure, their own education and their own public works according to Irish ideas.[4]

Edmund Lamb, promised that 'no measure of Home Rule ... [could] be brought forward to the next Parliament'. Should such a measure be introduced, he pledged to oppose it. Charles Henry saw Gladstone's bills as 'a matter of past history and not of present policy'. William Thompson insisted that the notion of a separate and independent Dublin Parliament was 'finally and definitely abandoned'. Liberals who did not reject Home Rule *per se* restricted their ambitions for the foreseeable future to administrative devolution. To Bryn Roberts, 'the surest and speediest method of obtaining Home Rule' was to 'to go step by step'.[5] No more than one in fifteen Liberals openly advocated Gladstonian Home Rule; these mostly contested constituencies with a substantial Irish vote while, 50 or 10 per cent of candidates actually opposed it.[6] Irish electors in Britain were loyal to Liberal candidates whether or not they adopted a forthright Home Rule stance. Where it made an endorsement, the United Irish League of Great Britain supported official Liberal candidates in 95 per cent of constituencies.[7] Limits to Liberal intentions were expressed by the catch-phrase 'step by step', enabling individual candidates to interpret the commitment in differing ways.

After the outcome was known, Dillon outlined the Irish party agenda to the Chief Secretary. Dillon emphasised that the party wanted legislation on the land question, a labourers' housing act, repeal of coercion, improved financing of the development grant, some changes in the personnel of the Land Commission to induce a friendly attitude towards tenant interests, action to aid the remaining evicted tenants and financial and official encouragement for the teaching of Gaelic in schools. In addition, he expressed disapproval of Sir Horace Plunkett retaining his now anomalous position (he had lost his parliamentary seat as long ago as 1900) as Vice-President of the Department of Agriculture and Technical Instruction.[8] Most parts of this programme might be undertaken by Conservatives. The Irish leadership was particularly insistent on the issues of land legislation, coercion and a University bill at an early moment. Bryce's response was 'very shaky' on the first two questions.[9]

Bryce aimed to erase grievances, but the Queen's Speech made scant reference to Ireland, stating merely that the new administration 'have under consideration plans for improving and effecting economies in the system of government in Ireland and for introducing into it a means for associating the people with the conduct of Irish affairs'.[10] By early February 1906 the Under-Secretary, Sir Antony

MacDonnell, had drawn up a draft proposal for administrative devolution based on the ill-fated plan of 1904. Furthermore, the Queen's Speech professed a 'desire that the government of the country, in reliance upon ordinary law, should be carried on, so far as existing circumstances permit, in a spirit regardful of the wishes and sentiments of the Irish people ...'.[11] By March the Irish party leaders were becoming restive at the government's inactivity. Faced by growing pressure from William O'Brien, Redmond appealed to Bryce to bring in a good labourers' bill. In March Bryce informed Redmond that he proposed to deal with the university question by appointing a Royal (Fry) Commission to investigate the workings of the University of Dublin. It was appointed on 2 June 1906. Redmond was invited to submit two names for it. The terms of reference were not altogether congenial to Dillon and Redmond who considered opposing the Commission. They met Bryce on 5 May to outline their views. Other problems between the Liberals and Irish popped up early in 1906. To the chagrin of the Irish leaders, twenty-two out of twenty-seven assistant sub-commissioners on the Land Commission were reappointed.[12] Compounding this setback Bryce refused to oust Plunkett who many Liberals thought was doing good work (he did not resign until May 1907).

Major government concessions were not forthcoming until May and June 1906. The Town Tenants bill, proposed by William McKillop and J. J. Clancy on 18 May was given ministerial assistance at the beginning of June. Though not passed until 20 December, it had negotiated most of the committee stages by the close of July. This act improved the legal position of urban tenants, giving them some of the rights of their rural counterparts. The Town Tenants' Association, which had 130 affiliated and some 60 unaffiliated branches, was emerging as an influential pressure group; Dillon and Michael Davitt backed its programme. Advocacy of town tenants' rights helped the party demonstrate that it was not devoted exclusively to rural interests. The Labourers' Housing bill, introduced on 28 May received the royal assent on 3 August, fulfilling a plank in the national programme and easing its difficulties in Munster where there was a substantial labourers' movement. Local authorities were allowed to secure loans at 3.25 per cent interest for the erection of labourers' cottages. A Treasury grant of £50,000 was appropriated while the Urban and District Councils were empowered to borrow up to £4.5 million for the construction of dwellings. Ultimately, 30,000 dwellings were built. Though reluctant to embark on land legislation, Bryce, in June, appointed a Royal Commission, the Dudley Commission, to investigate the question, especially the problem of congestion. Dillon supported the commission because 'they could go back to the people and say there was going to be an enquiry', though in private he confessed, 'the more I see of the administrative proceedings of Sir Antony and Bryce the less I like them'.[13] Concessions to the national party were vital for preserving a semblance of co-operation, particularly because of their differences over amending the Education Act of 1902. The Irish party was under pressure from the Catholic hierarchy to vote against the Education Bill of 1906 devised by Augustine Birrell to alter the 1902 Education Act because that legislation had provided funds for denomination schools. It ceased opposition when the government made sufficient concessions to Catholic schools. Gains during 1906, however, appealed to special interests and did not elevate the national question. By later August Dillon worried about the enervating effect, urging 'an effort must be made to put life into the movement. At present it is very much asleep, and Sinn Féiners, Gaelic League, etc. etc., are making great play.'[14] Reacting to O'Brien's pressing of agrarian issues, Dillon thought: 'it will be necessary for us to start a vigorous campaign on the evicted tenants question – as there is almost a deadlock on it'.[15]

Administrative reform, valuable in its own right, emerged in the context of Liberal and Irish party needs. For the Irish party it was a way to secure a non-sectional reform. A sound plan would boost support and help improve financial subscriptions. During 1906 Bryce sought to meet the demand for administrative reform with a plan known as the council scheme. This was meant to be a corollary to the Local Government Act of 1898 and was based in part on the proposals of the Earl of Dunraven in 1904 (see pp. 185–7 and 198–9). In the course of the year the plan was revised several times. O'Brien raised Bryce's hopes that modest administrative devolution would receive a warm welcome. In August he told MacDonnell that creation of an elective body to supervise a large portion of, but not all, local services was the maximum expected in Ireland.[16]

Bryce normally consulted Irish leadership on other questions, but he kept them in the dark about the council proposal, following Liberal precedents when dealing with institutional reforms. In June a draft proposal was circulated to the Cabinet and a committee was appointed to scrutinise it. In late July Redmond was assured that 'nothing will be done in the direction of reducing it to a draft bill' until he had seen it.[17] In response to rumours that a scheme was about to be introduced, Redmond in September then again at the beginning of October disclaimed any knowledge of it, reminding Liberals of the claim to full Home Rule. Anxious about Redmond's attitude, Bryce on 8 October explained the plan to him: a council with fifty-five members, two-thirds indirectly elected and one-third nominated, would be vested with limited administrative functions.[18] 'At first sight it seemed beneath contempt, in Redmond's estimation.'[19] Redmond and Dillon saw Bryce on 16 October but their concerns were not alleviated. Bryce reported that Redmond 'conceives that the creation of a new body in Ireland created irrespective of the existing Irish members would totally reduce the importance of the latter and practically deprive them of the power of criticising most branches of the Irish administration.'[20] Irish leaders viewed the plan as 'absolutely *Impossible*', suspecting that it must inevitably undermine the position of the Irish party, for 'under a system of double elections and different constituencies, temptation is held out to attacks on the policy of the Irish national party in accepting a modest instalment of Home Rule'.[21] On 15 December 1906 the Cabinet considered the proposal. Dissenting from the proposed bill yet subscribing to its principle, Irish leaders set the scene for another round of the councils proposal.

Campbell-Bannerman's first year in office held uncertain portents. Valuable legislation was enacted, Irish leaders had access to the Chief Secretary, but Bryce's administration enlarged party difficulties as well. Ireland found merely a limited place in the Liberal agenda and the Irish leadership was handed few trophies to display at home as a consequence of its influence. But the session was far from barren. In addition to the labourers' and town tenants' measures, general proposals also won approval from the Irish party which normally supported the 'new liberalism'. On 7 December John O'Connor spoke in favour of the Education (Provision of Meals) bill as they were 'ready to associate themselves in the general desire to feed the children of the poor no matter what schools they happened to be in'. William Redmond, too, was in favour of the measure, calling upon the government to employ the guillotine against parliamentary opposition: '[I] have had some experience in days gone by of minorities struggling to make their position felt, but [I] would have been ashamed to be one of the 17 [obstructionists].' On 10 December O'Connor spoke in favour of the Street Betting bill, which he saw as removing a 'great scandal which existed in the streets'. On 13 December O'Connor and Redmond supported the Workmen's Compensation bill.[22]

Four problems haunted Liberal–Irish entente – the personality of the Chief Secretary, the operations of the Castle Administration, differing religious outlooks over education and the limitations of specific Irish reforms. Each in some way exposed the fault line that had bedevilled relations since 1886. Irishmen anticipated getting more from Liberals, but found their expectations unrealised. After the close of the parliamentary session, to the relief of the Irish leadership, Bryce, who Dillon thought 'nearly as feeble an administrator as John Morley was',[23] and Redmond who deemed him 'a pedant, and as pigheaded as he can be, and obstinate to the last degree',[24] vacated Ireland to become the Ambassador to the United States. Bryce's work at the Irish Office has seldom received positive recognition. Examination of his correspondence reveals a Chief Secretary attentive to business who genuinely sought to balance the obligations of office with the conflicting demands of Irish factions. His perhaps insurmountable difficulty was that the nationalists did not value even-handedness, but wanted a Chief Secretary who promoted their interests.

Birrell, the new Chief Secretary set out to repair relations. Under his management of the abortive Education bill he had had extensive negotiations with the Irish leaders. A change of Chief Secretary did not auger reversal of the 'step by step' approach and he sometimes bruised Irish feelings much as Bryce had done. In April 1907, for instance, appointments to the Land Commission were dismissed by Redmond as 'an outrage'.[25] Birrell's major Irish work in 1907 was to revamp the council plan. In late January at Foxford, Mayo, Dillon cleared the ground for a limited bill:

> [T]hey had a right to demand that it should be at least a substantial advance on the road to complete Home Rule; that, to use the words of the Prime Minister at Stirling, it would be consistent with a lead up to the larger policy. What was the larger policy? It was Irish freedom and complete Home Rule. He had no doubt that a measure which they could recommend to the acceptance of Irishmen, not as a final settlement, but as a substantial instalment of their claims and leading up to the larger policy, would be introduced by the Government during the coming Session.[26]

Liberals were circumspect about the latitude of this reform. Lloyd George at Belfast on 9 February stressed that 'the supremacy of the Imperial Parliament must be maintained. They might depend upon it no scheme would be introduced by this Parliament which would impair in the slightest degree the true predominance and supremacy of the Imperial Parliament.'[27] In the Queen's Speech on 12 February the government announced only a small parcel of Irish legislation, pointing specifically to bills for improved administrative procedures and university education.[28] This last was much desired by the Catholic hierarchy; Redmond saw Birrell at the end of January in order to stress its importance. On 1 February at Waterford he stated that his party approved Bryce's university proposal of the previous year. Linkage of administrative and university measures would shield the Irish party from criticism at home. An Irish party amendment to the Queen's Speech on the evicted tenants helped keep this grievance in the spotlight. The amendment drew from Birrell an undertaking to legislate, thus easing the path for the council proposal.[29] Redmond on 16 March allowed that the expected institutional reform would be 'no bar, but a help and a further advance, to complete Home Rule'.[30] After consulting Redmond and Dillon in March, Birrell redrafted the measure to meet several of their objections but resisted having Irish MPs comprise the popular element of the council. Redmond probably saw the proposed measure for the first time on 10 April when he urged further alterations, particularly concerning the elective element. Interspersed between private negotiations concerning a Council bill, the party introduced a Land bill of its own which passed its second reading on 19 April 1907. Although it died because the government refused to allot it time during the session, the Irish party gained a psychological triumph when the government acknowledged the case for amending the Act of 1903.

The Chief Secretary altered provisions of the proposed Council bill, but not to make Irish MPs constitute the elective element, holding instead that 'to inspire confidence, and to conciliate moderate opinion in Ireland the Council must be recruited from the more business-like and substantial men that the country affords'. To achieve this end 'an infusion of new blood is essential if the scheme is to work'.[31] MacDonnell's hand shaped much of the proposal; his priority was a measure that would be passed by the House of Lords. Redmond's objections to aspects of the plan were circulated to the Cabinet on 29 April. Though not entirely satisfied, Dillon conceded, 'we have won three-fours of the battle. But there was a pretty hard fight, and we have not all. The bill as it now stands is so much improved that it bears no resemblance to the original scheme.' Yet, he foresaw that 'nevertheless, it will not be easy for us to decide our attitude towards it'.[32]

On 7 May the bill was introduced. It made provision for a council of 107 members comprising 82 elected on the existing local government franchise (which included peers and women) along with twenty-four nominated members and the Under-Secretary sitting in an ex officio capacity.[33] It would take control over eight of the forty-five departments, including local government, agricultural and technical instruction, the congested districts board, national education, intermediate education, reformatories and industrial schools, and the office of Registrar-General. The Council was to have an initial grant of £650,000 plus an annual sum. Considerable veto and other powers remained in the Lord Lieutenant's discretion. Birrell's assurance that the scheme 'does not contain a touch or a trace, hint or a suggestion of any legislative power' along with Campbell-Bannerman's characterisation of it as a 'little, modest, shy, humble effort to give administrative powers to the Irish people' no doubted relieved Liberal worries but did little to advertise the plan's virtues in Ireland.[34]

Redmond gave the bill a cautious reception and commented on several deficiencies, choosing also to recite Ireland's claim to Home Rule, though as *The Times* subsequently pointed out, he left the impression that the Irish party would accept the proposal.[35] Despite his reservations, Redmond declared that the Irish party would support the bill in the division lobby until it had been considered on 21 May by the National Convention of the United Irish League. Edward Blake was concerned about the lack of popular control, the powers reserved to the Lord Lieutenant, absence of effective executive power over departments and officials, appointment of chairmen of committees by the Lord Lieutenant without any influence on the part of the council and the inadequate financial provision.[36] Sometime prior to the Convention, Redmond decided to oppose it. He, Dillon and Joseph Devlin 'practically came to the conclusion that the best thing for the party and movement is to reject the bill'.[37] With criticism mounting, the party leadership's options correspondingly narrowed. Clerics objected to secular control of education, though priests numbered only 107 of the 3,000 convention delegates. None the less Church interests were well represented among secular participants. Newspaper support was thin on the ground with seventeen (including *The Freeman's Journal*) out of twenty-six rejecting the bill and merely five in favour, while Sinn Féin and, more ominously, O'Brien and Healy, were hostile. Resolutions attacking the scheme were passed by numerous District and Urban Councils, Boards of Poor Law Guardians and a myriad of national organisations. Thirty-five local bodies reported in *The Freeman's Journal* between 9 and 20 May, sixteen instructed delegates to oppose the bill, while merely five supported it and fourteen others deputised their representatives to follow Redmond's recommendation.[38] Most members of the Irish party, too, were hostile; T. M. Kettle called it a 'contemptible and vicious measure'.[39] The popular mood was captured by a ballad:

Is it this you call Home Rule,
Says the Shan Van Vocht;
Do you take me for a fool,
Says Shan Van Vocht.
To be sending round the hat
Five and twenty years for that
Isn't good enough for Pat
Says the Shan Van Vocht.[40]

Redmond's opening speech at the Convention condemned the bill; stressing the unity of the party and movement were his first priorities. Echoing his earlier concerns, he observed that 'there would be [the] greatest possible danger that the Council would constitute a sort of rival body to the Irish National party', insisting that 'the Liberal party must once and for all drop the Roseberyite idea of settling the Irish question. They must come back to the standard of Gladstone.'[41] While denying that there was or could be an alliance with the Liberals at least until the English party adopted Home Rule as its programme, Redmond called upon the government to deal with the evicted tenants, to pass a University bill along the lines of Bryce's plan and to implement a new land measure. After the Convention Birrell lamented: 'our mistake was ever to have touched *Devolution* at all. *Home Rule* we could not give. We should have contented ourselves with *Land* Reforms and the *University Question*.'[42]

The council episode caused the Liberals considerable embarrassment; there was some coolness towards Redmond and his party over the ensuing months, though, significantly, no abandonment of liberal unionist policy. Nor, in fact, did Liberals rule out a fresh version of the council scheme for the future. An outcome of the incident revealed the Liberals as more interested in institutional modifications than were members of the Irish party; the latter showed greater concern for social and economic reform.

The main losers were MacDonnell, whose influence rapidly diminished (he retired in July 1908), and Redmond. A. C. Hepburn suggests that only MacDonnell of the main participants was interested in the scheme for its own sake. The other participants, he argues, were guided by strategic ramifications.[43] His argument underestimates the extent to which devolution and liberal unionist ideas survived afterwards. At the National Liberal Federation on 6 June A. H. Acland expressed his regret that the Council bill had been rejected, declaring they must carry on with 'Liberal healing and reconciling work'.[44]

Following the Council bill fiasco, both the government and, especially, Redmond began a salvage operation. On 27 May 1907 the government announced that it would bring in an Evicted Tenants bill. On the following day Redmond pressed Birrell to introduce the University bill, even though he appreciated it would not be possible to pass it during the present session, arguing that it would ease the measure's path next year.[45] Redmond might have added that it would relieve his own predicament. Campbell-Bannerman made clear Liberal disappointment on 3 June, announcing in the House of Commons that the bill would be withdrawn:

> [T]he Irish Council bill, although intentionally and designedly a measure limited in its scope, was, after all, a great measure, because it was so framed as to place under direct control of the Council of which by far the largest part was elected, and elected on the most extended franchise, all the chief Irish Administrative Departments. … The bill also contains financial provisions that would have

enabled this Council, had it been erected, to make great additions to the efficiency of the public services in Ireland. We believe that this measure was one which the Irish people would have done well to give greater attention, in its details, than appears to have been bestowed upon it at the recent Convention.[46]

Stating that no large university measure would be introduced, he observed that the Chief Secretary would look at the question in the autumn while promising that the government would proceed with the Evicted Tenants bill. Redmond, responding for his party, called for legislation to deal with the university, evicted tenants and land questions.[47] The Irish were to get something, though less than they wanted. Sir Thomas Esmonde on 7 June demanded that either the government make a declaration for Home Rule or the parliamentarians return to Ireland to set up a self-governing Constitution. Failing both, he advocated vigorous opposition to the government in the House of Commons. Alfred Webb, in the passage cited at the beginning of the chapter, wondered whether Home Rule had broken loose from its moorings. At the meeting of the National Directory on 20 June Redmond was faced with the a motion advocating withdrawal from Westminster. While this was repelled, doubts about the value of parliamentarianism abounded in the coming months. C. J. Dolan resigned from the party on 23 June; Esmonde withdrew as party whip on 16 July, citing doubt 'that anything would be gained from the English Parliament under existing conditions'.[48]

While Redmond and the Convention seemed to have shut the door on the proposed Council bill, it was soon apparent that a better plan would prove acceptable. On 6 June at the Oxford Union, when outlining the case for Home Rule, Redmond gave a long historical discourse on Irish history, explaining that the claim was made on two distinct grounds – 'natural and historical right' and 'upon the failure of England to govern Ireland satisfactorily'.[49] Interestingly, Redmond then spoke about the flaws in the council plan, suggesting that a proper measure of devolution would be welcomed. The Irish leader cited the 1898 Local Government Act as an example of sound institutional reform and by implication signalled his continued adherence to the 'step by step' formula. During his lengthy address he stated:

> [W]e never have rejected, and never would be foolish enough to reject, an extension of National self-government on liberal and democratic lines which offered us the chance of successfully working it. But for this bill of Mr Birrell's, which touched only a small portion of the administration of Ireland and did not touch legislation at all, over every portion of that bill was written in large characters distrust of the people. Why, when the Tory government gave the Local Government Act of 1898 they trusted people as fully as

they did here in England, and we got a system of local government in Ireland the same as you have in England. I say that any proposal to confer any further self-government upon Ireland which is based upon liberal and democratic principles, and which, of course, offers a chance of being worked successfully, will be accepted as a weapon to get more.[50]

Meanwhile, the Evicted Tenants bill was introduced on 27 June, passed its third reading on 2 August and received the Royal Assent on 28 August. The Irish party was not consulted during the drafting stage. This act allowed the Estate Commissioners to acquire land for either evicted tenants or their representatives. If they were returned to the original holding, land could be acquired for tenants – planters in patriotic rhetoric – who were displaced. Some 26,000 acres were purchased with approximately 3,500 tenants benefiting under the act.[51]

Conservatives and Irish Unionists did not stay wholly outside the fray though the United Ireland League Convention decision, rejecting the council proposal precluded any need for a more concerted campaign. In any case the Unionist alliance was in disarray in the wake of the electoral defeat and internal differences over tariff reform were more important than Irish questions. Resistance to Home Rule had been the cement holding Unionists together but they had and continued to hold varying opinions on other Irish measures. After 1906 these differences widened not least because so long as Liberals shied away from Home Rule there was no question of keeping Unionists singing from the same hymnal. Dissension within Unionism erupted during autumn 1906 when some tried to revive the matter of MacDonnell's and Wyndham's roles in the 1904 devolution fracas. Balfour did not look kindly upon this freelance operation. True, the peers amended Irish bills in 1906 but these suffered no worse fate, indeed, got off lightly, compared to many strictly British measures. A proposal such as the Council bill was certain to meet some resistance but it was far from sure that it would encounter a united Unionist response. Unionists did not remain wholly silent. In the debate on 7 May, several were critical of Birrell's scheme. After it was withdrawn Dicey condemned it as 'at bottom nothing else than a Home Rule bill, but it is a Home Rule bill drafted by politicians who dare not act up to their faith in Home Rule'.[52] Dicey saw that there was an absence of commitment and agreement among Unionists. He pointed out, 'what Unionists must now dread is not enthusiasm for Home Rule, but indifference to the maintenance of the Union'. In his estimation the only means to ward off the threat was for the Unionist party to heal its internal divisions and stand united. Walter Long, the late Conservative Chief Secretary, also tried to sound the traditional clarion call against self government, arguing that 'devolution would produce chaos in government, would weaken the bond which binds Ireland to Great Britain [and] would undoubted pave the way for Home Rule'.[53] Despite these voices, Unionism remained uncertain about devolution. For them, as for Liberals, the idea exerted an appeal that would resurface in the future.

Economic and social reform, mid-1907–November 1909

From mid-1907 Redmond was faced with dissension, low morale, declining numbers of United Irish League branches, falling income and increased criticism of his leadership. To resurrect his position, he resorted to a fourfold strategy. First, he attempted to reassert the primacy of Home Rule and to extract a clear commitment to support it from the Liberals; second, he tried to use the looming ranch war in the west to his best advantage; third, he sought to get significant Irish legislation passed by the government; and fourth, he reciprocated O'Brien's overture to rejoin the party. On 6 July at Battersea he sounded his keynote theme:

> I want a great Home Rule movement this autumn and winter. The people of this country, many of them, have been allowed to keep the illusion too long that our movement in Ireland is a mere agrarian movement; that we should have been satisfied by the mere removal of grievances. I ask for a movement this autumn and winter which will show to England that no removal of the material kind of grievances will touch the soul of our national movement and that the real Irish demand is a demand for the recognition of our nationality.[54]

Redmond also endorsed 'a widespread and vigorous campaign' on the land question. At this point he tried to link Home Rule and the land crusade.

Soon Redmond had misgivings about the new land campaign,. arising from dissatisfaction with the Land Act of 1903, especially the rise in land prices which Home Rulers attributed to the generous treatment of landlords and the zone system for determining the value of property, the near exhaustion of funds for purchase which was causing a slow-down in the rate of tenant acquisition, and the problem of congestion which remained scarcely touched. This last had become very sensitive. It had long been national orthodoxy that pasture – ranches – must be broken up and redistributed into small tillage farms. This, they contended, would increase prosperity and stem emigration. Since the land war ranching had increased, especially in the poor western counties. During 1907 a more active anti-ranching agitation gained momentum. Its controversial feature, 'cattle driving', removed animals for their farms, allowing them to scatter. This, of course, was bound to bring the agitation into conflict with the law. Intimidation and outrages began to rise just when the government, by permitting the Arms Act to lapse, surrendered one valuable weapon against violence. 'Cattle driving' commenced in April, but remained at a low level until September when it escalated. The agitation exposed a chasm in the national movement. Some supported it; others were opposed. Redmond briefly saw the struggle as a means to divert attention from party problems, a way to apply pressure on the government. His initial enthusiasm quickly cooled. He had no wish to confront the government. Moreover it was soon clear that this agrarian agitation was a dagger thrust into the heart of the national coalition. Ranching was practised by large farmers, shopkeepers, clerics and local speculators, the backbone of the movement's active rank-and-file support. Unlike in the 1880s, the struggle did not routinely pit Catholic tenants against Protestant landlords. Instead it often took place within the Catholic community – an acquisitive provincial bourgeoisie and covetous land-hungry peasants. Rather than reversing sagging fortunes, the ranch war was poised to make matters worse. Emphasising Home Rule could turn attention away from the agitation.

Once Parliament rose Redmond delivered a series of speeches intended to revive his movement's morale. In January 1908 a selection of these were published under the title, *Some Arguments for Home Rule*. Redmond's announced purpose was to make the Home Rule case again. Unusually for him, these speeches were pithy and economical. At Ballybofey in his first trip to Donegal in twenty years, he referred at the outset to the great improvement in the country since his last visit as a consequence of land, labourers', town tenants, and local government legislation. He stated that the 'great need at this moment is for the country to pull itself together, and not to allow what is, perhaps, a natural feeling of disappointment to degenerate into apathy or despair'. Redmond then laid down the conditions of an effective parliamentary representation: 'first of all, the party must be the mouthpiece of a united, organised, and determined people at home'.[55] The other conditions necessary were a unified, pledge-bound, completely independent party composed of honest, capable men. Redmond proclaimed: 'we have no alliance with the present Liberal party. We would make no alliance with them except upon one condition, and that is that they would not only determine to introduce a full Home Rule bill for Ireland, but that they would make it the first and paramount item in their programme.' The Irish chairman offered an assurance:

[W]ith such a party as I have described, united, pledge-bound, disciplined, independent of all English parties, composed on honest and capable men, and, above all, representing a determined and organised and united people at home – with such a party it is my profound conviction that we can in the future, as we have done in the past, win great ameliorative reforms for the people of Ireland; and further, that we can in a comparatively short space of time, win for this country the right of full national self-government. ... Ireland has, in my opinion at this moment such a party, and it would be sheer mid-summer madness, it would be folly worthy of a nation of children, if this great weapon which has won so much in the past were now to be laid aside because it has not succeeded in winning in a couple of years from the present government a full measure of national self-government.[56]

In conclusion he commended the value of the Evicted Tenants Act and favourably appraised prospects for land legislation in the next session if Irish unity were maintained.

These and other themes were articulated in subsequent speeches. On 4 September 1907 in Dublin Redmond declared that only Home Rule could meet Ireland's aspirations:

[T]hat national demand, in plain and popular language, is simply this, that the government of every purely Irish affair shall be controlled by the public opinion of Ireland, and by that alone. We demand this self-government as a right. ... Resistance to the Act of Union will always remain for us, so long as that Act lasts, a sacred duty, and the method of resistance will remain for us merely a question of expediency. There are men today – perfectly honourable and honest men – for whose convictions I have the utmost respect, who think that the method we ought to adopt is force of arms. Such resistance, I say here, as I have said more than once on the floor of the House of Commons, would be absolutely justifiable if it were possible. But it is not under the present circumstances possible, and I thank God there are other means at our hands. The demand for National self-government is, therefore, founded by us, first of all, upon right, and we declare that no ameliorative reforms, no number of Land Acts, or Labourers Acts, or Education Acts, no redress of financial grievances, no material improvements or industrial development, can ever satisfy Ireland until Irish laws are made and administered upon Irish soil by Irishmen.[57]

He promised that Home Rule would be raised in the next session 'by us ... in unmistakable fashion' and also emphasised the benefits of parliamentarianism. At Longford on 15 September he discussed the over-taxation of Ireland, pledging to raise the question as soon a Parliament reassembled. At this meeting he responded to O'Brien's pleas for unity, observing he was ready 'to welcome any Irishmen, of any creed, or class, or politics, who chooses to come and give assistance upon this or any other Irish question'.[58] At Wicklow on 29 September he considered the university demand, suggesting that the party was happy to support any scheme granting equality of treatment to Catholics. Except for Home Rule, this issue was 'the most urgent and vital of Ireland's demands at the present moment'.[59]

The land question played only a subordinate part in the series of speeches. At Portumna on 6 October Redmond argued that new legislation was necessary, giving guarded support to the current agitation without specifically endorsing 'cattle driving'. Redmond chose to stress the importance of unity asserting, 'we can get an amending land bill next session, and I believe we can almost at once obtain a settlement of the evicted tenants question; but I warn you, if the people themselves allow their organisation to be weakened or their party to be discredited, they will get nothing, and they will deserve to get nothing.'[60] Succeeding speeches treated the system of justice, extravagance of the Irish administration, housing of the working classes, the means of successfully operating local government and the defects of the poor law system. Speeches at Cavan and Sligo on the 26 and 28 October are especially revealing. At Cavan he claimed to know 'of no more pressing need in Ireland today than the reform of the poor law system'. Redmond justified rejection of the Council bill on the ground that it 'would be a hindrance and a delay in the achievement of Home Rule', a point amplified at Glasgow on 29 November where he contended, 'the Imperial Parliament having passed such a bill, would have felt it had done its duty for some time to come'.[61] To stem criticism that he was proselytising a doctrine of materialism, Redmond retorted:

> Home Rule, and Home Rule alone, can settle the Irish question. ...
> This is a Home Rule meeting. That is the meaning of this meeting, and from that point of view I commend to Mr Birrell, and the Government he represents, and to the English people, the consideration of the fact that these great gatherings have come together not for any particular social reform. The necessity of those social reforms have been urged, as it has today, at these only as an argument for Home Rule.[62]

Nevertheless, a few days later at Sligo, Redmond once again reverted to social problems. Noting that the urban population was under-represented in Parliament, he promised that the party would press on the government a practical reform for dealing with working-class housing. He thought the 'artisans and labourers of the towns should organise themselves', waxing lyrical:

> Ireland has made great sacrifices for the farmers and agricultural

labourers and certainly the town labourers and artisans have an equal claim upon the country. Without their assistance, I believe, it would be impossible to have reformed the Irish Land Question. Without their assistance, I believe it would have been impossible to sustain the great national movement during the last generation; and the least we may expect from the country is that the country will assist in obtaining some measure, at least, of their rights; and I promise the artisans and labourers of the towns here today that the Irish party and National Organisation will turn their full force on this question, so as to secure an extension of the Town Tenants Act, and to obtain money sufficient out of the millions due to Ireland to provide decent habitations for the best Nationalists in Ireland – the artisans in her cities and towns.[63]

Punctuating Redmond's speeches, Birrell in late November 1907 spoke at several meetings in Ulster where he defended government policy, the council proposal and affirmed the liberal unionist creed. At the Ulster Liberal Association on 23 November Birrell made clear that the Council bill was not a Home Rule proposal but 'would have associated the Irish people with the task of Irish administration', declaring 'unhesitatingly that was the one thing the Irish people wanted. The one thing they ought to have at the earliest possible moment was the responsibility of the administration.'[64] Birrell's intervention increased Redmond's predicament. Replying three days later at Cardiff, he offered lukewarm support for 'cattle driving', insisting that the remedy was to remove its cause. He proclaimed that 'they could not enter into any sort or kind of alliance with any English party that did not put Home Rule in the front of their programme', professing that the 'Liberal party, whether they liked it or not were back to the old alternatives of coercion or Home Rule'.[65] Following this Redmond gave an assurance that reform proposals would get fair play. At Motherwell on 1 December, he gave a further qualified endorsement to 'cattle-driving', but sought to focus attention on the national question, insisting that Ireland would suffer 'no half-measure, and they must get back to the standard of Gladstone's Home Rule bill'.[66]

Redmond's speeches were directed at an Irish audience. He sought to revitalised morale, confound critics of parliamentarianism, restore unity and lay out the party's programme. He emphasised Home Rule as the foremost aspiration, but the party additionally had a positive function in seeking reforms essential to the welfare of the country. Redmond's formula allowed the party to fudge its position on agrarian agitation.[67] Stressing the inviolate nature of the self-government demand in the public arena was crucial to restoring Redmond's standing. Behind the scenes he tried to secure Ministerial support for a Home Rule resolution in the new parliamentary session. His endeavour met with little favour from Birrell who on 30 October informed Campbell-Bannerman: 'it seems to me impossible'.[68] Yet, Ministers had no wish to destroy Redmond's credibility. They were anxious to legislate in several areas and there was a revived interest in devolution. As Birrell informed the Prime Minister, they must find measures that might be adopted, for 'unless ... our programme contains something too good to be lost, we must bid farewell to Irish support'.[69] The Chief Secretary wanted to promise legislation on the university and land questions for the next session. In early January Haldane pointed to the council measure as having been constructed along 'true lines', noting that 'the public opinion of the country was against the extreme step of Home Rule'.[70]

O'Brien's interest in rejoining the party eased Redmond's predicament. Following up earlier soundings, O'Brien in later November expressed his 'considerable hope that all nationalist representatives might soon be brought together in the same camp and under the same flag'.[71] Dillon was frosty to O'Brien's bid, but Redmond saw advantages to absorbing him into the movement. O'Brien's reformist impulses chimed nicely with Redmond's autumn speeches. In December O'Brien defined four principles for the party:

1. The attainment of the fullest measure of Home Rule should be the first object of the party;
2. That pending the settlement of the question the party should work to obtain a Land Amendment Bill and a University Bill next session;
3. That the assistance of others outside the Party should not be rejected if offered; and
4. That every member of the party should be pledge-bound and that the pledge should be defined.[72]

Discussions floundered in late December over the fourth point, and because of O'Brien's demand that the unification be ratified at a national convention. These negotiations established the degree of agreement on party priorities, especially in advocating practical legislation. Although the discussions ended in disagreement, O'Brien, Healy, D. D. Sheehan, A. Roche, J. O'Donnell, and Esmonde rejoined the party in mid-January 1908.

Prior to the opening of the session, Redmond again sought to commit the government to support of a Home Rule resolution, but Ministers were hesitant. In the Queen's Speech on 29 January 1908 the government foreshadowed bills on university education and land purchase,[73] and Redmond's reply focused on these issues. His remarks on Home Rule were brief; he attempted to defuse allegations of agrarian crime resulting from the ranch war.[74] Limits to expectations were admitted by Healy, who noted in late February: 'Parliament is now sitting a month and while both the big English bills have been introduced, nothing is heard of the University bill. I should be satisfied if we got that this year.'[75] Redmond's Home Rule resolution scheduled for 17 February was postponed because of Campbell-Bannerman's rapidly declining health, but was debated on 30 March. As an occasion for invigorating morale in Ireland and demonstrating Liberal commitment to Home Rule, the debate was a failure.

The extent of ministerial interest in Home Rule and grip of liberal unionist ideas were readily visible. Birrell thought that sooner of later there 'must be very substantial modifications made in our relations with Ireland in our form of governing that country'.[76] Then the Chief Secretary expressed his feeling that the Council bill merited 'fuller, freer, and fairer discussion'. Acknowledging that the Liberals were a Home Rule party, he stated: 'it is not in the power of anybody to say how or to what extend Home Rule can be made a practical issue at the next election.' Birrell challenged the Irish to 'make it perfectly clear and plain what their proposals are and what they will accept', demanding as well 'what the safeguards are for the minority in Ireland'.[77] Formulating and promoting Home Rule was now an Irish party responsibility. Another, speaker stated that after the pledges given at the last election they could not attempt to pass a Home Rule bill in the present Parliament, 'and he for one would be content to accept any smaller measure which would take them even a little way towards the end they had in view, which was the government of Ireland, by Irishmen, in Ireland and not here'.[78] But Asquith struck the heaviest blow to national hopes. He could not support the motion as it stood 'because I find in it no explicit recognition of what to my mind has always been the governing condition in regard to this matter – Imperial supremacy'. Moreover, he held that they could not propose Home Rule without an electoral mandate, stating 'the utmost that could be done, consistently with the promises and assurances we gave, we attempted to do last year in the Irish Councils bill'. That proposal, he affirmed, 'was not inconsistent with further changes of a Constitutional kind, but it did not involve them as a necessary practical effort or logical consequence'. Asquith proceeded to defend the Council bill:

> I think myself that it would have brought great financial and administrative benefit to Ireland, and that in its working it would have stimulated British opinion in favour of a larger measure of devolution. But by, as I think, an unhappy conjuncture of circumstances we were obliged to drop it and so far as the present Parliament is affected, we have exhausted our powers with regard to the problem

of Irish government. I hope that I have made myself clear upon the point.[79]

According to him, he adhered to Gladstone's view, which was 'whatever legislative powers were given to an Irish Assembly should be exercised in subordination to and not in co-ordination with this Parliament', ending with an expression of sympathy for imperial federalism.[80]

Asquith's declamation did not reveal much sympathy for the Irish demand, but just the reverse. If Home Rule were to be forwarded by a Liberal Cabinet, it must have a favourable electoral verdict and, in all probability, be proceeded by a smaller, 'step by step' scheme. Healy, speaking on behalf of the party, took exception to Asquith's remarks.[81] Although the resolution passed it was amended to state that an Irish regime would be 'subject to the supreme authority of the Imperial Parliament'. Twenty Liberals voted against it and many more abstained. Dillon thought the debate had been 'in every sense a failure'.[82] Instead of quieting opposition, the resolution handed it fresh ammunition. Withdrawal from the House of Commons or at least an attempt 'by all means, fair or foul' to put the government out of office, was urged by one of the leader's correspondents.[83] Redmond attempted to put the best possible complexion on the situation. Though acknowledging that Asquith's speech had been bad and Birrell's worse, he pointed out that the overwhelming number of Liberals supported full Home Rule.[84] Up and down the country United Irish League branches vied with one another to express outrage over the treatment of the resolution. Redmond countered by insisting that much remained to be gained from parliamentary participation; beneficial legislation, especially the University bill, would be jeopardised by withdrawal.

As in the previous year, circumstances and the Liberals threw him a lifeline. Asquith's elevation to the Premiership on the resignation of Campbell-Bannerman in 1908 occasioned a Cabinet reshuffle. Churchill entered the Cabinet necessitating a by-election in his marginal constituency, Manchester North-West, which had a considerable Irish electorate. There was considerable doubt about the advice the United Irish League of Great Britain would give to these voters. After terse negotiations, Churchill issued a statement intended to meet Irish requirements but which also ruled out Liberal introduction of Home Rule before a general election:

But when this Parliament has reached its conclusion I am strongly of opinion, and I say this with the full concurrence and approval of my right hon. Friend the Prime Minister, I am strongly of opinion that the Liberal party should claim full authority and a free hand to deal with the problem of Irish self-government without being restricted to measures of administrative devolution of the character of the Irish Council bill.[85]

On 30 April and 4 May Asquith substantiated Churchill's decree. The latter, after losing the Manchester by-election, repeated his position in Dundee where he stood successfully. This Delphic statement might have failed to satisfy a more discerning audience, but the Irish party was desperate, choosing to interpret it as a Liberal commitment to introduce Home Rule in the next Parliament. Because Asquith and senior Liberals did not publicly reject Redmond's assertion, preferring to say as little as possible, the Irish leadership was able to retain credibility on the Home Rule question in Ireland though knowing that the Liberal pledge was tissue-thin.

Anxious to outflank critics, in April the National Directory of the United Irish League issued a circular defending the achievements of the party in the House of Commons.[86] According to this, the Evicted Tenants Act, improvements in rural and urban housing, the Town Tenants Act, improved salaries for teachers in the national schools (ultimately to the tune of £114,00) and grants for the construction and repair of school buildings, repeal of the Arms Act, the ending of coercion, the Irish universities legislation and the inclusion of Ireland in the Pensions bill were all the result of party endeavour.

The defence of parliamentarianism bore fruit, helping preserve party influence. As the circular anticipated, coercion virtually disappeared, while the Housing of the Working Classes Act, sponsored by the Irish party, facilitated construction of urban dwellings. Most significantly, the Irish Universities bill introduced on 31 March 1908 was enacted on 1 August. It was acclaimed by Dillon as 'one of the greatest services to the Irish nation which it has ever been given to an English statesman to render'.[87] This legislation provided the foundation of the modern Irish university system. Trinity College was left alone, the Queen's College at Belfast became free-standing, colleges at Galway and Cork augmented by the Catholic University in Dublin, were clustered into the National University of Ireland. In this arrangement, Trinity remained a Church of Ireland stronghold, Queen's University, Belfast, though secular, retained its close ties with Presbyterians, and the National University, was a *de facto* Catholic establishment. The National University was given substantial state funding.

The main legislative endeavour in 1908, though, was the Old Age Pensions Act (1 August). Irish MPs sometimes worried about the financial obligation this and other social legislation held for a future Home Rule administration. Their guarded reception masked the part

Irish members played in its inception. Historians, typically, portray Irish party support for the 'new liberalism' as stemming from a tactical need to sustain the Liberal alliance rather than from ideological commitment, though, in fact, examination of the record suggests their role is underestimated. J. C. Flynn stated that legislation on old age pensions enjoyed wide support in Ireland; T. P. O'Connor saw the measure as a 'long overdue arrears of social reform'.[88] Other MPs spoke in favour of the pensions plan, many being concerned with qualifying procedures. After its passage, Irish representatives were exceptionally diligent, raising individual instances of constituents being denied a pension. They were generally successful with these claims; indeed, more than a quarter of all claims came from Ireland. As of 31 December 1910, 411,489 pensions had been paid in England and Wales, 76,889 in Scotland, while the number stood at 180,974 in Ireland.[89] This represented 44.7 per cent of people aged 70 and older in England and Wales, 53.8 per cent in Scotland and an astounding 98.6 per cent in Ireland. Under the terms of the act anyone who earned more than 10 shillings per week or who had received relief between 1 January 1908 and 31 December 1910 was ineligible. Official returns in March 1911, the first after the relief disqualification had been lifted, revealed that 201,783 people in Ireland received pensions. The census of 1911 enumerated only 191,720 people in the country age 70 and above, though this is certainly an inaccurate count. However disproportionate, the number of Irish recipients reflects a combination of government intention to treat Ireland's cases favourably and the vigilance of official organisations, north and south. In 1911 the value of pension receipts in Ireland exceeded £2.5 million.

The Old Age Pensions Act was as important for Ireland as any other single measure. This and other legislation solidified the service function of the national movement. The act came just at a moment when the fortunes – indeed the morale – of the Irish party was at a low ebb following the council fiasco, when it was accused of insincerity in its devotion to self-government principles and with Sinn Féin making some headway in elections. But the Irish party hit back, claiming the gratitude of ordinary people, especially as the pension payable was uniform throughout the United Kingdom and, therefore, the purchasing power this money commanded went further in Ireland where the cost of living was often lower.

In 1909 the land amendment was passed. The Land Act of 1909 (3 December) supplemented funds available for purchase but made selling less attractive.[90] Vendors were now to be paid in stock, not cash, at 3 per cent interest; the 12 per cent bonus was replaced by a sliding scale ranging from 3 to 18 per cent, but generally working to the disadvantage of sellers; tenant annuities were increased from 3.25

to 3.5 per cent and the Congested Districts Board (CDB) received a larger grant. In the original bill the CDB was to have powers of compulsory purchase, but this section was deleted by the House of Lords. Remuneration in stock was unattractive, as its actual worth was less than face value. The measure retarded the pace of purchase. The Irish party welcomed the passing of the Labour Exchanges Act and supported the Development and Road Improvements bill for financing public works projects to relieve unemployment. In August 1909 T. P. O'Connor threw his influence behind the latter proposal after Lloyd George promised that Ireland would receive its share of the funds. O'Connor declared: 'though I do not profess myself an entirely blind advocate of state interference … we have something to learn from Continental countries with regard to internal development … we welcome this Bill.'[91] He urged that funds for the drainage of the Barrow and Bann river areas be made available immediately.

Substantial legislative results did not silence detractors. Activists in the Gaelic revival movement disliked the political focus and obsession with Home Rule. After 1906 Gaelic League membership had declined. Sinn Féin, founded by Arthur Griffith in 1905, was more successful for a period. It attacked the Westminster strategy, demanding that MPs withdraw or refuse to take their seats:

> [Its policy was to pursue] national self-determination through the recognition of the duties and rights of citizenship on the part of the individual, and by the aid and support of all movements originating from within Ireland, instinct with the National tradition, and not looking outside Ireland for the accomplishment of their aims.[92]

Sinn Féin made limited gains, mainly when the Irish party was at a low ebb. In 1907 and 1908 it reached an apogee, winning parliamentary by-elections and achieving some success in district and particularly urban council contests. The policy of abstention from Westminster did not convert many to its standard. Sinn Féin's popularity subsided after 1908. Early that year James Larkin contributed a complicating ingredient with the formation of an Independent Labour party, advocating the demands of urban working men. If successful, his party, like the House League and labourers' agitation movement of earlier times, or the Land and Labour Association, might challenge the rural bourgeois fabric underpinning the movement. Dillon recognised that 'Irish politics is and has been for a considerable time, a much more complex problem than it used to be'.[93] A more potent menace came from inside the Home Rule ranks. On 9 February 1909 William O'Brien was shouted down at the National Convention. He retorted by calling an All-for Ireland League meeting in Cork on 20 March 1909, where he anticipated a sympathetic hearing. As earlier, he differed on the way to win reform. He advocated abandoning strict adhesion to the Liberal alliance, proposing to replace this with co-operation between Irishmen of all shades of opinion. He believed that reforms achieved by this means would be more durable. But O'Brien's health collapsed, and instead of inaugurating a fresh movement, he resigned his seat in April, leaving Ireland to recuperate in Italy. O'Brien's ideas on the diet of required reform did not diverge in any remarkably way from that of the Irish party. This and the other challenges increased the party leader's sense of urgency to induce Liberals to make a Home Rule declaration which, it was reasoned, would reverse the present dilapidated state of party finance and slumping numbers of United Irish League branches, which by 1909 had fallen to half the 1902 total.[94]

New possibilities were presented in 1909 as a consequence of Lloyd George's 'Peoples' Budget'. It was introduced on 30 March and finally thrown out by the peers on 30 November, precipitating the constitutional crisis. Lloyd George's fiscal measure was prompted by the need for additional revenue to pay for the social programmes and the cost of constructing dreadnoughts. He proposed to raise taxes on land and other items, including spirits. Drink questions were controversial for the national movement. Additionally, the new landed class in Ireland – prosperous Catholics – were opposed to the land tax. Irish loyalties were strained. O'Brien and Healy attacked the budget, focusing on Irish party support for Liberals. Dillon recognised the threat, prophesying that should no concessions or promises be forthcoming from Asquith before the next general election, 'the effect on our position will be most serious'.[95] A stalemate was reached when the budget was thrown out. Parliament was dissolved on 28 November and the Liberals prepared to put the matter to a general election.

The crisis in Parliament, November 1909–December 1910

In late 1909 the leaders of the Irish party strove for a stronger self-government commitment than they had in 1905–06. Liberals would have preferred to evade the question once more. Redmond threatened, however: 'the political conditions in Ireland are such that unless an official declaration on the question of Home Rule be made, not only will it be impossible for us to support Liberal candidates in England, but we will most unquestionably have to ask our friends to vote against them.'[96] Asquith obliged reluctantly and on 10 December at the Albert Hall he repeated substantially his stance of the previous year:

[I stand behind] a policy which while explicitly safeguarding the supreme and indefeasible authority of the Imperial Parliament, will set up in Ireland a system of full self-government in regard to purely Irish affairs. There is not, and there cannot be, any question of rival or competing supremacies, but subject to those conditions that is the Liberal policy. For reasons which I believe to be adequate the present Parliament was disabled in advance from proposing any such solution. But in the new House of Commons the hands of the Liberal Government and the Liberal majority will be in this matter entirely free.[97]

Precisely how a Liberal government would interpret Home Rule was undisclosed. Asquith did not speak on the topic again during the campaign; his remarks at the Albert Hall were brief, occupying only a small part of the speech.

Throughout the election campaign Liberals, especially Cabinet Ministers, tried to minimise the Home Rule issue. Election addresses show that while 70 per cent of Labour candidates specifically endorsed Home Rule, only 39 per cent of Liberals did so and a quarter actually opposed all varieties of self-government, including devolution of the 1907 variety.[98] Asquith's position was, after all, less explicit than Campbell-Bannerman's at the previous general election, though, as one of his colleagues made clear, Home Rule 'has never ceased to be the policy of the Lib. Party since 1886, though there have been differences of opinion as to methods, and as to whether, self-govt should come about gradually or by a single measure'.[99]

The outcome of the contest held between 15 and 28 January 1910 was a qualified Liberal victory. Liberals returned 275 MPs, and Unionists won 273 seats. Also, the new Parliament contained 40 Labour members, 83 Home Rulers and 21 Irish Unionists. The Irish party numbered 71, including T. P. O'Connor who sat for the Scotland Division of Liverpool, 8 represented O'Brien's All-for-Ireland League (not yet a formal organisation) and there were 3 other Home Rulers. Liberals lost numbers but were still stronger than at any time since 1885. With the inclusion of Labour, the government could now count on 315 votes. Against this was arraigned a total Unionist alliance of 294. Home Rulers held the balance, but this was no balance of terror. Irish party rhetoric about throwing out the Asquith government was hollow, for the outcome would be a Unionist government. Irish influence increased, pointing to a further harvest of social legislation but not necessarily to realisation of Home Rule.

A matter that loomed large in subsequent Home Rule debates came to the fore in 1910 – Ireland's over-representation. In 1885 the country had been allowed to retain all 103 seats, even then an over-representation; the scheme in 1893 would have reduced Irish numbers to 80. In 1900 Ireland's representation was exaggerated by approximately 30 seats, rising yet higher, perhaps to 40, by 1910. In January 1910 the *Spectator* complained: 'the Government will be very largely dependent on the gross electoral anomaly and injustice, the over-representation of Ireland. ... It cannot be doubted that if electoral justice were done as between England and Ireland the majority for the government if it did not disappear altogether, would be reduced to insignificant proportions.'[100] Within Ireland there was a further anomaly: rural Catholic areas enjoyed an advantage over urban Protestant districts. Had Ireland's numbers been reduced by 30–40 seats in 1910 the overall picture of the House of Commons would have been different. Neal Blewett makes the ingenious argument that because Conservatives in Britain tended to sit for less populous constituencies, Ireland's representation rectified the position. Blewett's curious analysis begs the question of the consequences of Irish over-representation on post-1910 politics.[101]

During the session of 1910 the budget veto and the status of the House of Lords were in the forefront. Yet, in everyone's minds, the Irish dimension was also near the surface. Because Home Rulers understood that the prospects of self-government were blocked by the House of Lords, they were anxious shrink the powers of the upper chamber. On 4 March Redmond stated the national party ultimatum: 'no veto, no budget'.[102] If Liberals declined to curtail the peers' ability to thwart measures passed by the elected House, the Irish party would not vote for the budget. To many this smacked of unacceptable dictation, though the Cabinet did, in fact, shortly adopt an analogous position. Redmond's pivotal position, if it existed at all, quickly evaporated. However, readiness to curb the veto of the peers did not necessarily imply that Liberals also would promote a Home Rule bill. Lord Wolverhampton, for one, believed that it was more unpopular than ever, predicting that Home Rule would be 'more bitterly fought than it was in Mr Gladstone's time and I am afraid will break up the Liberal Party'.[103]

Meanwhile, O'Brien's return to political life had significant implications. On 31 March the long adumbrated All-for-Ireland League was formed.[104] It proposed to promote self-government, the completion of land purchase, relief from over-taxation and the conciliation of Irish Protestants. Except for the last, the issues scarcely differed from the Irish party's aims. O'Brien's movement and indeed those of the other critics did not flourish in the new atmosphere, which favoured Redmond. Political polarisation coupled with Asquith's statement on Home Rule at the Albert Hall, no matter how tentative, stifled opponents.

On 6 May 1910 Edward VII died and was succeeded by his son

George V, then aged 44 and relatively inexperienced. The new monarch proposed a truce and soon afterwards the idea of an inter-party conference was canvassed. It marked an eighth stage in Liberal disengagement of Home Rule (see p. 167). On 17 June eight Unionist and Liberal leaders, four representing each party, met.[105] The Irish party was not invited to join the discussions and remained largely ignorant of the content of these deliberations. Redmond and Dillon warily watched a process that threatened to leave them in the lurch. Between June and early November the Conference held twenty-two sessions. In August Lloyd George had set afoot a scheme for a coali-tion which, as one objective, would marginalise the Irish party. According to him, 'the advantages of a non-party treatment of this vexed problem are obvious. Parties might deal with it without being subject to the embarrassing dictation of extreme partisans, whether from Nationalists or Orangemen.'[106] As a way out of the impasse, he floated the idea of 'Home-Rule-All-Round' for the four countries of the United Kingdom. Redmond, acutely aware that the Home Rule question might be settled over his head, warned at Limerick on 10 September: 'we demand full executive and legislative control of purely Irish affairs. More than that we are not asking, and less than that we will never accept', decreeing, 'devolution is as dead as a doornail.'[107] The coalition idea, like the Conference, collapsed, but devolutionary and federalist schemes did not vanish with it. The Conference came to grief when Unionists failed to win guarantees that a plan to resolve future conflicts over finance questions and other matters by a conference of representatives of the two Houses would not be extended to include Home Rule. Unionists demanded that when the Commons and peers disagreed on constitutional bills these should be resolved by a referendum, a proposition put forward in 1893 by Chamberlain. Liberal refusal to include Home Rule in this procedure led to Conservatives withdrawing from the Conference. However, the Conference came close to agreement; its breakdown did not bring to a close hopes for securing agreement on Ireland.

Some Unionists, in fact, doubted the wisdom of flatly opposing the extension of all forms of devolution in Ireland. Alfred Milner, in the extract quoted at the beginning of the chapter, thought that it was bound to come in some shape and he was anxious that when devo-lution was implemented, it should accord with Unionist ideas. To him, the vital distinction was between provincial and national Home Rule; Unionists could accept the first but not the second. If Unionists confined themselves to a blanket opposition, they would find that they had little influence over the type of Home Rule Ireland received. A joint Liberal–Unionist agreement on Ireland using a federalist approach might provide a solution. Spearheaded by the Round Table circle, federalist views found a considerable audience between September and November. Irish leaders were suspicious of federalism, but O'Brien was favourable. He, predictably, cared less for structures than at arriving at self-government by agreement. Motivation for right-wing federalism could be found in ideas for imperial integration; United Kingdom federalism was just an initial phase in the grand design. F. S. Oliver, who authored several federalist articles in *The Times* under the pseudonym 'Pacificus', was, like O'Brien, anxious to deal with Ireland by consent and mutual compromise. For Oliver, 'the chance of getting the Irish question as well as the House of Lords question settled (amicably even!) in the year of the Coronation – possibly before the Coronation – would appeal to the popular imagination not only at home, but in our Dominions.'[108] J. L. Garvin, editor of the *Observer* and a leading force behind federalism, nevertheless in early October labelled it 'hocus-pocus all round'.[109] Nevertheless, his scepticism was temporary. On 17 October Garvin expressed the view of many younger Unionists when he informed Balfour: 'thinking the present Dublin Castle system now untenable – some form of devolution inevitable – I cannot think it now impossible to frame a safe constructive compromise between Gladstonian Home Rule which has perished ... and the old Unionist position which has now lost so much of its old basis'.[110] The Conservative leader, while prepared to listen to federalist appeals, was not persuaded. He declined 'to recognise that one phase of the Irish question is closed forever, and that a new phase is opened', holding that federalism in America, Canada, Australia and the Cape 'is a stage in the process from separation towards unification; while Federalism in the United Kingdom would be a step from unification towards separation'.[111] Although not slamming the book shut, Balfour and traditional Unionists did not find federalism an alluring solution. Dicey at end of October pointed out:

> Unionism means today what it meant in 1886 [and] is a fact on wh[ich] no Unionist leader ought to allow for a moment to be doubted. That any man should change his opinions, because he believes them to have been proved erroneous, is of course, no disgrace. But there is something shocking to common sense and to political morality in any statesman trying to persuade himself that he can remain a Unionist while adopting Home Rule under the alias of Federalism.[112]

This phase of federalism was linked to the Conference. It faded when the talks failed and the general election was called. But it soon resurfaced under Liberal tutelage. The federalist interlude revealed divisions within Unionism on devolution showing also a considerable groundswell of opinion in favour of resolving the Irish demand by consent.

The January 1910 election placed a heavy call on Irish party finances. With another one looming, Redmond, T. P. O'Connor and Joseph Devlin went to North America to raise money. They returned with $100,000. The mission forced Redmond to define both his Home Rule ideas and timetable for its achievement more closely, increasing his dependence on a commitment from the Liberals. The mission enabled Unionists to portray Redmond as the 'dollar dictator', Garvin proclaiming, 'he comes with the money of America to wipe England out. He comes with the money of Protected millionaires. ... He comes with the subscriptions from the country which has the strongest Constitutional safeguards in the world ... Above all he comes with his Republican cash to extort from the British Crown his guarantees.'[113]

On 10 November 1910 the failure of the interparty Conference was made public; on 18 November, while discussions about reform of the House of Lords were taking place, Asquith announced a dissolution. Home Rule featured more prominently in Conservative addresses and speeches than earlier in the year.[114] Liberals preferred whenever possible to evade the question. Nine of the sixteen Ministers issuing addresses in the two general elections of 1910 did not mention Home Rule; only 84 out of 272 successful candidates did so.[115] The outcome replicated the January result. Although 56 seats changed hands, in the balloting held between 3 December and 13 January Liberals ended up with 271 MPs, Labour had 42, Conservatives 272, Home Rulers 84 and there was one independent Conservative. Redmond once more held a paper balance of power.[116]

Conclusion

Between 1905 and late 1909 the Liberal government gave Ireland an accelerated version of what was handed to them by previous Conservative regimes. Between 1895 and 1910 spending in Ireland for domestic Irish purposes rose by 90 per cent.[117] By 1910–11 expenditure in the country exceeded its tax revenue by one million pounds. Ireland had made impressive strides since the 1890s, especially under the Liberal administration. But these gains did not include a commitment to implement Home Rule and were undertaken within a liberal unionist framework. The council incident showed the fragility of the national movement, its uneasy burden of balancing Home Rule ideology and the demand by the dominant elite that it perform as a service organisation.

When the budget crisis enabled Redmond to press Asquith in

December 1909 to pronounce for Home Rule, the triumph was illusory. Liberals might in theory support self-government, but they also showed little readiness to translate this idea into a reality. Even the collapse of the interparty Conference did not make Home Rule more likely. The House of Lords was only one obstacle, and perhaps not the most decisive impediment to the implementation of Home Rule.

Notes

1   Alfred Webb to John Redmond, 4 June 1907, Redmond MS 15,231 (5).

2   Quoted in John Kendle, *Ireland and the Federal Solution: The Debate over the United Kingdom Constitution, 1870–1921* (Kingston and Montreal, 1989), p. 112.

3   Quoted in T. M. Healy, *Letters and Leaders of My Day* (London, 1928), II, p. 476.

4   Quoted in Randolph S. Churchill, *Winston S. Churchill: Young Statesman 1901–1914* (London, 1967), II, pp. 442–3.

5   Lamb, Henry, Thompson and Roberts quoted in A. K. Russell, *Liberal Landslide: The General Election of 1906* (Newton Abbot, 1973), p. 74.

6   *Ibid.*, p. 75.

7   *Ibid.*, p. 190.

8   F. S. L. Lyons, *John Dillon: A Biography* (London, 1968), p. 283.

9   Denis Gwynn, *John Redmond* (London, 1932), p. 121.

10   *Parliamentary Debates [PD]*, 4th Series, 152 (1906), c. 23.

11   *Ibid.*

12   Lyons, *John Dillon*, p. 285.

13   Quoted in A. C. Hepburn, 'Liberal Policies and Nationalist Politics in Ireland, 1905–10', University of Kent at Canterbury, Ph.D., I, pp. 434, 442.

14   Quoted in Lyons, *John Dollon*, p. 288.

15   Quoted in Hepburn, I, 'Liberal Policies', p. 447.

16   A. MacDonnell to James Bryce, 4 and 15 August 1906, James Bryce Papers, National Library of Ireland, MS 10013..

17   John Redmond to John Dillon, 26 July 1906, Redmond Papers, National Library of Ireland, MS 15182.

18   Lyons, *John Dillon*, p. 289.

19   Quoted in Margaret A. Banks, *Edward Blake, Irish Nationalist: A Canadian Statesman in Irish Politics 1892–1907* (Toronto, 1957), p. 309.

20   Bryce to Campbell-Bannerman, Sir Henry Campbell-Bannerman Papers, British Library, MS 41,211.

21   Draft Memorandum by Redmond, Dillon and T. P. O'Connor [n.d. December 1906], Hepburn Thesis, I, p. 233; 3 December 1906, John Kendle, *Ireland and the Federal Solution*, p. 100.

22   *PD* 166, (1906), cc. 1430–2, 1669–70; 167, (1906), cc. 709–11.

23   Quoted in Lyons, *John Dillon*, p. 267.

24   Quoted in J. O. Baylen, '"What Mr Redmond Thought": An

Unpublished Interview with John Redmond, December 1906', *Irish Historical Studies*, XIX (September, 1974), p. 182.
25 Lyons, *John Dillon*, p. 293.
26 *The Freeman's Journal*, 28 January 1907.
27 *Belfast News-Letter*, 11 February 1907.
28 *PD*, 169 (1907), c. 3.
29 *Ibid.*, cc. 364–71.
30 *The Freeman's Journal*, 17 March 1907.
31 Cabinet Memorandum, 27 April 1907, Public Record Office, London, CAB (1907) 37/88.
32 Quoted in A. C. Hepburn, 'The Irish Council Bill and the Fall of Sir Antony MacDonnell, 1906–7,' *Irish Historical Studies*, XVII (September 1971), p. 486, see, also, p. 488.
33 *PD*, 174 (1907), cc. 78–103.
34 *Ibid.*, c. 78; Lyons, *John Dillon*, p. 294.
35 *PD*, cc. 112–28; *The Times*, 22 May 1907.
36 Banks, *Edward Blake*, p. 322.
37 Quoted in *ibid.*, p. 323.
38 Hepburn, 'The Irish Council Bill', pp. 488–95, 491.
39 *Weekly Freeman's Journal*, 18 May 1907.
40 Quoted in Joseph V. O'Brien, *William O'Brien and the Course of Irish Politics, 1881–1918* (Berkeley and Los Angeles, 1976), p. 175.
41 *The Times*, 22 May 1907.
42 Birrell to Campbell-Bannerman, 24 May 1907, Campbell-Bannerman Papers, MS 41,239.
43 Hepburn, 'Irish Council Bill', p. 484.
44 *The Times*, 7 June 1907.
45 Redmond to Birrell, 28 May 1907, Redmond MS 15,169.
46 *PD*, 4th Series, 175 (1907), c. 323–4.
47 *Ibid.*, cc. 336–41.
48 *Weekly Freeman's Journal*, 29 June 1907.
49 *The Freeman's Journal*, 7 June 1907.
50 *Ibid.*
51 Lyons, *John Dillon*, p. 298.
52 *The Times*, 8 June 1907.
53 Quoted in John Kendle, *Walter Long, Ireland, and the Union, 1905–1920* (Kingston and Montreal, 1992), p. 46.
54 *Weekly Freeman's Journal*, 13 July 1907.
55 John E. Redmond, *Some Arguments For Home Rule: Being a Series of Speeches Delivered in the Autumn of 1907*, with a preface and notes by J. G. Swift MacNeill, (Dublin, 1908), pp. 5–14.
56 *Ibid.*
57 *Ibid.*, pp. 15–22.
58 *Ibid.*, pp. 23–8.
59 *Ibid.*, pp. 29–34.
60 *Ibid.*
61 *Ibid.*, pp. 73, 183.
62 *Ibid.*, pp. 78–9.

63 *Ibid.*, p. 66.
64 *The Times*, 25 November 1907; also see his speech at Ballymoney, *ibid.*, 26 November 1907.
65 *Ibid.*, 28 November 1907.
66 *Ibid.*, 2 December 1907.
67 See, David Seth Jones, *Graziers, Land Reform, and Political Conflict in Ireland* (Washington, DC, 1995), pp. 197–8.
68 Birrell to Campbell-Bannerman, 30 October 1907, Campbell-Bannerman Papers, MS 41,240.
69 Quoted in Leon Ó Broin, *The Chief Secretary: Augustine Birrell in Ireland* (London, 1969), pp. 17–18.
70 *The Times*, 10 January 1908.
71 *Weekly Freeman's Journal*, 30 November 1907.
72 J. V. O'Brien, *William O'Brien*, pp. 181–3.
73 *PD*, 183 (1908), c. 4.
74 *Ibid.*, cc. 112–38.
75 Quoted in Healy, *Letters*, II, p. 482.
76 *PD*, 183 (1908), cc. 156.
77 *Ibid.*
78 *Ibid.*, c. 175–7.
79 *Ibid.*, cc. 222–7.
80 *Ibid.*
81 *Ibid.*, cc. 228–34.
82 Dillon to Redmond, 23 April 1908, quoted in Lyons, *John Dillon*, p. 304.
83 See, Gwynn, *John Redmond*, p. 155.
84 *The Times*, 21 April 1908.
85 *Ibid.*, 23 April 1908.
86 Lyons, *John Dillon*, p. 304.
87 *PD*, 188 (1908), c. 840.
88 *PD*, 190 (1908), cc. 750–3, 906.
89 B. B. Gilbert, *The Evolution of National Insurance in Great Britain* (London, 1966), pp. 227–8.
90 J. V. O'Brien, *William O'Brien*, 188.
91 *PD*, 5th Series, 10 (1909), cc. 938, 140.
92 *United Irishmen*, 9 December 1905.
93 Quoted in Lyons, *John Dillon*, p. 313.
94 J. V. O'Brien, *William O'Brien*, p. 191.
95 Dillon to Redmond, November 1909, quoted in Gwynn, *John Redmond*, p. 166.
96 *Ibid.*, p. 172.
97 *The Times*, 11 December 1909.
98 Neal Blewett, *The Peers, The Parties and the People: The General Elections of 1910* (London, 1972), pp. 317.
99 Quoted in Patricia Jalland, *The Liberals and Ireland: The Ulster Question in British Politics to 1914* (Brighton, 1980), p. 26.
100 Quoted in Blewett, *The Peers*, p. 367.
101 *Ibid.*, pp. 365–71.

102 Quoted in Gwynn, *John Redmond*, p. 174.
103 Quoted in Jalland, *Liberals and Ireland*, p. 16.
104 J. V. O'Brien, *William O'Brien*, p. 197.
105 See, John D. Fair, *British Interparty Conferences: A Study of the Procedure of Conciliation in British Politics, 1867–1921* (Oxford, 1979), pp. 77–102.
106 Quoted in *ibid.*, p. 91.
107 Kendle, *Ireland and the Federal Solution*, p. 116.
108 Quoted in John E. Kendle, *The Round Table Movement and Imperial Union* (Toronto and Buffalo, 1975), p. 139.
109 Quoted in Alfred M. Gollin, *The Observer and J. L. Garvin 1908–1914: A Study of a Great Editorship* (London, 1960), p. 202.
110 *Ibid.*, p. 214.
111 *Ibid.*, pp. 209, 217.
112 Quoted in Kendle, *Walter Long*, pp. 59–60.
113 Gollin, *The Observer*, p. 241.
114 Blewett, *The Peers*, p. 327–9.
115 Jalland, *Liberals and Ireland*, p.29.
116 Jalland's assertion that the Liberals held a majority independent of Home Rulers is inaccurate. She bases her subsequent argument on the existence of a Liberal majority. Jalland, *ibid.*, pp. 27–8.
117 See, E. Strauss, *Irish Nationalist and British Democracy* (New York, 1951), p. 201.

9

Third Home Rule bill, 1911–14

In our opposition to them we shall not be guided by the considerations or bound by the restraints which would influence us in an ordinary Constitutional struggle. We shall take the means, whatever means seem to us most effective, to deprive them of the despotic power which they have usurped and compel them to appeal to the people whom they have deceived. They may, perhaps they will, carry their Home Rule Bill through the House of Commons but what then? I said the other day in the House of Commons and I repeat here that there are things stronger than Parliamentary majorities. (Andrew Bonar Law, 27 July 1912, Blenheim Palace Meeting)[1]

Introduction

The events of 1910 brought Home Rule back to the fore, but until the powers of the peers were defined, there was no certainty about the timing of a fresh bill or its contents. From the perspective of the Irish party, any bill labelled Home Rule was an imperative. Augustine Birrell recognised in 1911 'how tremendously important it is for Redmond and his friends not to fail and how far they will go to meet us if they can'.[2]

The third Home Rule incident bore superficial similarities to 1886 and 1893. As before, the first stage consisted of using the issue as a parliamentary device framed to fit the political context of the Liberal party, sparking a drawn-out debate in the House of Commons where the opposition made much of the running; second, the struggle was directed at influencing public opinion and each camp sought to occupy the high moral ground. But there were crucial distinctions as well. The parliamentary struggle merged into the public arena under

240

different circumstances and to the preliminary stages were added third, fourth and fifth stages: behind-the-scenes negotiations, the threat of physical resistance and the passing of the bill under the impress of war. Ulster took on much greater importance, as did the associated question of whether the state might employ force to impose Home Rule upon an unwilling populous in the north-east. Ireland's over-representation in the House of Commons received greater emphasis and led to the assertion that the parliamentary majority was 'illegitimate'. Unionists insisted that with the passage of the Parliament Act the Constitution was in suspense and that Home Rule had to be endorsed by an electoral or referendum verdict, while the concept of citizenship and whether the people of Ulster could be deprived of it was argued with intense vigour.

As with the earlier bills, a chronological analysis of their content and context yield illuminating insights. Typically, historians, as strikingly illustrated by George Dangerfield's *Strange Death of Liberal England* (1935), see Ulster Unionists and Conservatives as the stumbling block to Home Rule – groups refusing to abide by liberal democratic norms – a view recently given renewed emphasis in Jeremy Smith's evaluation of Andrew Bonar Law.[3] Patricia Jalland reverses the argument, making the case that the government, particularly Asquith, should have anticipated the Ulster problem. By adopting a 'wait and see' attitude and ignoring the question in 1912 Liberals were culpable. In losing the initiative Asquith made resolution of the crisis more difficult. Six points are stressed in the present account. First, like its predecessors, the bill began as a parliamentary device but gravitated into a public agitation, in part, because this was the only avenue open to opponents under the Parliament Act. Second, it contained as many or more flaws than the earlier models, presenting opponents with soft targets; sustained opposition, especially in 1893, had made the bill's rejection easier and Unionists understandably chose to replicate this example but found that the defects were difficult to convey, whereas Ulster was comprehensible and had resonance. Third, because of pronounced schisms within the Conservative party and also in Irish Unionism over Home Rule, Liberals had little incentive to invent solutions. Fourth, the degree of Ulster resistance was unprecedented. Fifth, the dispute was waged mainly within and between British parties, with Irish Home Rulers consigned to the sidelines. Finally, it is suggested that only two groups were certain about their objectives – the Irish party which wanted Home Rule in any form and Ulster Protestants who rejected the governance of a Dublin regime. In this instance, both were in a position to secure their objects – the first by doing almost nothing, the second as a consequence of a tremendous agitation on the ground. These roles were the obverse of the more usual pattern – vigorous national agitation in the country and Unionist reliance upon constitutional forms.

Preparation of the third Home Rule bill, January 1911–10 April 1912

The main order of business of the House of Commons which opened on 31 January 1911 was the Parliament bill introduced on 22 February. The third reading negotiated the House of Commons on 15 May, the Lords on 10 August and on 18 August it received the royal assent. The new act introduced a number of significant changes: it limited the House of Lords veto to three years; if a bill unaltered in major details passed through the House of Commons in three successive sessions, though not necessarily within the lifetime of the same Parliament, it would become law; after the first passage, a bill could only be amended by means of 'suggestions', requiring the assent of both Houses; additionally, the upper chamber surrendered its veto over finance bills; parliaments were reduced from seven to five years' duration. The powers of the peers were curtailed by the act, but not eliminated; the procedure for overriding a veto played a major part in the third Home Rule dispute, but it was not just the way in which the Parliament Act structured the episode that was vital. Conservatives after 1906 were transformed into defenders of the Constitution.[4] For them, it seemed that Liberals were on the verge of effecting its destruction, appearing to seek government by a single chamber. It was alleged that as a consequence of Liberal actions the two chamber system was breaking down and the constitutional balance was being undermined. As a partial remedy they turned to the idea of 'referral' or the use of 'referendum' as a check upon the powers of the House of Commons, also focusing on the notion of citizenship, a concept destined to feature largely in the Home Rule dispute. Home Rule from 1912 was not simply about governmental institutions, but symbolised many of the concerns Conservatives held about Liberal destruction of the Constitution.

Interest in Home Rule in 1911 revived in the context of the political climate at Westminster. Some of those who took the largest part in the unfolding drama, like Churchill, held highly individualistic notions about its purposes.[5] Anticipation of Home Rule caused a resurgence of interest in federalism. While Irish MPs saw virtues in the concept, Dillon and Redmond 'were unwilling to complicate the Irish part of the question in that way'.[6] Their preference arose from the experience of the Council bill and an appreciation that only Gladstonian Home Rule was intelligible to the Irish and British public.

Planning for a fresh bill began in January 1911 when a Cabinet committee of Birrell, Lloyd George, Churchill, Haldane, Herbert Samuel, Sir Edward Grey and Lord Loreburn (chairman) was established. Several members of the committee, other members of the Cabinet and the party generally were lukewarm about Irish Home Rule, appreciating the limits of its appeal to the country. Perhaps a majority of the committee was attracted to federalism. Two issues dominated discussions – finance and Home Rule All Round. Ulster received little attention until February 1912. The full group did not tackle the financial aspect, which was the domain of a non-political committee of fiscal experts chaired by Sir Henry Primrose. Primrose was concerned about the level of Irish expenditure which by 1910–11 exceeded revenue by nearly £2 million per annum; the cost to the British Exchequer must rise to pay for social legislation. He guided the committee towards proposals intended to make the Irish responsible for the high and increasing expenditure.

Certain Liberals, including Birrell, were alert to the Ulster dimension. Churchill on 24 February 1911 circulated a paper advocating federalism.[7] On 27 February Lloyd George presented a more restricted plan, whereby Ireland would have immediate Home Rule; Wales, Scotland and England would be given parliamentary grand committees for parochial business. Responding to criticisms of his first paper, Churchill on 1 March suggested a federal scheme that would divide the United Kingdom into ten jurisdictions, each with a legislature and administration. An initial draft of a bill was produced in June; Lloyd George's grand committee plan was incorporated in a further version in August. In the interval there was a good deal of lobbying for and against the federal idea. C. P. Scott saw O'Connor, Dillon and Redmond in the second half of July. Birrell, the committee's most persistent critic of federalism, opposed any species of Home Rule All Round, stating on 20 July his intention 'to pave the way for Home Rule (on more or less Gladstonian lines) and to do all that in me lay to make any other solution of the problem *impossible*'.[8] At Cabinet in mid-August he protested 'against Irish Home Rule being included in a devolution Federal scheme for Wales and Scotland which the country had never discussed'.[9] His attitude to Ulster was less settled. On 26 August he wrote to Churchill, a letter also intended for Lloyd George's eyes, suggesting the possibility of each county in the province of Ulster deciding individually whether to join or remain outside the Home Rule regime for a period of time. This was known as the county option formula.

> [W]ere the question referred to Ulster county by county, it is probable that all Ulster save Antrim and Down would by a majority support Home Rule and it might then be suggested and agreed to that for the

nsitional period, say 5 years, Antrim and Down might stand out nd that at the end of that time there should be a fresh referendum to settle their fate. If this was done, there could be no Civil War.[10]

The Chief Secretary did not share his apprehensions, but a hint of the unease felt by some Liberals surfaced on 4 October when Churchill explained publicly: 'it is our duty to exhaust every effort which sympathy and earnestness can inspire to understand the reasonable difficulties of Ulster and to allay unfounded alarm'.[11]

The Primrose Committee report was handed to the government on 27 October.[12] It proposed to give the Irish government complete control over its own revenue and expenditure, but the Imperial Exchequer would meet the £2 million deficit by assuming liability for Irish pensions already granted (amounting to over half the shortfall). Only Birrell supported it. Herbert Samuel, the Postmaster-General, was given the task of framing the financial provisions. Although he sent numerous detailed memoranda on finance to the committee, few understood these and the constitutional and fiscal parts continued to be treated separately.

Opponents, especially in Ulster, did not remain idle. Edward Carson had assumed the leadership of the Ulster Unionist party on 21 February 1910. In March and April the Union Defence League was reactivated. From an early juncture Ulster Unionists realised that a huge effort was necessary to secure public sympathy in Britain. Four types of activities were directed at enlisting the support of people there: the production and distribution of literary propaganda; organisation of demonstrations; canvassing; and maintenance of follow-up services and tours of Ireland. Between September 1911 and mid-July 1914 they organised more than 5,000 meetings in England, canvassed nearly 1¼ million doubtful voters in more than 200 English constituencies and assisted at 23 contested by-elections; additionally, in Scotland they held 3,843 meetings, canvassed 205,634 electors and aided at 20 contested by-elections.[13] An estimated 6 million booklets were distributed in Great Britain. From 1911 to 1914 the number of Ulster Unionist Clubs formed rose from a mere 14 to 371. Conservatives were not united on what ought to be resisted or how this should be undertaken. In June Walter Long laboured to stifle federalist tendencies. Carson and James Craig in July began a determined campaign against Home Rule. Patrick Buckland observes that this and associated activities raised three questions: what did they mean by resort to force? were they justified? what price was paid for the success of their methods? He suggests that inflexibility was a key outcome and it may be added that this tendency was accentuated as Ulster assumed the most prominent position in the debate.[14] Yet, confusion lingered about what Unionists opposed. The fourth Marquess of Salisbury in early September was against Home Rule All Round but 'glorified County Council devolution' was another matter.[15] Ulster Unionists directed their efforts to stiffening Conservative support for themselves. As part of the effort to show unity and determination, 50,000 people gathered to hear Carson and others speak against Home Rule at Craigavon on 23 September. The meeting resolved:

> to frame and submit a constitution for a Provisional Government for Ulster, have due regard to the interests of the loyalists in other parts of Ireland, the powers and duration of such Provisional Government to come into operation on the day of the passage of any Home Rule Bill, to remain in force until Ulster shall again resume unimpaired her citizenship in the United Kingdom and her high position in the British Empire.[16]

Though the Irish party and Liberals preferred to downplay the fumigations of the 'Robespierre-Carson',[17] it was a magnificent publicity stunt. During the autumn the Union Defence League began to campaign in earnest. Balfour's equivocation brought from Long a complaint on 29 September that the leader was confusing Unionists:

> You indicate that Home Rule must be opposed *so long as we are entitled to assume that it is Gladstonian Home Rule.* Now, is it not inevitable that the inference drawn from this must be that there is one form of Home Rule to which you, as leader of the Party, would not offer relentless opposition? *The majority* of your supporters are opposed to Home Rule in any form: all your supporters hate the 'splitting of straws': the bulk of your followers in the country (the electors) have not the time or the knowledge sufficient to enable them to discriminate between one kind of Home Rule or another: and what they all ask for – and I speak of what I know – is clear, distinct guidance: a plain policy and straightforward statements appeal to the people and will win, but qualifications and doubts, 'ifs and ands' mystify and make them ask in their agony – for no other word describes it – for a clear indication of what the leaders of the Party mean to do.[18]

Law became leader of the Conservative party on 13 November. He was an unusual Tory figure – a Glasgow industrialist from Ulster stock who was born and spent his early years in New Brunswick where his father was a Free Presbyterian minister. Growing up on the ethnic/religious frontier, his sense of belonging to a threatened community was reinforced by summers spent with relatives near Coleraine. Bonar Law's wife had died; Lady Londonderry, a staunch Unionist, took charge of his social obligations. Conservative leaders had kept Ulstermen at arms length, but law, who shared much more of their outlook, worked closely with them. For him, the Union and especially Ulster's place in it was a passionate commitment not a political convenience. Carson, Craig and Law ensured that Ulster's case would be heard, that the fight would be carried into the public arena in ways exceeding the polite norms of the Establishment political mores.

Samuel's financial plan presented to the Cabinet on 4 December differed from the recommendations of the Primrose Committee, proposing instead extensive imperial control over Irish finance.[19] The entire proceeds of Irish taxes would be paid into the Imperial Exchequer until the £2 million Irish deficit was extinguished. An annual block grant of approximately £6 million would be transferred to the Irish Exchequer for the purposes of purely local expenditure, other than the 'reserved services', which the United Kingdom government would control and fund. These services included such items as pensions, national insurance, land purchase and tax collection. Should the Irish government elect to assume responsibility for any reserved services, the annual grant would be increased proportionately. When Irish revenue exceeded expenditure for three consecutive years, the arrangement would be reviewed. The Irish Parliament would have limited powers to vary customs and excise duties or on new taxes imposed by the Westminster Parliament.

The draft of a Home Rule bill was discussed at Cabinet on 7 December. Lloyd George's grand committee scheme met opposition; John Burns noted in his diary, 'what was not needed was a welter of parochialisms'.[20] Nevertheless, the idea was included in a draft the Cabinet decided to show to Redmond and Dillon for comment. Their first glimpse was on 12 January when they were told it 'was not the result of serious consideration, but had been thrown hurriedly together and was not to be regarded as expressing the settled view of the Cabinet'.[21] Parliament opened on 14 February 1912 and the Queen's Speech made the sparse announcement that 'a measure for the better Government of Ireland will be submitted to you'.[22] It was not the only controversial bill to be brought forward. Other legislation outlined included a franchise measure and a plan for the disestablishment of the Welsh Church.

A Cabinet meeting on 25 January learned that the Irish leaders were unhappy with Samuel's financial scheme, did not care for the grand committee proposal and wanted a bill that followed those of 1886 and 1893.[23] Between February and April Birrell regularly consulted Redmond and Dillon about the provisions; the Irish leaders made only minor suggestions, except to demand fiscal autonomy which was refused. Innovations, such as federalism, gradually disappeared.

During February 1912 Lloyd George and Churchill raised the

Ulster question. In Cabinet on 6 February they urged county option in Ulster. This was set aside, but Asquith informed the Irish leadership that the government remained free 'to make such changes in the Bill as fresh evidence of facts, or the pressure of British opinion, may render expedient'. In his letter to the monarch he clarified this:

[I]f, in the light of such evidence or indication of public opinion, it becomes clear as the Bill proceeds that some special treatment must be provided for the Ulster counties, the Government will be ready to recognise the necessity, either by amendment of the Bill, or by not pressing it on under the provisions of the Parliament Act. In the meantime, careful and confidential inquiry is to be made as to the real extent and character of the Ulster resistance.[24]

On 5 March Samuel's fiscal plan was incorporated into the latest draft of the bill. When the Cabinet met the next day Churchill again raised the question of the exclusion of Ulster. Several leading Liberals began to despair of ever passing a bill, and decided to proceed, as Loreburn put it, because they 'must stay & go down fighting', and according to Birrell, 'we are bound to the Irish'.[25] As in 1892–93, they foresaw the damage to the Irish party of not bringing forward a bill. Between January 1911 and April 1912 construction of the measure was affected by internal Liberal party requirements, the need to present a bill of some shape during 1912 no matter whether it passed, and the very strong preference of the Irish leaders for the Gladstonian formula. A large demonstration held in the outskirts of Belfast on Easter Tuesday signalled that when a definite scheme was presented Ulster Unionists would be ready. Nevertheless, Conservatives had difficulty opposing anything more than the principle of Home Rule before they learned what was proposed. Liberals braced for a battle along the lines of 1886 and 1893 where they anticipated Ulster would be raised but as a subordinate issue.

The bill, 11 April 1912

Asquith introduced the Home Rule bill on 11 April without broader federalist structures, though he anticipated that self-government for Ireland was merely the first instalment of constitutional reconstruction.[26] He justified Home Rule as the democratic demand of the Irish people expressed at every general election since the widening of the franchise in 1885. The new bill resembled that of 1893. Ireland was to be given a bicameral subordinate legislature, having 'power to make laws for the peace, order, and good government of Ireland', but where 'the supreme power and authority of the Imperial Parliament is to remain unimpaired and unchallenged'.[27] The executive would be

247

responsible to the Irish Parliament. A House of Commons consisting of 164 members would be elected by the existing constituencies – Ulster's 59 members, Leinster's 41, Munster's 37, Connaught's 25 and 2 university seats divided into 128 county MPs, 34 sitting for boroughs and the 2 university representatives. There was to be a nominated second chamber (Senate) of 40 members, initially appointed by the Imperial Executive for an eight-year term. When members retired in rotation, replacements would be selected by the Irish executive. If the two houses could not agree on any bill they would then sit together (40 plus 164 for a total of 204) where a majority vote would be decisive. An Irish Parliament's jurisdiction excluded matters affecting the Crown, war and peace, the army and navy, treaties, dignities, treason, control of general taxation, 'reserved services' – land purchase, old age pensions, national insurance, Royal Irish Constabulary (for six years), the post office savings bank, public loans and collection of taxes – and it was prohibited from infringing on religious liberty or endowing any sect. Catholics were to be eligible for the Lord Lieutenancy and this official retained substantial power, including the exercise of a veto on the authority of the Imperial Parliament. He would have a fixed term of six years. The Irish Parliament could not repeal or amend the act unilaterally and a Judicial Committee of the Privy Council was vested with the power to determine the validity of Irish-made laws. Ireland's representation at Westminster was to be retained, though reduced to 42 seats – 34 would be county members and 8 (Belfast 4, Dublin 3, Cork 1) borough representatives. Asquith estimated that there would be 34 Nationalists and 8 Unionists. There was no special provision for Ulster, but the Prime Minister pointed out that Unionist MPs outnumbered Home Rulers by only 17 to 16 (a position reversed in January 1913), arguing:

[T]hese figures in themselves are quite sufficient to show the misleading character of the pretence that Ulster would die rather than accept Home Rule. I have never under-estimated the force, and I have never spoken with disrespect of the motives of the strong and determined hostility which is felt to Home Rule by the majority in the north-eastern counties of Ulster, reinforced, I agree, by a powerful minority in other parts of the province. It is a factor which sane and prudent statesmanship cannot and ought not to leave out of account. I hope presently to show that we have not ignored it in the framing of this Bill. But we cannot admit, and we will not admit, the right of a minority of the people, and relatively a small minority – particularly when every possible care is being taken to safeguard their special interests and susceptibilities – to veto the verdict of the vast body of their countrymen.[28]

The financial aspects devised by Samuel were complex (see p. 246). Dicey found them so opaque that he urged Long to arrange for an accountant to appraise them.[29] According to Asquith, the provisions 'will be, among other things, a means of adjusting Irish finance to Irish needs, and giving Irishmen a direct interest in economy … and a direct responsibility for waste … and so gradually reducing the deficit'.[30] His reasoning resembled Gladstone's.

A Joint Exchequer Board consisting of five British representatives, two from Ireland and a chairman who was to be nominated by the Crown, would oversee arrangements. When Ireland achieved a surplus in three successive years, the Joint Exchequer Board could ask that a body composed of MPs based on the relative populations of the two countries – the 42 Irish MPs plus an appropriately larger number of British MPs – to set Ireland's contribution to Imperial expenses. Few Liberals liked the scheme; Redmond and Dillon were unhappy with it, but unable to mount an effective opposition. Any opt-out of Ulster was rendered more difficult because this would upset the financial calculations.

As a constitutional formula, the proposed bill was less satisfactory than its predecessors. It was devised primarily to suit Liberal tactical needs and only secondarily those of the Irish party; the practical mechanics of a regime in Ireland was of considerable less importance. Maintenance of Liberal unity required a proposal that retained extensive Imperial control, while the Irish were anxious merely to secure any measure called 'Home Rule'. Leaving aside Ulster, it contained ten significant flaws:

1 The financial provisions made tighter Treasury control implicit, thereby having the opposite effect from the de-centralising idea of Home Rule.
2 The financial structure was intended to reduce Imperial expenditure in Ireland, causing either a reduction in services or increased local taxation.
3 The Joint Exchequer Board would be dominated by Britain's representatives.
4 The body to set Ireland's Imperial contribution was weighted in favour of Great Britain and set up another tier of authority.
5 Having a Lord Lieutenant who did not leave office on a change of government, acting on behalf of, but not automatically responsible to a Cabinet created division of authority.
6 An Imperial-dominated Privy Council limited the discretion of the Irish government.
7 The Irish government was going to be a new institutional layer, costing a considerable sum of money but possessing only limited

revenue raising powers.

8 The allocation of representation ensured rural dominance and, as in the previous bills, the temptation to raise revenue from northern commerce would be considerable. This was now more likely than earlier because land was rapidly being transferred to former tenants.

9 Retention of Ireland's representation at Westminster, especially in view of the limited authority of the Irish government, invited fresh difficulties rather than relieving the business of the House of Commons.

10 The Senate, which was to safeguard property and the minority could cease performing this function when the Irish government assumed the nomination of its members.

These and other deficiencies gave hostages to fortune. In 1893 opponents had exploited the weak points in the bill, building a case for its rejection in the House of Lords. Unionists would follow a similar tactic this time even if the ground rules had changed; there was still strategic value in attacking the contents of the measure in order to legitimise its delay. As the new procedure established in the Parliament Act was untested, few were sure how in practice it would work. Unionists were handed a choice opportunity, but this raised the problem of settling on the most effective line of attack. They believed that the public in Britain was bored with Ireland and no longer cared very deeply about Home Rule. Nor were opponents of a single mind. They had both to ignite public interest and to unite their own fragmented ranks. Unionists could try to undermine Liberal support for the bill, force the ministry to make worthwhile concessions and pressurise or demoralise the government into agreeing to have a general election or referendum on the issue. Many of the bill's features were too technical to grasp – the question of Ulster had the virtue of being comprehensible and best designed to win public sympathy. It also brought to the fore the ambiguous notion of 'citizenship'. Could British subjects be arbitrarily deprived of their citizenship? This would be expressed effectively by C. F. D'Arcy, who said: 'to deprive a community, against its will, of the citizenship and liberties into which its members were born would be a political outrage.'[31]

Initial responses, April–June 1912

Carson answered for Unionists on the first of three days allotted to the first reading of the bill between 11 and 16 April 1912. Although the bill had not been printed yet, the leader of the Ulster Unionist party immediately identified several defects, criticising its rationale, technical aspects such as the nominated Senate, the impact of the financial clauses, the implied promise of federalism, retention of Ireland's MPs at Westminster and the status of the Lord Lieutenant. He attacked the logic of the financial aspects, observing: 'what is the object of the United Kingdom? As I understand it, it is that all parts of that Kingdom should be worked together as one whole; under one system, and with the object that the poorer may be helped by the richer, and the richer may be stronger by the co-operation of the poorer', a view reiterated by Balfour four days afterwards.[32] 'What argument is there that you can raise for giving Home Rule to Ireland that you do not equally raise for giving Home Rule to that Protestant minority in the north-east province? I believe there is none', Carson pointedly insisted.[33] In contrast, the answer of Irish Home Rulers came on 23 April when a convention held in Dublin accepted the measure.

During the second reading Liberal misgivings about Ulster seeped out. Two Ministers conceded that compromise might be required; several Liberals expressed reservations about the plan as it stood. On 2 May Thomas Agar-Robartes explained that he would vote with his party on the second reading, though he believed:

> [T]here is only one way out, and that is to leave the North-East of Ulster out of your scheme. ... The people of this country are bored to tears by the Irish question. They want to see it settled somehow; they wish to get rid of it; they wish to deal with their own affairs; and therefore it is for that reason, and that reason alone, that I shall give a vote for the Second Reading of this Bill, in order that it may be thrashed out in Committee. But, unless you can really reconcile Ireland as a whole by this Bill – and I mean by Ireland, Protestants as well as Roman Catholics – and unless you can emancipate this House from the pernicious influence of forty-two votes always for sale to the highest bidder, then I say, with reluctance, but with a clear conscience, when the Bill reaches its final stage in this House, I shall certainly reconsider my vote.[34]

Unionists had uncovered a chink in Liberal armour during the initial test of strength despite the fact that the second reading division on 9 May was carried by 372 votes to 271.

Ulster's position, June 1912–March 1913

Concern about Ulster broke out more completely during the committee stage. On 11, 13 and 18 June an amendment put forward by Agar-Robartes to exclude Antrim, Armagh, Londonderry and Down from an Irish Parliament was debated. This step introduced considerable disarray among both government and opposition, though

Unionists decided to support the amendment. Patricia Jalland sees this as the point when the bulk of British Unionists tacitly conceded Home Rule on the condition that all or part of Ulster was excluded.[35] (Subsequently, Jalland ascribes this acceptance to the Carson amendment debated on 1 January 1913 – see p. 253.) Though a moot point, it is certainly the moment when a sharp rift over Ulster opened amongst Liberals, ensuring that the question took on increased prominence. Unionists still wanted Home Rule scuttled altogether at this stage, and Ulster's position seemed the surest path towards that larger objective. On 13 June Bonar Law simply accepted the possibility of Ulster's exclusion as a useful improvement in a bad proposal, saying 'but while we oppose the Bill root and branch ... bad as the Bill seems to us to be [exclusion] would make it less bad then it was before the Amendment was introduced'.[36] Redmond voiced the nationalist position:

> [T]his idea of two nations in Ireland is to us revolting and hateful. The idea of our agreeing to the partition of our nation is unthinkable. We want the union in Ireland of all creeds, of all classes, of all races, and we would resist most violently as far as it is within our power to do so ... the setting up or permanent dividing lines between one creed and another and one race and another.[37]

Though uncompromising in tone, a reading between the lines hinted at a more accommodating attitude, if such proved necessary to secure a Home Rule bill. Discussion of the amendment revealed a reservoir of Liberal sympathy for Ulster. Lloyd George developed the official view that exclusion required something that had not yet been formulated, namely a definite proposal with details, limits, conditions and a workable geographical boundary.[38] This established a leading Liberal theme – a concrete proposal had not been offered as yet and if one were made it had to come from the Ulster members, not the government. Although the amendment was defeated, the government's majority fell, with sixty-two supporters absent. Unionists now saw Ulster as the Achilles' heel.

The House of Commons rose on 2 August 1912, beginning the second phase of the episode: mobilisation of public opinion. On 27 July approximately 13,000 people assembled at Blenheim for an anti-Home Rule rally, at which Law, Carson and F. E. Smith spoke. The first warned:

> [I]f an attempt were made without the clearly expressed will of the people of this country, and as part of a corrupt Parliamentary bargain, to deprive these men of their birthright they would be justified in resisting by all means in their power, including force ... if the attempt be made under present conditions I can imagine no length

of resistance to which Ulster will go in which I shall not be ready to support them.[39]

Though Liberals queued up to condemn Law's speech, a passage from which heads the chapter, the Blenheim demonstration encouraged some members of the government to see the Ulster demand in sharper focus. The battle thus far was being waged with tough-sounding words and these bore fruit. Churchill on 21 August wrote to Lloyd George: 'the time has come when action about Ulster must be settled. We ought to give any Irish county the option of remaining at Westminster for a period of 5 or 10 years, or some variant of this', and to Redmond on the 31 August:, 'something should be done to afford the characteristically Protestant and Orange counties the option of a moratorium of several years before acceding to the Irish Parliament'.[40] At Dundee on 12 September he ventilated his earlier idea of a federal reconstruction of the United Kingdom.[41] Carson arrived in Ulster two days later to give a lead to opinion. Between 18 and 28 September a series of mass meetings culminated in Ulster Day, when nearly half a million people in the northern province gathered to sign 'Ulster's Solemn League and Covenant'. Such highly effective publicity gimmicks spread unease among Liberals.[42]

Meanwhile Redmond and the Irish party faced criticism engineered by William O'Brien over acceptance of the financial clauses. O'Brien had stated his objections when the bill was introduced; now he amplified these. The General Council of the Irish County Councils endorsed this condemnation. Redmond appreciated that the soft spot was Ulster and set out during the autumn recess to assuage Protestant fears. In doing so, he inadvertently concentrated attention on the Ulster question.

Shortly after Parliament reassembled in October a cloture resolution was implemented. The Home Rule bill still required twenty-seven more days for the committee stage, seven for the report to the full House of Commons and two for the third reading. It finally negotiated the committee stage on 12 December, but not before an amendment on 22 November, in which the government was defeated by 228 votes to 206, deleted the power of the Irish Parliament to reduce customs duties. On 28 December an amendment sponsored by Carson and two other Ulster members to exclude the nine Ulster counties was placed on the order paper. Previously, Asquith had resisted exclusion because the demand had not emanated from Ulster MPs. Jalland views this moment as the tacit concession of the principle of Home Rule by British and Irish Unionists (but see p. 252) though both still sought to dismantle the bill altogether.[43] The Cabinet determined to resist the amendment, though several members, especially

Churchill, Lloyd George and to a lesser degree Birrell, were unhappy with the decision. On 1 January 1913 Carson spoke for exclusion, but to allay the fears of southern Unionists and many Conservatives he urged support for the amendment on the tactical grounds of defeating the bill in its entirety.[44] Redmond took a conciliatory line observing: 'within certain well-defined limits, there are no limits that for my part I would not be willing to go in order to conciliate the opposition'. He stated his two conditions – that the proposal must be genuine and not one simply to wreck the bill and that it must be 'of a reasonable character, and not inconsistent with the fundamental principle of national self-government'. Like Carson, he had to reassure elements among his own following. Redmond went on to state:

> Ireland for us is one entity. It is one land ... our ideal in this movement is a self-government Ireland in the future, when all her sons, of all races and creeds, within her shores will bring their tribute, great or small, to the great total of national enterprise, national statesmanship, and national happiness.
>
> Men may deride that ideal; they may say that it is a futile and unrealisable ideal, but they cannot call it an ignoble one. It is an ideal that we at any rate will cling to, and because we cling to it, and because it is there, imbedded in our hearts and natures, it is an absolute bar to such a proposal as this amendment makes – a proposal which would create for all times a sharp, eternal dividing-line between Irish Catholics and Irish Protestants, and a measure which would for all time mean the partition and disintegration of our nation. To that we, as Nationalists, can never submit.[45]

Following a vigorous discussion, the amendment was defeated by 294 votes to 197, but 77 Liberals did not vote. According to C. P. Scott, Redmond was 'prepared to go almost any length in the direction of Home Rule within Home Rule for the North-Eastern counties provided always that Ulster remained within the Bill as a part of Ireland'.[46] After 52 days of consideration the bill passed on the third reading on 16 January 1913 with a majority of 110, and on 30 January it was rejected in the House of Lords by 326 votes to 69. On the same day, a Home Ruler captured the by-election at Londonderry, giving them a 17 to 16 edge in Ulster representation. On 7 March Parliament was prorogued. Since the previous April, more certainly from June, Ulster had become the central question, but there was no emergent consensus even within parties about how to deal with it, while the Home Rule bill was now hemmed in by the terms of the Parliament Act.

Towards agreement by consent, March 1913–March 1914

The new session that opened on 10 March lasted until 15 August. During 1913 Liberals' morale suffered as a result of the Marconi scandal, discouraging by-election performances and the abandonment of social legislation. Unionist reactions became sharper at the same time. On 27 March the British League was formed under the impetus of Baron Willoughby de Brooke, a moving spirit behind resistance to the Parliament Act. This new association was supported by 200 peers and 120 MPs.[47] Because amendments were not allowed, the government dispensed with the committee and report stages of the bill in this second cycle of its passage through the House of Commons. Only three days were allowed to debate the bill which passed its third reading on 7 July by 352 votes to 243. Unionist arguments remained unchanged, though the leadership adopted the tactic of demanding that Home Rule be submitted to the electorate. Its claim was built upon the idea that the Constitution was in suspense as a result of the Parliament Act; major constitutional innovations required endorsement by the electorate. Birrell and Asquith did not offer an Ulster proposal but stated they were prepared to consider any reasonable 'suggestion' consistent with the principle of the bill. It was defeated a second time by the peers on 15 July. The crisis now entered a third phase centring on behind-the-scenes negotiations. There were three broad means of resolving the Ulster difficulty – federalisation of the United Kingdom, Home Rule within Home Rule (self-government for all or part of Ulster within an otherwise unified Ireland) and exclusion. Numerous British figures leaned towards the first, the Irish party albeit reluctantly preferred the second and Ulster Unionists favoured the last. The case of exclusion raised several questions: what geographical area was involved, and how were its boundaries to be determined; would this be a permanent or a temporary arrangement; and would jurisdiction over the excluded region be retained by the Westminster Parliament or would a separate Ulster legislature be created? On 24 July Birrell told the King that 'perhaps an arrangement could be made for Ulster to "contract out" of the Home Rule Bill, say for 10 years, with the right to come under the Irish Parliament, if so desired, after a referendum by her people, at the end of that period.'[48] To the sovereign's concern that Redmond would refuse, Birrell answered that he 'could be squeezed', using the threat of dissolution.

Unionists focused on winning wider public sympathy by keeping up the pressure on Liberal leaders, by agitation on the ground in Ulster and through a vigorous campaign across Great Britain. This campaign had gained a substantial degree of success, with the King, army and public accepting that Ulster should receive separate treatment. Buckland sees the period of autumn 1913 to August 1914 as the first of four stages (the subsequent ones being the attempted settlement of 1916, the Irish Convention of 1917–18 and the Act of 1920) in the development of the Ulster debate.[49] In this feverish atmosphere proposals for a settlement by consent came from several directions: the rank and file of both British parties, the monarch, southern Irish Unionists and advocates of federalism. On 11 August and again on 22 September the King pressed on Asquith the need for a dissolution of Parliament, which the Prime Minister in three separate responses adroitly refused. However, the temperature in Ulster became warmer.

While staying at Balmoral Bonar Law had a private meeting with Churchill. Reporting their conversation on 18 September to Carson, the Conservative leader stated: 'I have long thought that it might be possible to leave Ulster as she is, and have some form of Home Rule for the rest of Ireland. ... The whole question as to the exclusion of Ulster really turns upon this – whether or not it would be regarded as betrayal by the solid body of Unionists in the South and West.'[50] Carson concurred, responding 'on the whole things are shaping towards a desire to settle on the terms of leaving "Ulster" out. A difficulty arises as to defining Ulster and my own view is that the whole of Ulster should be excluded but the minimum would be the 6 Plantation counties and for that a good case could be made.'[51] Exclusion received a chilly reception from Lord Lansdowne, a leading light among southern Unionists. Lloyd George saw T. P. O'Connor on 30 September, informing him that Conservatives were prepared for a settlement if Ulster were excluded. O'Connor appraised Dillon of what had passed. Dillon, ever wary of settlements by consent, on 2 October urged discretion upon O'Connor, foreseeing the difficulty for their party if four counties were to opt out, while worrying that any sign of weakness 'might be used to force Redmond to make some irreconcilable declaration on the subject'.[52] To Lloyd George, O'Connor disclaimed the ability to accept Ulster's exclusion. In early October Bonar Law learned from Carson that Southern Unionists might be receptive to an Ulster solution and, as he then wrote to Lansdowne on 8 October, 'I am more hopeful than I was of a settlement of that kind'.[53] Speaking at Dundee, Churchill suggested: 'our bill is not unalterable, and the procedure of the Parliament Act renders far-reaching alterations possible. But only upon one condition – there must be agreement.'[54] Lansdowne shortly afterwards conceded that they might be 'driven to this kind of settlement', but found 'it difficult to believe that Redmond would accept it'. Nevertheless, he thought it 'worth risking a good deal to obtain a settlement by con-

sent and if Redmond shipwrecks such a settlement we shall find ourselves in a much better tactical position'.[55] Redmond, though,
adopted a moderate line at Limerick on 12 October, pointing out

> that Irish nationalists can never be assenting parties to the mutila-
> tion of the Irish nation. ... The two nation theory is to us an abomi-
> nation and a blasphemy. Ulster is as much a party of Ireland as
> Munster ... [although] it is true that within the bosom of a nation,
> there is room for diversities of the treatment of government and of
> administration, but a unit Ireland is and Ireland must remain.[56]

On 14 October Asquith and Bonar Law had the first of three private
interviews, from which Asquith understood that Conservatives
would agree to Home Rule going through if Ulster were excluded.[57]
At Ladybank on 25 October Asquith invited Unionist leaders to 'an
interchange of views and suggestions, free, frank, and without prejudice'. His conditions were that there must be a measure of Home
Rule, it must be granted now and 'nothing must be done to erect a
permanent and insuperable bar to Irish unity'.[58] Two days later Earl
Grey advocated the idea of 'Home Rule within Home Rule', explaining that this would be administrative devolution for the Protestant
counties.[59] On 6 November, when the two party leaders met again,
the various forms of exclusion were discussed without reaching
agreement.[60] The Cabinet considered the position on 12 and 13
November. At the first meeting it learned of Asquith's talks with
Bonar Law and that Conservatives might accept Ulster exclusion. On
the second day Lloyd George presented an exclusion proposal limited to a defined period. Asquith undertook to see Redmond. Before
they conferred, Redmond at Newcastle restated his objections to
Ulster's exclusion, while promising not to 'shut the door to a settlement by consent'.[61]

When Redmond and Asquith met on 17 November the Irish chairman was invited to submit his views. Lloyd George met Dillon the
same day and found him friendly to some scheme satisfactory to
northern Unionists. Six days later Redmond stated his objections to
caving in to Orangemen. These were considered by the Cabinet and
a reply was given by Lloyd George, who had taken over many of the
functions of the Chief Secretary:

> [T]hat the Cabinet were quite unanimous in agreeing the argument
> in ... [Redmond's] memorandum, that the making of any sugges-
> tions or proposals by the Government at the present juncture would
> be a fatally wrong step in tactics, and therefore, that no such pro-
> posals or offers would be made for the present. He went on to say,
> however, that he thought the time would come when some offers
> would have to be made – sooner than we thought.[62]

On 26 November Asquith informed Redmond that no proposal would be made to Bonar Law at present, but 'we must, of course, keep our hands free, when the critical stage of the Bill is ultimately reached to close with any reasonable proposal ensuring Home Rule by consent'.[63] Birrell attempted to ease Redmond's mind, assuring him that the Cabinet had made no decisions. However, the balance within the Cabinet in favour of exclusion had shifted during the autumn while Lloyd George, who had long favoured an accommodation, had assumed many of the Chief Secretary's policy prerogatives.[64] Asquith explained to Bonar Law at their third meeting on 10 December that the Cabinet leaned towards the Lloyd George scheme, advocating automatic inclusion of Ulster after a specified period. Bonar Law demurred, saying that the only basis for settlement was inclusion by plebiscite after a prescribed period.

Carson met Asquith twice on 16 December.[65] A week later the Prime Minister sent him a paper with his own 'suggestions', a variant on Home Rule within Home Rule, which Carson rejected on 27 December. On 10 January 1914 Carson reported to Asquith that he had declined the invitation to further discussions; on 15 January Bonar Law affirmed publicly that the negotiations were ended. On 2 February Asquith saw Redmond, outlining his dealings with Carson and informing him of the 'suggestions'. Two days afterwards Redmond responded, urging that nothing be done at present, for he 'might be forced into closing the door on proposals which, if they came at a later stage in the struggle, and under other circumstances, I might be in a position to consider in a different spirit'.[66]

Events during the previous autumn had effectively narrowed the ground, exclusion in principle being accepted by all parties. During the year opponents had stressed two elements – Asquith's inflexibility and the necessity of an electoral mandate for major constitutional innovation. Liberals as well as Conservatives supposed that Home Rule, if presented at a referendum or general election, would be rejected. Meanwhile, by November 1913 76,757 men had joined the Ulster Volunteer Force and there were many reports of large-scale importation of rifles. In Dublin a counter-force, the National Volunteers, was organised on 25 November.

The new session of Parliament opened on 9 February 1914 with Home Rule on everyone's mind. That day Birrell informed Redmond that the Cabinet 'won't be willing to wait *very long* before making up their minds as what *ought* to be offered publicly to Ulster'.[67] Unionists put down an amendment demanding an election on Home Rule, which was debated on 10 and 11 February. Asquith in response declared that the government intended to submit 'suggestions' for altering the bill in order to end the discord. Carson, Bonar Law and

Redmond expressed conciliatory views about this announcement. Asquith repeated his promise on 16 February. On the same day Lloyd George sent Asquith a revised version of his November plan. Its main features included the right of counties to opt out where this was favoured by a simple majority in a plebiscite – at the end of a specified period these counties would be incorporated into an Irish Parliament 'unless the Imperial Parliament in the meantime provided otherwise'; there would be one general election at least in the interval. Interviews with Dillon and Redmond on 27 February and 2 March were meant to clear the ground. Redmond reluctantly agreed after the second meeting on condition that a three-year exclusion must be the Ministry's last word and that Unionists must accept the offer. His followers were prepared for exclusion, he wrote, 'as the price of peace'.[68] After the Cabinet meeting on 4 March, where it was agreed to promote the exclusion plan, Asquith wrote to Redmond that this would be the Liberals' position without binding themselves regarding 'matters of detail'.[69] Under further pressure Redmond concurred, writing 'we feel we cannot refuse to consent to an extension to five years', which the Prime Minister immediately raised to six in order to allow space for a second general election to have taken place.[70]

Physical resistance, March–August 1914

On 9 March 1914 Asquith announced the government's intention in the House of Commons. Carson's reply was a mixture of defiance and conciliation. After assurances that 'we will never agree to the sacrifice of the people of the south and west, whatever may be the benefits which may be offered to Ulster', he said, 'I frankly admit we have made some advance this afternoon by the acknowledgement of the principle of exclusion ... the moment you admit the principle of exclusion the details of the principle may be a matter that may be worked out by negotiation.'[71] But he went on to attack the time limit, saying 'Ulster wants this question settled now and for ever. We do not want sentence of death with a stay of execution for six years.' Despite evidence of conciliation, the Unionist attitude angered several Ministers, including Churchill and Lloyd George, persuading them that they might after all have to proceed with the original bill. It also pressed the government to consider and improve their organisation in the event of any armed resistance in Ulster on passage of a bill. At this juncture the fourth phase of the third Home Rule bill began – the actual possibility of armed conflict.[72] By 19 March, when the government had still not presented details of its proposal, Bonar Law moved for a referendum on the question. Asquith then resumed a private correspondence with the Tory leader.

On 20 March a bomb exploded at the Curragh camp in County Kildare when officers stated their intention to resign rather than use force against Ulstermen.[73] After the incident it was clear that the military could not be used to impose Home Rule upon Ulster. Over the next four weeks Ministerial efforts to explain away the incident as a 'misunderstanding' instead added fuel to the flames, giving credence to suspicions of a government 'plot' against Ulster Unionists. Carson's hand was strengthened by the Curragh episode, while it made Liberals increasingly anxious to find a solution. Jalland argues that the ensuing landing of 35,000 rifles at Larne in an operation organised by the Ulster Volunteer Force on 24–5 April confirmed the shift of balance towards Carson and Ulster Unionists. After a series of Cabinet meetings it was determined on 30 April not to prosecute the organisers. Jalland maintains that the Home Rule policy was undermined more effectively by the Curragh episode than from the events of the First World War, though subsequent events do not warrant this conclusion.[74]

On 23 May the government decided to introduce an Amending bill in the House of Lords to receive the royal assent simultaneously with Home Rule. This new bill would provide for counties to opt out for six years. On 25 May the third reading of the Home Rule bill passed in the House of Commons. The Amending bill was introduced in the upper chamber on 23 June, and on 2 July the peers substituted the permanent exclusion of nine counties without a plebiscite. An impasse was reached, for though the Home Rule bill could pass, the Amending bill needed Unionist co-operation. Carson told the Ulster Unionist Council on 10 July that the Amending bill was unlikely to pass through the House of Commons. Faced with these difficulties, Asquith agreed to George V's suggestion of an all party conference, including Home Ruler representatives. Between 21 and 24 July Asquith, Lloyd George, Lansdowne, Bonar Law, Redmond, Dillon, Carson and Craig met at Buckingham Place to see if a solution could be hammered out.[75] Redmond insisted on the county opt-out option, Carson on a 'clean break'. Bonar Law on the second day advocated the exclusion of six counties. The conference broke up without an agreement on the question of the area to be excluded, and the time period for exclusion was not discussed. On 26 July a National Volunteers' gunrunning attempt at Howth ended when troops, having failed to impound the weapons, fired upon a crowd in Bachelors Walk in Dublin, killing four people and wounding thirty-seven. Threats of violence had progressed into actual physical action, though thus far it was only from the hands of the British soldiers.

Passage of the bill, August–September 1914

The immediate crisis came to an halt when on 4 August Britain declared war on Germany. While the outbreak of the European conflagration is often cited as stopping civil war in the United Kingdom, less frequently mentioned is that it abruptly moved Unionists from an offensive to a defensive posture.[76] The effect was to enact the original bill in the face of Unionist opposition. On 30 July 1914 Asquith accepted an offer from Carson and Bonar Law to postpone the Amending bill again. Redmond on 3 August insisted on the necessity of getting the royal assent for Home Rule, of promising an Amending bill in the winter session and of ensuring that no step whatever will be taken to put the original Home Rule measure into operation until the Amending bill was secured.[77] When the Irish party chairman met Carson the next day he found his opposite number was not in a compromising mood. However, a day later Asquith informed Redmond: 'my intention and that of my colleagues to see the bill on the statute book this session is absolutely unchanged.'[78] The Cabinet committee on 7 September elected to proceed with Home Rule and a suspending bill. Unionists believed Asquith engaged in sharp practice under the guise of the war. When Conservatives meet at the Carlton Club on 14 September anger poured forth over the government's attitude.[79] The next day, in protest, Bonar Law led Unionists out of the House of Commons. Meanwhile, Asquith reported his intention that 'the Home Rule bill will not come into operation until Parliament has had the fullest opportunity, by an Amending bill, of altering, modifying, or qualifying its provisions in such a ways as to secure the general consent both of Ireland and of the United Kingdom.' To coerce Ulster, in his much quoted words, was 'absolutely unthinkable'.[80] On 18 September an act suspending Home Rule for one year or the duration of the war was followed by the Government of Ireland Act. Home Rule was a legal, if not an actual reality (see document 8).

In the end, passage was achieved under cover of a political truce. The Irish party rather than Ulster Unionists had their way, or at least so it seemed. Unionists were entombed by their patriotism. Outbreak of war had reversed the relative fortunes of the Irish party and Ulster Unionists. Enactment of the original bill may have marked a triumph, but it also became the determining impulse in the next round. It brought neither Home Rule nor peace; the contest was delayed not resolved. But there was no telling what the future would bring, when the problem would re-appear or how it ultimately would be worked out.

Conclusion

The Parliament Act was decisive as the frame of reference for the third Home Rule episode. This crisis went through five phases – beginning as on previous occasions as a parliamentary formula, it progressed to being a contest for public opinion; there followed behind-the-scenes negotiations, quasi-military intimidation and finally, the passage of the bill under the impress of war. The third, fourth and fifth stages distinguish the incident from 1886 and 1893. The question evolved in ways not predictable at the outset. Politicians did not invent the anti-Home Rule sentiment in Ulster, though they gave it form and expression. Ulster became the crux of the dispute because Protestants on the ground there knew what they did not want, the issue was intelligible, Unionist leaders were less divided over it than on other elements and from an early date some Liberals revealed leanings towards exclusion. Like Ulster Unionists, the Irish party, too, knew what it wanted – any bill that could be characterised as Home Rule. But, as in 1886 and 1893, the battle saw the Irish party shoved to the fringes, a spectator rather than a central player. However, it continued to exploit Question Time and to use other procedures at the House of Commons to express the grievances of constituents. When all is said and done Home Rule had made the decisive leap to acceptance.

In chapter 1, eight groups were identified, each one necessary to the legitimacy of Home Rule. In 1914 Home Rule was supported by at least six of these groups: Catholics in Ireland, the Liberal Party, the House of Commons, wider sections of the press, the British public and, albeit reluctantly, a significant segment of Unionists on the condition that the north-eastern region were excluded. At the same time the peers' authority had been trimmed and the influence of southern Unionists nullified. Even Unionist unity over how to secure Ulster exclusion was conditional, another portent of the future. Lord Selborne deserves the last word. Writing to Austen Chamberlain on 12 August 1914 he conceded:

> I could never follow Bonar Law in accepting the present Government of Ireland bill with the complete exclusion of the six Ulster counties as a final settlement of the Irish constitutional question (even if I thought it would work, which I don't) and I cannot conceive it possible that Redmond either should accept it as a final settlement.[81]

Notes

1   *The Times*, 29 July 1912.
2   Quoted in Patricia Jalland, *The Liberals and Ireland: The Ulster Ques-*

tion in British Politics to 1914 (Brighton, 1980), p. 70.

3 See, Jeremy Smith, 'Bluff, Bluster and Brinkmanship: Andrew Bonar Law and the Third Home Rule Bill', *Historical Journal*, 36 (March 1993), pp. 161–78.

4 D. George Boyce, 'Rights of Citizenship: The Conservative Party and the Constitution, 1906–1914', in Alan O'Day (ed.), *Government and Institutions in the Post-1832 United Kingdom* (Lewiston, NY/Queenston, Ont/Lampeter, Wales, 1995), pp. 215–25.

5 Andrew R. Muldoon, 'Making Ireland's Opportunity England's: Winston Churchill and the Third Home Rule Bill', *Parliamentary History*, 15, pt. 3 (1996), pp. 309–31.

6 Quoted in John Kendle, *Ireland and the Federal Solution: The Debate Over the United Kingdom Constitution, 1870–1921* (Kingston and Montreal, 1989), p. 140.

7 *Ibid.*, pp. 138–39; Jalland, *Liberals and Ireland*, p. 38.

8 Quoted in Jalland, *Liberals and Ireland*, p. 39.

9 Quoted in Kendle, *Ireland and the Federal Solution*, pp. 140–1.

10 Quoted in Jalland, *Liberals and Ireland*, p. 59.

11 Quoted in Randolph S. Churchill, *Winston S. Churchill: Vol. II: Young Statesman 1901–1914* (London, 1967), p. 460.

12 Jalland, *Liberals and Ireland*, pp. 45–6.

13 Patrick Buckland, *Irish Unionism: One: The Anglo-Irish and the New Ireland 1885–1922* (Dublin, 1972), p. 246; *Irish Unionism: Two: Ulster Unionism and the Origins of Northern Ireland 1886–1922* (Dublin, 1973), pp. 49, 70.

14 Buckland, *Irish Unionism: Two*, pp. 66–8.

15 Quoted in Kendle, *Ireland and the Federal Solution*, p. 132.

16 Quoted in Denis Gwynn, *The Life of John Redmond* (London, 1932), pp. 194–5.

17 Quoted in Jalland, *Liberals and Ireland*, p. 57.

18 Quoted in John Kendle, *Walter Long, Ireland, and the Union, 1905–1920* (Montreal and Kingston, 1992), p. 65.

19 Jalland, *Liberals and Ireland*, pp. 46–7.

20 Quoted in Kendle, *Ireland and the Federal Solution*, p. 143.

21 Quoted in Jalland, *Liberals and Ireland*, p. 41.

22 *Parliamentary Debates [PD]*, 5th Series, 34 (1912), c. 6.

23 Kendle, *Ireland and the Federal Solution*, p. 144.

24 Asquith to George V, 7 February 1912, Asquith MS 38, ff. 95–6.

25 Quoted in Jalland, *Liberals and Ireland*, p. 42.

26 *PD*, 36 (1912), cc. 1399–426.

27 *Ibid.*, c. 1408–9.

28 *Ibid.*, c. 1401.

29 Kendle, *Walter Long*, p. 70.

30 *PD*, 36 (1912), c. 1417.

31 Quoted in Buckland, *Irish Unionism: Two*, p. 65.

32 *PD*, 36 (1912), c. 1432; 37 (1912), c. 48.

33 *Ibid.*, c. 1440.

34 *Ibid.*, 37 (1912), cc. 2162, 1265–6.

35 Jalland, *Liberals and Ireland*, p. 94: see, John Campbell, *F. E. Smith*,

First Earl of Birkenhead (London, 1991), p. 325.

36   *PD*, 39 (1912), c. 780.

37   *Ibid.*, 1086–7.

38   *Ibid.*, cc. 1119–28.

39   *The Times*, 29 July 1912.

40   Quoted in Randolph S. Churchill, *Winston S. Churchill, Vol. II, Companion, Part 3, 1911–1914* (London, 1969), p. 1396; Churchill to Redmond, 31 August 1912, Redmond MS 15175.

41   *The Times*, 13 September 1913.

42   See St John Ervine, *Craigavon Ulsterman* (London, 1949), pp. 233–8.

43   Jalland, *Liberals and Ireland*, p. 108.

44   *PD*, 46 (1912), cc. 377–91.

45   *Ibid.*, cc. 401, 405–6.

46   Quoted in Kendle, *Ireland and the Federal Solution*, p. 157.

47   Buckland, *Irish Unionism: Two*, p. 86.

48   Quoted in Harold Nicolson, *King George the Fifth: His Life and Reign* (London, 1952), p. 220.

49   Buckland, *Irish Unionism: Two*, pp. 95–6.

50   Quoted in Robert Blake, *The Unknown Prime Minister: The Life and Times of Andrew Bonar Law 1858–1923* (London, 1955), p. 156.

51   Quoted in Jalland, *Liberals and Ireland*, p. 147.

52   Quoted in F. S. L. Lyons, *John Dillon: A Biography* (London, 1968), pp. 321–2.

53   Quoted in Blake, *The Unknown Prime Minister*, p. 160.

54   Quoted in Jalland, *Liberals and Ireland*, p. 151.

55   Quoted in Blake, *The Unknown Prime Minister*, p. 160.

56   *The Freeman's Journal*, 13 October 1913.

57   Blake, *The Unknown Prime Minister*, pp.161–3.

58   *The Freeman's Journal*, 27 October 1912.

59   Jalland, *Liberals and Ireland*, p. 165.

60   Blake, *The Unknown Prime Minister*, pp. 164–5.

61   Quoted in Jalland, *Liberals and Ireland*, p. 170.

62   Quoted in Gwynn, *John Redmond*, p. 135, see, pp. 233–9.

63   Quoted in Jalland, *Liberals and Ireland*, 172.

64   *Ibid.*, p. 143.

65   See, Ian Colvin, *The Life of Lord Carson* (London, 1934), II, pp. 262–7; H. Montgomery Hyde, *Carson: The Life of Sir Edward Carson, Lord Carson of Cuncairn* (London, 1974), pp. 344–5.

66   Memorandum of meeting on 2 February 1914, Redmond MS 15165.

67   Birrell to Redmond, 9 February 1914, Redmond MS 15169.

68   Redmond to Asquith, Asquith MS 39, ff. 134–41; Redmond MS 15257.

69   Asquith to Redmond, 4 March 1914, Redmond MS 15165.

70   Redmond to Asquith, 7 March 1914, Asquith MS 39, ff. 145–6; see, Lyons, *John Dillon*, p. 348.

71   *PD*, 59 (1914), cc. 806–18 [Asquith]; cc. 933–4 [Carson].

72   See, A. T. Q. Stewart, *The Ulster Crisis* (London, 1968) where developments on the ground are examined.

73 See, Elizabeth A. Muenger, *The British Military Dilemma in Ireland: Occupation Politics, 1886–1914* (Lawrence, KA, 1991), pp. 164–204.

74 Jalland, *Liberals and Ireland*, p. 247.

75 For a summary of the discussions, see, John D. Fair, *British Inter-party Conferences: A Study of the Procedure of Conciliation in British Politics, 1867–1921* (Oxford, 1980), pp. 114–19.

76 See, D. George Boyce, 'British Conservative Opinion, the Ulster Question, and the Partition of Ireland, 1912–21', *Irish Historical Studies*, XVII (March, 1970), p. 90; Patricia Jalland and John Stubbs, 'The Irish Question after the Outbreak of War in 1914: Some Unfinished Party Business', *English Historical Review*, XCVI (October, 1981), pp. 778–807; John O. Stubbs, 'The Unionists and Ireland, 1914–18', *Historical Journal*, 33, 4 (1990), pp. 867–93.

77 Jalland and Stubbs, 'The Irish Question', p. 783.

78 Quoted in Gwynn, *John Redmond*, pp. 363–4.

79 Jalland and Stubbs, 'The Irish Question, p. 802.

80 Quoted in Ervine, *Craigavon Ulsterman*, p. 305.

81 Quoted in D. George Boyce, *The Crisis of British Unionism: Lord Selborne's Domestic Political Papers, 1885–1922* (London, 1987), p. 115.

10

Attempts to implement Home Rule, 1914–18

With all the Unionist press except the 'morning post' in full cry for a settlement and the bulk of the Unionist Members as well as all the other parties in the House being on the same track and unwilling to listen to Irish or Ulster Unionists, the situation was so unpromising that we were strongly advised to agree to the suggested terms, as the party which refused to agree to Lloyd George's arrangement will be the party that will stink in the nostrils of the patriotic British public. (Hugh de Fellenberg Montgomery to C. Montgomery, 9 June 1916)[1]

[I]f we make the attempt and again fail the position will be worse, as it was after the last attempt ... we have decided that ... it is worth while for us ... to make another attempt. (Andrew Boner Law, 22 March 1917)[2]

Introduction

In view of the militancy of Unionists between 1912 and 1914, not to mention the opposition mounted to Home Rule throughout the years after 1886, the two quotations from sources usually unfriendly to national aspirations seem at first sight to be an anomaly. The turnabout is less remarkable than it appears and demands examination. Explanations advanced include a transformation in British public opinion, which ceased to be interested in Home Rule and was impatient for a solution; political leaders were anxious to remove impediments to the war effort; coalition government and the common sacrifice on the battlefield eased party strife; and American and Dominion pressure made an attempt to meet Irish aspirations essential. In spite of these influences favourable to a settlement, one did not emerge during the war primarily because two of the eight groups identified in chapter 1 – first, southern Irish Unionists in 1916 and, second, Ulster Unionists in 1918 – were not mollified. Also, in the latter case national representatives stuck to demands that complicated the attempt at settlement. Detailed analysis of the projected Home Rule settlement of 1916 and the Irish Convention of 1917–18 illustrates the difficulty of achieving a solution so long as the question was treated as a whole.

Three themes are advanced – first, the thinking underlining the proposed settlements was broadly consistent with earlier ideology; second, Ulster Unionists were vulnerable; and third, even when the Westminster elite scarcely had time to spare, Ireland occupied substantial space in the political calendar.

Abeyance, September 1914–April 1916

Redmond from conviction and tactical appreciation of the situation committed Ireland's Catholics to the war effort, encouraging the National Volunteers to serve under the British flag. His stance enraged a section of the national movement, precipitating a split in the Volunteers, with some 12,000 of approximately 180,000 withdrawing to establish a separate body. The bulk of Catholics in Ireland supported Redmond's mission. During the early months of the conflict thousands of Irishmen of every creed enlisted. Momentarily, it seemed that war might consummate a marriage between Irish people and draw them closer to Britain and the imperial family. But even if the *raison d'être* of the Irish party was approaching an end, this did not herald its extinction. The party could anticipate the gratitude of Catholics; no credible rival waited in the wings; its middle-class rural base corresponded to the realities of Irish life; it was a multi-issue movement, an organ of social integration with vampire characteristics, absorbing local groups which obligingly pledged fidelity to it and the national political culture.[3] Moreover, the Irish party exerted influence over government patronage, always a matter of interest to the local bourgeoisie. Until April 1918 individual MPs remained active in the House of Commons, pursuing a myriad of matters pertinent to their constituents. This diligent attention to local concerns had long been the cornerstone of the party's parliamentary existence, providing a critical link between Westminster politics and local elites. The Irish party was not a moribund movement merely waiting for the *coup de grâce*.

Liberals, and Asquith especially, retained ambivalent feelings about the Irish party and its leaders, which did not dissolve in the common war effort. During 1914 and early 1915 the military offensive became bogged down; glaring deficiencies in munitions production and economic organisation caused embarrassment. Enthusiasm for the conflict waned in Ireland. Redmond's suggestions, notably his desire to have a specifically Irish regiment formed from the National Volunteers, received a chilly response for many months. Lord Kitchener was a consistent obstacle. Initially he was reluctant to sanction the Ulster Volunteer Force's transfer into a specifically Ulster regiment, but Carson and James Craig met him on 7 August 1914 and shortly afterwards their request was granted. This decision was endorsed on 3 September by the Ulster Unionist Council. Establishment of an Ulster regiment (36th Division) made the rebuff to Redmond's request the more galling to Catholics in Ireland; Redmond bombarded Asquith with complaints during the autumn of 1914. Ultimately, Redmond's wish found satisfaction in creation of the 16th Division.

Relations with Birrell remained close, but the Chief Secretary was increasingly isolated within the Cabinet. Home Rule received little attention though it was not completely forgotten and thinking in some quarters returned to the possibilities of a federalism approach in the post-wat years. O'Brien on 10 March 1915 pointed out: 'the Unionists alone can solve the Irish difficulty with success, and, of course, on Federal United Kingdom lines, leaving the larger question to work itself out later.'[4] He pointed out that the first step was for Ireland 'to be favourably disposed'. Asquith, aware of concerns about the progress of the war, on 18 May 1915 issued an invitation to all parties to form a coalition government. This was to be a national as opposed to a party administration. Redmond was invited to join, but declined; Bonar Law and Carson accepted and the first coalition was formed on 26 May. Unionists, as a result, found themselves at the centre of government; Irish party influence, meanwhile, soon began to dip. 'The incomers claimed their share [of places] in Ireland', Birrell observed soon afterwards.[5] The change, though, was gradual. A leading Ulster Unionist newspaper late in the year carped: '[Unionists] have responsibility without power while Mr Redmond has power without responsibility.'[6] Likewise, southern Unionists were dissatisfied with the distribution of patronage during the first coalition.[7] David Fitzpatrick traces a decline in local support and the collapse of ancillary organs from this time.[8]

Few in Dublin Castle or outside anticipated the rebellion that commenced on Monday, 24 April 1916 – the Easter Rising. It was principally confined to Dublin, and initially officials had difficulty identifying the participants, their aims or potential reservoirs of support. Correspondence and reports to Asquith testify to this official mystification; Sir Horace Plunkett's papers reveal similar confusion on the ground in Dublin. On 27 April Carson and Redmond denounced the rebellion in the House of Commons; over the following weeks they co-operated in suppressing lingering rebel elements.[9] Redmond believed the revolt was aimed as much at the party as against British rule; Carson worried about the implications for order throughout Ireland. The rebellion was suppressed swiftly, and General Sir John Maxwell arrived on 28 April. Armed with martial law powers, he possessed wide authority, including the right to hold military court martials without reference back to the Cabinet. Patrick Pearse, as provisional President of the Irish Republic, surrendered on 29 April. Jeers and a hail of rotten fruit and vegetables from hostile crowds greeted the rebels as they were marched to captivity. Fifteen leaders were executed (fourteen in Dublin between 3 and 12 May, followed by the hanging of Sir Roger Casement on 3 August at Pentonville Prison, London). Redmond protested against further executions to Asquith on 3 May; the Prime Minister assured him that the number would be few. In the House of Commons on 11 May Dillon registered a stronger protest.[10] Already sympathy began to flow in favour of the rebels. The detention of suspected sympathisers during the next few weeks increased hostility towards Britain, hardening popular opinion and damaging the standing of Redmond and the Irish party.

Settlement by consent, 24 April–27 July 1916

Nicholas Mansergh observes that 'one cannot remind oneself too often that the Easter Rising came as a great surprise'.[11] Rather than stiffening anti-Home Rule feeling, the Rising induced a fresh attempt to bring about a settlement. This fourth effort to implement a Home Rule scheme merits careful analysis and is identified by Patrick Buckland as the second of four steps towards an Ulster solution (see p. 256). It is distinguished from early attempts in crucial ways – it was a product of intense private negotiations and not subject to close parliamentary scrutiny; public opinion played a minor part and was enrolled on the side of an agreement; a section of influential Unionists, including Bonar Law, Carson and Balfour, supported the proposed solution; the gap between Irish factions was nearly bridged; and failure resulted from internal resistance from southern Irish Unionists rather than because of British party pressures and intrigues or the hostility of Ulster.

Birrell was widely blamed for failing to keep colleagues abreast with the unrest that fuelled the revolt. 'Since this Cabinet was formed last May Birrell has never once mentioned the subject of Ireland and we have no knowledge whatever of the state of affairs there', complained Lord Selborne.[12] Birrell resigned on 1 May; Sir Matthew Nathan, the Under-Secretary followed suit two days later. A Commission of Inquiry was established to affix responsibility for the rebellion. Resignations and the Inquiry allowed the coalition to distance itself from the incident, freeing it to promote a remedy. Redmond's position was not yet gravely weakened in Ireland or with the government. He was able to prevent either Robert Cecil or Walter Long succeeding Birrell, as it would mean 'the instalment of an Ulster Government in Dublin Castle'.[13] In the longer term Birrell's departure deprived Redmond of a sympathetic Chief Secretary, leaving him more isolated from the Cabinet and strengthening Unionist influence in Dublin Castle.[14] Patronage increasingly fell into Unionist hands. Asquith temporarily added the Irish Office to his own portfolio.

A Cabinet meeting on 6 May considered the policy on punishment of rebels, dispatching an ambiguous telegram to Dublin, but Maxwell proceeded to put two more insurgents – including James Connolly, severely wounded and suffering from gangrene, who had to be propped up on a stretcher – before firing squads. Reassessment of Irish policy had five strands – enlisting public support if only in a limited way; an official inquiry; initiating negotiations; getting Carson and Redmond to agree on a settlement; and persuading the Cabinet and Parliament to endorse an agreement. Concern that Ireland detracted from the war focus, poisoning relations with the United States and Dominion governments, gave negotiations urgency. Influential sections of the press prepared the ground for a fresh initiative.[15] Lord Northcliffe wrote to Cecil Harmsworth: 'this damnable business needs to be settled now otherwise the hotheads will get to work, both in Ulster and elsewhere.'[16] On 11 May 1916 Asquith stated in the House of Commons that he was going to visit Ireland to assess opinion, and 'I hope I may arrive after consultation at some arrangement for the future which may commend itself to the general consent of Irishmen of all parties and of the House of Common'.[17] His intervention was the first of three stages of the episode in which an agreed formula was the objective.[18] In 1914 the division between Ulster Unionists and the Irish party had been narrowed to the precise area to be excluded and the period of time for this exclusion. The principle of exclusion had been accepted, albeit reluctantly by Redmond, by both sides.

Lloyd George began his own diplomatic initiative. Writing on 19 May, T. P. O'Connor reported him as saying: 'if I am allowed to make some arrangement about Ulster I can promise to get you Home Rule for all the rest of Ireland.'[19] Following his trip, Asquith believed that the Ulster Unionists were ready for a settlement. Lloyd George was offered the Chief Secretaryship but declined, though he was prepared to mediate an Irish solution. There was ample goodwill for his endeavour. Writing on 23 May, Long assured him that 'my influence with my friends will be entirely at your service'.[20] At the Cabinet meeting on 24 May Lloyd George was commissioned to negotiate an arrangement based on bringing into operation as soon as possible the act of 1914, with the exclusion of six counties (plus the parliamentary boroughs of Belfast, Londonderry and Newry). In the House of Commons the next day Asquith announced that Lloyd George would seek a solution through negotiations.[21] Although not yet seeing any proposals, a meeting on the following day of Unionist peers and MPs from the southern provinces expressed misgivings about reopening the issue of Home Rule during the war. Viscount Middleton conveyed this opinion to Lloyd George, and was told that Home Rule was 'the price the Irish Unionists must pay to the Empire for the war'.[22]

Lloyd George saw Dillon at his club about his ideas. On 29 May he showed the proposals to Carson and Redmond, leaving the first with the understanding that partition was permanent and the second that it would be for a temporary period (see document 9). For Carson's benefit he put down on paper: 'we must make it clear that at the end of the provisional period Ulster does not, whether she wills it or not, merge in the rest of Ireland.'[23] Lloyd George laboured under two presumptions – the urgency of solution and the belief that if Carson and Redmond could agree, everyone else would follow. George Boyce points out that Carson and Redmond were as anxious as Lloyd George to reach an agreement.[24] But the equation was not two-sided but three-dimensional. Lloyd George also met Middleton, Lord Desart and George Stewart, informing them of his negotiations, and on the same day, Long appraised Lloyd George of the necessity of gaining the consent of southern Unionists; the following day he was shown a rough draft of the proposal.[25]

Negotiations could never be conducted in a vacuum. In the naval Battle of Jutland on 31 May heavy losses were incurred. Southern Unionists with telling effect contended throughout the episode that the moment was not ripe for the introduction of Home Rule. Lansdowne and Long voiced their objections on 1 June. The following day the latter declared that only 'idiots or traitors' would consent to turn over Irish government at present.[26] On 2 June Middleton's group affirmed the need for the continuation of martial law, condemning Lloyd George's proposals as unworkable.[27]

While southern Unionist resistance mounted, northern Catholics opposed the settlement from the opposite camp. Joseph Devlin found that 'everywhere outside Belfast the proposed terms were rejected with contempt. Everybody absolutely refuses to discuss or consider them.'[28] At a meeting of the Ulster Unionist Council on 6

June Carson defended the settlement. In spite of obstacles, Lloyd George secured the support of both Carson and Redmond. Balfour and Bonar Law concurred with Carson and stuck with him throughout the negotiations. Balfour was conscious of placating American opinion; Bonar Law wished to appease General Smuts and the Dominions. Confronted with such pressure, one reluctant Unionist on 9 June, as noted in the quotation at the beginning of the chapter, recognised the inability to thwart Home Rule directly.

In spite of bumps, prospects were promising. Speaking in Dublin on 10 June Redmond stated that it was 'a proposal which we may fairly regard as the proposal of the government'.[29] Long was outraged, writing to Lloyd George 'that the time was not right' and in a memorandum the next day directed to Unionist colleagues he pointed out: 'it was never suggested, and I never realised that we were asked to agree to the final acceptance of any proposals without consulting English Unionists or for that matter English Home Rulers, and obtaining their views upon the proposals.'[30] However, two days later the Ulster Unionist Council sanctioned continued negotiations. In Dublin, meanwhile, Redmond stated that the exclusion would be temporary, and at the same time Lloyd George published the results of his negotiations with Carson and Redmond.

Southern Unionists, though disliking the scheme, were obliged to acquiesce so long as sufficient safeguards were incorporated.[31] The Irish party remained intent on securing an agreement. Devlin played down distinctions between Carson and Redmond: '[A]s to the apparent difference of opinion between Mr Redmond and Sir Edward Carson whether exclusion is permanent or temporary … [I think] this is more apparent than real, that it actually represents two legitimate views of the same proposal, and may easily be cleared up afterwards.'[32] Although increasingly critical, Unionists were still unwilling to accept responsibility for jettisoning the plan. Until 18 June only Long, Lansdowne and Carson among Cabinet members saw details of the scheme. This was the beginning of a second phase of the episode, when southern Unionist concerns intruded onto the scene. At a meeting of Conservative members of the government held at Curzon's house on 20 June three conditions were laid down – insurance of sufficient protection for southern Unionists; guarantees that Home Rule would not endanger the war effort; and the permanent exclusion of the designed counties – but they did not prejudge how these were to be met. When the Cabinet met that day it was determined to establish a subcommittee to devise further safeguards.

During this time Redmond tried to secure his own flank. He met the northern bishops on 16 June in preparation for the Ulster conference of national supporters to consider the scheme.[33] A week later the conference met, approving the scheme by 475 votes to 265. The meeting consisted of a priest from each parish, representatives of national organisations, the Ancient Order of Hibernians and the Irish National Foresters. Redmond attended and spoke in favour of acceptance of the plan, but it remained highly controversial. Most of its support came from Belfast, an area under Devlin's control. Of the 270 delegates 183 came from Fermanagh. Tyrone and Derry City voted on the losing side and episcopal influence was thrown on the scales against it as well.[34] The Irish party needed a speedy solution before widespread resistance developed.

At this juncture momentum stuttered. Backbench Conservatives were dubious about the plan. Within two weeks of the formation the Imperial Unionist Association was supported by 76 peers and 98 MPs.[35] Balfour continued to pump for the proposal. On 24 June he observed: 'personally, I do not think there is the least chance of the Irish representatives deliberately making themselves willing instruments in the hands of our enemies.'[36] The former Prime Minster appreciated that the Irish party and middle-class Catholics generally would throw their weight against Sinn Féin and pro-German elements. He professed to see this as a unique opportunity to satisfy Ulster Unionists. Unionists were not fully satisfied, but realised that Home Rule could not be derailed indefinitely. On 26 June a memorandum prepared for the Cabinet by Lord Robert Cecil argued that Home Rule should be granted but that the Dublin Parliament when it met should then adjourn until the conclusion of the war.[37] This, in his view, guaranteed that there would be no attempt to withdraw Home Rule from the political agenda. A delegation of southern Unionists saw Lloyd George on 27 June and while expressing doubt about the immediate implementation of his scheme promised after the war to attend an Imperial Conference 'with an open mind'.[38] Cabinet meetings on 27 and 28 June revealed deep cleavages. Following a heated discussion, Lloyd George tried to salvage the plan by suggesting a further Cabinet committee.

The war again intruded. On 1 July the battle of the Somme began; 79 officers and 1,777 men were killed, while another 102 officers and 2,626 soldiers were wounded. Ulstermen fell in droves. On 5 July the Cabinet again was locked in disagreement. Balfour, Bonar Law and Carson on the Unionist side stood squarely behind the scheme, repeating their support at a party meeting on 7 July.[39] Selborne, who had tendered his resignation on 16 June had now suspended the decision, left the Cabinet. Long and Lansdowne agreed not to follow him, though on the expressed understanding that during the war the imperial executive would remain supreme in Ireland. The Cabinet did agree to draft a bill. In the House of Commons on 10 July Asquith described it in general terms and Lloyd George stated that the settlement was provisional. In the House of Lords the next day Lansdowne contradicted these statements, insisting that it was 'permanent and enduring' and emphasising the need to exercise emergency powers in Ireland, reduce the country's representation at Westminster and that exclusion of the Ulster counties was not open to alteration.[40] His expression of confidence in Maxwell, now a target of Irish party criticism, gave further offence. To make matters worse he followed up his comments four days later in a letter published by *The Times*. Writing to Selborne, he pointed out: 'the Irish "settlement" bogs down under its own weight ... and we are well out of it'.[41] On 17 June the Imperial Unionist Association endorsed the stance of Lansdowne and Long.[42]

The same day the Cabinet drew up the 'Headings of a Settlement as to the Government of Ireland'. After modification, the Act of 1914 was to be brought into force as soon as possible; it would not apply to the six counties which would be administered by a Secretary of State; Ireland would retain its 103 seats in the Imperial Parliament; the act would be in force for twelve months, but could be extended; Irish representation at Westminster would be reduced when the Dublin Parliament was established; and a final settlement was reserved for a post-war Imperial Conference. At the Cabinet meeting on 19 July Unionists enforced two amendments to the draft bill – permanent exclusion and reduction in Ireland's representation in the House of Commons. This decision opened the final phase of the episode: Irish party rejection of the formula. Redmond was told by Lloyd George on the 22 July that exclusion must be permanent; in the House of Commons two days later the Irish chairman reviewed the negotiations, announcing: 'if they introduce a bill ... I will oppose it at every stage', so ending prospects of an agreed settlement.[43]

Southern Unionists were always opposed to reopening Home Rule. Their persistent pressure, Buckland observes, caused a crisis of confidence in the Cabinet.[44] These machinations did not win them many friends. The *Daily Telegraph* on 25 July wished for a further effort, 'when we hope that public opinion will range itself even more unmistakably on the side of those who are working to bring peace and not a sword to Ireland'; the following day the *Daily Mail* castigated 'Lord Lansdowne and his friends [who] are living in the seventeenth century ... it is preposterous that these people who represent nobody but themselves, should be allowed any longer to stand between Ireland and a measure of self-government.'[45] The government bowed to the combined opposition of southern Unionists and the Irish party, finally abandoning the scheme on 27 July.

The attempted settlement is seen as a forlorn effort to reach agreement, a last chance to save something like Gladstonian Home Rule and with it the Irish party. Lloyd George is portrayed as engaging in sharp practice, deceiving Redmond. Boyce exonerates Lloyd George, arguing that Redmond rejected the plan because southern and British Unionists backed him into a corner where he was obliged to take a stand he otherwise would have avoided.[46] Lloyd George, Boyce notes, pushed ahead without first establishing support from Cabinet and Unionist colleagues. Chastened by the experience, he ensured that he had their support next time round.[47] Mansergh points out five differences from the position in 1914: first, Asquith in 1914 did not move beyond county opt-outs, but in 1916 he accepted exclusion *en bloc* of the six counties; second, without Lloyd George's dexterity there could be no settlement; third, Lloyd George advocated postponing fundamental questions until the conclusion of the war, opening a new tactical pathway; fourth, the difference between temporary and permanent exclusion was politically – as opposed to psychologically – rendered minimal or non-existent, since what the Ulster Unionists once obtained, they would not have abandoned; and fifth, the Cabinet would have been split if the plan proceeded.[48] St John Ervine, Craig's biographer, contends that the Cabinet decision on 22 July – that exclusion must be permanent – was the beginning of partition, but later events show that this judgement is premature, a verdict that must be applied also to John Kendle's assertion that from this time Home Rule was effectively dead.[49] The stance of Carson, Bonar Law and Balfour suggested that outstanding differences were now minor though of sufficient consequence to delay a settlement, while an important section of Unionist press and public opinion for the first time swung behind Home Rule. This incident came at a delicate moment in the military conflict, but none the less showed the continuing potency of Home Rule in Westminster affairs. American and Dominion opinion played some part in the jigsaw puzzle, but the intricacies of Irish and Westminster alignments proved decisive. This fourth attempt to introduce Home Rule nearly succeeded and it was the first occasion when a significant segment of Unionists accepted it.

Keeping the 'negotiating' spirit alive, late July 1916–21 May 1917

The breakdown of negotiations injured Redmond and the Irish party but it did not vitiate efforts to secure self-government. On 28 July Asquith wrote to Redmond: 'I think it is of great importance (if possible) to keep the "negotiating" spirit alive.' He saw only two distinctions between Redmond's and Carson's respective positions; minimising these, he wrote to the Irish party chairman:

(4) The real point is the future of the excluded area. Carson (naturally) wants safeguards against the possibility of 'automatic inclusion'. You (with equal reason) desire to keep open, and effectively open, the possibility of revision and review at an early date.

(5) I hope and believe that point (4) which is the crux of the whole matter may be got right.[50]

H. E. Duke was appointed Chief Secretary on 30 July. On 31 August William O'Brien wrote to Lloyd George to urge a conciliation conference.[51] The following months were dominated by a desire to keep communications afloat and by late September Long was preparing the groundwork for fresh negotiations.[52]

In the House of Commons on 18 October Redmond introduced a motion 'that the system of government at present maintained in Ireland is inconsistent with the principles for which the Allies are fighting in Europe, and has been mainly responsible for the recent unhappy events and for the present state of feeling in the country', which was defeated by 303 votes to 106.[53] During the debate Devlin stated: 'if there are any outstanding difficulties, and if by Irishmen meeting together either in their own country or here we can come to an agreement which will receive the sanction of the Irish people, we will be only too delighted to meet and endeavour to grapple with these difficulties and end this long and weary conflict.'[54] Members from all sections of the House rushed to identify themselves with renewal of attempts to find an agreed settlement. Devlin's plea, which contained the seeds of what became the Convention idea was taken up by Herbert Samuel who pointed out that the government 'are not prepared to contemplate armed coercion in Ireland [of Ulster]. If they [Irish party] are not willing to leave Ulster out until she is ready to come in, and if they are not prepared to wait for Home Rule until Ulster is ready to come in, then what is their proposal? That is the difficulty ... that is the dilemma in which we are placed.'[55] He proceeded to welcome Devlin's idea of a conference among Irishmen, promising government support.

Concern about the conduct of the war, and the devastating German U-boat sinking of British merchant shipping, enforced concentration on the military conflict. Redmond's grassroots support ebbed away without corresponding enthusiasm for his opponents who were preoccupied by opposition to him rather than bonded together by a common programme.[56] The Irish party retained a seat in a by-election on 16 November, an indication that it still had vitality. Later in the month Irish MPs opposed the government over the sale of Nigerian enemy property.[57] Between the end of July and early December 1916 Ireland had been discussed in the House of Commons about half a dozen times.

Asquith resigned on 5 December and the following day Lloyd George was requested to form a government. The second coalition had a more Unionist complexion. On 9 December Redmond conferred with Lloyd George, who told him he had 'no intention at present of making any move for settlement of the Irish question'.[58] The Irish chairman inveighed against conscription without Home Rule, demanded suspension of martial law and the release of untried prisoners. Despite the initial reluctance of the new Premier, Ireland soon seeped back into view, not least because the creation of his own secretariat, known as the 'Garden Suburb', brought to the fore the influence of men who 'took more responsibility for the substance of Irish policy than it did with respect to any other subject'.[59] Members, especially W. G. S. Adams, had a disposition towards federalism. Redmond's vulnerability was exposed when Count George Noble Plunkett, with Sinn Féin backing, defeated the official Irish party candidate in the Roscommon North by-election on 3 February 1917. A week later the Cabinet held a preliminary discussion on Ireland.[60] Redmond on 12 February sought a day to discuss O'Connor's motion:

> [W]ith a view to strengthening the hands of the Allies in achieving the recognition of the equal rights of all nations and the principle of nationality against the opposite German principle of military domination and government without the consent of the government, it is essential without further delay to confer upon Ireland the free institutions long promised.[61]

L. S. Amery's memorandum on 18 February advocated a convention to treat the Irish question.[62] A parliamentary debate on the issue was scheduled for 7 March. In the interval the government looked at ways to restart the dialogue between differing Irish interests. Events in Ireland, not least difficulties arising from deportations of suspected republicans, made an Irish agreement attractive. There were three possible courses – a British negotiated settlement, an imposed solution following the report of a commission established to make changes in the Act of 1914, or a conference of Irishmen. The first had already failed, the second was full of difficulties and the third, though successful in 1903, had not worked in 1914 (the Buckingham Palace Conference had not been an exclusively Irish affair). Amery's conference idea found favour with Lloyd George's 'Garden Suburb', which pressed its virtues on the Prime Minister.

On 2 March, in preparation for the debate in the House of Commons, Lloyd George met Bonar Law and Carson; based on what he learned, he then approached O'Connor.[63] In the debate Redmond called for an imposed solution: 'put the Home Rule Act into operation with such additions, amendments, and changes as the passage of time and the altered circumstances render necessary. Do that on your own responsibility. Come forward on your own responsibility, and do not ask us into your back parlours for any more negotiations.'[64] He then led the Irish party out of the chamber in protest. After their departure Lloyd George responded: 'I laid down the principle that the government were prepared to put into immediate operation that self-government, Home Rule, should be granted to that part of Ireland which clearly demanded it, but we could not take any action to enforce Home Rule on the part of Ireland to which it was repugnant.' He then observed that there were 'two ways of dealing with details. One was a conference of Irishmen, which, I confess, I should have liked to see ... [and the other was to] set up a commission in order to consider the adjustments that would be necessary to put these principles in operation.'[65] Behind the scenes the mood warmed up for a settlement. On 20 March the Church of Ireland Archbishop of Dublin indicated his support for a Convention of Irishmen. Carson's memorandum the same day stated: 'I do not believe Ulster would agree to come in on any conditions; but I think the conditions which could be offered to her should be ascertained and should be included in any amending bill, so dealing with matters of interest to whole of Ireland.'[66] As a way forward he suggested a 'consultative assembly' for matters germane to the whole island. This was the germ of the Council of Ireland. On 22 March the Cabinet agreed to establish a commission, and Bonar Law in the House of Commons supported the need for a settlement, as quoted at the head of the chapter. After urging the Irish not to press him further about precise details for another attempt at present, Bonar Law took issue with his colleague, Lord Hugh Cecil:

> I do not agree ... that the only thing you have to think of in the government of Ireland is to set up government that will govern in the best way. I do not think that at all. I think very often a very bad form of government if it is with the consent and good will of the people governed, will work infinitely better than a much better system without that consent and good will.[67]

The Conservative leader had arrived at Gladstone's proposition that laws to be effective must be promulgated by the appropriate people.

On 17 April a bill to prolong the life of the present Parliament was due for debate amidst concern that the Irish party would resort to obstruction. When the Cabinet considered Ireland again that day it accepted four realities – the Act of 1914 was outmoded in certain respects; the government was committed to attempt a settlement; the Irish party would not enter negotiations; and though no one wished to see partition made permanent, any attempt to include the proposed excluded area in a measure would end in failure.[68] It also concluded that a commission would not be acceptable to any of the parties. Ulster Unionists were unwilling to allow their 'rights' to be adjudicated by a commission. The idea of county option was refloated, but Carson immediately took exception.[69] The Cabinet determined to prepare a bill containing a county opt-out clause which would be submitted to an Irish conference during its committee stage. Individual counties could seek inclusion in the Dublin Parliament if they secured 55 per cent of votes. A subcommittee, comprising Curzon, Christopher Addison and Duke, was given the task of drafting the bill; it reverted to Carson's preference for a 'clean cut' for six counties for a three-year period after the end of the war, but also provided for periodic meetings of Ulster MPs and representatives of the Dublin Parliament.

Momentum continued to build for a new approach, increasing sharply because of America's entry into the war on 17 April 1917, a narrow Sinn Féin success (1,493 votes to 1,461) over the Irish party candidate in a parliamentary by-election on 9 May for Longford South, Redmond's threat of obstruction in the House of Commons, imperial pressure and a growing need for conscription in Ireland.[70] Lloyd George met Devlin and O'Connor on 29 April and found them interested in finding a solution. Long was among those who urged action, writing to Lloyd George on 15 May: 'you are on the edge of a precipice as regards Ireland'.[71] At a banquet in honour of Smuts, Redmond had a useful informal talk with Lord Crewe which was quickly relayed to the Prime Minister. Two Cabinet meetings on 16 May discussed Ireland without agreeing; Lloyd George continued to seek a way out of the impasse. Writing to Redmond that same day, he offered implementation of Home Rule with exclusion of the Ulster counties to be reconsidered by Parliament after five years. His new feature was a Council of Ireland, comprising equal numbers from both parts of the country; it would have the power to extend or initiate an end to exclusion.[72] In a postscript, as 'a last resort', Lloyd George offered him 'a convention of Irishmen of all parties for the purpose of producing a scheme of Irish self-government'. Redmond already had the benefit of O'Connor's opinion in a letter on 10 May that the government and House of Commons would retreat from the proposal to exclude the six counties to one that would give each county an option, thus facilitating the inclusion of Tyrone and Fermanagh into the Irish Parliament. Redmond, sensing an advantage, replied the next day, throwing cold water on the proposed solution but agreeing to a conference. No doubt he preferred a conference to shouldering responsibility for the Prime Minster's plan, relieving him of criticism for accepting it on his own. On the 21 May Lloyd George announced: 'Ireland should try her hand at hammering out an instrument of government for her own people.' It was promised that 'should substantial agreement' be arrived at, the government would 'accept responsibility of taking all necessary steps to enable the Imperial Parliament to give legislative effect to such conclusions of the conference'.[73] The next day the *Daily Mail* breathed a sigh of relief, commenting that 'so far as Great Britain is concerned the last obstacle to a settlement of Irish Question is removed. It is now solely and wholly in the hands of the Irish themselves.'[74]

After the end of July 1916 the public hiatus in Irish affairs had concealed a good deal of behind-the-scenes manoeuvring to keep the 'negotiating' spirit alive. The idea for a conference was not new nor was restricting its membership to the Irish an innovation. It had three attractions in the spring of 1917 – it would throw responsibility for an arrangement on the Irish, it would conciliate American and Dominion opinion and the Westminster government would be relieved of direct involvement at a moment when no effort could be spared from the war. But it was only one of two options offered to Redmond. The chairman of the Irish party chose the conference when the Prime Minister professed to be ready to implement Home Rule with the exclusion of six counties. In a sense, then, Home Rule could have been put in place in spring 1917 on lines sufficiently close to what was almost universally expected without the interlude of a conference. Redmond was guided by two considerations – reluctance to shoulder the burden of exclusion and a strong hope that the area excluded would be narrowed, its term of exclusion limited.

The Irish Convention, 22 May 1917–9 April 1918

The Irish Convention was the fifth attempt to implement Home Rule and marks Buckland's third step toward a solution of the Ulster question (see p. 280). The first of four phases to the unfolding of the Convention was construction of its membership and format. It remained to be seen who would attend the Convention, how representative the delegates would be, whether they could reach agreement and, not incidentally, if people in Ireland would adopt its settlement. Middleton indicated that southern Unionists would attend if represented in sufficient numbers. On 28 May Carson, in an attempt to secure Ulster Unionist participation, reminded Hugh Montgomery: 'above all things it must be remembered that under the Home Rule Act Ulster is "included" *and remains included until some compromise is agreed and carried through Parliament.*'[75] On 8 June 350 delegates to the Ulster Unionist Conference sanctioned attendance subject to the stipulation that 'nothing in any way binding [be accepted] ... without consultation with the Ulster people'.[76] Sinn Féin declined as early as 18 May to send representatives, demanding instead elections based on adult suffrage to choose delegates, insisting as well that the Convention must have the right to declare Ireland independent and that decisions be ratified by a majority vote. The government was not discouraged. On 15 June Bonar Law announced amnesty for political prisoners 'in order that the Convention may meet in an atmosphere of harmony and goodwill'.[77] On the following day 120 prisoners were released (including Countess Markievicz).

Healy and O'Brien also declined invitations, the latter believing that the conclave would make 'a hateful bargain for the partition of the country under a plausible disguise'. What was needed instead was not a 'heterogeneous assembly ... but a small round-table of representative Irishmen'.[78] The Dublin Trades Council, the Cork Trade and Labour Council, the Gaelic and National Leagues also refused. Ninety-five men agreed to attend including fifty-two representing national interests. On the other side there were two Liberals, nine southern Unionists, twenty-four Ulster Unionists plus J. P. Mahaffery and Plunkett. Fifty-three were Catholic, forty-two were Protestant. Thirty-two delegates were chairman of county councils (only Kerry declined to send a representative) and a further eight were chairman of urban district councils, making a total of forty-six. The majority of these were members of the Irish party. Edward MacLysaght, a government nominee, was in close touch with Sinn Féin. Though not strictly a 'representative', Convention delegates could reach an agreement that commanded general assent. The popularity of the Irish party had dipped, but Sinn Féin could not automatically succeed it. Fitzpatrick's study of County Clare shows that when Sinn Féin triumphed it did so as a reconstituted version of the Irish party. Possibly the Irish party itself was beyond resuscitation, but a successful conclusion to the Convention might derail Sinn Féin hopes to fill the vacuum.

On 6 July the Irish party candidate was unopposed at a parliamentary by-election in Dublin South but four days later de Valera captured East Clare (by 5,010 votes to 2,035) in a parliamentary by-election resulting from Major Willie Redmond's death on the Western Front (7 June). Also, before the Convention was convened the National Volunteers passed into the control of Sinn Féin. The opening session under Plunkett's chairmanship was held in Trinity College on 25 July, discussions by the full Convention began on 8 August and formal presentations commenced two weeks later. However, in the interval William Cosgrave on 10 August at Kilkenny City won another parliamentary by-election for Sinn Féin (by 772 votes to 392).

Two decades earlier Plunkett had logged a huge success with his handling of the Recess Committee. That group had worked quickly and efficiently. Plunkett interpreted his brief in 1917 to allow all opinions to be aired fully, not to hurry delegates and through the process of letting everyone have a say in order to reach a consensus. In his view, 'anyone who really understands Ireland can get the most antagonistic elements to combine once they consent to meet'.[79] Lord Southborough thought this 'personal intercourse might wear the Ulstermen's feelings down'.[80] Plunkett followed an agenda, initially focusing on matters commanding near unanimity. This approach would narrow the potential differences on contentious questions. The presentation stage lasted for eighteen sittings (twelve in Dublin, three in Belfast and three in Cork). In September an outside observer who held hopes for a successful outcome thought: 'if the Convention produced an Irish Parliament they [Sinn Féin supporters] will be quite satisfied and the extremists will soon be discounted. Unionists and Nationalists expect and hope that the Convention will produce something in the end, and even Sinn Féiners would be glad if it did.'[81] At the close of the first stage Plunkett believed 'the discussion had been really fruitful in hardening the heart of the south and softening the head of the north'.[82]

On 25 September the Convention adopted a new procedure, establishing a grand committee of nine to meet in October charged with framing a scheme to 'meet the views and difficulties expressed by various speakers during the course of the debates'. This shift began a second phase of the episode when divisions within the Convention were exposed. This committee was also 'for the purpose of negotiation between leaders on the vital issues in dispute'.[83] Its sessions commenced on 11 October. Differences over whether Ireland should have complete fiscal autonomy or the customs and excise duties retained by the Imperial Parliament soon emerged and threatened to disrupt the Convention. Meanwhile, on 25 and 26 October, the Sinn Féin Ard-Fheis elected de Valera President and adopted the policy of seeking recognition for the Irish republic; at the same time de Valera became President of the Irish Volunteers. In theory the Convention was a wholly Irish affair. However, Plunkett and Redmond began appealing to the Prime Minister, the Irish chairman on 19 November pointing out that it is 'up to you and the government ... to step in and avert the serious disaster ... of a break-down of the Convention'.[84] On 22 November Middleton introduced a compromise allowing the Irish Parliament control of internal taxation, including excise duties, but allowing the Imperial Parliament to retain customs. From around this time national representatives and southern Unionists drew closer together while significant cracks appeared in the alliance between southern and Ulster Unionists. At this point most of the activity was within the committee and private discussion. By early December the full Convention had not met for two months.

During December Lloyd George became more directly involved, opening a third phase of the Convention. Middleton and the Church of Ireland Archbishop, Bernard, had an interview with the Prime Minister on 5 December to press him to support the proposed compromise fiscal scheme. Redmond wrote to Lloyd George on 11 December asking for 'definite assurance' that 'if we could come to an arrangement in the House of Commons' he would 'fight the Ulster Unionists'.[85] The Prime Minster pointed out that it would be essential 'to meet in the most reasonable way the difficulties of Ulster'. On 18 December the Ulster delegates met to consider Middleton's plan. They insisted on two conditions – that the Imperial Parliament would have a right to impose conscription and it would control excise duties as well as customs. In spite of the evident discord, R. B. McDowell points out that in December there was justification for believing that the Convention was moving towards an agreed settlement.[86]

On 4 January 1918 Redmond addressed the Convention in favour of accepting Middleton's proposal so long as it was adopted and given legislative effect by the government. At this juncture the Prime Minster was hopeful of a successful outcome, but exasperated by the Ulster Unionists, observing to Bonar Law on 12 January 1918: 'if the little Protestant community of the south, isolated in a turbulent sea of Sinn Féinism and popery, can trust their lives and their property to Middleton's scheme, surely the powerful communities of the north might take that risk for the sake of Empire in danger.'[87] Redmond found himself confronted with powerful internal opposition, especially from Bishop O'Donnell, and on the 15 January he distanced himself from Middleton's solution. Carson left the Cabinet over differences about the conduct of the war on 21 January.

From late January the government's role in the negotiations escalated. Also, an Irish party triumph over Sinn Féin on 2 February at Armagh South (by 2,324 votes to 1,305) appeared to reverse the slide in Redmond's fortunes. On 6 February the Prime Minster, Bonar Law and Curzon met Middleton, Bernard and Desart. Lloyd George observed: 'if Ulster stood out it would be difficult to describe the residual majority as substantial'.[88] The southern Unionists insisted that 'the one thing all Ireland (outside Belfast) would not allow was partition', a sentiment warmly endorsed by the Prime Minster. On 13 February he met a delegation from the Convention, pointing out that he was guided by three considerations – the impossibility of legislating as freely in wartime, thereby necessitating control of the police from Westminster and fiscal relations remaining as they were at present until its conclusion; a settlement was only possible if partition was ruled out ('it would be idle to propose partition again'); and there had to be safeguards for the Ulster Unionists ('Labour must be protected against the peasant').[89] To Hugh Barrie, the leader of the Ulster delegation, he wrote on 21 February, imploring his side to seek a solution. On 25 February in a lengthy letter to Plunkett, which was read to the Convention the following day, Lloyd George outlined his formula for a compromise – customs and excise would remain in the control of the Imperial Parliament until two years after the war; at the conclusion of the war a Royal Commission would consider the fiscal question; during the conflict all revenue raised in Ireland would be returned there after the appropriate deductions for Imperial purposes; there would be an increase in Unionist representation in the Irish legislature; and an Ulster Committee in the Irish Parliament would be empowered to modify or veto legislative or administrative action 'not consonant with the interests of Ulster'.[90] As part of the package he promised a bill to settle land purchase and to make 'a substantial provision' for dealing with the urban housing problem.

Lloyd George's letter made a limited impression on Ulster Unionists and a segment of southern Unionists outside the Convention were unhappy with Middleton's apparent readiness to strike a bargain. With his health deteriorating rapidly, Redmond on 26 February wrote to Dillon resigning the party chairmanship; he died on 6 March, and a week later Dillon succeeded him. In spite of the difficulties with the Convention there was still a general belief that some formula would emerge. On 9 March Chamberlain opined:

> [N]ow that half this country has given up the idea of maintaining the Union as it stands we cannot get 'resolute government' for the time necessary to let the Home Rule idea die out, even if it would ever die out after all the encouragement it has had. And federalism is the only thing which could make Home Rule safe and the only form of Home Rule which Ulster could be got to accept, whilst for us devolution would seem to have become necessary when you think of the mass of work which lies before Parli[ament] in the near future.[91]

Like Bonar Law, his thinking was swinging around to Gladstone's direction in 1886.

Immediate prospects for an agreed solution among the Irish received a setback on 12 March when Ulster Unionists presented the Convention with a plan for the exclusion of nine counties. This opened the third phase of the Convention: decisions by majority vote and its report. The fiscal question was dealt with on 13 March and by the following week twenty-one resolutions of provisional agreement had been adopted. On 22 March the Irish party candidate, John Redmond's son Captain William Archer Redmond, defeated the Sinn Féin nominee in at parliamentary by-election to fill his seat at Waterford (by 1,242 votes to 745). British Unionist MPs remained anxious that agreement be secured. At the end of March they received a circular, asking 'if a Home Rule Bill is introduced, would you oppose it or give it support if it is drafted on Federal lines', which attracted a hundred favourable replies.[92]

Just at this moment Home Rule became hostage to the military position; the largest German offensive of the war broke through the allied lines on 24 March. Between 21 March and the end of April the British Army lost more than 300,000 men. Resolution of the Irish question became intertwined with the need for military manpower and this marked the final phase of the Convention's labours.[93] Lloyd George now linked Home Rule to the imposition of conscription in Ireland, which was applied on 25 March. At a further session three days later the Prime Minister spelt out the 'essential element of a settlement – single legislature for a united Ireland'.[94] At the same time the Irish party took heart from its candidate's success over Sinn Féin in the parliamentary by-election for Tyrone East (by 1,802 votes to 1,222). A Cabinet meeting on 5 April determined on introducing Home Rule and conscription simultaneously. On 5 April the Convention report was carried by 44 votes to 29; it and two accompanying minority reports along with five 'Notes' were presented to Parliament on 9 April and published three days later. The result could not be represented as 'substantial agreement'. Robert Cecil observed: 'If I vote for Home Rule it is because I hope thereby to get conscription.'[95]

Chamberlain was invited to join the Cabinet to aid in preparing the Home Rule measure; he favoured giving the Irish Parliament wide powers.[96] Despite a disappointing outcome the Convention narrowed the ground yet further. It is certainly an exaggeration to dismiss it as 'an example of elitist politics at its most ineffectual'.[97] Failure of the Convention forced the government to look in another directions for a solution. The Convention is often pictured as a device to assuage American opinion, get the problem out of London and to buy time. In May 1917 most people, including Lloyd George, expected that it would achieve a substantial agreement and until 12 March 1918 at least this seemed a probable outcome. Ulster Unionists and national representatives had reached a measure of accommodation in 1916; Carson's idea of a 'consultative assembly' had the makings of structure to maintain the nation's unity. What the Convention demonstrated was that Anglo-Irish affairs were triangular: London could not stay on the sidelines. This fifth attempt at Home Rule revealed that its principle had been firmly entrenched. The problem was to find a formula to make Home Rule a reality.

Conclusion

Home Rule was enshrined in the Government of Ireland Act of 1914. Although the war and other factors melted away the hard core of Unionist opposition, self-government did arrive swiftly in spite of vigorous efforts to find a formula for its introduction. Throughout the post-Rising period, politicians laboured for an agreed solution. Unlike earlier self-government attempts this was less a parliamentary problem than one of satisfying Unionists in the Cabinet and the two major Irish factions. Discovering exactly the right balance to achieve a result remained elusive even after the effects of British party strife were moderated.

Notes

1 Quoted in John D. Fair, *British Interparty Conferences: A Study of the Procedure of Conciliation in British Politics, 1867–1921* (Oxford, 1980), p. 125.

2 *Parliamentary Debates [PD]*, 91 (1916), c. 2133–7.

3 David Fitzpatrick, *Politics and Irish Life 1913–1921: Provincial Experience of War and Revolution* (Dublin, 1977), pp. 85–6, 100.

4 Quoted in John Kendle, *Ireland and the Federal Solution: The Debate over the United Kingdom Constitution, 1870–1921* (Kingston and Montreal, 1989), p. 176.

5 Denis Gwynn, *The Life of John Redmond* (London, 1932), pp. 426–7.

6 Quoted in Lawrence W. McBride, *The Greening of Dublin Castle: The Transformation of Bureaucratic and Judicial Personnel in Ireland 1892–1922* (Washington, DC, 1991), p. 205.

7 John Kendle, *Walter Long, Ireland, and the Union, 1905–1920* (Montreal and Kingston, 1992), p. 92.

8 Fitzpatrick, *Politics and Irish Life*, p. 112.

9 Fair, *British Interparty Conferences*, p. 121.

10 Gwynn, *John Redmond*, p. 480; David Harkness, *Ireland in the Twentieth Century: Divided Island* (London and Basingstoke, 1996), p. 29.

11 Nicholas Mansergh, *The Unsolved Question: The Anglo-Irish Settlement and its Undoing 1912–72* (New Haven and London, 1991), p. 81.

12 Selborne to his wife 26 May 1916, Selborne Papers, Bodleian Library, MS 102/195.

13 John Redmond to John Dillon, 1 May 1916, Redmond Papers, MS 15,182 (22).

14 McBride, *Dublin Castle*, pp. 219–21.

15 D. George Boyce, 'British Opinion, Ireland, and the War,

1916–1918', *Historical Journal*, XVII, 3 (1974), pp. 578–9.
  16 Quoted in Reginald Pound and Arthur G. Harmsworth, *Northcliffe* (London, 1959), p. 501.
  17 *PD*, 5th series, 82 (1916), cc. 959–60.
  18 For a catalogue of events from Asquith's vantage-point, see, Roy Jenkins, *Asquith: Portrait of a Man and an Era* (New York, 1966), pp. 397–404.
  19 Quoted in F. S. L. Lyons, *John Dillon: A Biography* (London, 1968), p. 395.
  20 Quoted in Fair, *Briths Interparty Conferences*, p. 123.
  21 Bentley Brinkerhoff Gilbert, *David Lloyd George; A Political Life: Organizer of Victory 1912–1916* (London, 1992), p. 322.
  22 Quoted in Kendle, *Walter Long*, p. 101; Trevor Wilson (ed.), *The Political Diaries of C. P. Scott, 1911–1928* (London, 1970), pp. 206–7.
  23 Quoted in Ian Colvin, *The Life of Lord Carson* (London, 1936), III, p. 166.
  24 Boyce, 'British Opinion', pp. 579–80.
  25 Kendle, *Walter Long*, pp. 99–102.
  26 Quoted in David W. Savage, 'The Attempted Home Rule Settlement of 1916', *Éire-Ireland*, II, (Autumn, 1967), p. 139.
  27 See, Patrick Buckland, *Irish Unionism: One: The Anglo-Irish and the New Ireland 1885–1922* (Dublin, 1972), pp. 54–92.
  28 Quoted in Lyons, *John Dillon*, p. 389; for the background to northern national politics, see A. C. Hepburn, *A Past Apart: Studies in the History of Catholic Belfast 1850–1950* (Belfast, 1996).
  29 *The Times*, 12 June 1916.
  30 Quoted in Fair, *British Interparty Conferences*, p. 131.
  31 Buckland, *Irish Unionism: One*, p. 57.
  32 Quoted in Boyce, 'British Opinion', p. 581.
  33 David W. Miller, *Church, State and Nation in Ireland 1898–1921* (Dublin, 1973), p. 337.
  34 Eamon Phoenix, *Northern Nationalism: Nationalist Politics, Partition and the Catholic Minority in Northern Ireland 1890–1940* (Belfast, 1994), pp. 30–1; Mary Harris, *The Catholic Church and the Foundation of the Northern Irish State* (Cork, 1993), pp. 54–7; R. B. McDowell, *The Irish Convention 1917–18* (London, 1970), pp. 53–4.
  35 *The Times*, 18 June 1916.
  36 Quoted in Catherine B. Shannon, *Arthur J. Balfour and Ireland 1874–1922* (Washington, DC, 1988), pp. 219–21.
  37 McDowell, *The Irish Convention*, p. 58.
  38 Quoted in *ibid.*, pp. 54–4.
  39 PRO, CAB41/36/25.
  40 *PD*, 5th series, Lords, 22, cc. 645–52, Middleton's speech, cc. 635–41; *The Times*, 14 July 1916.
  41 Quoted in Shannon, *Arthur J. Balfour*, p. 223.
  42 Kendle, *Walter Long*, p. 128.
  43 *PD*, 84, c. 1432–4.
  44 Buckland, *Irish Unionism: One*, p. 69.

45 Quoted in Boyce, 'British Opinion', p. 584.
46 *Ibid.*, pp. 580–1.
47 D. George Boyce, 'How to Settle the Irish Question: Lloyd George and Ireland 1916–21', in A. J. P. Taylor (ed.), *Lloyd George: Twelve Essays* (London, 1971), p. 141.
48 Mansergh, *The Unsolved Question*, p. 95.
49 St John Ervine, *Craigavon Ulsterman* (London, 1949), p. 324; Kendle, *Federal Solution*, p. 179.
50 Quoted in Gywnn, *John Redmond*, pp. 522–3.
51 J. V. O'Brien, *William O'Brien and the Course of Irish Politics, 1881–1918* (Berkeley and Los Angeles, 1976), p. 224.
52 Kendle, *Walter Long*, p. 135.
53 *PD*, 86 (1916), c. 581.
54 *Ibid.*, c. 641.
55 *Ibid.*, c. 692.
56 Sheila Lawlor, *Britain and Ireland 1914–23* (Dublin, 1983), p. 14.
57 Wilson (ed.), *C. P. Scott*, p. 239.
58 'Notes on Discussion', Redmond MS 15,189; see, Gwynn, *John Redmond*, pp. 531–5.
59 John Turner, *Lloyd George's Secretariat* (Cambridge, 1980), p. 85.
60 PRO, CAB23/1; Ronan Fanning's assertion that between February 1917 and March 1918 the War Cabinet discussed Ireland only twice is incorrect. See, Ronan Fanning, 'Britain, Ireland and the End of the Union', in Robert Blake, *Ireland After the Union* (Oxford, 1989), p. 108.
61 *PD*, 90 (1917), c. 277.
62 McDowell, *The Irish Convention*, p. 69.
63 Turner, *Secretariat*, p. 88.
64 *PD*, 91 (1917), c. 480.
65 *Ibid.*, cc. 485–6.
66 Colvin, *Lord Carson*, II, p. 244.
67 *PD*, 91 (1916), c. 2133–7.
68 McDowell, *The Irish Convention*, pp. 73–4.
69 PRO CAB23/2.
70 See, John O. Stubbs, 'The Unionists and Ireland, 1914–18', *Historical Journal*, 33, 4 (1990), p. 884; see, also, Alan J. Ward, *Ireland and Anglo-American Relations 1899–1921* (London, 1969), pp. 141–268; F. M. Carroll, *American Opinion and the Irish Question 1910–23* (Dublin, 1978), pp. 36–193; Stephen Hartley, *The Irish Question as a Problem in British Foreign Policy, 1914–18* (Basingstoke, 1987).
71 Quoted in John Turner, *British Politics and the Great War: Coalition and Conflict 1915–1918* (New Haven and London, 1992), p. 184.
72 D. Lloyd George to Redmond, 16 May 1917, Redmond MS 15,215.
73 *PD*, Lords (1917), cc. 198–9.
74 Quoted in Boyce, 'British Opinion', p. 586.
75 Quoted in Fair, *British Interparty Conferences*, p. 203.
76 Quoted in McDowell, *The Irish Convention*, p. 81.
77 Quoted in Colvin, *Lord Carson*, III, p. 299.
78 Quoted in McDowell, *The Irish Convention*, p. 83, see, p. 85.

79 Quoted in *ibid.*, p. 105.

80 Quoted in *ibid.*, p. 106.

81 William Ormsby-Gore to W. Adams, 11 September 1917 quoted in Turner, *Great War*, p. 245.

82 Quoted in McDowell, *The Irish Convention*, pp. 113–14.

83 Quoted in *ibid.*, pp. 117, 119–20.

84 Quoted in Gwynn, *John Redmond*, p. 570.

85 Redmond MS 15,189.

86 McDowell, *The Irish Convention*, p. 136.

87 Quoted in Patrick Buckland, *Irish Unionism: Two: Ulster Unionism and the Origins of Northern Ireland 1886–1922* (Dublin, 1973), p. 110.

88 Quoted in McDowell, *The Irish Convention*, pp. 157–8.

89 Quoted in *ibid.*, pp. 158–9.

90 Quoted in *ibid.*, pp. 165–6.

91 Quoted in Kendle, *Federal Solution*, p. 193.

92 Quoted in *ibid.*, p. 195.

93 Trevor Wilson, *The Downfall of the Liberal Party, 1914–1935* (London, 1966), p. 107.

94 PRO CAB23/14.

95 PRO CAB23/6.

96 David Dutton, *Austen Chamberlain: Gentleman in Politics* (Bolton, 1985), p. 142.

97 Turner, *Great War*, p. 285.

11

Home Rule and Dominion status, 1918–21

In principle Home Rule has passed beyond the scope of discussion. While its character, its extent and its limitations have to be reviewed afresh, we are all Home Rulers today. (*The Times*, 26 March 1919)[1]

To establish one Parliament for the three southern provinces and a second Parliament for Ulster, together with a Council of Ireland composed of members of the two Irish Parliaments, to discharge certain immediate functions, but mainly to promote as rapidly as possible and without further reference to the Imperial Parliament, the union of the whole of Ireland under a single legislature. (Long Committee, 4 November 1919)[2]

Introduction

Self-government was implemented by a Unionist-dominated coalition that strove to maintain a façade of a united Ireland. While this shift was born of necessity, closer analysis suggests that the change was not so dramatic; it was a refurbishing of traditional organic Unionist ideology. In this last leg of the journey Irish political leaders continued to be marginalised. John Turner asserts: 'during the war it was the Irish party which fell victim; after the war as a direct consequence of the extinction of the Nationalists, the Union itself broke down.'[3] Instead, it is argued that displacement of the Irish party was less important than coalition politics for reordering the Union. The Union, if broken down, had reached that point under the Government of Ireland Act in 1914. Three innovations took place: marginalising southern Unionists, breaking the question into two segments and the granting of Dominion status.

Preparatory discussions for self-government, 10 April 1918–3 November 1919

In the next round the problem was to find a formula to implement self-government in a way acceptable to the coalition rather than trying to get rival Irish factions to reach an accord. The Cabinet meeting on 11 April 1918 established a committee to draw up a bill, comprising Long (chairman), Duke, Curzon, Smuts, Chamberlain, Addison, George Barnes, Herbert Fisher, George Hewert and Sir George Cave. This group had strong federalist inclinations. Federal ideas had an important function over the coming months, affording Unionists a means to square anti-Home Rule ideology with the construction of an Irish solution. Their problem, John Kendle points out, was to preserve the Union and to protect both Ulster and southern Unionists while giving self-government to the Irish majority.[4] Federalism held three attractions: Ireland would only be one portion of a wider United Kingdom and Dominion restructuring; Ulster could be treated as part of a larger reconstruction and not specifically as a portion of Ireland; and self-government was a means of improving efficiency not a concession to nationalism. Writing to Lloyd George on 10 April Chamberlain observed: 'the time has come when the only safe and practicable solution of our difficulty is to be found in a federal organisation of the United Kingdom. I believe this is now required for the satisfactory conduct of business of Great Britain; but I believe also that it is the only scheme which would make Irish Home Rule safe and the union of Ireland possible.'[5] Long's thinking, expressed in a memorandum on 14 April, was moving in an analogous direction:

> While very valuable results have followed from the deliberations of the [Irish] Convention it is hopeless to try and bring Nationalists, Southern Unionists and Ulstermen together, and that to provoke a controversy is to lose the bill. Can we not device a scheme which would if necessary be adopted as a basis for Federation of United Kingdom and flight it on these lines?[6]

The committee met on 15 and 16 April. At the second session the chairman wanted advice on three matters – the situation of the Catholic minority in Ulster, finance and Irish representation at Westminster.[7] That same day the government pushed its Military Service (Amendment) bill through the House of Commons. In protest, Dillon led the Irish party out of the chamber, working with Sinn Féin against conscription.[8] The next day the Cabinet under pressure from several sources, accepted a voluntary recruiting campaign, deciding against imposing conscription for the time being.[9] On 19 April the Sinn Féin candidate was elected unopposed at the King's county parliamentary by-election. A general strike in Ireland on 23 April showed the depth of revulsion against conscription in the southern provinces. At a Cabinet meeting on the same day Long and Chamberlain favoured a federal solution, but were opposed by Balfour and Curzon. Long was given charge of drafting a new bill for Ireland, as it could be delayed no longer. On 9 May Long's draft – minus financial proposals – was discussed by the Cabinet committee. Support for a settlement permeated rank-and-file Conservatives as well. As a test of opinion Conservative Central Office enquired of district agents:

1. whether Unionist feeling was hostile to any Home Rule proposal;
2. whether it was felt that provided Ulster was properly safeguarded, such proposals should be entertained, and
3. whether a Home Rule measure would be more acceptable if it were consistent with the application of the federal principle to all parts of the United Kingdom.[10]

The responses gave scant encouragement to federalists; sixteen districts were sampled and only three expressed definite hostility to Home Rule. Lord Hugh Cecil put it simply: 'the truth is that colouring federalism with nationalism is like painting a rat red; it kills the animal'.[11]

Ministerial interest in self-government was somewhat torpid in the fevered conditions of spring 1918. Growing support for Sinn Féin led the government to arrest leaders on 17 May for alleged complicity with Germany. Evidence of their involvement was insubstantial. The impact was counter-productive, increasing pro-Sinn Féin sentiment among Catholics. On 4 June the Cabinet postponed introduction of a Home Rule measure. Long believed that any bill would be opposed by Ulster and Viscount Middleton.[12] On 19 June the Cabinet maintained the dual policy of Home Rule and conscription, but decided that the timing and method of application would be judged by the government. Meanwhile, on 20 June Arthur Griffith, standing for Sinn Féin, defeated the Irish party candidate at a parliamentary by-election (by 3,795 votes to 2,581). By the end of June Long had drafted a federal scheme. Writing to the Prime Minister a month later he declared that the old sort of Home Rule was 'as dead as Queen Anne. Federalism is the only substitute.'[13] Lloyd George on 25 July announced that there was no intention to proceed with Home Rule in the immediate future and at Cabinet a few days later this was reaffirmed. But on 6 August Long's committee discussed the relative merits of proceeding with the bill of 1917 or basing a measure on the Convention report. On the ground Sinn Féin continued to entrench itself.

By September the German offensive had passed; the war's end was imminent. On 4 October Germany appealed for an armistice; it took effect on 11 November. This raised the spectre that the Home Rule Act of 1914 would come into force automatically when the final peace treaty was signed. On 14 November the coalition government called a general election; Parliament was dissolved on 25 November. Ireland was not the central issue of the campaign. Lloyd George and Bonar Law worked out an agreed formula:

> [W]e regard it as one of the first obligations of British statesmanship to explore all practical paths towards the settlement of this grave and difficult question, on the basis of self-government. But there are two paths which are closed – the one leading to a complete severance of Ireland from the British Empire, and the other to be forcible submission of the six counties of Ulster to a Home Rule Parliament against its will. In imposing these two limitations, we are only acting in accordance with the declared views of all English political leaders.[14]

This was a declaration of principle, however, rather than a commitment to a precise formula.

The Franchise Act of 1918 more than doubled the electorate and granted the ballot to women over the age of 30. Nominations closed on 4 December. Polling, except for soldiers and the universities, took place on a single day for the first time; results were announced a fortnight later on 28 December. The coalition scored a smashing triumph capturing 475 of 707 seats (339 Conservatives and 136 Liberals); Asquith Liberals were reduced to 26. In Ireland the long dominance of the Irish party ended; it won only 6 compared to Sinn Féin's 73 of 105 constituencies. Unionists lifted their number to 23. Sinn Féin won 23 contests unopposed. Unionists took 28.4 per cent of ballots, the Irish Party 22 per cent and Sinn Féin 47 per cent, with others accounting for the remaining 2.6 per cent. Sinn Féin pledged to refuse to sit in the Westminster Parliament. Twenty-eight of its elected members who were not in prison met at the Mansion House in Dublin on 21 January 1919, constituting themselves as the Dáil Éireann (it met six times in 1919, six in 1920, and six in 1921). On the same day republican violence escalated when an Irish Volunteer unit of Dan Breen, Séan Tracey and Seámus Robinson murdered two policemen at Soloheadbeg, Tipperary. Sinn Féin repudiated Home Rule, seeking instead a republic. The election outcome had four implications: the Coalition was Conservative-dominated; there was no longer a need to negotiate with the Irish party; Sinn Féin abstention lessened problems in the House of Commons; and, the government could strike an agreement with Ulster Unionists first, and deal with national representatives afterwards.

During the first half of 1919 Lloyd George was immersed in the peace conference. He was at Versailles between 12 January and mid-February, returning again in early March and staying until the end of June. The political and military situation in Ireland worsened. De Valera escaped from Lincoln prison on 3 February; between 6 and 10 March the remaining Sinn Féin prisoners were released; on 1 April the second session of the Dáil opened and de Valera was elected President; on 18 June the Dáil established arbitration courts;[15] on 12 September Dáil Éireann was declared a dangerous association; on 20 September republican newspapers were suppressed; and on 15 October Sinn Féin and the Irish Republican Army were outlawed. Isolating republicans created more freedom for the Cabinet to deal with Ulster, though, as events would show, this did not mean Ulster Unionists were handed a blank cheque. Carson on 12 July made it clear that Ulster would not tolerate a revival of the Act of 1914. *The Times* in the second half of July predicated that the next bill would make provision for two parliaments.[16]

During 1919 Ireland's future was briefly entangled with growing support for federalism. It was debated in the House of Lords in March and in the House of Commons in July. Long on 24 September prepared a memorandum 'the situation in Ireland' for Cabinet consideration.[17] On 7 October the Cabinet concluded, 'at any early stage in the parliamentary session, some declaration of policy by the government would be expected', and the Long committee was revived with a membership of twelve 'to examine and report on the probable effect on Ireland and on the United Kingdom and on opinion abroad of each of the possible Irish policies'.[18] It was also charged with drafting a bill along federalist lines. The first meeting was held on 15 October when a decision was made to create distinct legislatures for Ulster and the southern provinces linked by a common council, comprising representatives from both. At this time a Parliamentary Inquiry chaired by the Speaker of the House of Commons was set up to consider the federalist option.[19] It met initially on 23 October and made a final report on 27 April 1920. However, its part in the Irish solution was constrained by the fact that Ireland was specifically placed outside the ambit of the body.

The Government of Ireland measure,
4 November 1919–22 June 1921

On 4 November Long's committee presented a report, surveying three alternatives. County option was ruled out and an all-Ireland Parliament rejected, while the committee pumped for a third alternative: two Parliaments plus an overarching Council of Ireland composed of twenty members from each Parliament. In the first year it would look after transport, health, agriculture and similar matters, afterwards working towards unity of the country. Irish representation at Westminster was to be reduced to sixty-four seats. The report observed: 'the Imperial Parliament can compel Irishmen to govern themselves by the simple expedient of withdrawing its own officials. But once it gives Ireland self-government it cannot compel Ireland to unite. Irish unity can then only come from unity in Ireland itself.' The objective was to do 'everything possible to promote unity'. The committee preferred two parliaments because then 'no nationalists would be retained under British rule. All Irishmen would be self-governing.' Finally, it argued:

> [I]f the withdrawal of British rule and the establishment of local legislature in Ulster is necessary to heal the feud which has estranged Ireland and Great Britain for so many decades, and which is now seriously imperilling the relations of Great Britain both with the rest of the Empire and with the United States of America, the sacrifices which Ulster will be called upon to make in assuming control of its own local affairs is one which the Imperial government and Parliament is clearly entitled to ask its people to make.[20]

This report brought the question full circle, adopting Gladstone's moral purpose by providing a framework to make Irishmen reach accommodation among themselves. John McColgan argues that the logic of government policy stemming from the Long Committee was partition, not unity, but the repeated efforts to induce Ulstermen to accept the principle of an all-Ireland Parliament belie his assertion.[21] The Long committee report became the basis of the Government of Ireland Act of 1920, marking the start of the sixth attempt to introduce Home Rule; it is also the beginning of Buckland's fourth phase in finding an Ulster solution (see p. 256). This time it was conceived of in two parts. On 29 November Long in a letter to A. V. Dicey explained the reasoning behind dividing the question: 'as regards Ireland under a Federal plan, if the three Southern provinces declined to adopt it, the only alternative that I can see would be to include Ulster and govern the other three provinces on some different plan and this I believe will be forced upon us so long as Sinn Féin controls the majority of the people as it does at present.'[22]

Cabinet on 11 November considered the Long Committee paper, directing his group to refine the scheme. It submitted four reports between 4 November and 2 December. On 21 November the draft of the financial proposals was completed and this was circulated a few days later. At the next Cabinet discussion on 3 December it was determined that the Westminster Parliament would retain responsibility for the Crown, foreign affairs, defence, dignitaries, treason, external trade and the wireless. Other functions were to be transferred to the Dublin Parliament.[23] Provisionally, the whole province of Ulster was excluded. James Craig was unhappy about the size of the area, realising that the nearly balanced numbers of Catholics and Protestants would render control tenuous. When conferring with Lloyd George on 19 December Craig pressed his objections, arguing for the exclusion of just six counties. The Prime Minister responded with the idea of a boundary commission.

On 22 December Lloyd George outlined the scheme in the House of Commons.[24] The legislation was guided by three principles – the impossibility of severing Ireland from the United Kingdom; Irish national opposition to British rule; and the north-east's opposition to Dublin government. Every opportunity would be given to effect unity, he explained, 'but the decision must rest with them'. A Council of Ireland would have twenty representatives from each legislature plus the chairman, having authority for private bills and able to proceed towards unity without further reference to the Westminster Parliament. He did not propose to lay down what resources the Council would control. The individual legislatures would follow the 1914 principle with specified powers reserved to the Imperial Parliament. Reservation of services maintained a degree of unity in the Irish administration.[25] The two jurisdictions would not possess separate judiciaries; for the time being the judiciary would be nominated by the Imperial authorities. On 17 January 1920 Sir Henry Robinson urged the transfer of approximately twenty services to the Council of Ireland so as to give it purpose.

Long took wider soundings, as he was anxious to make the bill watertight. He and the government were concerned also about the turbulent condition of Ireland. On 25 January he was made chairman of a Cabinet Committee on the 'state of affairs' in Ireland. In January 1920 Long visited Dublin and Belfast, coming away with the view that 'because the Unionist Party realise that if a settlement can be obtained now, they will secure infinitely better terms than they could hope for from a new Parliament, in which, in all probability the Labour Party would have much stronger representation'.[26] His observations were sent to Lloyd George on 3 February, and circulated to the Cabinet a week later. Meanwhile, on 30 January the subcommittee dismissed Robinson's proposal, as it 'might be regarded as an infringement of the pledge to Ulster'.[27] The Cabinet on 14 February determined that 'the area of Northern Ireland shall consist of the parliamentary counties of Antrim, Armagh, Down, Fermanagh, Londonderry and Tyrone and the parliamentary boroughs of Belfast and Londonderry'.[28] The Long Committee continued to prefer a nine-county Ulster Parliament, advocating this again on 17 February. Long learned the following day that the Ulster people wanted a separate judiciary and that if this was not granted they would try to wreck the measure; on 20 February Long reported to Bonar Law that the measure would be redrafted.

The bill was read for the first time on 25 February, but no discussion followed. It was the most carefully constructed Home Rule measure, being praised by George Boyce as 'an inspired piece of drafting'.[29] It closely followed Lloyd George's announcement on 22 December, creating two co-equal responsible Parliaments: a Council of Ireland 'with a view to the eventual establishment of a Parliament for the whole of Ireland, and to bring about harmonious action between the parliaments'.[30] However, if one half of either House of Commons declined to take their seats in the Council, it could be adjourned by the Lord Lieutenant without prejudice to either. Following the recommendation of the Irish Convention, members of each Parliament were to be elected by proportional representation in multi-members constituencies, in theory, providing that minorities secured seats.

Originally, the legislatures were unicameral, but on 3 November 1920 the bill was amended to include a Senate for each Parliament. In the north, with the exception of seats reserved for the Lord Mayors of Belfast and Londonderry, Senators were elected by the lower house; in the south, as recommended in the Report of the Irish Convention, they were nominated. The Parliaments could only legislate on matters pertaining exclusively to their designated territorial jurisdiction and were prohibited from abrogating rights of religious practice and citizenship. No laws discriminating on the basis of religion were permitted; no property could be appropriated without compensation. The franchise, distribution of members and proportional representation could not be amended for three years. Distribution had to be done with regard to population enumeration. Other exclusions included conferment of titles, the laws of treason, naturalisation, domicile, trade with outside areas, interference with cable and wireless, air navigation, lighthouses, coinage, negotiable financial instruments, weights and measures, trade marks, copyright and patents, along with similar matters. There was a distinction between 'reserved' and 'exempted' services, and the legislative authority of the Northern Ireland Parliament, the only one to come into effective operation, differed for the two categories. Also, it could not impose or collect customs, excise duties, income tax or surtax, purchase tax, and tax on profits or any general tax on capital. Both new states had limited powers, especially over finance. Westminster retained 88 per cent of revenue derived from Northern Ireland, controlling as well 60 per cent of expenditure.[31] From an Ulster Unionist vantage point there were three objections: admission of the principle of Home Rule; reduction of Ulster representation to twelve in the Westminster House of Commons; and the substantial number of Protestants left outside the excluded area.[32]

Unlike earlier bills only a small quantity of parliamentary time was consumed by this measure. Debates and divisions were sparsely attended. National representatives in and outside the House of Commons had little influence. Northern bishops rejected the bill out of hand, but to no avail.[33] Debates on the second reading took place on 29, 30 and 31 March, when it was carried by 348 votes to 94 and went into committee. Chamberlain pointed out: 'it is a paradox that the only hope of union in Ireland is to recognise her present division'. He advanced the now almost standard Unionist view that 'the cure lies in the hands of the Irish themselves. It can come only from them.'[34] Carson on 31 March denounced the whole idea of Home Rule. Although the Council of Ireland was devised to effect unity, the ethnic purpose of the new regimes received confirmation from the Prime Minister when he pointed out that 'Ulster is not a minority to be safeguarded. Ulster is an entity to be dealt with.'[35] On 6 April Hugh Montgomery explained privately that it was futile to mount an open opposition:

[I]n view of the conduct of the English Unionist party, the strength of the Coalition government and many other circumstances, frontal attack would lead to disaster to ourselves. It would either fail or end in our bringing upon ourselves a worse measure of Home Rule than that offered. To attempt to organise sufficient votes to kill the bill is hopeless, but the ultimate success of the bill can be made impossible by establishing in Ireland of an impregnable Protestant and Unionist rule. The only available means to defeat the present conspiracy are the seizing of the impregnable Pale offered to us under the bill.[36]

A number of changes took place in late spring. During May new officials were posted to Dublin Castle to improve the functioning of the Irish administration.[37] Several had national sympathies and were inclined towards giving Ireland Dominion status. From this time, too, the tempo of violence in Ireland and calls for repression accelerated, leading to the Restoration of Order Act, passed on 1 August. Owing to poor health, Bonar Law retired from the Cabinet on 17 May, also relinquishing the Conservative leadership to Chamberlain. On 27 May the bill passed a major hurdle when it was approved by the Ulster Unionist Council. Against this was a background of Ulster Unionist estrangement arising from the growing disorder in Ireland and also the problem of a summer of sectarian riots in the north.

Despite slow progress with the bill, Lloyd George on 13 October revealed his continued desire for its success:

> [He was] still a Gladstonian Home Ruler, and wished to keep Ireland as an integral part of the United Kingdom, and that was the way he hoped the present bill would be proceeded with. The bill was a good and generous one, and under it, it was possible to keep the United Kingdom, which was a small country, together and in some sort of unity, and enable it to face the future. He would stand by the bill until someone with real authority in Ireland appeared with whom it was possible to negotiate.[38]

The bill emerged from committee nearly unscathed, other than the inclusion of Senates, carrying the third reading on 11 November by 183 votes to 52 in a thinly attended House of Commons. The peers' amendments were considered by the lower chamber on 16 December, with the royal assent conferred on 23 December. It was to come into force on 3 May 1921 (see document 10).

The 1920 Government of Ireland Act was a substantial achievement in many respects but it could not make stable and efficient institutions on its own. It proposed to divide Ireland in a way never done previously, raising a series of difficulties. There was no administrative apparatus in place in Northern Ireland.[39] In September 1920 Sir Ernest Clark was appointed to prepare a detailed scheme for a bureaucracy. Unlike their southern counterparts, Clark and other appointed officials generally sympathised with Ulster Unionism. He reported on 7 February, giving the new state little time to get started. In preparation for the change Carson was succeeded by Craig on 4 February 1921 as leader of the Ulster Unionists. At the same time Craig was nominated by the Ulster Unionist Council as the designated head of government and he and Clark worked closely during the coming months. Elections for both new parliaments were held on 24 May with results announced three days later. The franchise was the same as for the United Kingdom, but in the north there were 11 constituencies each electing 4–8 members returned by proportional representation based on the single transferable vote. For all parties partition was the abiding issue. Turnout in the north was 89 per cent; Unionists captured 40 of 52 seats. On 31 May the incoming Cabinet was announced. The House of Commons met on 7 June and Craig formed a ministry. Sinn Féin and Nationalist members did not attend and both declined to make nominations to the Senate. George V on 22 June attended and addressed the ceremonial opening of the Northern Ireland Parliament. Northern Ireland was effectively a one-party sectarian state, though this outcome was not the inevitable consequence of the act. In the south Sinn Féin used the election as a referendum for its own policy, winning unopposed 124 of the 128 seats. Only the four representatives from Trinity College and fifteen Senators nominated by the Lord Lieutenant took their seats in the southern parliament; it opened on 18 June, adjourning on 13 July never to sit again.

Motivations for this sixth attempt to implement Home Rule were varied, even confused. By late 1920 the war and American pressure had subsided, but the situation in Ireland plus a general acceptance that self-government was inevitable pushed the Unionist-dominated coalition onwards.[40] The Long Committee report of 4 November 1919 and Unionist speeches during the debates reveal the dual influence of federalist thinking and Gladstone's legacy. David Harkness criticises the act on the basis that it was a solution agreed between Unionists at Westminster and therefore represented the worst of all worlds.[41] This misrepresents both the quality of drafting and context for passing a measure. Although the financial clauses posed problems for Northern Ireland, this bill was more workable than its predecessors. Rather than precipitating a parliamentary battle, the main dispute was within the Cabinet. Yet, readiness to find a solution was not a sudden development. This had existed since 1913–14. What differed this sixth time round was that the government only had to satisfy one Irish party, the Ulster Unionists. Past efforts had been hampered by trying to satisfy too many interests at one stroke.

Dominion status, 23 June–7 December 1921

The Government of Ireland Act was intended as a settlement for the whole island; Sinn Féin's refusal to accept the measure rendered it redundant in the south. By mid-1921 Sinn Féin could authentically claim to be the voice of the Catholic nation, having emerged victorious from the general election, performed impressively in local and municipal elections held in January and June 1920 and again in the elections to the southern Parliament in May 1921. During 1920 and early 1921 the situation on the ground in Ireland became ugly. With the formation of the Black and Tans, made up of ex-military personnel in January 1920, the scene was set for the nastiest phase of the conflict. In late October Terence McSwiney died while on hunger strike and on 1 November Kevin Barry, a young medical student, was hanged; both incidents provided republicans with propaganda material. In January 1921 the Labour party declared: 'things are being done in the name of Britain which must make our name stink in the nostrils of the whole world.'[42] Negotiations with Sinn Féin leaders slipped into the background while the government dealt with the Government of Ireland measure. However, after 23 June the combined effects of Home Rule's rejection and public concern, including within Conservative ranks, over the policy of reprisals made a fresh attempt at settlement in the south imperative.[43] By mid-1921 Sinn Féin leaders, too, were anxious to find an 'honourable' solution.

In spring 1921 British leaders hoped that with Home Rule about to come into place, Craig and de Valera could reach an understanding. The two met in Dublin on 5 May. On 24 and 25 May the Cabinet was encouraged that further meetings seemed likely. However, de Valera had concluded that the Anglo-Irish quarrel could not be settled 'through a prior agreement with a Unionist minority'. In his view the question was 'an Irish-English one for which the solution 'must be sought in the larger general policy of English interest'.[44]

The government used the King's visit to Northern Ireland to signal readiness for compromise. His conciliatory speech was widely applauded.[45] The seventh attempt to implement self-government began. For Lloyd George the problem still was to devise a solution acceptable to a Conservative Cabinet, Ulster Unionists and Sinn Féin leaders. On 24 June he invited both Craig and de Valera to London for discussions. Negotiations with the republications for a truce began on 5 July, were agreed to four days later and the truce came into force on 11 July. Northern Ireland was a significant factor in discussions.

Lloyd George seized the initiative by inviting de Valera to London;[46] the President and Craig both arrived on 14 July and met separately with the Prime Minister but did not confer together. The Irish delegation contained Arthur Griffith, Robert Barton, Austen Stack and Erskine Childers, but Lloyd George met de Valera alone four times between 14 and 24 July. Lloyd George swiftly spelt out the British position – continued loyalty to the crown, prohibition of an Irish navy and airforce, complete freedom of trade between Ireland and the United Kingdom and no coercion of Northern Ireland. Two issues separating Britain and de Valera were pinpointed – the formal unity of Ireland and the country's future relationship to Great Britain. The Prime Minister was flexible on both and de Valera, too, adopted a moderate attitude. When he saw Craig on 18 July, the Prime Minister made five 'suggestions' concerning modification of Northern Ireland that might accommodate de Valera. Craig was unwilling, stating 'it now merely remains for Mr de Valera and the British people to come to terms regarding the area outside that of which I am Prime Minister'.[47] From this time Craig, appreciating that Northern Ireland was not secure despite the Government of Ireland Act, laboured to get an administration up and running in order to reduce the risk of it being dissolved in a wider settlement. On 20 July Lloyd George wrote to de Valera offering Dominion status, with a prohibition on a navy, erection of hostile tariffs and no coercion of the excluded area.[48] On 22 July the Northern Ireland Cabinet rejected the proposals. De Valera responded on 10 August: 'we cannot admit the right of the British government to mutilate our country, either in its own interest, or at the call of any section of our population.' Nevertheless, he affirmed: 'we do not contemplate the use of force.'[49] While demanding that partition be abandoned, he also suggested 'free association' between Ireland and Great Britain.

After de Valera's return to Dublin there was a steady flow of letters and telegrams between the leaders. During the following weeks it became apparent that the republican leadership contained shades of opinion on both Northern Ireland and Dominion status. In Dáil sessions on 22 and 23 August de Valera returned to the idea of county option. It seemed there was an atmosphere conducive to successful negotiations. On 7 September the Cabinet agreed to invite Sinn Féin to attend a conference to 'ascertain how the association of Ireland with the community of nations know as the British Empire can best be reconciled with Irish national aspirations'.[50] On 27 September Lloyd George invited de Valera to attend; he accepted the following day.

On 11 October the conference began in London, but de Valera declined to attend in person. The Irish plenipotentiaries were Griffith (chairman), Michael Collins, Eamonn Duggan, Barton, Sir George Gavan Duffy and Childers (Secretary). They began with the position that 'the unimpaired unity of Ireland is a condition precedent to the conclusion of a Treaty of Association between Ireland and the nations of the British Commonwealth'.[51] On 14 October the negotiations reached the section of Lloyd George's letter to de Valera of 20 July on Northern Ireland. Three days later a Sinn Féin proposal came back from Dublin, demanding either the abandonment of the Act of 1920, or that the Northern Ireland Parliament be made subordinate to the all-Ireland legislature. On 29 October the Irish delegates were prepared to accept the Crown but the *sine qua non* was unity.[52] Two days later the Prime Minister had to face a hostile motion of censure on his Irish policy in the House of Commons.

Craig was summoned to meet Lloyd George in London on 5 November, where he learned that the Prime Minister believed Northern Ireland should come under an all-Ireland Parliament. This was rejected by the Northern Ireland Cabinet. In order to quieten critics Lloyd George agreed to transfer services to Northern Ireland. An Order in Council by the sovereign on 9 November designed 22 November, 1 December, 1 January and 1 February as the handover dates. McColgan sees the transfer as crucial to the implementation of partition, though its importance largely eluded Sinn Féin which lodged no protest.[53] On 10 November Craig was presented with an outline of a possible agreement and the reasons why Northern Ireland should relinquish its separate status. Bonar Law was sufficiently disturbed by the negotiations: 'if L.G. goes on with his present proposals I will oppose them. I shall try to get the Conservative party to follow me.'[54] On 12 and 13 November Griffith, with an eye to the Conservative party conference scheduled for the following week, was persuaded to accept a document containing the idea of a boundary revision, which Lloyd George prophesied would so enervate Northern Ireland as to undermine its viability.[55] On 17 November Craig resisted further pressure from Lloyd George. Meanwhile Craig was intent upon putting the administration of Northern Ireland on a solid footing as quickly as possible, despite considerable resistance from Britain. The judiciary had been established in October. Control of the police was handed over to Northern Ireland on 21 November. Four days later Craig met Lloyd George and again reiterated his opposition to bringing the Northern Ireland Parliament under a Dublin regime. During the autumn Ulster Unionists were intensely unpopular in Britain, but their refusal to be swayed left the Prime Minister with limited options beyond securing the best agreement he would with Griffith's delegation. Finally, Lloyd George threatened the Irish with resumption of the military conflict unless they reached an agreement, preserving the position of Northern Ireland and the formal link through the Crown in exchange for virtual autonomy in internal affairs. Certain other matters were reserved. Except for the Irish share of the budget deficit, it would enjoy the same status as Canada. Dominion status was accorded to all of Ireland even though it only came into existence in the south. On 7 December 1922 Northern Ireland exercised its right to opt out.

The treaty was signed on 6 December, ratified by Parliament on 16 December after little discussion, and accepted by the Dáil on 7 January 1922 by 64 votes to 57, following an acrimonious debate. It was then signed on 14 January 1922 (see document 11). In the end the Irish wrangled among themselves about the symbolic status of the Crown; the excluded area and the precise powers accorded under self-government received less attention. Lloyd George had been open to several possibilities, including modification of the Act of 1920. However, he ensured that he carried his colleagues with him and included influential Unionists – Lord Birkenhead (F. E. Smith) and Chamberlain – in the negotiations. By dividing the Irish self-government question in two he was able to focus on bilateral negotiations, achieving success a second time.

Conclusion

The Government of Ireland Act of 1920 and the Treaty of 6 December demanded time, patience and negotiating skill. The first took the better part of a year to enact and the second only became feasible in the aftermath of the 1920 legislation and owed much to Lloyd George's prowess. After 1914 Irish self-government was less a parliamentary problem than one of satisfying Unionists in the Cabinet and the two major Irish factions. Negotiations in 1916 and 1918 broke down over differences between Irishmen; they succeeded in 1920 and 1921 because southern Protestants and northern Catholics were left outside the negotiations, while the claims of Ulster Unionists and southern nationalists were treated separately. Perhaps Griffith had the most appropriate, though not the last word, when he defended his acceptance of the Treaty: 'the principle that I have stood on all my life is the principle of Ireland for the Irish people. If I can get that with a Republic I will have a Republic; if I can get that with a monarchy, I will not sacrifice my country for a form of government.'[56]

Notes

1 *The Times*, 26 March 1919.

2 PRO, CAB27/68.

3 John Turner, *British Politics and the Great War: Coalition and Conflict 1915–1918* (New Haven and London, 1992), p. 177.

4 John Kendle, *Ireland and the Federal Solution: The Debate over the United Kingdom Constitution, 1870–1921* (Kingston and Montreal, 1989), p. 208.

5 Quoted in Sir Charles Petrie, *The Life and Times of the Right Hon. Sir Austen Chamberlain* (London, 1940), II, pp. 114–15.

6 Long memorandum, 14 April 1918, Arthur Balfour Papers, British Library MS 49,777.

7 Kendle, *Federal Solution*, p. 197.

8 See, Alan J. Ward, 'Lloyd George and the 1918 Irish Conscription Crisis', *Historical Journal*, XXVII, 1 (1974), pp. 107–29.

9 CAB23/14.

10 D. George Boyce, 'British Opinion, Ireland, and the War, 1916–1918', *Historical Journal*, XVII, 3 (1974), p. 588; Ronan Fanning, 'Britain, Ireland and the End of the Union', in Robert Blake, *Ireland After the Union* (Oxford, 1989), p. 110.

11 Quoted in Nicholas Mansergh, *The Unsolved Question: The Anglo-Irish Settlement and its Undoing 1912–72* (New Haven and London, 1991), p. 112.

12 Keith Middlemas (ed.), *Thomas Jones: Whitehall Diary* (London, 1969), III p. 65.

13 Quoted in Kendle, *Federal Solution*, p. 207.

14 Quoted in D. George Boyce, *The Irish Question and British Politics 1868–1986* (London and Basingstoke, 1989), p. 59.

15 See, Arthur Mitchell, *Revolutionary Government in Ireland: Dáil Éireann 1919–22* (Dublin, 1995).

16 Eamon Phoenix, *Northern Nationalism: Nationalist Politics, Partition and the Catholic Minority in Northern Ireland 1890–1940* (Belfast, 1994), p. 67.

17 PRO, CAB24/89.

18 *Ibid.*, CAB23/12.

19 Kendle, *Federal Solution*, pp. 210–33.

20 PRO, CAB27/68.

21 John McColgan, *British Policy and the Irish Administration 1920–22* (London, 1983), p. 47.

22 Quoted in Kendle, *Federal Solution*, p. 212.

23 PRO, CAB23/18.

24 *Parliamentary Debates [PD]*, 123, cc. 1169–83.

25 McColgan, *British Policy*, p. 40.

26 Quoted in John Kendle, *Walter Long, Ireland, and the Union, 1905–1920* (Montreal and Kingston, 1992), p. 186.

27 PRO, CAB23/23.

28 *Ibid.*, CAB23/20.

29 Boyce, *Irish Question*, p. 62.

30 *PD*, 123 (1919), cc. 1169–83.

31 Patrick Buckland, *Irish Unionism: Two: Ulster Unionism and the Origins of Northern Ireland 1886–1922* (Dublin, 1973), p. 133.

32 *Ibid.*, p. 115.

33 Mary Harris, *The Catholic Church and the Foundation of the Northern Irish State* (Cork, 1993), p. 80.

34 *PD*, 123 (1919), c. 981; Ian Colvin, *The Life of Lord Carson* (London, 1936), III, p. 384.

35 *Ibid.*, 127, cc. 1332–4.

36 Quoted in T. G. Fraser, *Partition in Ireland, India and Palestine: Theory and Practice* (London, 1984), p. 36.

37 Eunan O'Halpin, *Head of the Civil Service, a Study of Sir Warren Fisher* (London, 1989), pp. 85–90.

38 Quoted in McColgan, *British Politics*, p. 46.

39 Bryan A. Follis, *A State under Siege: The Establishment of Northern Ireland, 1920–1925* (Oxford, 1995), pp. 6–25.

40 See, Charles Townshend, *The British Campaign in Ireland 1919–1921: The Development of Political and Military Policies* (Oxford, 1975); also, see, Colm Campbell, *Emergency Law in Ireland 1918–1925* (Oxford, 1994), pp. 8–148.

41 David Harkness, *Ireland in the Twentieth Century: Divided Island* (London and Basingstoke, 1996), p. 37.

42 Quoted in McColgan, *British Policy*, p. 48.

43 Mitchell, *Revolutionary Government*, pp. 289–91; Kenneth O. Morgan, *Consensus and Disunity: The Lloyd George Coalition Government 1918–1922* (Oxford, 1979), p. 131.

44 Quoted in John Bowman, *De Valera and the Ulster Question* (Oxford, 1982), p. 48.

45 Harold Nicolson, *King George the Fifth: His Life and Reign* (London, 1952), pp. 348–54.

46 Kenneth O. Morgan, 'Lloyd George and the Irish', in Robert Blake, *Ireland After the Union* (Oxford, 1989), p. 96.

47 Quoted in D. George Boyce, *Englishmen and Irish Troubles: British Public Opinion and the Making of Irish Policy, 1918–1922*, p. 144.

48 Fraser, *Partition in Ireland*, p. 48.

49 Quoted in Dorothy McCardle, *The Irish Republic* (3rd impression; London, 1938), pp. 506–7; a rich documentary source for the negotiations.

50 Quoted in Fraser, *Partition in Ireland*, pp. 50–1.

51 Quoted in *ibid.*, p. 51.

52 *Ibid.*, p. 53.

53 McColgan, *British Policy*, p. 69.

54 Quoted in Fraser, *Partition in Ireland*, p. 55.

55 Earl of Longford, *Peace by Ordeal: An Account, from First-hand Sources of the Negotiations and Signature of the Anglo-Irish Treaty 1921* (London, 1972), pp. 174–5.

56 *Dáil Éireann, Proceedings*, 1921 (7 January 1922), p. 344.

12

Epilogue

The Irish Government bill is a much better piece of *workmanship*, than that of 1886, and presents, in my judgement, fewer *secondary* points for attack. But, of course, the new Parliamentary constitution, which it gives to *Great Britain and the Empire*, opens an entirely new field of principles and probable consequences and is much worse than the simple exclusion of Irish members proposed in 1886. (Lord Selborne, 22 February 1893)[1]

[It is the] equivalent to shutting a man in a tiger's cage and advising him to make himself as comfortable as possible. (Revd Colthurst to Walter Long, 18 February 1920)[2]

Neither the evolution of self-government in both parts of Ireland nor the Irish problem ended in December 1921. But, Home Rule as an integral feature of British political culture was over. When Ireland reared its head in British politics thereafter it did so under different conditions, never becoming so central or the stuff of party warfare again. Home Rule no longer galvanised ideological concerns; its symbolic status was a relic of the past. Self-government concluded much as it began – a response to the threat of revolution in Ireland. Six of the seven attempts to introduce national self-governing institutions were the labours of British politicians; even the Irish Convention, a partial exception, sought the embrace of London leaders. Self-government schemes were never exclusively about institutions or even about Ireland; a myriad of considerations prohibited treating the issue in isolation. Each plan arose in a specific context and was shaped to fit the demands of its environment. Principles matter, of course, but these were just one part of a complex equation. It was only when self-government was stripped of accruements and compartmentalised that it was implemented. The tempo of Home Rule solutions speeded up – five of the seven attempts came between 1912 and 1921 – just at the point when the representatives of Catholic Ireland were increasingly marginalised. Irishmen may have initiated the demand but the problems of definition, structures, timing and areas included or excluded were in the hands of British policy-makers.

Whether Home Rule or some variant could have satisfied Catholics in Ireland or reconciled competing traditions within the island is a moot point. Older analyses are burdened by sentimentality and wishful thinking. Recent scholarship, in contrast, is cynical about the motives and content of the schemes. The first three plans had many defects, as Lord Selborne observed in the quotation at the start of the chapter; from a structural point of view the third Home Rule bill was the least satisfactory. The two versions actually implemented had the virtues of superior drafting. Good construction is essential, but does not make for successful government though it can have the opposite effect. Workable democratic government, as Gladstone and Bonar Law ultimately came to appreciate, requires consensus, but also a readiness to accommodate differences, especially profoundly antagonistic aspirations. Gladstone refused to accept that the two Irish traditions were irreconcilable; Bonar Law recognised the nature of the differences and promoted solutions, taking account of these. Gifted though he was as a negotiator – and the final outcome owes much to his skill – it is difficult to find much principle in Lloyd George's manoeuvres. He emerges with credit, but a trickster none the less. Perhaps if Home Rule had been introduced earlier the dreams of its advocates would have been realised, but there is no means to test this hypothesis. The evidence at hand does not give excessive cause for optimism on this score.

Home Rule has seven ironic outcomes. First, its founders conceived of self-government as a means to resolve differences between Ireland's peoples. In practice it was a formula for constructing an ethnic and then ultimately two ethnic states, neither having a notable appetite for accommodation. Polarisation in Ireland was actually exacerbated by Home Rule. Second, some prominent early advocates were southern Protestants who saw in Home Rule a way to make Ireland safe for their order. These figures, always a minority among Protestants, had a colonial identity, seeking to reconcile their status and place. Miroslav Hroch, as noted in chapter 1, gives attention to the importance of this element. However, southern Irish Protestants were the biggest losers, though in their individual capacities they or their progeny may have fared well elsewhere. This was not the outcome that southern Protestant proponents of Home Rule had in mind, and the tiger's cage referred to at the start of the chapter proved distinctly uncomfortable for them. Third, Home Rule was promoted as a measure of decentralisation and a means to stop the Irish from looking to London. Its impact on decentralisation is dubious and the controversy actually increased the tendency to look to Westminster. Fourth, Home Rule was a democratic aspiration; Gladstone and Asquith, then latterly Austen Chamberlain and Bonar Law, recognised it as the will of Catholics in Ireland. It was pursued, though, by a movement intent upon suppressing any hint of dissent or rival political parties – the building blocks of democracy. Under the impress of Home Rule Ireland dissolved into two one-party regions defined by religious headcounts. Tom Garvin notes that the power-brokers in Catholic Ireland accepted electoral procedures but held an ambiguous attitude about democracy.[3] Democratic politics and self-government alike were employed by a section of the Irish Catholic bourgeoisie to secure its own dominance. Fifth, just when the British public came to accept Home Rule, the Irish lost interest.[4] Sixth, self-government was granted by Unionists who latterly adopted many of the assumptions articulated by Gladstone. And finally, the part of Ireland most resistant to Home Rule in any guise, Northern Ireland, had it foisted upon it.

Home Rule was a symbol for the expression of grievances and contained a coded message. It afforded an umbrella under which competing claims could shelter and priorities be established; the opposition operated as a mirror image. The Irish party and the wider national movement possessed ideologues determined that nothing divert it from its grand mission, but much energy within national groups was directed towards achieving materialist ends. Linking Home Rule and reform worked satisfactorily for most of the movement's existence despite the internal tensions this generated. After 1912 the party was less well placed to straddle Home Rule and reform; by mid-1916 this was increasingly impossible. All was not lost, however. Sinn Féin began as an ideological movement but soon took on characteristics of a party of social integration, seeking materialist ends. Unionism followed a similar course with its most militant strand, the Ulster people, gaining their primary objective – exclusion from the Dublin Parliament.

Theoretical constructs of national movements in Europe are examined in chapter 1. Much of this literature skirts the Irish dimension. The main lines of the Irish experience conform to patterns elsewhere. If the Home Rule debate is an Anglo-Irish event, it is also a European one. Catholic national ambitions to build an ethnic community have numerous parallels in the middle, south-eastern and eastern portions of Europe. Great Britain's desire for a multi-ethnic national state has its parallels in Western Europe and the English-speaking nations overseas. This often overlooked European dimension receives welcome emphasis in Brian Walker's *Dancing to History's Tune*.[5] The Home Rule controversy was an international as well as a national laboratory for debate about the most appropriate means to deal with the conflicting ambitions of large states and their restless minorities. This episode also amplifies Anthony D. Smith's conditions necessary for entrenching national identity among a significant section of inhabitants and George Boyce's four manifestations of nationalism: colonial identity, cultural identity, national identity and nationalism.[6] Home Rule in the broad sense became what Ernest Gellner calls 'high culture' (see p. 16). In Donegal, what began as a 'high' or 'Home Rule' culture was remoulded into a localised Catholic national identity. Individuals identified with Home Rule because this served their interest.[7] Michael Hechter and Margaret Levi's suggestion that ethnic solidarity arises in regions developed as internal colonies where there is a hierarchical cultural division of labour determining life's chances is borne out.[8] Solidarity, as in Ireland, increases when members interact within the boundaries of their own group. The movement's durability, however, depended on the ability to deliver on its promises. Home Rulers capitalised on the claim that they delivered the economic goods, building upon this to promote the national idea of self-government. John Hutchinson's emphasis upon blocked mobility in the early twentieth century affords an insight into why Conservative reforms failed to defuse Home Rule; he argues that the rate of Catholics advancement did not keep pace with escalating expectations. He also demonstrates that blockage became acute at the beginning of the twentieth century (see pp. 17–18). Hroch's point about the importance of a completed social structure for a political movement prioritising political demands, and that until a late point in its progression autonomy not independence is the focus of national movements, is sustained in the case-study of Ireland; his typology is relevant to Irish experience, also (see p. 16). Home Rule, as theorists of economic nationalism observe, had 'value-added' benefits for groups receiving fewer of the direct material compensations.

Notes

1 Quoted in D. George Boyce, *The Crisis of British Unionism: Lord Selborne's Domestic Political Papers, 1885–1922* (London, 1987), p. 16.

2 Quoted in Richard Murphy, 'Walter Long and the Making of the Government of Ireland Act, 1919–20', *Irish Historical Studies*, XXV (May, 1986), p. 95.

3 Tom Garvin, *1922 The Birth of Irish Democracy* (Dublin, 1996), pp. 29–39.

Epilogue

4 D. George Boyce, 'British Opinion, Ireland and the War, 1916–1918', *Historical Journal*, XVII, 3 (1974), p. 591.

5 Brian Walker, *Dancing to History's Tune, History, Myth and Politics in Ireland* (Belfast, 1996), pp. 34–56.

6 Anthony D. Smith, *National Identity* (London, 1991), p. 14; D. George Boyce, *Nationalism in Ireland* (3rd edn; London, 1995), pp. 18–19.

7 Albert Breton, Gianluigi Galeotti, Pierre Salmon and Ronald Wintrobe (eds), *Nationalism and Rationality* (Cambridge, 1995).

8 Michael Hechter and Margaret Levi, in John Hutchinson and Anthony D. Smith, *Nationalism* (Oxford, 1994), pp. 184–95.

Epilogue

4 D. George Boyce, 'British Opinion, Ireland and the War, 1916–1918', *Historical Journal*, XVII, 3 (1974), p. 591.

5 Brian Walker, *Dancing to History's Tune, History, Myth and Politics in Ireland* (Belfast, 1996), pp. 34–56.

6 Anthony D. Smith, *National Identity* (London, 1991), p. 14; D. George Boyce, *Nationalism in Ireland* (3rd edn; London, 1995), pp. 18–19.

7 Albert Breton, Gianluigi Galeotti, Pierre Salmon and Ronald Wintrobe (eds), *Nationalism and Rationality* (Cambridge, 1995).

8 Michael Hechter and Margaret Levi, in John Hutchinson and Anthony D. Smith, *Nationalism* (Oxford, 1994), pp. 184–95.

311

Documents

Document 1
Proclamation of an Irish Republic, 1867

We therefore declare that, unable longer to endure the curse of Monarchical Government, we aim at founding a Republic based on universal suffrage, which shall secure to all the intrinsic value of their labour.

The soil of Ireland, at present in the possession of an oligarchy, belongs to us, the Irish people, and to us it must be restored.

We declare, also, in favour of absolute liberty of conscience, and complete separation of Church and State.

We appeal to the Highest Tribunal for evidence of the justness of our cause. History bears testimony to the integrity of our sufferings, and we declare, in the face of our brethren, that we intend no war against the people of England – our war is against the aristocratic locust, whether English or Irish, who have eaten the verdure of our fields – against the aristocratic leeches who drain alike our fields and theirs.

Republicans of the entire world, our cause is your cause. Our enemy is your enemy. Let your hearts be with us. As for you, workmen of England, it is not only your hearts we wish, but your arms. Remember the starvation and degradation brought to your firesides by the opposition of labour. Remember the past, look well to the future, and avenge yourselves by giving liberty to your children in the coming struggle for human liberty.

Source: Alan O'Day and John Stevenson (eds),
Irish Historical Documents since 1800 (Dublin, 1992), p. 77.

Document 2

Resolutions of the Home Rule Conference, November 1873

1. That as the basis of the proceedings of this conference, we declare our conviction that it is essentially necessary to the peace and prosperity of Ireland that the right of domestic legislation on all Irish affairs should be restored to our country.

2. That, solemnly reasserting the inalienable right of the Irish people to self-government, we declare that the time in our opinion has come when a combined and energetic effort, should be made to obtain the restoration of that right.

3. That, in accordance with the ancient and constitutional rights of the Irish nation, we claim the privilege of managing our own affairs by a Parliament assembled in Ireland and composed of the Sovereign, the Lords, and the Commons of Ireland.

4. That, in claiming these rights and privileges for our country, we adopt the principle of a federal arrangement, which would secure to the Irish Parliament the right of legislating for and regulating all matters relating to the internal affairs of Ireland, while leaving to the Imperial Parliament the power of dealing with all questions affecting the Imperial Crown and Government, legislation regarding the colonies and other dependencies of the crown, the relations of the empire with foreign states, and all matters appertaining to the defence and stability of the empire at large, as well as the power of granting the supplies necessary for Imperial purposes.

5. That, such an arrangement does not involve any change in the existing constitution of the Imperial Parliament, or any interference with the prerogatives of the crown or disturbance of the principles of the constitution.

6. That to secure to the Irish people the advantages of constitutional government, it is essential that there should be in Ireland an administration for Irish affairs, controlled, according to constitutional principles, by the Irish Parliament, and conducted by ministers constitutionally responsible to that Parliament.

7. That in the opinion of this conference, a federal arrangement, based upon these principles, would consolidate the strength and maintain the integrity of the empire, and add to the dignity and power of the imperial crown.

8. That while we believe that in an Irish Parliament the rights and liberties of all classes of our countrymen would find their best and surest protection, we are willing that there should be incorporated in the federal constitution articles supplying the amplest guarantees that no change shall be made by the Parliament in the present settlement of property in Ireland, and that no legislation shall be adopted to establish any religious ascendancy in Ireland, or to subject any person to disabilities on account of his religious opinions.

9. That this conference cannot separate without calling on the Irish constituencies at the next general election, to return men earnestly and truly

devoted to the great cause which this conference has been called to promote, and who in any emergency that may arise may be ready to take counsel with a great national conference, to be called in such a manner as to represent the opinions and feelings of the Irish nation; and that, with a view of rendering members of Parliament and their constituents more in accord on all questions affecting the welfare of the country, it is recommended by the conference that at the close of each session of Parliament the representatives should render to their constituents an account of their stewardships.

10. That in order to carry these objects into practical effect, an association be now formed to be called 'The Irish Home Rule League' of which the essential and fundamental principles shall be those declared in the resolutions adopted at this conference, and of which the object, and the only object, shall be to obtain for Ireland by peaceable and constitutional means, the self-government claimed by those resolutions.

Source: Edmund Curtis and R. B. McDowell (eds),
Irish Historical Documents 1172–1922 (London, 1943), pp. 276–8.

Document 3
Provincial Councils; printed for the Cabinet, 7 April 1882

Constitute Provincial Councils for the Management of certain Classes of Local Affairs.

Constitution of Provincial Councils.
1. For the purposes of this Act there shall be established four Provincial Councils. Each of such Councils shall be called the Provincial Council of the Province to which it belongs, and shall consist of such number of Representatives for each County in the Province as are set opposite to the name of such County in the schedule to this Act. Each Provincial Council shall be a Body Corporate with power to acquire and hold lands for the purposes of this Act.

Powers of the Council.
2. There shall be transferred to the Provincial Council of each Province all the powers and duties connected with National Education in such Province of the Commissioners of National Education.

All moneys provided by Parliament after the commencement of this Act for the purpose of National Education; or for the purpose of contributing towards the salaries of medical officers of workhouses and dispensaries, and sanitary officers acting in execution of the Public Health Act, or for the purpose of contributing towards the cost of District Lunatic Asylums, or for Reformatory and Industrial Schools, shall be apportioned by Parliament between the Provinces in the proportions in which the moneys provided for the same purposes were expended in the Provinces respectively on the average of the three years ending 31 March 1882.

Documents

The amount appropriated by Parliament in each year after the commencement of this Act for each of the Provinces for the several purposes aforesaid shall be applied by the Provincial Council of the Province for the purpose for which it is provided, in such manner as the Council thinks most expedient.

No greater sum shall be voted by Parliament in any year after the commencement of this Act for any of the purposes aforesaid than the sum voted for the same purpose for the year ending 31 March 1882. ...

Supplemental Provisions

Election of Provincial Council
7. Each Provincial Council shall consist of so many Representatives for each County in the Provinces as are set opposite the name of the County in the schedule to this Act. The persons qualified to vote at an election of Members to represent the County shall be [the persons who are qualified to vote at an election of Guardians under the Acts for the Relief of the Poor; and at such election each such person shall have so many votes in respect of each vacancy then to be filled up as he would have at an election for a Guardian.]...

Source: J. L. Hammond, *Gladstone and the Irish Nation*
(new impr.; London, 1964), pp. 259–62.

Document 4
Parnell's speech at the National League Convention, 29 August 1883

I am also glad to bring encouraging tidings as the result of our Parliamentary labours in London during the past session (applause) We opened the session under circumstances of the greatest possible discouragement. I do think that no body of men were ever assailed with so much vituperation as that which we were compelled to meet last February and March, and I am glad that we are able to say there today, as we can say, that we have lived it down, and triumphed over it successfully (applause). And not only that, but that we have been able to turn the announced intentions of Parliament – intentions announced at that time of a session of neglect for Irish interest – we have been able to turn those announced intentions and that programme of neglect for the interests of Ireland in to a result which has afforded us several most valuable measures in the interests of the Irish people (hear, hear). I do not think when I point to the Fisheries (Ireland) Act, with which the name of Mr Blake is honourably identified, to the Labourers' (Ireland) Act, the passing of which is due to the ability and untiring energy of Mr T. P. O'Connor (applause); and lastly, though, not least to the Tramways Act – I do not think I exaggerate when I say that I consider that it is probable that the result of these measures, if judiciously, wisely, and prudently worked, will be valuable only in a second degree to the Irish Land and Arrears Acts of the sessions of 1881 and 1882. The Fisheries Act, I trust, will result

315

in the building of a number of much-needed harbours, and boat slips on the West Coast of Ireland, which will enable the hardy Irishmen to reap the harvest of the sea, which is only waiting to be taken. The Labourers' (Ireland) Act will, I hope, result in affording to every industrious, sober, and hardworking labourer in Ireland a home and a small plot of ground upon which to grow vegetables for the support of himself and his family (hear, hear). Of course unforeseen friction may occur, some local bodies may prove themselves unworthy of the trust which the provisions of that measure confide to them, and I trust that the branches of the Irish National League throughout the country ... I trust that the members of the National League throughout the country will encourage the Poor Law boards and boards of town commissioners to set the highly beneficial provisions of this measure in action with as little delay as possible. If the Poor Law authorities do their duty great benefit will undoubtedly result to Ireland and to both the farmers and the labourers, from the suitable working of the Labourers' Act. We have seen that what I may call the normal emigration from Ireland has been going on now for many years; at the rate of one million a decade. Much of this emigration is due to the utter impossibility that the labourers find of obtaining any appropriate settlement at home. ... Under the provisions of this act it will be possible to provide suitable settlements for the labourers in the country, it will be possible to take them from the back streets and slums of the town and give them locations near the scene of their labours, and that without rendering it necessary for their employers to do that which in many cases seemed most obnoxious to them, namely to give to them a bit of land on the farm of the employer himself. I look to the Labourers' Act as being most important, and most likely to take in a great deal of the normal emigration which has been going on, and which has resulted in depriving the farmers of the labour of a great deal of the bone and sinew of the country, and in some parts to render it almost impossible for them to get in the present valuable harvest. The promotion of light lines of railways and steam tramways will be beneficial beyond a doubt in many parts of the country; but I look to the second part of the act with every hope that it will bring a means of solving a problem which must have occupied the attention of every thinker on the land question during the course of the great movement of the last few years. It has often been said, and with truth, that the Irish Land Act did not touch the condition of the smaller tenants in the west of Ireland; that it did not better the condition or provide any remedy for the sufferings of the small cottier tenants in the congested districts of the county of Mayo, and cradle of the land movement; and that although the sufferings and the labours of these men brought about the passing of the Land Act, and certainly set on foot the movement which brought about the passing of the Land Act, yet that practically nothing whatever was done under the operation of the measure for the benefit of those unfortunate people (hear, hear). A scheme of emigration was proposed last session, and under the provisions of the scheme many persons have been emigrated from the west of Ireland. ... It was proposed by the Government, in the Tramways Act, that a further sum of

£100,000 should be devoted to the purpose of proceeding with this emigration scheme. With considerable difficulty we obtained half of this sum of £100,000 for the purpose of trying a plan of migration (hear, hear). If this plan of migration be successful it will give us an unanswerable argument for the application of further and larger sums next session in the same direction. It will bring about a redistribution of the population in those congested districts on other lands which are available, and are better suited for the purpose, speaking from an agricultural point of view, than for any other purpose. It will lead to the revival, I trust, of industries in the western districts, to the increased prosperity of many of the smaller and larger towns; and above all it will check the projects of emigration which are being put forward as the only panacea for improving the distressed condition of the population in those overcrowded districts. I look with every hope to the successful working of the provisions of part two of the act. ... I have every confidence that we shall be able to show practically this winter that is possible to migrate, or remove, and resettle families in such a way as to enable them to be a benefit and advantage to the country, and with every prospect that they will never again become a charge upon the rates. ... It is now no longer a question with the great body of Englishmen whether the Irish people shall have self-government, but as to the amount of self-government they will be willing to accept (hear, hear). I think that when we have placed the national question – the question of legislative independence – on the same footing that the land question was placed before the introduction of the Irish Land Act of 1881; that is to say, when we have induced the English government themselves to bring forward a proposal of their own for settling this question, we shall have brought it very near a final and successful issue. I have always held that it was most undesirable for the Irish people to make proposals on such questions as Irish land and Irish self-government; but that we should rather, by agitation and organisation, set our English rulers and governors to work to consider these matters, and to make their own propositions. I have every hope that before long a measure in the direction of local self-government will be laid before Parliament; and, though it may not go the whole distance that we go, yet, undoubtedly, it will give considerable further powers to the Irish people, and train them in those habits of self-government and self-reliance which are of so much advantage and of such vital importance in forming a nation (applause).

Source: *The Freeman's Journal*, 30 August 1883

Document 5
A proposed constitution for Ireland (prepared at Parnell's direction –
30 October 1885)

An elected Chamber with power to make enactments regarding all the domestic concerns of Ireland, but without power to interfere in any Imperial matter.

The Chamber to consist of three hundred members.

Two hundred and six of the number to be elected under the present suffrage, by the present Irish constituencies, with special arrangements for securing to the Protestant minority a representation proportionate to their numbers; the remaining 94 members to be named in the Act constituting the Chamber.

The principle of nomination regarding this proportion of the first Chamber.

The number of elected members, suffrage, and boundaries of constituencies for election of succeeding Chamber to be capable of alteration by the preceding Chamber, excepting those special arrangements for securing to the Protestant minority a proportionate representation, which arrangements shall be fixed and immutable.

The first Chamber to last for three years, unless sooner dissolved by the Crown.

The Chamber shall have power to enact laws and make regulations regarding all the domestic and internal affairs of Ireland, including her sea fisheries.

The Chamber shall also have power to raise a revenue for any purpose over which it has jurisdiction by direct taxation upon property, by Customs duties and by licenses.

The Chamber shall have power to create departments for the transaction of all business connected with the affairs over which it has jurisdiction, and to appoint and dismiss chief and subordinate officials for such departments, to fix the term of their office, and to fix and pay their salaries; and to maintain a police force for the preservation of order and the enforcement of the law.

This power will include the constitution of Courts of Justice and the appointment and payment of all judges, magistrates, and other officials of such Courts, provided that the appointment of judges and magistrates shall in each case be subject to the assent of the Crown.

No enactment of the Chamber shall have the force of law until it shall have received the assent of the Crown.

A sum of one million pounds sterling per annum shall be paid by the Chamber to the Imperial Treasury in lieu of the right of the Crown to levy taxes in Ireland for Imperial purposes, which right would be held in suspense so long as punctual payment was made of the above sum.

The right of the Imperial Parliament to legislate regarding the domestic concerns and internal affairs of Ireland will also be held in suspense, only to be exercised for weighty and urgent cause.

The abolition of the office of Lord Lieutenant of Ireland and all other offices in Ireland under the Crown connected with domestic affairs of that country.

The representation of Ireland in the Imperial Parliament might be retained or might be given up. If it be retained the Speaker might have power to decide what questions the Irish members might take part in as Imperial questions, if this limitation were thought desirable.

Such Naval and Military force as the Crown thought requisite from time to time would be maintained in Ireland out of the contribution of one million pounds per annum to the Imperial Treasury; any excess in the cost of these forces over such sum being provided for out of the Imperial Revenue (i.e. by Great Britain).

The Militia would also be levied, controlled, and paid by the Crown, and all the forts, military barracks, posts, and strong places of the country would be held and garrisoned by the Crown forces.

No volunteer force to be raised in Ireland without the consent of the Crown and enactment of the Imperial Parliament, and, if raised, to be paid for and controlled by the Crown.

Source: J. L. Hammond, *Gladstone and the Irish Nation* (new impr.; London, 1964), pp. 422–3.

Document 6
Government of Ireland bill, 1886

Legislative Authority
2. With the exceptions and subject to the restrictions in this Act mentioned, it shall be lawful for Her Majesty the Queen, by and with the advice of the Irish Legislative Body, to make laws for the peace, order, and good government of Ireland, and by any such law to alter and repeal any law in Ireland.
3. The Legislature of Ireland shall not make laws relating to the following matters or any of them:
  (1) The status or dignity of the Crown, or the succession to the Crown or a Regency.
  (2) The making of peace or war.
  (3) The army, navy, militia, volunteers, or other military or naval forces; or the defence of the realm.
  (4) Treaties and other relations with foreign States, or the relations between the various parts of Her Majesty's dominions.
  (5) Dignities or titles of honour.
  (6) Prize or booty of war.
  (7) Offences against the law of nations, or offences committed in violation of any treaty made or hereafter to be made between Her Majesty and any foreign State; or offences committee on the high seas.
  (8) Treason, alienage, or naturalisation.
  (9) Trade, navigation, or quarantine.
  (10) The postal and telegraph service, except as hereafter in this Act mentioned with respect to the transmission of letters and telegrams in Ireland.
  (11) Beacons, lighthouses, or sea marks.
  (12) The coinage, the value of foreign money, legal tender, or weights and measures; or
  (13) Copyright, patent rights, or other exclusive rights to the use or profits of any works or inventions.

Documents

4. The Irish Legislature shall not make any law:
   (1) Respecting the establishment or endowment of religion, or pro-
       hibiting the free exercise thereof; or
   (2) Imposing any disability or conferring any privilege on account of
       religious belief; or
   (3) Abrogating or derogating from the right to establish or maintain
       any place of denominational education, or any denominational
       institution or charity; or
   (4) prejudicially affecting the right of any child to attend a school
       receiving public money, without attending the religious instruc-
       tion at that school; or
   (5) Impairing, without either the leave of Her Majesty in Council
       first obtained, on an address presented by the Legislative Body of
       Ireland, or the consent of the corporation interested, the rights,
       property, or privileges of any existing corporation, incorporated
       by Royal Charter or local or general Act of Parliament; or
   (6) Imposing or relating to duties of Customs and duties of Excise as
       defined by this Act, or either of such duties, or affecting any Act
       relating to such duties, or either of them; or
   (7) Affecting this Act except in so far as it is declared to be alterable
       by the Irish legislature.
       Source: Alan O'Day, *Parnell and the First Home Rule Episode*
       (Dublin, 1986), pp. 254–5.

Document 7
Government of Ireland bill, 1893

Legislative Authority
2. With the exceptions and subject to the restrictions in this Act mentioned, there shall be granted to the Irish Legislature power to make laws
for the peace, order and good government of Ireland in respect of matters exclusively relating to Ireland or some part thereof. Provided that,
notwithstanding anything in this Act contained, the supreme power and
authority of the Parliament of the United Kingdom of Great Britain and
Ireland shall remain unaffected and undiminished over all persons, matters, and things within the Queen's dominions.
3. The Irish Legislature shall not have power to make laws in respect of
the following matters or any of them:
   (1) The Crown, or the succession to the Crown, or a Regency; or the
       Lord Lieutenant as representative of the Crown; or
   (2) The making of peace or war or matters arising from a state of war;
       or the regulation of the conduct of any portion of Her Majesty's
       subjects during the existence of hostilities between foreign states
       with which Her Majesty is at peace, in respect of such hostilities;
       or
   (3) Navy, army militia, volunteers, and any other military forces, or
       the defence of the realm, or forts, permanent military camps,

magazines, arsenals, dockyards, and other needful buildings, or any places purchased for the erection thereof; or

(4) Authorising either the carrying or using of arms for military purposes, or the formation of associations for drill or practice in the use of arms for military purposes; or

(5) Treaties or any relations with foreign States, or the relations between different parts of Her Majesty's dominions, or offences connected with such treaties or relations, or procedure connected with the extradition of criminals under any treaty; or

(6) Dignities or titles of honour; or

(7) Treason, treason-felony, alienage, aliens as such, or naturalisation; or

(8) Trade with any place out of Ireland; or quarantine, or navigation, including merchant shipping (except as respects inland waters and local health or harbour regulations); or

(9) Lighthouses, buoys, or beacons within the meaning of the Merchant Shipping Act, 1854, and the Acts amending the same (except so far as they can consistently with any general Act of Parliament be constructed or maintained by a local harbour authority); or

(10) Coinage; legal tender; or any change in the standard of weights and measures; or

(11) Trade marks, designs, merchandised marks, copyright, or patent rights. ...

4. The powers of the Irish Legislature shall not extend to the making of any law:

(1) Respecting the establishment or endowment of religion, whether directly or indirectly, or prohibiting the free exercise thereof; or

(2) Imposing any disability, or conferring any privilege, advantage, or benefit, on account of religious belief, or raising or appropriating directly or indirectly, save as heretofore, any public revenue for any religious purpose, or for the benefit of the holder of any religious office as such; or

(3) Diverting the property or without its consent altering the constitution of any religious body; or

(4) Abrogating or prejudicially affecting the right to establish or maintain any place of denominational education or any denominational institution or charity; or

(5) Whereby there may be established and endowed out of public funds any theological professorship or any university or college in which the conditions set out in the University of Dublin Tests Act, 1873, are not observed; or

(6) Prejudicially affecting the right of any child to attend a school receiving public money, without attending the religious instruction at that school; or

(7) Directly or indirectly imposing any disability, or conferring any privilege, benefit, or advantage upon any subject of the Crown on account of his parentage or place of birth, or of the place where

any part of his business is carried on, or upon any corporation or institution constituted or existing by virtue of the law of some part of the Queen's dominions, and carrying on operations in Ireland, on account of the persons by whom or in whose favour or the place in which any of its operations are carried on; or

(8) Whereby any person may be deprived of life, liberty, or property without due process of law in accordance with settled principles and precedents, or may be denied the equal protection of the laws, or whereby private property may be taken without just compensation; or

(9) Whereby any existing corporation incorporated by Royal Charter or by any local or general Act of Parliament may, unless it consents, or the leave of Her Majesty is first obtained on address from the two Houses of the Irish Legislature, be deprived of its rights, privileges, or property without the due process of law in accordance with settled principles and precedents, and so far as respects property without just compensation. Provided nothing in this subsection shall prevent the Irish Legislature from dealing with any public department, municipal corporation, or local authority, or with any corporation administering for public purposes taxes, rates, cess, dues, or tolls, so far as concerns the same.

Source: Arthur Mitchell and Pádraig Ó Snodaigh (eds), *Irish Political Documents 1869–1916* (Dublin, 1989), pp. 87–9.

Document 8
Government of Ireland act, 1914

Legislative Authority

1. (1) On and after the appointed day there shall be in Ireland an Irish Parliament consisting of His Majesty the King and two houses, namely, the Irish Senate and the Irish House of Commons.

(2) Notwithstanding the establishment of the Irish Parliament or anything contained in this act, the supreme power and authority of the Parliament of the United Kingdom shall remain unaffected and undiminished over all persons, matters, and things in Ireland and every part thereof.

2. Subject to the provisions of this act, the Irish Parliament shall have power to make laws for the peace, order, and good government of Ireland with the following limitations, namely, that they shall not have power to make laws except in respect of matters exclusively relating to Ireland or some part thereof, and (without prejudice to that general limitation) that they shall not have power to make laws in respect of the following matters in particular, or any of them, namely:

(1) The Crown, or the succession to the Crown, or a Regency ....

(2) The making of peace or war or matters arising from a state of war ...

(3) The navy, the army, the territorial force, or any other naval or mil-

Documents

itary force, or the defence of the realm ...
(4) Treaties, or any relations, with Foreign States, or relations with other parts of His Majesty's dominions ...
(5) Dignities, or titles or honour ...
(6) Treason, treason felony, alienage, naturalisation ...
(7) Trade with any place out of Ireland (except so far as trade may be affected by the exercise of the powers of taxation given to the Irish Parliament, or by the regulation of importation for the sole purpose of preventing contagious disease, or by steps taken, by means of inquiries or agencies out of Ireland, for the improvement of Irish trade or for the protection of Irish traders from fraud): the granting of bounties on the export of goods; quarantine; or navigation, including merchant shipping (except as respects inland waters, the regulation of harbours, and local health regulations);
(8) Any postal services ...
(9) Lighthouses, buoys, or beacons ...
(10) Coinage ...
(11) Trade marks ...

3. In the exercise of their power to make laws under this act the Irish Parliament shall not make a law so as either directly or indirectly to establish or endow any religion, or prohibit or restrict the free exercise thereof, or give a preference, privilege, or advantage, or impose any disability or disadvantage, on account of religious belief or religious or ecclesiastical status, or make any religious belief or religious ceremony a condition of the validity of any marriage, or affect prejudicially the right of any child to attend a school receiving public money without attending the religious instruction at that school, or alter the constitution of any religious body expect where the alteration is approved on behalf of the religious body by the governing body thereof, or divert from any religious denomination the fabric of cathedral churches or, except for the purpose of roads, railways, lighting, water, or drainage works, or other works of public utility upon payment of compensation, any other property ...

8. (1) The Irish Senate shall consist of forty Senators nominated as respects the first Senators by the Lord Lieutenant subject to any instructions given by His Majesty in respect of the nomination, and afterwards elected by the four provinces of Ireland as separate constituencies.

(2) The election of Senators shall be according to the principle of proportional representation, the electors being the same electors as the electors of members returned by constituencies in Ireland to service in the Parliament of the United Kingdom ...

9. (1) The Irish House of Commons shall consist of 164 members, returned by the constituencies in Ireland ...

11. (1) If the Irish House of Commons pass any public bill which is sent up to the Irish Senate at least before the end of the session and the Irish Senate reject or fail to pass it, or pass it with amendments to which the Irish House of Commons will not agree, and if the Irish House of Commons in the next session again pass the bill with or without any amend-

ments which have been made or agreed to by the Irish Senate, and the Irish Senate reject or fail to pass it, or pass it with amendments to which the Irish House of Commons will not agree, the Lord Lieutenant may during the session convene a joint sitting of the members of the two houses.

(2) The members present at any such joint sitting may deliberate and shall vote together upon the bill as last proposed by the Irish House of Commons, and upon the amendments (if any) which have been made therein by the one house and not agreed to by the other; and any such amendments which are affirmed by a majority of the total number of members of the two houses present at the sitting, shall be taken to have been carried ...

15.(1) The Irish Parliament shall have power to vary (either by way of addition, reduction, or discontinuance) any imperial tax so far as respects the levy of that tax in Ireland, and to impose in Ireland any independent tax not being in the opinion of the joint exchequer board substantially the same in character as an imperial tax, subject to the following limitations:

(a) The Irish Parliament shall not have power to impose or charge a customs duty, whether an import or an export duty, on any article unless that article is for the time being liable to a customs duty of a like character levied as an imperial tax, and shall not have power to vary, except by way of addition, any customs duty levied as an imperial tax or any excise duty so levied where there is a corresponding customs duty; and ...

(f) The Irish Parliament shall not, in the exercise of their powers of taxation under this provision, make any variation of customs or excise duties the effect of which will be, in the opinion of the joint exchequer board, to cause the customs duty on an article of a class produced, prepared, or manufactured in Ireland, to exceed the excise duty by more than an amount reasonably sufficient to cover any expenses due to revenue restrictions, or any variation of customs or excise drawbacks or allowances which would cause the amount of drawback or allowance payable in respect of any article to be more than reasonably sufficient, in the opinion of the joint exchequer board, to cover the duty paid thereon and any expenses due to revenue restrictions ...

Source: Edmund Curtis and R. B. McDowell (eds),
Irish Historical Documents 1172–1922 (London, 1943), pp. 292–5.

Document 9
Headings of a settlement as to the Government of Ireland, 1916

1. The Government of Ireland Act, 1914, to be brought into operation as soon as possible after the passing of the Bill, subject to the modifications necessitated by these instructions.

2. The said Act not to apply to the excluded area, which is to consist of the Six Counties of Antrim, Armagh, Down, Fermanagh, Londonderry, and Tyrone, including the Parliamentary Boroughs of Belfast, London-

derry, and Newry.

3. As regards the excluded area, the executive power of His Majesty to be administered by a Secretary of State through such officers and departments as may be directed by Order of His Majesty in Council, those officers and departments not to be in any way responsible to the new Irish Government.

A Committee to be appointed on which both of the Irish parties are to be represented, to assist the Government in preparing the necessary Orders in Council.

4. The number of Irish representatives in the United Kingdom House of Commons to remain unaltered.

5. The Irish House of Commons to consist of the Members who sit in the United Kingdom House of Commons for constituencies within the area to which the Act applies.

6. A reduction to be made in the number of Irish Senators proportionate to the population of the excluded area. The Senators to be nominated by the Lord Lieutenant, subject to instructions from His Majesty.

7. The Lord Lieutenant to have power to summon conferences between the members for constituencies in the excluded area, and the members for constituencies in the rest of Ireland.

8. A deduction to be made from Item(a) of the Transferred Sum (cost of Irish Services) when ascertained proportionate to the population of the excluded area.

9. Provision to be made for permanent sittings of the Irish High Court in Belfast as well as in Dublin, or for the constitution of a new court in Belfast with the same jurisdiction as that of the high Court but locally limited.

All appeals, both from the courts in the excluded area, and those in the rest of Ireland, to go to the Appeal Court in Dublin, which is to be composed of judges appointed in the same manner and having the like tenure of office as English judges.

The appeals from the Court of Appeal in Dublin, whether as respects cases coming from the excluded area or from the rest of Ireland, to go to the same tribunal of appeal in England – whether it should be the House of Lords or the Privy Council is for the present immaterial.

10. Section thirty of the government of Ireland Act to be extended to any disputes or questions which may arise between the excluded area and the new Irish Government.

11. His Majesty's power of making Orders in Council for the purposes of the Act to be extended so as to include power to make the necessary adjustments and provisions with respect to the Government of the excluded area and relations between that area and the rest of Ireland and Great Britain, etc.

12. Amongst the various questions to which attention must be directed in this connection will be the question of fixing fair rents under the Irish Land Acts. It is proposed that there should be two Commissioners specially allotted for fixing rents in the excluded area and appointed by the British Government.

13. All Orders in Council under the new Act to be laid before both Houses of Parliament in the same manner as Orders under the Government of Ireland Act.

14. The Bill to remain in force during the continuance of the war, and a period of twelve months thereafter, but if Parliament has not by that time made further and permanent provision for the Government of Ireland, the period for which the bill is to remain in force is to be extended or Order in Council for such time as may be necessary to enable Parliament to make such provision.

It is also understood that at the close of the war there should be held an Imperial Conference with a view to bringing the Dominions into closer co-operation with the government of the empire, and that the permanent settlement of Ireland should be considered at that Conference.

Source: F. S. L. Lyons, *John Dillon: A Biography*
(London, 1968), pp. 484–5.

Document 10
Government of Ireland Act, 1920

An Act to Provide for the Better Government of Ireland, 23 December 1920

Be it enacted by the King's most Excellent Majesty, by and with the advice and consent of the Lords Spiritual and Temporal, and Commons, in this present Parliament assembled, and by the authority of the same as follows: Establishment of Parliaments for Southern Ireland and Northern Ireland and a Council of Ireland.

1. (1) On and after the appointed day there shall be established for Southern Ireland a Parliament to be called the Parliament of Southern Ireland consisting of His Majesty, the Senate of Southern Ireland, and the House of Commons of Southern Ireland, and there shall be established for Northern Ireland consisting of His Majesty, the Senate of Northern Ireland, and the House of Commons of Northern Ireland.

(2) For the purposes of this Act, Northern Ireland shall consist of the parliamentary counties of Antrim, Armagh, Down, Fermanagh, Londonderry and Tyrone, and the parliamentary boroughs of Belfast and Londonderry, and Southern Ireland shall consist of so much of Ireland as is not comprised within the said parliamentary counties and boroughs.

2. (1) With a view to the eventual establishment of a Parliament for the whole of Ireland, and to bringing about harmonious action between the Parliaments and governments of Southern Ireland and Northern Ireland, and to the promotion of mutual intercourse and uniformity in relation to matters affecting the whole of Ireland, and to providing for the administration of services which the two parliaments mutually agree should be administered uniformly throughout the whole of Ireland, or which by virtue of this Act are to be so administered, there shall be constituted, as soon as may be after the appointed day, a Council to be called the Council of Ireland.

(2) Subject as hereinafter provided, the Council of Ireland shall consist of a person nominated by the Lord Lieutenant acting in accordance with instructions from His Majesty who shall be President and forty other persons, of whom seven shall be members of the Senate of Southern Ireland, thirteen shall be members of the House of Commons of southern Ireland, seven shall be members of the Senate of Northern Ireland, and thirteen shall be members of the House of Commons of Northern Ireland.

The members of the Council of Ireland shall be elected in each case by the members of that House of the Parliament of Southern Ireland or Northern Ireland of which they are members. The election of members of the Council of Ireland shall be the first business of the Senates and Houses of Commons of Southern Ireland and Northern Ireland....

3. (1) The Parliaments of Southern Ireland and Northern Ireland may, by identical acts agreed to by an absolute majority of members of the Houses of Commons of each Parliament at the third reading (hereinafter referred to as constituent acts), establish, in lieu of the Council of Ireland, a Parliament for the whole of Ireland consisting of His Majesty and two houses. ...

(2) On the date of Irish union the Council of Ireland shall cease to exist and there shall be transferred to the Parliament and government of Ireland all powers then exercisable by the Council of Ireland ...

4. (1) Subject to the provisions of this act, the Parliament of Southern Ireland and the Parliament of Northern Ireland shall respectively have power to make laws for the peace, order, and good government of Southern Ireland and Northern Ireland with the following limitations, namely, that they shall not have power to make laws except in respect of matters exclusively relating to the portion of Ireland within their jurisdiction, or some part thereof, and (without prejudice to that general limitation) that they shall not have power to make laws in respect of the following matters ...

7. (1) The Council of Ireland shall have power to make orders with respect to matters affecting interest both in Southern Ireland and Northern Ireland, in any case, where the matter:

(a) Is of such a nature that if it had affected interests in one of those areas only it would have been within the powers of the Parliament for that area; and

(b) Is a matter to affect which, it would apart from this provision, have been necessary to apply to the Parliament of the United Kingdom by petition for leave to bring in a private bill ...

9. (2) The following matters, namely:

(a) the postal service; (b) the Post Office Savings Bank and Trustee Savings Bank; (c) designs for stamps, whether for postal or revenue purposes; (d) the registration of deeds and the Public Record Office of Ireland; shall be reserved matters until the date of Irish union ...

10.(2) With a view to the uniform administration ... any powers (not

Documents

being powers relating to reserved matters) exercisably by any department of the government of the United Kingdom at the appointed day with respect to railways and fisheries and the contagious diseases of animals in Ireland and the power of making laws with respect to railways and fisheries and the contagious diseases of animals shall, as from the appointed day, become powers of the Council of Ireland ...

21.(1) The power of the Parliaments of Southern Ireland and Northern Ireland to make laws shall include power to make laws with respect to the imposing, charging, levying, and collection of taxes within their respective jurisdictions, other than customs duties, excise duties on articles manufactured and produced, and excess profits duty, corporation profits tax, and any other tax on profits, and (except to the extent hereinafter mentioned) income tax (including super-tax), or any tax substantially the same in character as any of those duties or taxes ...

38.The supreme court of judicature in Ireland shall cease to exist, and there shall be established in Ireland the following courts, that is to say, a court having jurisdiction in Southern Ireland, a court having jurisdiction in Northern Ireland, to be called the supreme court of judicature in Northern Ireland, and a court having appellate jurisdiction throughout the whole of Ireland, to be called the high court of appeal for Ireland ...

Source: Edmund Curtis and R. B. McDowell (eds),
Irish Historical Documents 1172–1922 (London, 1943), pp. 297–302.

Document 11
Articles of agreement for a treaty Between Great Britain and Ireland, 6 December 1921

1. Ireland shall have the same constitutional status in the community of nations known as the British Empire as the Dominion of Canada, the Commonwealth of Australia, the Dominion of New Zealand, and the Union of South Africa, with a Parliament having powers to make laws for the peace and good government of Ireland and an executive responsible to that Parliament, and shall be styled and known as the Irish Free State.

2. Subject to the provisions hereinafter set out the position of the Irish Free State in relation to the Imperial Parliament and government and otherwise shall be that of the Dominion of Canada, and the law, practice and constitutional usage governing the relationship of the crown or the representative of the crown and of the Imperial Parliament to the Dominion of Canada shall govern their relationship to the Irish Free State.

3. The representative of the crown in Ireland shall be appointed in like manner as the governor-general of Canada, and in accordance with the practice observed in the making of such appointments.

The oath to be taken by members of the Parliament of the Irish Free State shall be in the following form: 'I do solemnly swear true faith and allegiance to the Constitution of the Irish Free State as by law established and that I will be faithful to H.M. King George V, his heirs and successor by law in virtue of the common citizenship of Ireland with Great Britain

328

and her adherence to and membership of the group of nations forming the British Commonwealth of nations'.

5. The Irish Free State shall assume liability for the service of the public debt of the United Kingdom as existing at the date hereof and towards the payment of war pensions as existing at that date in such proportion as may be fair and equitable, having regard to any just claims on the part of Ireland by way of set off or counter-claim, the amount of such sums being determined in default of agreement by the arbitration of one or more independent persons being citizens of the British empire ...

7. The government of the Irish Free State shall afford to His Majesty's imperial forces:

    (a) In time of peace such harbour and other facilities as are indicated in the annex hereto, or such other facilities as may from time to time be agreed between the British government and the government of the Irish Free State; and

    (b) in time of war or of strained relations with a foreign power such harbour and other facilities as the British government may require for the purposes of such defence as aforesaid ...

12. If ... an address is presented to His Majesty by both houses of the Parliament of Northern Ireland ... the powers of the Parliament and government of the Irish Free State shall no longer extend to Northern Ireland and the provisions of the Government of Ireland Act, 1920 (including those relating to the Council of Ireland), shall so far as they relate to Northern Ireland, continue to be of full force and effect. ...

Provided that if such an address is so presented a Commission consisting of three persons, one to be appointed by the government of the Irish Free State, one to be appointed by the government of Northern Ireland, and one who shall be chairman to be appointed by the British government shall determine in accordance with the wishes of the inhabitants, so far as may be compatible with economic and geographic conditions the boundaries between Northern Ireland and the rest of Ireland, and for the purposes of the Government of Ireland Act, 1920, and of this instrument, the boundary of Northern Ireland shall be such as may be determined by such Commission. ...

14. After the expiration of said month, if no such address as is mentioned in article 12 hereof is presented, the Parliament and government of Northern Ireland shall continue to exercise as respects Northern Ireland the powers conferred on them by the Government of Ireland Act, 1920, but the Parliament and government of the Irish Free State shall in Northern Ireland have in relation to matters in respect of which the Parliament of Northern Ireland has not the power to make laws under that act (including matters which under the said act are within the jurisdiction of the Council of Ireland) the same powers as in the rest of Ireland, subject to such other provisions as may be agreed in the manner hereinafter appearing.

15. At any time after the date hereof the government of Northern Ireland and the provisional government of Southern Ireland hereinafter constituted may meet for the purpose of discussing the provi-

sions subject to which the last foregoing article is to operate in the event, of no such address as is therein mentioned being presented, and those provisions may include:

(a) Safeguards with regard to patronage in Northern Ireland.
(b) Safeguards with regard to the collection of revenue in Northern Ireland.
(c) Safeguards with regard to import and export duties affecting the trade or industry of Northern Ireland.
(d) Safeguards for minorities in Northern Ireland.
(e) The settlement of the financial relations between Northern Ireland and the Irish Free State.
(f) The establishment and powers of a local militia in Northern Ireland and the relation of the defence forces of the Irish Free State and of Northern Ireland respectively,

and if at any such meeting provisions are agreed to, the same shall have effect as if they were included amongst the provisions subject to which the powers of the Parliament and government of the Irish Free State are to be exercisable in Northern Ireland under Article 14 hereof ...

16. Neither the Parliament of the Irish Free State nor the Parliament of Northern Ireland shall make any law so as to either directly or indirectly to endow any religion or prohibit or restrict the free exercise thereof or give any preference or impose any disability on account of religious belief or religious status or affect prejudicially the right of any child to attend a school receiving public money without attending the religious instruction at the school or make any discrimination as respects state aid between schools under the management of different religious denominations or divert from any religious denomination or any educational institution any of its property except for public utility purposes and on payment of compensation. ...

Source: Arthur Mitchell and Pádraig Ó Snodaigh (eds), *Irish Political Documents 1916–1949* (Dublin, 1985), pp. 117–20.

Bibliographical essay

Writings on Home Rule are voluminous and the main themes contained in them are discussed in chapter 1. Many references to other valuable books and articles can be found in the notes. General accounts on Ireland and Anglo-Irish problems abound. Only Pauric Travers, *Settlements and Division: Ireland 1870–1922* (Dublin, 1988) corresponds almost exactly to the period covered in this book but a number of wider studies devote considerable attention to it. Particularly useful are D. George Boyce, *Nationalism in Ireland* (3rd edn; London, 1995), *Ireland 1828–1929* (Oxford, 1992), *Nineteenth-Century Ireland: The Search for Stability* (Dublin, 1990) and *The Irish Question and British Politics* (Basingstoke and London, 1988). To this impressive labour should be added his edited volume *The Revolution in Ireland, 1879–1923* (Basingstoke and London, 1988). Other works include R. F. Foster, *A Modern History of Ireland* (London, 1988), K. Theodore Hoppen, *Ireland since 1800: Conflict and Conformity* (London, 1989), Joseph Lee, *The Modernisation of Irish Society 1848–1918* (Dublin, 1973), *Ireland 1912–1985* (Cambridge, 1989) and F. S. L. Lyons, *Ireland since the Famine* (London, 1971). Books more specifically focused on the self-government question are John Kendle, *Ireland and the Federal Solution: The Debate over the United Kingdom Constitution, 1870–1921* (Kingston and Montreal, 1989) and Alan J. Ward, *The Irish Constitutional Tradition* (Washington, DC, 1994). J. L. Hammond, *Gladstone and the Irish Nation* (London, 1938) remains indispensable. A short survey aimed at students is Grenfell Morton, *Home Rule and the Irish Question* (Harlow, Essex, 1989).

Several general volumes of documents on Irish history supplement this reading. These include, Edmund Curtis and R. B. McDowell (eds), *Irish Historical Documents 1172–1922* (London, 1943), Arthur Mitchell and Pádraig Ó Snodaigh (eds), *Irish Political Documents 1869–1916* (Dublin, 1989) and *Irish Political Documents 1916–1949* (Dublin, 1985), along with Alan O'Day and John Stevenson (eds), *Irish Historical Documents since 1800* (Dublin, 1992). Selections of pertinent documents can also be found in Morton, cited above, and A. C. Hepburn, *The Conflict of Nationality in*

331

Irish Home Rule

Ireland (London, 1980). A more specialised collection is Patrick Buckland (ed.), *Irish Unionism 1885–1923* (Belfast, 1973). Biographies of the main participants in the home rule struggle abound. Recent treatments of key British figures are H. C. G. Matthew, *Gladstone* (Oxford, 1995) and Peter March, *Joseph Chamberlain: Entrepreneur* (New Haven and London, 1994). Parnell is examined in Paul Bew, *C. S. Parnell* (Dublin, 1980), F. S. L. Lyons, *Charles Stewart Parnell* (London, 1977), Robert Kee, *The Laurel and the Ivy* (London, 1993) along with two multi-contributor works, D. George Boyce and Alan O'Day (eds), *Parnell in Perspective* (London, 1991) and Donal McCartney (ed.), *Parnell: The Politics of Power* (Dublin, 1991). Other leaders are portrayed in F. S. L. Lyons, *John Dillon* (London, 1968), Tim Pat Coogan, *Michael Collins* (Dublin, 1990) and *Eamon de Valera* (Dublin, 1993), Frank Callanan, *T. M. Healy* (Cork, 1996), Joseph V. O'Brien, *William O'Brien and the Course of Irish Politics* (Berkeley and Los Angeles, 1976), Mark Tierney, *Croke of Cashel: The Life of Archbishop Thomas William Croke* (Dublin, 1976), Trevor West, *Horace Plunkett, Co-operation and Politics* (Gerards Cross, 1986), Alvin Jackson, *Colonel Edward Saunderson* (Oxford, 1995). Several of the Gill's Brief Lives are valuable: see, especially, Leon Ó Broin, *Michael Collins* (1980), T. Ryle Dwyer, *Eamon de Valera* (1980), Patrick Buckland, *Sir James Craig* (1980), A. T. Q. Stewart, *Edward Carson* (1980) and Calton Younger, *Arthur Griffith* (1980). The Life and Times series of the Historical Association of Ireland contains succinct accounts of *Sir Edward Carson* (1995) by Alvin Jackson, *Justin McCarthy* (1996) by Eugene J. Boyle and *John Redmond* (1996) by Paul Bew. Additional figures are treated in older biographies and many of these are referred to in the notes.

Home Rule, politics, organisation and electoral machinery is considered in Philip Bull, *Land, Politics and Nationalism* (Dublin, 1996), David Thornley, *Isaac Butt and Home Rule* (London, 1964), Lawrence J. McCaffrey, *Irish Federalism in the 1870s* (Philadelphia, 1961), Conor Cruise O'Brien, *Parnell and his Party 1880–90* (Oxford, 1957), Alan O'Day, *The English Face of Irish Nationalism* (Dublin, 1977) and *Parnell and the First Home Rule Episode* (Dublin, 1986), Alvin Jackson, *The Ulster Party* (Oxford, 1989), B. M. Walker, *Ulster Politics, The Formative Years* (Belfast, 1989), James Loughlin, *Gladstone Home Rule and the Ulster Question 1882–93*, F. S. L. Lyons, *The Irish Parliamentary Party 1890–1910* (London, 1951), Paul Bew, *Conflict and Conciliation in Ireland 1890–1910* (Oxford, 1987) and Patricia Jalland, *The Liberals and Ireland* (Brighton, 1980).

For post-1914 developments see Paul Bew, *Ideology and the Irish Question* (Oxford, 1995), D. G. Boyce, *Englishmen and Irish Troubles* (London, 1971), Patrick Buckland, *Irish Unionism I and II* (Dublin, 1972–3), T. G. Fraser, *Partition in Ireland, India and Palestine* (London, 1984), David Fitzpatrick, *Politics and Irish Life* (Dublin, 1977), Nicholas Mansergh, *The Unsolved Question* (New Haven and London, 1991), R. B. McDowell, *The Irish Convention* (London, 1970).

Index

Index